# Monetary Integration and Dollarization

'De cette manière, il y aura dans toute l'Europe uniformité de monnaie, ce qui sera d'un grand avantage pour le commerce.'

Napoleon Bonaparte
in a letter to his brother Louis, King of Naples, 6 May 1807

'The dollar is our currency, but it's your problem.'

John Connolly
Nixon's Treasury Secretary

# Monetary Integration and Dollarization

No Panacea

*Edited by*
Matías Vernengo

*Assistant Professor, University of Utah, Salt Lake City, USA*

**Edward Elgar**
Cheltenham, UK • Northampton, MA, USA

Published by
Edward Elgar Publishing Limited
Glensanda House
Montpellier Parade
Cheltenham
Glos GL50 1UA
UK

Edward Elgar Publishing, Inc.
136 West Street
Suite 202
Northampton
Massachusetts 01060
USA

A catalogue record for this book
Is available from the British Library

**Library of Congress Cataloguing in Publication Data**
Monetary integration and dollarization : no panacea / edited by Matias Vernengo.
    p. cm.
    Includes bibliographical references and index.
    1. Currency question—Developing countries. 2. Foreign exchange—Developing countries. 3. Monetary policy—Developing countries. 4. Dollar, American. 5. Europe—Economic integration. I. Vernengo, matias, 1968–

    HG1496.M63 2005
    332.4'564—dc22

2005054870

ISBN-13: 978 1 84376 896 8
ISBN-10: 1 84376 896 8

Typeset by Manton Typesetters, Louth, Lincolnshire, UK
Printed and bound in Great Britain by MPG Books Ltd, Bodmin, Cornwall

# Contents

# Figures

# Tables

# Contributors

| | |
|---|---|
| **Philip Arestis** | Cambridge University, UK |
| **Ronald G. Bodkin** | University of Ottawa, Canada |
| **Luiz Carlos Bresser-Pereira** | Fundação Getulio Vargas, Brazil |
| **Alcino F. Câmara Neto** | Universidade Federal do Rio de Janeiro, Brazil |
| **Paul Davidson** | New School University, New York, USA |
| **Barry Eichengreen** | University of California, Berkeley, USA |
| **Stephany Griffith-Jones** | Sussex University, UK |
| **William C. Gruben** | Federal Reserve Bank of Dallas, USA |
| **Kenneth P. Jameson** | University of Utah, USA |
| **Jahyeong Koo** | Federal Reserve Bank of Dallas, USA |
| **Carlos Medeiros** | Universidade Federal do Rio de Janeiro, Brazil |
| **Alain Parguez** | Université de Franche-Comté, Besançon, France |
| **Jean-François Ponsot** | Université Pierre Mendès, Grenoble, France |
| **Susan Pozo** | Western Michigan University, USA |
| **Malcolm Sawyer** | University of Leeds, UK |
| **Mario Seccareccia** | University of Ottawa, Canada |
| **Franklin Serrano** | Universidade Federal do Rio de Janeiro, Brazil |
| **Rogério Studart** | Inter-American Development Bank, USA |
| **Matías Vernengo** | University of Utah, USA |

# Acknowledgment

I would like to thank the Annals of the American Academy of Political and Social Science for allowing publishing portions of Chapter 8 that appeared in volume 579 in January 2002.

# Foreword

## Luiz Carlos Bresser-Pereira

The exchange rate is the most strategic of the four macroeconomic prices, and yet it is the least studied and the most misunderstood. The interest rate is the key price in every macroeconomic textbook; inflation is the main concern of macroeconomic policy-makers; and the wage rate is, rather, the object of microeconomic analysis. The exchange rate, however, has always occupied an awkward position in economic theory. Keynes knew well its strategic role, and probably for that reason opted for fixed exchange rates in the Bretton Woods agreements. For some time, economists were freed from concerns about it. Yet, after these agreements collapsed in the 1970s and open macroeconomics became a necessity, discussion on the exchange rate returned. Neoclassical and Keynesian economists debated for years about which exchange rate regime would be more appropriate for the world – fixed or floating. The discussion got nowhere because the rich countries, primarily the United States, were not interested in creating and backing an international organization that would work as a central bank in an international monetary union – as Paul Davidson demonstrates forcefully in his chapter. In the present state of the world, an attempt to form an international monetary union would involve the central banks in defining the 'rules of the game' that permit fixing exchange rates and in accepting or inventing a common reserve asset. And Davidson adds that even for some of the more developed nations this contractual agreement seems at present impossible to achieve.

This book is essentially about the exchange rate in a world where exchange rates are not fixed but floating. Countries that have arrived at full financial integration are those that have adopted a fixed and definitive exchange rate among themselves through the acceptance of a single currency. The European Union, with its euro, is the only case that falls into this category. Countries that have formally dollarized their economies are those that have given up managing their exchange rates and accepted being appended monetarily to the United States; and the same goes for countries that have adopted a currency board system.

But these are extreme forms of dealing with the exchange rate problem. Europe was able to adopt a single currency after a long and difficult process of economic and political integration. It is probably the most extraordinary example of political and economic engineering in the history of humanity. On the other hand, dollarization and currency boards are solutions adopted either by small countries or by countries that acknowledge their incapacity to deal with exchange rates. Big countries that opt for that solution are like the man who decided to blind himself because he was afraid to see. One of the many reasons that countries must retain control over their exchange rates is that they act as stabilizing mechanisms when exogenous factors produce a balance of payments problem.

An alternative solution as extreme as dollarization or the adoption of a currency board is a fully free floating rate. This option is actually more radical than a fixed exchange rate, given that, whereas we have examples of fixed exchange rates, I know of no country that has adopted a fully free float. Nevertheless, at least rhetorically, this is the dominant policy advocated by the conventional wisdom that reigns in the international financial markets and at present in the policies of the ancillary international institutions (though not necessarily in the papers of its best economists). In fact, rather than a policy, the conventional wisdom regards the free float as the only real possibility, since markets, but not governments, are able to determine the exchange rate in an international financial environment characterized by high capital mobility.

In fact, all countries that officially float their exchange rates manage them to some degree. For small countries, and sometimes for big ones, as in the case of France in relation to Germany in the 1980s, the more obvious option is to tie the national currency to a stronger one. Another alternative, which was common among developing countries in the recent past, was to peg the exchange rate to inflation. It was a way of keeping it fixed in real terms, but it was an inflationary way of doing so since it involved indexation.

Since managing the exchange rate is viewed as a 'sin' by the high priests of conventional wisdom, and as aggression by the governments of the rich countries that espouse it, no country acknowledges that it is doing so. Malaysia's decision openly to control capital flows in order to manage its exchange rate was an exception.

According to the conventional wisdom, the exchange rate should not and cannot be managed. If you try to manage it, you run into a succession of policy mistakes. You will be involved in competitive devaluations that provoke inflation while entrenching low productivity. You will keep the exchange rate either artificially undervalued or artificially overvalued, with negative consequences for the country.

In fact, this may well happen. As a trade-off, however, I suggest that, if we want to understand the enormous success of the East Asian countries since the Second World War, if we want to know their economic policy secret, we may come up with many answers, but the central one is that they used, and continue to use, their exchange rate strategically as a tool for economic growth. For developing countries, the exchange rate, when combined with fiscal austerity, is essentially a tool for economic growth, first, because it assures a country of balance of payments stability, and second, and principally, because it increases savings and investment.

This is not the usual view of the matter, and certainly is not what the conventional wisdom says. Conventional economic theory would agree with the first reason in so far as a competitive exchange rate stimulates exports and curbs imports, and keeps the current account in equilibrium. Yet, starting in the early 1990s, the conventional wisdom began to propose that developing countries pursue growth with foreign savings, that is, growth cum debt. Thus, it became uncomfortable with the idea of balance of payments crises caused by excessive international indebtedness. Before the 1990s, the standard procedure adopted by the IMF when a country faced a balance of payments crisis was to impose fiscal adjustment and to demand exchange-rate devaluation. Since the 1990s, the second part of the standard procedure has been abandoned: because depreciation would cause inflation if the exchange rate was fixed or because the market would automatically take care of the problem if the exchange rate was flexible. The fact that the market had not taken care of the problem – that, on the contrary, it had caused it through an artificial overvaluation of the exchange rate – was not considered.

The second reason a competitive exchange rate is a tool of economic growth – that it promotes savings and investments – is strange not only to the conventional wisdom but to economic theory in general. Probably some economists had already written about it, but if they had done so they have not have been listened to. It is obvious, however, that a competitive or relatively devalued currency stimulates savings. The transmission mechanism is simple. A competitive exchange rate keeps wages down. If aggregate consumption varies essentially with total wages, it too will be kept down. On the other hand, a competitive exchange rate creates opportunities for investment in export industries, promoting an increase in investment and in GDP that exceeds the relatively repressed increase in consumption. Thus, with a relatively devalued currency, the savings rate and the investment rate will increase, or, if they are already high, the relative depreciation will be small, and the savings and investment rates will remain high.

We may give all kinds of explanations for the high savings rates in the East Asian countries, but certainly one of them is their governments' exchange-rate policies. They deliberately keep the exchange rates relatively high in dollar terms in order to sustain high domestic rates of savings and investments, and also in order to avoid the possibility of a balance of payment crisis. For a few years, in the early 1990s, they came under the influence of what I used to call the Second Washington Consensus (capital account opening and growth cum foreign savings), and indulged in being net recipients of capital flows. But the

1997 crisis taught them that being 'emergent markets' could be disastrous, and they immediately returned to their classic exchange rate policy. Since capital flows, deriving not only from export surpluses, quickly resumed, they did not hesitate to adopt the policy of buying dollar-denominated bonds in order to increase international reserves and avoid the valorization of their currencies. In recent years, as these countries realized current account surpluses and financed the large current account deficit of the United States, they were doing exactly the opposite of what conventional wisdom proposes: they were growing with foreign dissavings, that is, with current account surpluses.

Conventional wisdom does not accept this kind of reasoning, on several grounds. First, it believes that the exchange rate, like every price, has a market equilibrium level – and this is the level that it will have to obey. Thus, it affirms that it would be either impossible or unsound for a government to strive for a relatively devalued exchange rate. As a matter of fact, however, what the conventional wisdom proposes is that developing countries' exchange rates be relatively overvalued, to the extent that it proposes that they grow with foreign savings. Since foreign savings are the opposite side of the coin of current account deficits, a country that has a current account deficit is a country whose market equilibrium exchange rate is lower than it would be if the current account was balanced. Additionally, conventional wisdom supports the use of the exchange rate as an anchor for price stabilization. Such a perverse role for the exchange rate likewise involves its relative evaluation.

Conventional wisdom prefers a relatively overvalued to a relatively devalued currency in developing countries because there is no bigger threat to the rich countries than a competitive exchange rate. They fear competition from the intermediate developing countries, which pushes down their wages and threatens their current account surpluses.

Yet, as we can see clearly in this book, particularly from the chapter by Rogério Studart, international financial markets, characterized by large and unstable capital flows, became extremely dangerous for developing countries. Studart argues that this instability was triggered by the abrupt and careless integration of financial markets, which caused the macro and financial imbalances of the 1990s, particularly in Latin America – a region that accepted the strategy of growth with foreign savings. Excessive capital flows create pressure to revalue the domestic currency. On the other hand, Studart sees consumption, not investment, increasing in Latin America with the opening of capital accounts and the surge of foreign capital. However, he gives a different explanation for it. Although foreign savings should, in principle, finance investments – and, in the case of direct investments, they directly do that – in the end what has been financed in Latin America is consumption. While macroeconomic uncertainties have restrained investors, consumer credit is highly rationed in the region, and responds rapidly to changes in the supply of credit. This financial explanation for the increase in consumption is interesting, and may be viewed as complementary to the real one related to the exchange rate.

What options are left for the developing countries, given the huge flows of capital that characterize the global system today? Barry Eichengreen discusses this question in his chapter. First, he remarks that the 1997 Asian crisis and its fallout in Latin America and Eastern Europe convinced many observers that soft currency pegs are crisis-prone and that emerging markets should embrace greater exchange rate flexibility. In other words, he is saying that conventional wisdom, which supported fixed exchange rates (through currency boards or dollarization), switched to favouring greater exchange rate flexibility.

Yet he is not satisfied with these two options, and searches for a third: to accept greater flexibility for the exchange rate, and to use inflation-targeting policy as a substitute for an exchange-rate anchor. In a footnote, Eichengreen recognizes that a further option, the adjustable peg, may be viable for countries with capital controls, as the experience of China and Malaysia has shown. Yet he dismisses this option on the grounds that trends in technology and policy (domestic financial liberalization in particular) will lead additional countries to liberalize their international financial transactions, thus limiting those countries to which this option is relevant.

Eichengreen includes in his chapter an interesting discussion of inflation targeting. He distinguishes strict inflation targeting from the flexible variety. Inflation targeting is strict when only inflation enters the central bank's objective function; it is flexible when a positive weight is given to other variables, like output, and when inflation caused by variations in the exchange rate is partially disregarded, or when the inflation target is a medium-range rather than a short-range target. Yet, in so far as the target is made more flexible, the substitute anchor loses strength.

The real question is to know whether using the exchange rate as an anchor to fight inflation is sound policy, or whether the country that adopts that policy is not just replacing one evil with a worse one. An outstanding Brazilian economist, Mario Henrique Simonsen, used to say that inflation cripples, and the exchange rate kills. More traditional policies, such as keeping the budget deficit under control, and raising the interest rate when excess demand materializes, as well as more innovative ones such as eliminating all mechanisms involving indexation of wages and other prices, probably make more sense as inflation controls than using the exchange rate as an anchor. If we have learned anything from the Argentinian crisis, it is that using the exchange rate as an anchor to fight inflation is disastrous.

Just as the exchange rate is a powerful source of economic growth, it is a powerful trigger of economic crises. An overvalued currency is tempting not only because it helps to control inflation, but also because it means 'exchange rate populism' in so far as it raises wages and consumption above the potential of the economy, and implies current account deficits. If fiscal populism is the state spending more than it collects in revenues, exchange rate populism is the nation spending more than it earns. When either budget deficits or current account deficits become chronic, one can be certain that economic crisis looms.

For a developing country that is small enough not to cause competitive devaluations, the ideal policy is to keep its exchange rate stable at a relatively devalued level. I mean by a competitive or relatively devalued exchange rate the rate that balances the current account or that allows the country to build reserves. If the country is highly indebted, it will be the rate that allows it to gradually repay its liabilities. There is no doubt that globalization and capital mobility limited the capacity of countries to control their exchange rates, but this does not mean that countries cannot or should not retain reasonable command over their exchange rates.

The globalist ideology that asserts that the developing countries are in a straitjacket, and have no alternative but to open their capital account, is false. Nation-states retain a considerable degree of freedom, as the Asian countries show. The idea that Mundell's triangle of incompatibilities represents a trilemma for the developing countries is also false, since it is not difficult to choose which of the three possibilities the country should dispose of. Indeed, it is impossible to conserve autonomy in monetary policy and in exchange rate policy, and keep the capital account fully open, but there is little doubt that it is preferable for them to keep control over the interest rate and the exchange rate, even at the cost of imposing some limits on capital inflows – not outflows. The real problem that developing countries face in today's global world is not a shortage of capital but an excess. Shortage, the suspension of the rollover of existing debt, occurs only in moments of crisis; excess supply of international finance is an everyday problem. Thus, when the country becomes 'fashionable' in the realm of international finance, and capital surges towards it, some administrative measures to control it should be considered. Such control should be preceded by a policy of building international reserves, but if this policy is not sufficient to avoid an undesirable overvaluation of the domestic currency given the inflow of speculative capital, the alternative of imposing administrative controls on capital inflows should be considered. The threat from international financial markets to the effect that such policy will involve loss of credibility is empty. As experience consistently demonstrates, the international credit of a country does not depend on its subservience to conventional wisdom, on confidence-building strategies, but on the soundness of its current account and of its fiscal performance.

Does this means that growth in developing countries should essentially be based on domestic savings, and that international finance has a limited role in this respect? Essentially, it does. International finance is essential for trade, but has a limited scope when investment is to be financed. Countries face a solvency constraint that makes it unwise for them to become indebted internationally. On some occasions, when the international interest rate is low, and the profit rate expected from investments is substantially higher, it may make sense to grow with debt. Yet this process will be necessarily limited in time, since countries soon reach the threshold of foreign indebtedness – between 1 and 1.5 times exports – and are supposed to balance their current account and stop borrowing.

When I refer to the conventional wisdom of the 1990s, based on financial liberalization and the strategy of growth with foreign savings as advocated by the Second Washington Consensus, I am being precise, because John Williamson's original or 'First' Washington Consensus did not include financial liberalization among the proposed reforms. When Williamson was asked why, he responded that developing countries were not ready for it. Yet, by responding in this way, he was suggesting something popular among reformers in Washington: the problem of sequencing. In their typical strategy of defining the agenda for the developing countries, they used to say that financial liberalization should come after trade liberalization. By saying that, the agenda was already defined. For the conventional wisdom, there is no doubt that developing countries must engage in financial liberalization; the only problem is when. The 'when', however, is crucial in this case. For them, the 'when' is just after capital liberalization; for me, much later. I agree that developing countries could and probably should open their capital accounts when they cease to be net debtors internationally, and have a per capita income near to that of the developed countries.

Philip Arestis and Malcolm Sawyer say something similar in this book when they observe that monetary union should come after integration has materialized in other respects. Financial integration is a beautiful thing but probably it will not happen while countries are able to create a world political authority, as the Europeans did with the European Union. For the moment, perspectives in relation to a world government are not realistic. Thus, small countries may opt for becoming just appendages of large developed countries. Most developing countries, however, have no alternative but to protect themselves, while participating in general agreements like the UN or the WTO. To protect themselves from balance of payment crises, unemployment, and low rates of growth, the best thing they can do is to keep control of their exchange rates: not to fix them, because that is impossible, but also not to fully float them. Instead, they should keep them relatively undervalued even if this involves lower wages in the short term.

# Monetary arrangements in a globalizing world: an introduction

## Matías Vernengo

### INTRODUCTION

This book is based on a conference held at Kalamazoo College Michigan. In 11–12 May 2001, on the lessons of the European Monetary Union (EMU) for the Americas. Much of the economic analysis of moving to EMU has been undertaken within the context of the Optimal Currency Area (OCA) paradigm, based on Mundell's (1961) seminal contribution. In that view money is viewed as having developed from a private sector cost minimization process to facilitate trading. Not surprisingly the main advantage of monetary integration in the OCA context is the reduction of transaction costs.[1] Yet the validity of OCA to analyse processes of monetary integration seems to be limited at best (Goodhart, 1998).

The discussions in the conference, that are partly reflected in the chapters of the book, try to go beyond the OCA model and understand the political economy of monetary integration by comparing the EMU with the dollarization (formal and informal) process in Latin America.[2] Although it is clear that no consensus was reached during the conference – something that was dubbed the Kalamazoo Dissensus by one participant – it was clear for all that monetary integration, from the more loose arrangements to the more tight including Currency Boards and formal dollarization, is no panacea.

The debate on monetary integration and dollarization is an extension of the debate on the appropriate exchange rate regime, but also is part of a broader discussion. The question is whether global financial integration would lead to fewer currencies and whether that is desirable. Cohen (2004) refers to the notion that the number of currencies around the world will shrink as the Contraction Contention, and he argues that that hypothesis is fundamentally incorrect.

Several authors have shown that territorial currencies controlled by national states are a relatively recent phenomena dating from the nineteenth Century.[3] However, it is clear that the advantages of national currencies outweigh the costs of forgoing a certain degree of monetary sovereignty, making resistance to monetary integration in all its forms a very likely strategy for national governments around the world. In this view, referred to as the Chartal (or Cartalist) view of money creation, the power of issuing money is central to the analysis, and the political relationship between control over money and political sovereignty is the key to understanding the future organization of international monetary arrangements.

Helleiner (2003) suggests that beyond the reduction of transaction costs in the domestic market the push towards national currencies in the nineteenth Century – facilitated by technical innovations in the minting process and improved capabilities against counterfeiting that led to a veritable coinage revolution – was caused by at least three additional motives. First, countries opted for territorial currencies because they desired to control monetary policy for domestic purposes.[4] Second, territorial currencies by providing seigniorage revenues increase the fiscal options of the state. Not surprisingly the typical complaint against monetary integration is related to the loss of seigniorage revenues (see Berg and Borensztein, 2000).

Helleiner (2003, p. 10) suggests that the fiscal advantages of monetary integration should not be reduced to the seigniorage gains, but more importantly to the reduction in the transaction costs associated with the management of complex fiscal bureaucracies. From a Chartal perspective, even more important would be the fact that the ability to enforce the currency in which taxes have to be paid allows governments to increase the acceptable levels of taxation. Not surprisingly Tanzi and Schuknecht (2000, pp. 52–3) show that the average level of government revenue for a list of developed countries was around 10 percent of GDP in 1870, at the time that national currencies had been recently established or were in the process of being established, while the same measure was close to 40 percent of GDP by the end of the twentieth Century.[5]

This suggests that the conventional OCA approach has downplayed the interaction between monetary and fiscal policy and consequently severely underestimated the costs of giving up monetary sovereignty. Not only national currencies seem to be associated with higher levels of taxation, but also high international transaction costs reducing foreign exchange transactions, historically allowed governments to maintain domestic interest rates at relatively low levels and finance public debt denominated in local currency at reduced cost. This was the basis for Keynes's position in favor of capital controls during the Bretton Woods negotiations (Vernengo and Rochon, 2000).

Furthermore, it appears that territorial currencies may be central for countries to pursue expansionary macroeconomic policies, but the ability to do so is restricted by the willingness of the hegemonic country to accept, and even promote as the USA did during the Bretton Woods period, a relatively closed international financial system. In that respect, the problems for peripheral countries are not only associated with the challenges to domestic currencies such as processes of monetary integration, but more broadly speaking their problems are related to the international financial regime.[6]

In other words, a country that maintains its national currency, but has a relatively open and deregulated capital account, allowing free movement of capital, will also retain its ability to pursue monetary and fiscal policy for domestic purposes.[7] The last important reason countries hold to territorial currencies, according to Helleiner, is that domestic currencies strengthen the national identity. By increasing the sense of national sovereignty territorial currencies may foster active national macroeconomic management.

This is clearly one of the major differences between the EMU and the extension of currency boards and dollarization throughout the periphery. The European experiment shares monetary sovereignty with all the participating members and it allows for significant fiscal transfers from the richer countries in the union to those in need. Clearly those arrangements are less than perfect, and some chapters in this book will emphasize the limitations, but the macroeconomic implications of monetary integration in the periphery are undeniably harsher. Hence, one would expect a lot of resistance to the elimination of domestic currencies in emerging markets, something that maybe termed the Resistance Contention.

The Contraction Contention built on the OCA framework disregards the limitations imposed on national macroeconomic policies and the political importance that these policies might have. For that reason, even though it is very likely that domestic currencies will continue to be popular for a long while, the OCA framework misses the point. Some evidence in favor of the Resistance Contention is visible in the diminished enthusiasm for dollarization since the conference was held, and also from the increased respectability for what Rudiger Dornbusch referred to as the BBC rules, that is, Band, Basket and Crawl, which reflect intermediary exchange rate arrangements (Williamson, 2000, p. 6).

The bipolar view, which claimed that developing countries in particular should either float their currencies or pursue a hard peg has been exaggerated as admitted by Stanley Fischer (2001, p. 5). Jeffrey Frankel (1999, p. 30) noted correctly that 'intermediate solutions are more likely to be appropriate for many countries than are corner solutions.' In addition, it has been noted that most countries that float their currencies actually intervene to avoid extreme fluctuations (Calvo and Reinhart, 2002). This suggests that capital controls – understood as measures that limit exchange rate volatility by reducing the size of the foreign exchange market – cannot be completely taken off the agenda.[8]

The Resistance Contention raises a broader question regarding dollarization. Dollarization may be seen as a specific monetary arrangement by which a country adopts a foreign currency (the dollar in most cases, hence the name) formally or informally. However, it is clear that since the Bretton Woods agreement and more so after its demise in 1973 the world economy has been under a dollar standard regime. The role of the US dollar as key currency in international financial markets can be seen as a more wide-ranging form of dollarization.

As noted by D'Arista (2004, p. 558) 'the share of dollar assets in international reserve holdings, the high level of dollar-denominated debt owed both to foreign and domestic creditors by borrowers in countries other than the United States, the amount of US currency held and exchanged outside the United States by residents of other countries, and the impact of changes in US interest rates and the value of the dollar on developments in the global economy are all among the pervasive manifestations of dollar dominance.' As US trade deficits increased and its net international liabilities mounted, questions about the sustainability of the global system became more unrelenting. Notwithstanding the resilience of the dollar has been incredible.[9]

This is probably the great paradox of our times. On the one hand, dollarization in a broad sense has been widespread for the last half-century, leading to increasing imbalances in the balance of payments accounts of almost every country. This has been forcefully pushed by the USA, in particular those that benefit from the dollar's position in financial markets, what Bhagwati called the Treasury-Wall Street complex. On the other hand, resistance in the periphery makes it less likely that a reduction of the number of currencies – *in extremis* dollarization in a narrow sense – will eventually take place. The US dollar will most likely remain in the midway limbo, without substituting other national currencies, but maintaining a dominant position in financial markets. The limits to this monetary arrangement are always being tested, and the fears are that a financial tsunami will drive the dollar, and the world economy, to a major crisis.

## AN OUTLINE OF THE BOOK

The contributions in this volume reflect the disagreements and the changing views on the proper monetary arrangements in a globalized world, and suggest that monetary integration and dollarization are not the solution for the great majority of countries around the world. The chapters in Part 1 deal with the European Monetary Union. In Chapter 1 Arestis and Sawyer briefly review the establishment in the European Union (EU) of the EMU and the single currency (euro) experiment as instituted in January 1999, and argue that the present arrangements governing the euro do not involve mechanisms for the reduction of the disparities of unemployment and GDP per head. They suggest that fiscal policy and a social security system operating at the level of the monetary union are required to promote a more equitable integration.

In Chapter 2 Ponsot describes the Eastern European experience with currency boards and the possibilities open by the EMU. In particular, the strict limitations imposed by the currency board arrangement, and the difficulty of reverting to a central banking system, indicate for him that the only possible way out seems to be euroization.

Parguez provides a severe indictment of the EMU, both of its theoretical foundations and of its effective achievements so far, in Chapter 3. In particular, the criticism is associated to the poor foundations provided by the OCA approach, and the economic straitjacket that is imposed on European societies. Hence, for Parguez the lesson is clear: there is no reason to create a monetary union in the Americas.

The chapters in Part 2 shift the attention to the problems of foreign exchange choice in North America. Gruben and Koo discuss in Chapter 4 whether NAFTA has moved North America closer to an optimal currency area. They argue that some change in business cycle synchronicity has occurred between Mexico and the United States, and that a similar, but less pronounced change might have occurred in between Canada and Mexico at least in comparison with previous periods. According to the authors this suggests that a positive move towards currency union has occurred.

In Chapter 5 Pozo tries to analyse the possible effects of dollarization in Mexico on illegal immigration into the United States. The conclusions derived are based on the reliability of the adjusted apprehension data as an estimate of illegal immigration into the USA from Mexico, and the notion that dollarization will result in greater stability in relative prices between Mexico and the USA. Under those assumptions, Pozo's results suggest that dollarization leads to a reduction in the level of illegal immigration.

Chapters 6 and 7 are dedicated to the discussion of whether the Canadian dollar should survive or not. Seccareccia argues that there are clear political forces at work in Canada, moving in the direction of greater monetary integration with the United States, who have employed OCA theory to further their specific political ends. However, Seccareccia suggests that OCA theory rests on terribly shaky foundations, and that the benefits of moving in the direction of greater monetary integration are highly uncertain. Bodkin agrees in his spirited contribution that the present Canadian system of foreign exchange rate regimes is probably not ideal, but that the majority of his fellow Canadian citizens prefer it anyway, and that should count for something.

Part 3 shifts the emphasis to the question of the appropriate exchange rate regime for developing countries, also known as emerging markets, despite the fact that several have literally submerged in the last decade under the pressure of several waves (tsunamis?) of financial crisis. For that reason the need for reforming the international financial architecture is also discussed. Eichengreen suggests in Chapter 8 that the Asian crisis and its fallout in Latin America and

Eastern Europe convinced many observers that soft currency pegs are crisis prone and that emerging markets should embrace greater exchange rate flexibility. In that case, inflation targeting provides a coherent alternative to exchange-rate-based monetary policy strategies that are overly restrictive and crisis prone.

In Chapter 9 Studart makes a case that the increase of financial flows between developed and developing economies is inherently destabilizing due to the wide differences between financial markets in mature and developing economies. For that reason he concludes that in the absence of substantive reforms of the international financial institutions, developing economies should be able to shelter from destabilizing effects of short-term volatile capital inflows.

Griffith-Jones argues in Chapter 10 that after several financial crises there is a broad consensus that fundamental reforms are required in the international financial system. Particularly problematic in her view is the lack of institutions that provide international liquidity, an international lender of last resort. Griffith-Jones points out that the International Monetary Fund (IMF) provides emergency financing but not liquidity, and, although the IMF has the capacity to create fiat money, through the issue of Special Drawing Rights (SDRs), those were used in the past only in a very limited way.

In Chapter 11 Medeiros and Serrano take a broader political economy view of the changes in the international economy. They argue that in the current floating dollar standard the balance of payments situation facing the emerging markets is characterized by a basic contradiction. On one hand, it is extremely easy to attract large amounts of foreign capital. On the other hand, it has become more and more difficult to deliver the fast growth of exports that is a necessary condition for the financial servicing of these inflows.

The last part of the book presents general reflections on the question of monetary integration and dollarization. Vernengo argues in Chapter 12 that dollarization – understood as the substitution of domestic currency for a foreign one – does not imply an automatic adjustment of the balance of payments. Further, the deflationary stance imposed on dollarizing countries is only a recent variation of a longer story. More importantly, the author argues that the collapse of Bretton Woods implies that dollarization is more rather than less widespread, and this has led to lower levels of growth, higher rates of interest, and has increased the degree of financial fragility of the world economy.

In Chapter 13 Davidson provides an interesting taxonomy for analysing dollarization processes. Davidson distinguishes between open and closed economies, on the one hand, and between unionized monetary systems and non-unionized monetary systems, on the other. Monetary integration and dollarization are forms of unionized monetary systems. If open economies decide to enter unionized monetary systems, then severe balance of payments can occur in the absence of a supra-national authority capable of providing fiscal transfers.

In Chapter 14 Jameson discusses the reasons for the diminished prospects of formal dollarization in the Western Hemisphere. He notes that at the time of the conference in May 2001, it seemed possible that the entire Western Hemisphere would soon move toward adopting the dollar as the uniform currency, but now a Western Hemisphere Monetary Union no longer seems likely; the dollarization momentum has diminished. The move toward greater exchange rate flexibility has been the result, to a great extent, of renewed capital flows to Latin America.

In the last chapter Câmara Neto and Vernengo try to determine the main lessons from the conference. Monetary unions and dollarization are sometimes suggested as solutions to excessive inflation, excessive foreign exchange risk and high interest rates, low levels of economic growth, too much illegal immigration and a variety of economic problems. However, it was clear from the discussions in the conference that in the real world monetary integration and dollarization are no panacea. They may solve some problems, but usually at high costs.

In particular, it seems that even though monetary integration and dollarization can deliver low levels of inflation – or at least bring inflation down to international levels, which is not necessarily the same – the costs in terms of growth and employment are high. In cases where fiscal policy can mitigate the effects on unemployment the costs of monetary unions are smaller and more bearable. Hence, in Europe a reform of the Stability and Growth pact allowing less stringent limits on budget deficits and debt would strengthen rather than weaken the monetary union. The lack of any program of fiscal transfers makes dollarization in North America and in other emerging markets less likely. The cries for reform in Europe and the renewed interest in intermediate solutions for exchange rate policy in the developing world suggest that those conclusions have been vindicated by events since the conference took place. The time elapsed since the conference, hence, has not diminished the value of the contributions here presented.

My interest on dollarization and monetary integration started with the adoption of the currency board in Argentina, and the implementation of a system of fixed exchange rates in Brazil slightly later. Lance Taylor suggested my name to the organizers of a conference at the Banco Central de Ecuador in 2000 that allowed me to meet moderate critics of the idea, such as Benjamin Cohen and Joseph Stiglitz and strong supporters like Eduardo Borensztein from the International Monetary Fund. I would like to thank Marco Baquero, Diego Mancheno and Pedro Paez for important discussions about the Ecuadorian experience.

Several participants enriched the discussions but their final contributions did not make it into the book. Robert Barro, Per Gunnar Berglund, Alfredo Calcagno, Jane D'Arista, José Maria Fanelli, Ricardo Hausmann, Jomo K.S., Marc

Lavoie and Carol Wise provided insights that are not completely lost in the remaining revised contributions. I thank them all for that.

A grant from the Ford Foundation made the conference possible. I would like to thank Manuel Montes for his incredible patience during the long gestation of the book. Marilyn Cake and several students at Kalamazoo College made the two-day conference possible and enjoyable. James Jones, the then president of the College, and above all Hannah McKinney, the department chair, supported the project in all possible ways. More importantly they showed, at a difficult point, that honesty and integrity are always rewarded. Chuck Stull, and his family, Suzan, Ricardo and Maria were incredible friends in the good and bad times of our Kalamazoo stay. Yongbok Jeon and Carlos Schonerwald da Silva, and the editorial staff at Edward Elgar were instrumental in preparing the final version of the book. Finally, Marcia and Piero provided the necessary dose of love to make it all worthwhile.

## NOTES

1. There is a catalogue of conditions that determine whether an area is an OCA or not. Two important issues are whether the whole area is affected by symmetric economic shocks, leading to the need of similar macroeconomic policies, and whether wage or labor flexibility can take the brunt of a regional balance of payments adjustment in the absence of exchange rate devaluations. De Grauwe (1997) provides a comprehensive and accessible introduction to the topic.
2. In that respect the focus is slightly different from the one pursued in Salvatore et al. (2003) and Levy Yeyati and Sturzenegger (2003).
3. See Helleiner (2003), Rochon and Vernengo (2003) and Cohen (2004).
4. Helleiner (2003) supposes that monetary policy has concentrated on the control of the money supply, fundamentally as a result of the need to follow the rules of the game of the gold standard. This reflects an incorrect perception of the functioning of that system. Current understanding of that system suggests that the control of the rate of interest and not monetary aggregates was at the center of policy decisions (Bordo and Kydland, 1996). For a critical perspective on the functioning of the gold standard see Vernengo (2003).
5. The list of countries includes Australia, France, Italy, Ireland, Japan, New Zealand, Norway, the United Kingdom and the United States.
6. Monetary integration refers to the use, in different degrees, of an external currency as a substitute for the national one. Financial integration corresponds to the degree of capital mobility. Countries may very well stay clear of monetary integration arrangements and still choose to integrate into financial markets by eliminating all types of capital controls.
7. The incompatibility between capital mobility, national autonomy in the conduct of monetary policy, and fixed exchange rate systems is well known in the literature. Here it is suggested that even with flexible exchange rates, capital mobility is incompatible with national autonomy in the conduct of both monetary and fiscal policies.
8. The literature on capital controls has surged lately. Wade (1998–9) and Dunn (2002) provide opposing views. For a defense of capital controls see also Vernengo and Rochon (2000).
9. Frank (2003, p. 252) suggests the resilience of the dollar is connected to American power to coerce other governments to hold dollar denominated assets, which ultimately is related to American military power.

# REFERENCES

Berg, A. and E. Borensztein (2000), 'The pros and cons of full dollarization,' IMF working paper No 00/50, Washington, DC.

Bordo, M. and F. Kydland (1996), 'The Gold Standard as a commitment mechanism,' in T. Bayoumi, B. Eichengreen and M. Taylor (eds), *Modern Perspectives on the Gold Standard*, Cambridge, UK: Cambridge University Press.

Calvo, G. and C. Reinhart (2002), 'Fear of floating,' *Quarterly Journal of Economics*, **117** (2), 379–408.

Cohen, B. (2004), *The Future of Money*, Princeton, NJ: Princeton University Press.

D'Arista, J. (2004), 'Dollars, debt, and dependence: the case for international monetary reform,' *Journal of Post Keynesian Economics*, **26** (4), Summer, 557–72.

De Grauwe, P. (1997), *The Economics of Monetary Integration*, New York: Oxford University Press, 3rd edition.

Dunn, Jr., R. (2002), 'The misguided attractions of foreign exchange controls,' *Challenge*, September–October, 98–111.

Fischer, S. (2001), 'Exchange rate regimes: is the bipolar view correct?' *Journal of Economic Perspectives*, **15** (2), Spring, 3–24.

Frank, E. (2003), 'The surprising resilience of the US dollar,' *Review of Radical Political Economy*, **35** (3).

Frankel, J. (1999), 'No single currency regime is right for all countries or at all times,' *Princeton Essays in International Finance*, no. 215 (August).

Goodhart, C. (1998), 'The two concepts of money: implications for the analysis of optimal currency areas,' *European Journal of Political Economy*, **14** (3), 407–32.

Helleiner, E. (2003), *The Making of National Money: Territorial Currencies in Historical Perspective*, Ithaca: Cornell University Press.

Levy Yeyati, E. and F. Sturzenegger (eds) (2003), *Dollarization: Debates and Policy Alternatives*, Cambridge: MIT Press.

Mundell, R.A. (1961), 'A theory of optimal currency areas,' *American Economic Review*, **53** (1), 657–64.

Rochon, L-P. and M. Vernengo (2003), 'State money and the real world: Chartalism and its discontents,' *Journal of Post Keynesian Economics*, **26** (1), Fall, 57–67.

Salvatore, D., J. Dean and T. Willett (2003), (eds), *The Dollarization Debate*, New York: Oxford University Press.

Tanzi, V. and L. Schuknecht (2000), *Public Spending in the 20th Century*, Cambridge, UK: Cambridge University Press.

Vernengo, M. (2003), 'The Gold Standard and centre–periphery interactions,' in L-P. Rochon and S. Rossi (eds), *Modern Theories of Money: the Nature and Role of Money in Capitalist Economies*, Cheltenham, UK and Northampton, MA, USA: Edward Elgar.

Vernengo, M. and L-P. Rochon (2000), 'Exchange Rate Regimes and Capital Controls,' *Challenge*, **43** (6), November–December, 76–92.

Wade, R. (1998–9), 'The coming fight over capital controls,' *Foreign Policy*, Winter, 41–54.

Williamson, J. (2000), *Exchange Rate Regimes for Emerging Markets: Reviving the Intermediate Option*, Washington, DC: Institute for International Economics.

PART 1

European Monetary Union

# 1. Reflections on the experience of the euro: lessons for the Americas

## Philip Arestis and Malcolm Sawyer

## INTRODUCTION

This chapter aims to review briefly the establishment in the European Union (EU) of the Economic and Monetary Union (EMU) and the single currency (euro) experiment as instituted in January 1999, and ask whether any lessons can be drawn for the Americas.

The euro was established for financial transactions with the exchange rates between those national currencies, which will be absorbed by the euro, fixed (to 6 significant figures) on 1 January 1999. The euro replaced the component national currencies for all transactions in the first two months of 2002. The value of the euro has declined through most of the first period of its existence from an initial value vis-a-vis the dollar of $1.18, to parity with the dollar in December 1999, an all-time low in November 2000 of $0.82, before starting something of a climb back and the time of writing (October 2003) is around the initial level vis-a-vis the dollar. We have explored the explanations for the initial decline elsewhere (Arestis et al, 2002, 2003). A brief summary of those papers would be that we find explanations based on 'bad luck' (in effect currencies go up and down in value and the first two years of the euro's existence happened to be a down) and adjustment to prior high value of the euro to be unconvincing. The euro declined well past any purchasing power parity or trade balance benchmark point. The notion that the weakness of the euro is merely the other side of strength of the dollar faces the problem of explaining the decline of the euro against other currencies such as the yen and sterling. The USA has run a large current account deficit (of the order of 4 per cent of GDP) whereas the Eurozone has run a substantial current account surplus (order of 2 per cent of GDP) and hence it is difficult to explain the decline of the euro in terms of the current account position. There seems though some plausibility in the view that perceptions of strength and profitability of the US economy generated capital inflows into the USA and away from the eurozone.

We have also argued that weaknesses in the eurozone (including the fudging of the convergence criteria for membership of the euro and the manner in which the ECB has operated) may have contributed to the decline in the value of the euro. We also emphasized the continuing divergent state of the eurozone especially in terms of variables such as unemployment rates and GDP per head as problematic for the future economic health of the eurozone. This is to emphasize the divergent *state* of the economies, rather than asking whether there has been a process of convergence or divergence in the past decade or so. The decline in the value of the euro confounded those who believed it would be a 'strong currency', and those who thought that the perceived strength of the Mark and reputation of the Bundesbank would be transferred to the euro and the European Central Bank.

The existence of the euro and the particular circumstances surrounding its launch (e.g. its existence for financial dealings but not for other transactions) precludes any firm assessment of the impact of the single European currency on the economic performance of the eurozone. We approach the question of the implications of the euro experience for dollarisation and monetary union in the Americas by considering some of the issues that have arisen in the context of the euro.

## OPTIMAL CURRENCY AREA CONSIDERATIONS

It would seem on the surface that the formation of a monetary union encompassing 12 politically independent countries each with their own currencies prior to the union would be much influenced by optimal currency area (OCA) considerations. The formation of the single currency and the eurozone provides one of the few occasions when a change in the scope of a currency area has been actively considered. The other recent cases that come to mind would be the reunification of Germany, and the splintering of Czechoslovakia, the Soviet Union and Yugoslavia. In each of those cases, the political considerations for the currency regime would dominate any OCA-type considerations (we return to the question of the relationship between monetary union and political union below). It is argued here that the OCA considerations had virtually no impact on the decision to introduce a single European currency nor on the conditions governing which countries were to be members.

The Maastricht Treaty provided convergence criteria that were intended to be met by those seeking to join the euro. These criteria were:

1.  Average exchange rate not to deviate by more than 2.25 per cent from its central rate for the two years prior to membership: what became known as the Exchange Rate Mechanism (ERM).
2.  Inflation rate not to exceed the average rate of inflation of the three community nations with the lowest inflation rate by 1.5 per cent.

3.  Long-term interest rates not to exceed the average interest rate of the three countries with the lowest inflation rate by 2 per cent.
4.  Budget deficit not to exceed 3 per cent of GDP.
5.  Overall government debt not to exceed 60 per cent of GDP.

Countries were also required to enact legislation for their Central Banks to become 'independent'.

In the event, these criteria were 'fudged' (as discussed in Arestis et al, 2001). The decision on membership of the euro and whether the convergence criteria were met was based on data available in March 1998. As we have shown elsewhere (Arestis et al, 2001), it was clear that France and Luxembourg were the only countries which, on a strict interpretation, satisfied all the convergence criteria for membership of the euro. However, nine more countries were deemed as meeting all the convergence criteria, even though they did not meet them on a literal interpretation. Seven of them – Belgium, Germany, Spain, Ireland, the Netherlands, Austria and Portugal – failed on the debt/GDP criterion, one on the ERM participation for at least two years (Finland), and one on both of these criteria (Italy).

These convergence criteria on economic performance variables related to convergence in nominal variables at a particular point in time, and made no reference to convergence in real variables (whether in terms of levels such as GDP per head or rates of change and position within the business cycle). Nor was there any reference to what could be termed structural convergence in terms of institutional and organizational arrangement.

The OCA literature suggests three conditions for an 'optimal currency area' (Mundell, 1961):

1.  factor mobility and openness of markets;
2.  relative price flexibility; and
3.  fiscal transfers within the monetary union.

It would be desirable for a single currency to be used in an economic area within which there is openness of goods markets and mobility of factors of production (labour, capital) as the mobility of factors is seen as one way in which adjustment is made to differences in economic performance. Further, member economies should share similar inflationary tendencies since a common currency imposes a common inflation rate.

The Single European Act of 1986 and the implementation of the single European market by the end of 1992 were steps in seeking to ensure the mobility of goods and services and of capital within the European Union. But it is well-known that effective labour mobility within the EU remains low, especially by comparison with the USA, despite the large differences in real wages and unemployment rates across the EU. Price flexibility (in terms of relative prices across countries) remains low. The differences in labour market institutions, notably over wage determination, mean that there are different inflationary tendencies and different responses to economic shocks. The convergence criteria ensured a convergence of inflation rates, which is not the same as convergence of inflationary mechanisms and tendencies. Indeed, similar rates of inflation across the eurozone countries in 1998 (the relevant year for the application of the convergence criteria) were accompanied by widely differing rates of unemployment from around 4 per cent in the case of Austria and the Netherlands to 17 per cent in the case of Spain (and the difference in unemployment between regions was much more marked from 3 per cent in the Oberösterreich region of Austria to 32 per cent in the Andulucia region of Spain and nearly 37 per cent in Reunion, France: these figures refer to 1997). The calculated output gap, as a sign of stage of the business cycle, varied (according to the OECD measure) from over +2 per cent in Ireland to –2 per cent in Italy (and there was a slight widening of the differences in 1999).

The EU budget is small (around 1.25 per cent of GDP), required to be always in balance and dominated by the Common Agricultural Policy (CAP). There is clearly little role for fiscal transfers from relatively rich countries to relatively poor countries, nor is there any possibility of the EU budget operating as a stabilizer. About half of the transfers which do occur will be set by the requirements of the CAP, although much of the remainder (in the form of regional policy) do involve transfers from rich to poor areas. There is currently no mechanism for the operation of an EU level fiscal policy which could have stabilizing effects (as an automatic stabilizer) over time nor which has any significant redistributive element across economic regions.

The optimists would tend to believe that the continuing effects of the single European market and the introduction of the euro will lead to further integration between the national economies. This integration could then be reflected in some convergence between national business cycles and (perhaps) some reduction in the extent of asymmetric shocks that impact on some countries but not on others. There could, in the fullness of time, be increased mobility of labour. But there seems little prospect of EU wide measures such as a common social security policy which would enhance the mobility of labour. There would also seem to be little prospect of significant fiscal transfers, even up to the level of public expenditure and taxation at the EU level of 7.5 per cent as recommended by the MacDougall Report (1977).

An OCA obviously introduces alongside a single currency a union-wide monetary policy. In much of the OCA literature the role of the common monetary policy is rather underplayed, but attention must be paid to the nature of the common monetary policy and who operates it, especially in an era when monetary policy has displaced fiscal policy as the main macroeconomic instrument.

In the eurozone context, this common monetary policy is operated by the ECB in pursuit of price stability in an environment where there is no union-level fiscal policy of any significance.

Fiscal policy can be differentiated, whether as a side effect of the design of the tax system (the obvious example being a progressive income tax system which has a degree of redistribution from rich areas to poor areas) or through the allocation of public expenditure. Fiscal policy has the capabilities of being differentiated and of transferring resources though those capabilities need not be exercized. But monetary policy cannot be differentiated – a common Central Bank discount rate must apply across all countries (or in the days of monetary targets, there is a single monetary aggregate to which the targeting applies). Monetary policy is likely to have differential effects on regions and countries. The mark-up of bank lending and mark-down of bank borrowing rates over the Central Bank discount rate may vary across countries (and also within countries). The responsiveness of aggregate demand in different regions is likely to vary, for example depending on the extent of fixed rate or variable rate borrowing. The difficulties of the 'one policy fits all' nature of monetary policy are well-known and come into play whenever there are differences between economic areas in terms of economic performance, stage of the business cycle or inflationary pressures. These differences are exacerbated at the eurozone level as economies with different financial institutions and arrangements are brought together under a single umbrella. It should be noted that there is a sense in which the EU has adopted a one-instrument approach to policy, namely the use of monetary policy. Fiscal policy is restricted to an overall balanced budget position, albeit with variations of the national budget deficit positions over the business cycle.

The difficulties with the use of one policy instrument is illustrated by the continuing dilemma for the ECB – the inflationary position (of over 2.5 per cent) points to raising interest rates whereas the warnings of economic slowdown point to reducing interest rates, though the objectives given to the ECB suggest that the former would have to dominate.

This brief discussion indicates to us that OCA considerations appear to have played little role in the formation of the eurozone. Further, if the OCA literature is correct, then the eurozone would appear not to be an optimal currency area. Some of the departures of the eurozone from an OCA arise from policy decisions (notably the absence of EU fiscal policy) whereas others (notably lack of labour mobility) are more deeply embedded and some attempts have been made to address them (e.g., by development of transferability of qualifications between countries). But to say that the eurozone is not optimal is not the same as saying that the eurozone is not better than the continuation of national currencies. However, we would argue that it is still the case that the criteria proposed by the OCA literature still have some relevance in judging whether the introduction of the euro is an improvement. Feldstein (1997) stated that 'what is clear to me is that the decision [on economic and monetary union] will not depend on the *economic* advantages and disadvantages of a single currency' (p. 23). This is a remark with which we would concur and we would say in particular that the OCA literature has been ignored.

## THE MACROECONOMIC POLICY OF A SINGLE CURRENCY

The adoption of the Stability and Growth Pact has accompanied the introduction of the euro. It governs the economic policies of the member countries that have joined the single currency and constrains the economic policy of those who did not join.

The lack of trust between Northern and Southern EU states has produced this pact, which increases the restrictions imposed on the freedom of EU countries to use fiscal policy (Miller, 1997).[1] The Stability and Growth Pact created four rules for macroeconomic policy. The ECB was granted independence from political influence from member governments, the European Commission or the European Parliament. There is the rule of 'no bail out' of national government deficits. The monetary financing of government deficits is prohibited. Finally, member states must avoid 'excessive deficits' which are defined as more than 3 per cent of GDP. This rule has been seen to imply a balanced budget or slight surplus over the course of the business cycle (given that the 3 per cent deficit cannot be exceeded during a downswing).[2]

The terms of the Stability and Growth Pact differ significantly from the Maastricht convergence criteria quoted above in that although the same figure of 3 per cent is used for the deficit to GDP ratio requirement, the convergence criteria referred to a moment in time whereas the Stability and Growth Pact refers to a maximum that implies an overall balanced budget. One (perhaps) minor side effect is that there appears to be no route to any expansion of base money: on average the budget is to be balanced or in surplus, and anyway any deficit (even a temporary one) cannot be directly monetized. The banking system (expanding at around 4.5 per cent per annum if the money supply reference level is achieved) would be operating with diminishing reserve ratios unless the ECB is generally engaging in open market operations which have the effect of buying in the debt of national governments.

The rationale for the 'no bail out' rule and the limits on budget deficits would appear to be some combination of seeking 'credibility' in the financial markets and dealing with possible externalities. The 'credibility' would be perceived to be gained through adherence to particular rules for economic policy as well as granting 'independence' to central banks, etc. Whatever the intention, the decline in the value of the euro does not suggest much success in gaining 'credibility'. The latter would arise if high levels of borrowing of euros by one government put upward pressure on the interest rate on bonds paid by that government which in turn could edge up the interest rate on bonds issued by other eurozone governments. But this would be based on some combination of the argument that there are limited funds for borrowing and that the risk premium attached to one eurozone country affects the risk premium of other eurozone countries. It can also be noted in this context that the eurozone differs from most (perhaps all) nation states where governments not only have the ability to raise taxes to finance interest payments and debt repayment but also the ability to create national currency to do so.

The eurozone is perhaps unique in having a 'high level' monetary authority (the ECB) and in effect no 'high level' fiscal authority, with fiscal policy residing at the national level (albeit constrained by the Stability and Growth Pact). There cannot be any substantive coordination of monetary and fiscal policies in these circumstances, and there is a sense in which the monetary authority has the last word in that interest rates are set frequently and can be adjusted to seek to offset any fiscal policy. It is also the case that the independence of the ECB and the national central banks places heavy constraints on any coordination of fiscal and monetary policy. For example, 'neither the ECB, nor a national central bank, nor any member of their decision making bodies shall seek or take instructions from Community institutions or bodies, from any government of a Member State or from any other body' (Article 7 of the Statute of the European System of Central Banks and of the European Central Bank).

One notable feature of the operation of the ESCB is the apparent absence of the lender-of-last-resort facility. The Protocols under which the ECB is established enable, but do not require, the ECB to act as a lender of last resort. The relevant article of the Protocol suggests that:

> In order to achieve the objectives of the ESCB and to carry out its tasks, the ECB and the national central banks may: operate in the financial markets by buying and selling outright (spot and forward) or under repurchase agreement and by lending or borrowing claims and marketable instruments, whether in Community or in non Community currencies, as well as precious metals; conduct credit operations with credit institutions and other market participants with lending being based on adequate collateral. The ECB shall establish general principles for open market and credit operations carried out by itself or the national central banks, including for the announcement of conditions under which they stand ready to enter into such transactions. (Protocol, No. 3 on the Statute of the European System of Central Banks and of the European Central Bank)

The lender-of-last-resort function requires that base money is essentially provided on request to the banking system by the Central Bank, and in particular would be supplied if reserves were low following an expansion of broader money. More generally, the lender-of-last-resort function recognizes the role of a central bank in securing a stable financial system, but the specific objective of stabilizing the financial system is not included in the remit of the ECB. It is clear that on occasions, the lender-of-last-resort function may require base money to be supplied when pursuit of a price stability target would point in the opposite direction.

In this context can there be any effective macroeconomic policy? The standard answer would be that there is and it is monetary policy. But monetary policy is heavily constrained in that the extent to which euro interest rates can be varied relative to say American interest rates is limited, especially over an extended period of time. Further how much impact would interest rates have, especially in the context of a quasi-closed economy such as the eurozone (where imports and exports are equivalent to circa 10 per cent of GDP). Interest rates may influence exchange rates, but in a quasi-closed economy changes in the exchange rate may have little impact on the level of output or on the rate of inflation. It could be argued that one of the paradoxes is that the creation of a monetary union reduces the effect of monetary policy in that the effect of exchange rate changes is reduced. Further it can be argued that fiscal policy becomes more potent in that there are fewer spill-over effects into other economies, and the boost from expansionary fiscal policy within the monetary union is enhanced.[3]

If the market economy is deemed to be stable around high levels of employment and the argument put that no guidance for the level of aggregate demand is required even in the short run, then there would be no need for either monetary or fiscal policy. But when such guidance is required (which we would assert is generally the case) then fiscal policy as well as monetary policy is required. Further, unless it can be asserted that there will always be sufficient private demand to maintain high levels of employment, then fiscal policy (in the form of budget deficits) will be required.

Although there is no significant EU-level fiscal policy, there are, of course, the national fiscal policies coordinated through the Stability and Growth Pact and the meetings of Ecofin (the EU Council of Economic and Finance Ministers). But the coordination of fiscal policies from that pact is not in the form of coordinated reflation or deflation to deal with EU-wide issues of unemployment or inflation. Nor is it a coordination that seeks to achieve an overall average high level of aggregate demand, but rather it is coordination of budgets to an average balance or a surplus.

> It is also necessary to ensure that national budgetary policies support stability oriented monetary policies. Adherence to the objective of sound budgetary positions close to balance or in surplus will allow all Member States to deal with normal cyclical fluctuations while keeping the government deficit within the reference value of 3% of GDP.

Further:

> Member States commit themselves to respect the medium-term budgetary objective of positions close to balance or in surplus set out in their stability of convergence programmes and to take the corrective budgetary action they deem necessary to meet the objectives of their stability or convergence programmes, whenever they have information indicating actual or expected significant divergence from those objectives. (Resolution of the European Council on the Stability and Growth Pact, Amsterdam, 17 June 1997)

Some recent experiences (e.g. the condemnation of Ireland for cutting taxes and raising public expenditure when output was above trend, and criticisms of Britain, even though outside the eurozone, for proposing public expenditure increases above the trend rate of growth of output) point to a general deflationary bias in the operation of the Stability and Growth Pact. It also means that 'governments could be required to raise taxes, or cut government spending, as the economy moves into recession, thereby exacerbating the downturn' (Currie, 1997, p. 13). This is illustrated by the recent recommendation in April 2001 to the British government (who are not formally governed by the Stability and Growth Pact) that in the event of a downturn in 2002, public expenditure should be reduced (below planned levels) to maintain the public expenditure to GDP ratio.

We may conclude this section by suggesting that macroeconomic policy at the EMU level has been designed in manner that tends be restrictive. It amounts to the absence of any fiscal policy (other than directives to member states emanating from the Stability and Growth Pact) and in terms of monetary policy, the ECB pursues extremely cautionary rules, presumably in its attempt to gain 'credibility' in the financial markets at the cost of any other objectives. A serious implication at this juncture is that with the US slowdown, which threatens to produce a world recession, EMU policy could potentially help to avoid it. The ECB policy stance at the moment does not appear to be geared to this objective.

## POLITICAL UNION?

The introduction of the euro provides one of the few examples where a monetary union does not coincide with a nation state. The cases of the reunification of Germany, and the splintering of Czechoslovakia, Soviet Union and Yugoslavia provide examples of where changes in the nation state were quickly paralleled by changes in the monetary union. There have been examples of monetary unions encompassing a number of nation states but with a poor survival rate. There are the examples of the Latin Union that started in 1865 but collapsed shortly after the First World War and the Scandinavian Monetary Union beginning in 1873 lasting until 1920. The monetary union between Ireland and the United Kingdom continued for sometime after political disunion and the final break between the Irish pound and the British pound came in 1979. The forms of monetary union imposed by colonialisation have usually not survived political independence. The only continuing examples of a monetary union which do not involve political union that we are aware of is the Francophone area of West Africa (but then this is only because the whole union is under the grip of the Bank of France), and the Eastern Caribbean Currency Union (which covers a total population of half a million).

This raises the obvious question as to whether a coincidence between the nation state and monetary union is virtually a necessity for the long run continuation of the monetary union. The reference in the OCA literature to the relevance of fiscal transfers suggests the requirement for political union (though it is possible to envisage fiscal transfers without formal political union).

A belief that a market economy will function effectively without government intervention and redistribution would obviate any need for eurozone economic policies. The eurozone contains considerable economic disparities. The idea that either they will be eliminated through a process of market competition or that such disparities are politically sustainable would indicate that there is little requirement for an effective political union. By effective political union here we mean significant EU-level taxation, social security and public expenditure programmes. We leave open the question as to whether that would entail a formal political union within a federal state, but we would argue that the effective operation of a market economy involves government intervention in that form. A common social security system would enhance labour mobility as well as involving elements of redistribution. A substantive fiscal policy would likewise aid economic integration and would involve significant fiscal transfers between regions and between countries.

The present arrangements governing the euro do not involve mechanisms for the reduction of the disparities of unemployment and GDP per head. The disparities of unemployment inevitably undermine the achievement of high levels of employment across the eurozone. When some regions are experiencing low unemployment and high rates of capacity utilisation, others still have high unemployment. Inflation pressures, actual or perceived, in the low unemployment regions will lead to high interest rates and attempts to slow down the eurozone economy.

A monetary union involves the imposition of a common currency across a number of nations with the requirement that the common currency is the only legal tender within the nations involved. In that trivial sense, a monetary union involves a degree of political agreement, if not political union. There is also the obvious requirement for a central bank for the monetary union, and in an era of dominance of monetary policy over fiscal policy, that central bank becomes the effective macroeconomic policy maker. Any requirements for an effective fiscal policy across the monetary union which would be redistributive across time and space, point to the emergence of a fiscal authority at the level of the monetary union. Further requirements such as measures to enhance trade or a common social security system to enhance labour mobility, again point towards policies being exercized at the level of the monetary union. It could be said that such policies can be introduced through the construction of institutions at the level of the monetary union without formal political union. But if there were to be fiscal, social security and other policies at the level of the monetary union, it comes close to being a political union.

Feldstein (1997) argued that 'there can be no doubt that eliminating individual currencies would be a major psychological and substantive step toward a European central government' (p. 24). The argument we are putting is a rather different one, namely that a monetary union may require considerable central government support to operate fiscal and social security policies across the eurozone. Whether the elimination of individual currencies will be a sufficient psychological step remains to be seen.

## TRANSPARENCY AND CONFLICT

One of the arguments for the way in which monetary union can be beneficial to economic performance (and here consumers in particular) is that there will be increased transparency of prices across the eurozone. A comparison between the price of the same item in country A and country B can be readily made without currency conversion calculations or taking account of transactions costs. The currency conversion and the transactions costs disappear with monetary union. There are then increased competitive pressures leading to equalisation of prices across countries. But there is also increased transparency in terms of wage levels and living standards. Although the introduction of a single currency does not change the ease of comparison, it would also be our guess that comparisons of unemployment levels and employment opportunities across nations will increase, especially if there is an evolution of wage determination towards the eurozone level. The question here is then whether this makes any difference to economic and political behaviour. This could range from increased migration to political campaigns to redistribute income and employment opportunities. 'These disagreements about monetary and fiscal policies may have broader effects on the relations among European countries, creating conflict rather than the political harmony that many of EMU's advocates seek'. Further, 'uniform monetary policy and inflexible exchange rates will create conflicts whenever cyclical conditions differ among member countries' (Feldstein, 1997, p. 41).

It could, of course, be argued that there are disagreements over monetary and fiscal policies within any existing monetary union, i.e. within any nation state. Any continuing nation state has to find ways of resolving and modifying those disagreements. The disagreements within the EMU can be seen as involving different dimensions compared with those within an existing nation state. First, the EMU has very limited room to make 'side payments' from one region to another since there are few transfers from rich regions to poor regions within the monetary union. Second, the economic disparities within the eurozone are considerable as hinted above. The disparities between the regions of the euro-zone (which number 65) and the states of the United States of America may provide a reasonable basis for comparison. For the USA, unemployment rates between states ranged from 2.2 per cent to 5.9 per cent in 2000, and per capita disposable income from $18 467 (Mississippi) to $31 697 (Connecticut) in 1999. For the eurozone, unemployment rates ranged, as indicated above, from 3 per cent to 37 per cent, and GDP per head (in 1998) from 6536 euros per head (Ipi-eros, Greece) to 40 353 euros per head (Hamburg), i.e. by a factor of 1:6. Third, there is not only incomplete convergence of business cycles across countries but also that the differing institutional arrangements mean that economic activity and inflation respond differently. Fourth, there are differences of views on ap-propriate economic policies. This, again, could be expected to occur within any monetary union, but may be greater when countries with different traditions and outlooks are brought together.

Some of the potential for disagreement is illustrated by a recent episode with the criticism of Irish budgetary policy adopted by the Ecofin on 12 February 2001 (based on recommendations from the European Commission). Far from tightening fiscal policy, the Irish government relaxed it in an attempt to contain inflationary wage increases. This episode illustrates three points. First, the Sta-bility and Growth Pact is seen to involve the notion that government budgets should be, on average, in balance or surplus in order to comply with the refer-ence value of 3 per cent of GDP for the budget deficit. The Maastricht Treaty required budget deficits to be pushed below 3 per cent at the time of the decision on euro membership, but this is now moved to a much more stringent aim of overall balance or surplus. Second, the Stability and Growth Pact is interpreted to say that budgets must be tightened rather than loosened when there is evi-dence of 'overheating', without regard to the budget position and without regard to the prospects for inflation. The European Commission argues that as the Irish budget plans for 2001 'will fuel demand but are likely to generate smaller supply effects in the short term, the overheating problem will worsen'. Third, there are some fundamental differences between governments on economic policy and the workings of the economy. In this instance the European Commission and a number of member governments seem to be saying that inflation is necessarily demand-led and should be met by fiscal demand deflation (even though monetary policy is supposed to be the policy instrument for the control of inflation), whereas the Irish government appears to be arguing that wage agreements can moderate inflation.

## CONCLUDING REMARKS

In a short chapter we can only touch on some of the issues that have arisen in the context of the creation of the European Monetary Union. We would summarize the implications of those issues for moves towards some form of monetary union on the American continent. From our discussion of the OCA literature we have concluded that decisions on monetary union are little influenced by the concerns of the OCA literature. The OCA literature could be seen as asking what alternatives exist to the exchange rate as an adjustment mechanism for a country experiencing economic performance that is markedly different from that of its trading partners. In the formation of the eurozone there seems little possibility of labour mobility or fiscal policy being used in this way. We see this as a considerable weakness in the formation of EMU, and would argue that any American monetary union should pay attention to those issues.

The creation of a monetary union obviously creates a union level monetary policy. It is widely recognized that monetary policy imposes a single policy applying across a diverse set of economic regions. A particular monetary policy may be appropriate to some economies but not to others given their position in the business cycle and the responsiveness of their economies to monetary policy, and the monetary policy is more likely to favour the most politically robust (even when operated by an 'independent' central bank). Further, monetary policy is constructed to deal with demand-induced inflation with interest rates raised (lowered) in response to inflation (actual or expected) above (below) the target rate, though we would doubt the effectiveness of monetary policy to significantly influence aggregate demand. But monetary policy cannot deal with other forms of inflation (e.g. cost-push inflation) nor with situations in which there is high (or rising) inflation combined with low (or falling) levels of economic activity. A monetary union requires a further set of policy instruments including fiscal policy.

In this chapter we have raised the question (but not supplied the answer) as to whether a sustainable monetary union requires a considerable degree of political integration (and perhaps political union). We have suggested that fiscal policy and a social security system operating at the level of the monetary union is required. The diversity of economic performance, institutional arrangements and beliefs concerning economic policy and the operation of market economies are all further difficulties in the construction of a monetary union.

In debates over financial liberalisation there has been concern over the sequencing of institutional and policy changes. It could be argued that a similar concern should arise with monetary union, namely whether monetary union should precede economic and political integration or come after considerable integration. Unlike current advocates of the European single currency, we are of the opinion that monetary union should come after other integration materializes. This is probably the most important question arising from the European experience that is of particular relevance for monetary union and dollarisation in the case of Americas.

## NOTES

1.  The 'growth' part of the Stability and Growth Pact is merely cosmetic. It was added to conciliate the French authorities who insisted on the inclusion of growth and other activity variables in the pact. They also managed to change the German proposal that any budget revenues should be used to pay off debts, to one that requires government financial positions to be close to zero or in surplus in the medium term.
2.  If there is an economic downturn and output has fallen by more than 2 per cent then the member state escapes any sanction automatically, but the deficit should be corrected once the recession has finished. If output falls between 0.75 and 2 per cent then the Council of Ministers can use discretion when making a decision on an 'excessive' deficit.
3.  It may be argued that the long-term effectiveness of fiscal policy is constrained by the inflation barrier of the NAIRU. If such a barrier exists then it also applies to monetary policy. The argument here is that fiscal policy becomes more effective and monetary policy less effective with the formation of a monetary union.

## REFERENCES

Arestis, P., I. Biefang-Frisancho Mariscal, A. Brown and M. Sawyer (2003), 'The decline of the euro in its first two years: is there a satisfactory explanation?', in Rochon, L.-P. and M. Seccareccia (eds), *Dollarisation: Lessons from Europe for the Americas*, London: Routledge.

Arestis, P., I. Biefang-Frisancho Mariscal, A. Brown and M. Sawyer (2002), 'Explaining the euro's initial decline', *Eastern Economic Journal*, **28** (1), Winter.

Arestis, P., A. Brown and M. Sawyer (2001), *The Euro: Evolution and Prospects*, Cheltenham, UK and Northampton MA, USA: Edward Elgar Publishing.

Currie, D. (1997), *The Pros and Cons of EMU*, July, London: HM Treasury (published originally by the Economist Intelligence Unit, January 1997).

European Commission (MacDougall Report) (1977), *Report of the Study Group on the Role of Public Finance in European Integration*, Brussels: European Commission.

Feldstein, M. (1997), 'The political economy of the European Economic and Monetary Union: political sources of an economic liability', *Journal of Economic Perspectives*, **11**, (4), 23–42.

Miller, M. (1997), 'Eurosclerosis, Eurochicken and the Outlook for EMU', *Warwick Economic Research Papers*, no. 482, Department of Economics, University of Warwick.

Mundell, R.A. (1961), 'A theory of optimal currency areas', *American Economic Review*, **53** (1), 657–64.

# 2. European experiences of currency boards: Estonia, Lithuania, Bulgaria and Bosnia and Herzegovina

## Jean-François Ponsot

## INTRODUCTION

> A currency board solution, therefore, is equivalent to the blood letting prescribed by 17th century doctors to cure a fever. Enough blood loss can, of course, always reduce the fever but often at a terrible cost to the body of the patient. Similarly, a currency board may douse the flames of a currency crisis but the result can be a moribund economy. (Davidson, 2000, p. 16)

The expression 'currency board' has two different meanings, describing as it does both a particular monetary arrangement, the currency board arrangement (CBA) – characteristic of the British colonial era – and the organization within this system entrusted with the monopoly of issuing local currency – in many cases the former central bank if already in existence. The activity of the currency board is governed by three strict rules:

1. an exchange rate rigidly pegged to a foreign reference currency;
2. the obligation for the currency issued to be freely and integrally convertible into this foreign 'reserve currency';
3. an obligation for the currency board to keep in its balance sheet assets a volume of foreign reserve currency equal to at least 100 per cent of the currency issued, i.e. the monetary base is made up of money in circulation plus bank reserves.

In the light of the financial crises striking the developing economies over the past ten years, a general consensus has emerged, denouncing the unsuitable character of the intermediate exchange rate systems and calling for the adoption of one or other of the two 'corner solutions' – the pure flexibility option or the currency board. The introduction of four CBAs in Europe – Estonia, Lithuania, Bulgaria, Bosnia and Herzegovina – predated this debate but the forces at work were much the same. Section 2 sets out the empirical and theoretical justifications for adoption of these CBAs together with the context in which they were introduced. The constraints inherent in the rigidity of the CBA are explored in Section 3, while their impact on each country is illustrated in Section 4. Section 5 lists the palliative measures adopted in an effort to re-establish certain discretionary margins and shows how these have contributed to the gradual distortion of the CBA. Now that the question of withdrawing the CBA has been raised, Section 6 examines the conditions for a successful withdrawal in terms of eventual integration in the EMU. Lastly, Section 7 looks at the conclusions and lessons to be drawn from the European experiences of CBAs for the Argentinean CBA.

## EMPIRICAL AND THEORETICAL JUSTIFICATIONS

### Transitions and Monetary Stabilization

#### Estonia, 1992
The determination of the Estonian authorities to distance themselves from the old system and the former USSR, and to embark on a process of rapid transition was apparent right from the date of independence in 1991. The CBA formed part of the logic of the economic stabilization program advocated by the IMF (July 1992–June 1993) and designed to halt the decline of activity, limit the rise of unemployment, balance the budget and guarantee the stability of the currency. On this last point, the Estonian authorities were quick to realize that the stability of the national currency was synonymous with a fixed exchange rate. The law of 20 June 1992 pegged the new national currency – the kroon – to the deutschmark (DM1 = EEK8). Since 1999 the kroon has *de jure* been pegged to the euro (E1 = EEK15.6456). The new central bank (Eesti Pank or BOE) cannot devalue and must ensure 100 per cent cover of the money it issues (Table 2.1).

#### Lithuania, 1994
The convincing results rapidly achieved by Estonia in terms of monetary stability prompted the Lithuanian leaders to abandon the system of managed floating which they had difficulty in controlling. In the years following 1992, the national currency lost over half of its face value against the dollar before rallying sharply. The rate of inflation exceeded 180 per cent. The determination to establish a strong and stable currency induced the Lithuanian monetary authorities to renounce explicitly all attempts to conduct a discretionary policy. Parity was fixed to the dollar by the Law on the Credibility of the Litas of 1 April 1994 ($1 = LTL4). The choice of the dollar was motivated by large-scale dollarization of the economy and the denomination of the major import – oil – in this currency.

Table 2.1  *Description of European CBAs (May 2001)*

| | Bosnia and Herzegovina | Bulgaria | Estonia | Lithuania |
|---|---|---|---|---|
| Date of establishment | August 1997 | July 1997 | June 1992 | April 1994 |
| Legal framework of the set-up | Constitution (Art. VII). Law on the CBBH of 1997 | Law on the BNB | Law of the Republic of Estonia on the Security for Estonia | Law on the Credibility of the Litas |
| Administrative agency | CBBH | BNB | Eesti Pank (BOE) | BOL |
| Official exchange rate | E0.51=DM1=BAM1 (DM1=BAM1) | Euro peg (DM1=BGL1000) | E1=EEK15.645 (DM1=EEK8) | US$1=LTL4 |
| Backing rule | The aggregate amount of CBBH's monetary liabilities shall at no time exceed the equivalent of its net foreign exchange reserves | 100% of monetary liabilities covered with foreign exchange reserves | 100% of monetary base covered with euro interest-bearing assets and gold | 100% of currency and BOL's liquid liabilities covered with foreign assets and gold |

| | | | |
|---|---|---|---|
| Power to change the exchange rate and backing rule | No | No | BOE: right to revalue the exchange rate. Devaluation needs to be voted by the Parliament | Since June 1994, the BOL may change the exchange rate in consultation with the government, but only 'under extraordinary circumstances' |
| LOLR facilities | No information | Liquidity assistance limited to the excess of foreign exchange reserves over the liabilities of the BNB and restricted to emergency situations | Restricted to systemic crises and limited to the foreign exchange reserves in excess | Restricted to systemic crises and limited to the foreign exchange reserves in excess (BOL intends to maintain them to an amount of around 15% of deposits in the banking system) |
| Reserve requirements (2000) | n.a. | n.a. | 10% | 10% |
| Other 'monetary instruments' | n.a. | n.a. | BOE's certificates of deposits (limited) | Treasury bills (since July 1994) |
| Credit to government | Prohibited | Prohibited (Art. 45) | Prohibited (Art. 16) | No special provisions |

*Sources:* BOL, BOE, BNB, CBBH, Balino et al. (1997), Tsang (1999)

## Bulgaria, 1997

Bulgaria established a CBA under the aegis of the IMF in the midst of the serious financial crisis of 1996–7. The country had been in the throes of a banking crisis since at least 1995. The closure of several banks, hyperinflation – running at a yearly rate of 2000 per cent in March 1997 – and the further decline of an already weak economic activity left the authorities with little choice but to adopt a monetary system capable of swiftly restoring confidence in the economy, following the failure of the stabilization attempt of July 1996 (Gulde, 1999: 6). In order to reinforce the transparency of the currency board, the BNB's balance sheet was reorganized on the Bank of England Model into an Issue Department and a separate Banking Department (Table 2.2). Despite the urgency of the situation, discussions between the IMF mission and the Bulgarian authorities were somewhat protracted (November 1996–July 1997), particularly with regard to the choice of the anchor currency. Advocates of the US dollar peg noted the widespread dollarization in informal transactions and as a store of value, but the deutschmark was finally retained. On 5 June 1997 the exchange rate was fixed at 1000 leva for one deutschmark. Then on 1 January 1999, the peg was changed to the euro. The statutes of the Bulgarian National Bank (BNB) were modified and the new system came into effect on 1 July of that year.

*Table 2.2   Bulgaria – structure of BNB's accounts*

|  | Assets | Liabilities |
|---|---|---|
| Issue department | Foreign reserves<br>• Foreign currency assets<br>• Gold | Monetary liabilities<br>• Notes and coins issued<br>• Commercial bank deposits and current accounts<br>• Government deposits |
| Banking department | *Deposit with Issue Department*<br>Credit to banks<br>Other assets | Credit from IMF<br>Other long-term liabilities<br>Provisions<br>Capital and reserves |

## Bosnia and Herzegovina, 1997

The Central Bank of Bosnia and Herzegovina (CBBH) was created under the aegis of the IMF, in the context of the Dayton Peace Accord bringing an end to the war in Bosnia and signed in 1995. The New Zealander, Peter Nicholl, was appointed as the first governor of the CBBH with a term of office of six years.

Under the terms of the Law on the CBBH, no citizen of Bosnia and Herzegovina or any neighboring state could hold this position until 2003 at the earliest. Of all the CBAs, the Bosnian system is the most transparent and the most faithful to the concept of a pure CBA. Indeed, its principles are directly enshrined in the national Constitution which stipulates that the transactions of the CBBH must be consistent with the principles of the Constitution itself (article VII of the Constitution). Article 32 of the Law on the CBBH establishes the at parity relation linking the new currency – the convertible marka – to the deutschmark (DM1 = BAM1). The choice of the deutschmark naturally reflects the fact that the currency was in common use in Bosnia and Herzegovina, but it was also a measure of the wish to draw nearer to the European Union. Since 1 January 1999, the marka has been *de facto* – but not yet *de jure*[1] – pegged to the euro (E0.51 = DM1 = BAM1).

## TOWARDS A GENERAL ADOPTION OF CBAS IN EUROPE?

The question of a CBA in Russia was raised in the early 1990s (Hanke et al., 1993). The project was turned down because it involved making concessions in monetary and political policy that were deemed too heavy – particularly the location of the currency board in Switzerland. Following the ruble crisis of August 1998, the debate has resurfaced (Barro, 1998; Boone et al., 1998; Hanke, 1998), despite the fierce opposition of the Russian authorities.

If a new CB is to emerge anywhere in Europe, it could well be in the Balkans. The disintegration of the former Yugoslavia has already given birth to the Bosnian system, soon perhaps to be joined by a similar system in Montenegro and Kosovo. Both these entities have already adopted the deutschmark but still entertain hopes of extending their sovereignty and issuing their own currencies linked to the euro. This plan could also embrace Serbia since Montenegro has just recently proposed monetary union – without the current Yugoslav dinar – in exchange for recognition by Serbia of a more autonomous or independent status.

### Theoretical Foundations

Over and above the empirical justifications, there are more theoretical arguments in favor of the CBA. The arguments invoked come from various horizons and sometimes place their authors in contradiction with their own theories.

### Contemporary free banking school
This school of thought, advocated by Selgin and Dowd defends the idea of a competitive system for creating bank money by referring in particular to the

banking principles defined by Adam Smith more than 200 years ago. While its advocates do not dispute the existence of a monetary base to interbank regulations, they are opposed to the idea of introducing a higher currency on monopoly grounds. They therefore suggest that monetary policies and central banks should be abolished. The latter are not the result of a spontaneous ordering of banking actions, but rather the consequence of an exogenous intervention on the part of the State, designed to finance its public deficit. The recourse to the CBA is a satisfactory solution insofar as the monetary base is not manipulated by a public authority and the action of the lender of last resort (LOLR) is excluded. The banks must be left free to define the level of their reserves. However, we can notice that present-day CBAs are somewhat removed from this model inasmuch as they contain a mechanism of required reserves.

**Monetarist view and multiplier**

In order to understand why certain monetarists (Friedman and Schwartz, 1963) have partially rallied to the idea of the CBA, it is important to remind ourselves of the implications of the monetarist approach with respect to monetary policy. The money stock $(M)$ is a multiple of the monetary base $(H)$, determined by the value of the monetary multiplier $(k)$: $M = k.H$. As a means of avoiding an excessive money supply and thus of circumscribing all sources of inflation, an automatic system for guiding monetary policy is deemed preferable to active intervention on the part of the central bank. Friedman recommends the adoption of a monetary rule consisting of maintaining a constant growth rate of the money supply in function of the increase of production in volume. The monetary rule contained within the CBAs and amounting to the annihilation of any form of monetary activism is attractive to monetarists. But their enthusiasm should be tempered for two reasons: (1) in the CBA, $H$ is determined by the movement of the balance of payments and not by the central bank; (2) monetarists traditionally tend to look favorably on flexible exchange rates.

The same ambiguity may be found in Dornbusch who has recently come to the defense of the CBA (Dornbusch and Giavazzi, 1999). At first sight, this is scarcely a matter for surprise, bearing in mind the degree to which the CBA mechanism corresponds to his basic model of 1973. However, this model differs from the CBA in that, where the model is concerned, adjustment calls for intervention – limited but nonetheless effective – on the part of the monetary authorities in order to maintain the fixed exchange rates, unlike the 'automatic' adjustment system of the CBA.

**The paradigm of credibility**

The CBA's most consistent supporters are to be found among economists of the New Classical School. R. Barro has recommended this solution on several occasions, particularly in the case of Russia (Barro, 1998). He remains faithful to the conceptions of the theory of rational expectations and sticks to his previous proposal (Barro and Gordon, 1983). His reasoning embraces the older conclusions established by Kydland and Prescott (1977) and other models concerning the dissociation between *rules* and *discretion*. Since any discretionary policy is doomed to failure and contain an inflationary bias, such policies must be replaced by strict, unchanging rules in order to guard against all sources of instability and inflation. In this view of things, the issuing rules contained in a CBA constitute an optimum solution. The question of monetary 'credibility' should no longer arise since the exchange rate and the regulation of the money supply are no longer under the control of the political and monetary authorities. Now that the 'paradigm of monetary credibility' is afforded greater importance in monetary analyses, the CBA is logically viewed more favorably by these authors.[2]

## Monetary Immobility and Apostasy of Central Banking

Despite differentiations in the proposed implementing frameworks and the diversity of analytical approaches, the objective remains the same: to establish a stable and convertible currency through the institutional adoption of a fixed parity and integral cover of the monetary base by foreign currency reserves (backing rule). The 'credibility in bottle' (Frenkel, 1999) contributed by the CBA is achieved at the cost of renouncing the chief responsibilities shouldered by the government authorities and the central bank in the sphere of exchange rate policy and central banking – the LOLR function and the regulation of interest rates. The exchange rate is frozen and monetary regulation is no longer the result of any discretionary power but of the automatic application of automatic rules.[3]

Regardless of whether the backing is applied solely to part or all of the monetary authority's balance sheet, central currency cannot be issued/destroyed without the counterpart of an increase/reduction of the foreign reserve currency. Contrary to what happens in a traditional central banking system, a 'pure' currency board's balance sheet assets cannot therefore accumulate any debt on the government or the economy – in domestic currency – thereby excluding any possibility of monetary financing of the budget deficit. The constitution of a CBA is thus considered as a pledge of monetary stability in that it signals the renouncement of all recourse to devaluation or inflation as a means of demonetizing debts. The CBA thus serves to reduce the level of uncertainty in both exchange rate and inflation. The forced monetary stability that it induces is supposed to favor the inflow of capital within a framework theoretically precluding speculative attacks.

**Disinflationary Efficiacy Despite a Failure to Respect the Initial Conditions**

A successful introduction of European CBAs would have required certain pre-conditions to be met. Of these, we may mention the following three:

1. The availability of foreign reserves in sufficient quantities. Such a state of affairs pertained in none of the countries concerning us here. In Estonia, the constitution of the reserve fund guaranteeing full convertibility was fa-cilitated by the return of old gold reserves, deposited in Sweden, with the BIS and in London, prior to the German and Soviet occupations. But these reserves were insufficient for the task and provisional use had to be made of 150 million dollars of 'Estonian forest bills' as a complementary guar-antee. The situation was similar in Lithuania where long-term resources were borrowed from the IMF. Indeed the Bank of Lithuania (BOL) had expressed to commence with excess coverage, which was necessary given the presence of weak banks and financial instability.
2. A general acceptance of the changes brought about by the CBA rules. While this condition still holds true in Estonia today, it has never been met in Lithuania, where the CBA has always encountered stiff opposition (includ-ing from those who, once in power, have nonetheless retained the system), or in Bulgaria.
3. The construction of a solid banking system prior to monetary reform. Un-fortunately, this final condition was not met by any of the transitional economies under review here. Subsequent consolidations, when they took place, were the result of bank crises that reshaped the financial landscape of these economies.

Notwithstanding the failure to meet these criteria, the CBAs have unquestion-ably succeeded in putting a stop to inflation. With the exception of the first years of the Estonian CBA, results have come swiftly, as may be seen from recent developments in Bulgaria or, over a longer period, the examples of the two Baltic countries (Tables 2.3, 2.4 and 2.5). An internal IMF study based on sta-tistical comparisons and an econometric analysis of the various fixed exchange rate systems reveals that the evolution of the consumer price index in a CBA is on average 3.5 points lower than the index in a standard fixed exchange rate system (Ghosh et al., 1998).

*Table 2.3   Bulgaria – main indicators*

|  | 1994 | 1995 | 1996 | 1997 | 1998 | 1999 | 2000 |
|---|---|---|---|---|---|---|---|
| Real growth of GDP (%) | 1.5 | 2.1 | –10.9 | –6.9 | 4.0 | 3.5 | – |
| Consumer price index (%) | 121.9 | 32.9 | 310.8 | 578.5 | 1.0 | 2.0 | – |
| Unemployment rate (%) | 12.4 | 11.1 | 12.5 | 13.7 | 12.9 | 13.3 | 15.6 |

*Sources*:   IMF, BNB

*Table 2.4   Lithuania – main indicators*

|  | 1994 | 1995 | 1996 | 1997 | 1998 | 1999 | 2000 |
|---|---|---|---|---|---|---|---|
| Real growth of GDP (%) | –9.8 | 3.3 | 4.7 | 7.3 | 5.1 | –4.2 | 2.7 |
| Consumer price index (%) | 45.0 | 35.5 | 13.1 | 8.4 | 2.4 | 0.3 | 1.1 |
| Current account balance (% GDP) | –2.1 | –10.2 | –11.4 | –10.2 | –12.1 | –10.8 | –6.9 |
| Credit to private sector growth (%) | – | 23.0 | –4.4 | 18.9 | 16.9 | 11.8 | –4.0 |
| Foreign direct investments inflows (million US$) | – | 72.6 | 152. | 354.5 | 925.5 | 486.5 | – |
| Unemployment rate (%) | 4.5 | 6.1 | 6.2 | 6.7 | 6.9 | 10.0 | 11.8 |

*Sources*:   BOL, BOFIT

*Table 2.5   Estonia – main indicators*

|  | 1992 | 1993 | 1994 | 1995 | 1996 | 1997 | 1998 | 1999 | 2000 |
|---|---|---|---|---|---|---|---|---|---|
| Real growth of GDP (%) | – | – | –2.0 | 4.3 | 3.9 | 10.6 | 4.7 | –1.1 | 5.4 |
| Consumer price index (%) | – | 89.8 | 47.7 | 29.0 | 23.1 | 11.2 | 8.1 | 3.3 | 4.0 |
| Current account balance (% GDP) | – | – | –7.2 | –4.4 | –9.2 | –12.1 | –9.2 | –5.8 | –5.5 |
| Unemployment rate (%) | 5.0 | 6.4 | 7.6 | 9.7 | 10.0 | 9.7 | 9.9 | 12.3 | 13.9 |

*Sources*:   BOE, IMF, BOFIT

## CBA CONSTRAINTS

Despite their ability to set up monetary stabilization, the CBA rules imply specific economic mechanisms which must be looked at in detail and whose negative effects need to be measured.

### Vulnerability of the Banking System and Restrictive Conditions of a Credit extension

The banking systems of the European CBAs are extremely vulnerable. Serious bank crises have emerged, notably in the Baltic CBAs – Estonia in 1992–4 and 1998–9; Lithuania in 1995–6. The banks' fragility is usually put down to behavior ill-suited to the new economic environment: mistaken assessments of market risks, poorly adapted loan regulations and banking supervision by the central bank, persistence of banking malpractices and incompetence (Fleming et al., 1997). Without denying the importance of these problems, we need to allow for the impact of a CBA on the process of monetary creation by commercial banks.

The 100 per cent backing rule applies solely to the currency issued by the CBA, and not to that created by the banks. The banking system is therefore not restricted by the principle of 100 per cent reserves – as described by Rothbard, Fisher or Allais. Commercial banks retain their power to create money of credit *ex nihilo*; but this power is nonetheless more limited than in the traditional system controlled by a central bank. In practice, the automatic character of the issue of high-powered money makes it impossible for the currency board to act on the financial system's liquidity. Its strict application exacerbates the liquidity constraint associated with banking practice, and the credit dynamic is thus drastically altered.

As with the theoretical model of the gold standard, the CBA places great emphasis on the mechanism governing the transmission from a dynamic of balance of payments to one of internal financing. The sequence may be expressed as follows:

$$BP \Rightarrow R \Rightarrow H \Rightarrow M$$

based on a triple relation of causality:

1.  from balance of payments ($BP$) towards foreign currency reserves ($R$);
2.  from R towards the monetary base ($H$);
3.  from H towards the stock of money ($M$).

When a commercial bank holds foreign reserve currency, for example as a result of export revenue received by a client, its liquidity position is improved. Indeed, if conversion into central currency – domestic reserve currency – is carried out with the currency board, the bank can use its reserves in excess to grant new credits in the local currency.

The latter relation of the sequence corresponds to the multiplier theory. The same conclusion is reached if we adopt an argument which does not involve recourse to this mechanism – for example if we argue within the framework of the post-Keynesian theory of the endogenous money that rejects the multiplier theory. The supply of money is by nature endogenous. In a modern capitalist economy, the banks' main role is the *ex nihilo* creation of credit money in the light of business credit requirements. Once the money has been created, the banks need to refinance themselves by turning to the central bank, which, in this case, is accommodating.[4] According to this logic, the currency board is aberrant since the central bank refuses refinancing *a posteriori*. It is an *unnatural system* in the sense that its functioning is in flat contradiction with the nature of money which is endogenous. It is true that banks may make use of financial innovations in responding to requests for finance with varying degrees of enthusiasm. But these innovations remain limited in scope in the emerging economies. Moreover, they only improve the redistribution of preexisting loanable funds, in other words the recycling of a stock of money that has already been created.

### The Search for Regular Inflows of Currency

Irrespective of the causality adopted – multiplier view or endogenous money approach – the central bank cannot intervene after money has been created. This restrictive situation highlights the financing constraint to which CBA economies are subjected. With the exception of the special case of Hong Kong CBA – and to a lesser degree that of Argentina, where there has been substantial development in capital markets and financial innovations – the regular inflow of foreign currency constitutes a central plank in the banks' ability to respond favorably to business financing needs.

The CBA thus obliges economies wishing to secure regular growth to ensure, in the medium and long term, a structural surplus of their balance of payments (Ponsot, 2001). One option is a current account surplus; but this is not the most common scenario in economies that are 'emerging' or striving to 'catch up'. If the current deficit is of manageable proportions, it can be compensated by stable inflows of capital, for example in the shape of foreign direct investments (FDI). The important thing is to maintain net capital inflows over the long term.

### Special Growth System

In short, the CBA's financing constraint points to two possible scenarios for financing economic activity by domestic credit: (1) the previous holding of foreign currency; and (2) foreign currency borrowing, but this latter solution comes at a price – debt servicing. The traditional process by which credit money is created by the banking system is altered as a result of the automatic character informing the issue of the central currency. In this scheme of things, changes in the volume of foreign currency reserves become of crucial importance in the process of financing production. Economic activity, influenced by movements in the balance of payments, may remain subdued in the event of a chronic deficit. At best, expansion depends on changes in the international monetary and financial climate which cannot be cushioned by any intervention on the exchange rate or interest rates.

This underlines the dual nature of the particular system of growth ushered in with the CBA. Either the economy in question is able to ensure a current surplus and/or to attract foreign capital, in which case it enjoys conditions favoring the domestic financing of activity through banking credit; or it is not able to do so, in which case there is a persistent stagnation or restriction of credits despite the monetary stability (Table 2.6).

*Table 2.6    CEECs – credit to the business sector (% GDP)*

| | |
|---|---|
| Slovenia | 53% |
| Czech Republic | 42% |
| Estonia | 21% |
| Lithuania | 15% |
| Bulgaria | 10% |
| Albania | 10% |

*Source*:   EBRD

**Vulnerability To Speculative Attacks and External Shocks**

Despite the guarantees offered by the CBA – in theory supposed to provide protection by virtue of improved credibility compared to other fixed exchange rate systems – recent experience has shown that the vulnerability persists. Sudden movements of capital have a deeply destabilizing effect. Since the CBA is unable to sterilize the effects of these flows, a massive flight of capital brings in its wake a shrinking of the monetary base, soaring interest rates and pressure on the banks, making it necessary to apply a recessive adjustment. It should be noted that the consequences of the opposite effect – i.e. resulting from the massive non-sterilized inflow of capital – are not in fact as inflationary as sometimes supposed. Indeed, the banks tend to take advantage of the situation to improve their liquidity position, and the impact on overall demand remains moderate.

External shocks, such as the Russian crisis of 1998 or interest rate increases in the economy issuing the anchor currency, quite clearly also have a considerable impact.

**Fiscal Austerity**

Deprived of exchange rate flexibility and the right to juggle with interest rates, the authorities should be tempted to use fiscal policy as a counter-cycle weapon. Budgetary activism is nevertheless limited: the statutes of the currency board (central bank) make it impossible to monetize public deficits; financing with the banking sector are considered as ill-advised owing to the possible eviction effect on the private sector; more generally, public debt, if it lasted, would increase pressure in favor of a devaluation or a default payment and damage the credibility of the monetary arrangement. Stringent fiscal policy must therefore remain the norm, even in times of economic slowdown.

**Real Recessive Adjustment and Unemployment**

Adjustment, in terms of economic activity and employment, tends to be particularly painful inasmuch as the appreciation of real exchange rates is recurrent in these economies. Since the CBA is very often introduced in a context of hyperinflation, it sometimes fails to provide an immediate answer to the inertia of inflation that continues to prevail for several months.

In point of fact, the effects of adjustment constraint are principally felt on prices and wages. The size of the nominal wages adjustment is usually smaller than that observed on prices. If wages flexibility proves insufficient, the volume of employment becomes the adjustment variable. The reversal of the cycle usually leads to an upswing in employment but this is not always enough to cut the unemployment rate that tends to remain high. Irrespective of whether there is weak growth of GDP – Bulgaria, Bosnia and Herzegovina – or strong growth notwithstanding a certain irregularity – Estonia – CBA economies are characterized by high rates of unemployment and precarious working conditions (Tables 2.3, 2.4 and 2.5).

## ILLUSTRATION OF CBAS' CONSTRAINTS

### The Unstable Vitality of the 'Baltic Tiger'

The country benefiting most fully from the growth system revitalized by the inflow of capital is Estonia. Growth was vigorous up to 1999 (see Table 2.5). As foreign direct investment (FDI) flowed freely into the country – largely as a result of such circumstantial factors as privatizations – the monetary base broadened quickly thanks to the increased foreign reserves of the CBA. Domestic credit reacted favorably to the influx of foreign capital, thus strengthening the growth impetus.

However, although monetary stability prompted renewed growth in Estonia from the end of 1994, it was unable to stem the rising tide of unemployment.

The years between 1997 and 1999, marked as they were by the rise of international financial instability, illustrate the rapid reversal of the climate brought about by the CBA, once financial conditions become unfavorable. The increased uncertainty slowed down considerably the inflow of capital and several speculative attacks were launched against the kroon despite repeated commitments in favor of the CBA. The CBA showed its ability to resist in an unstable environment and without the intervention of the monetary authorities (Lepik, 1999). The market adjustment mechanisms worked perfectly, particularly in the form of a surge of short rates. These have fallen back today, but the turbulence was a tough ordeal for the banking system. In addition to a fall in external financing, banks reduced the amount of internal credit to the private sector that in turn led to a marked slowdown in activity. The outcome was that, for the first time in several years, Estonia found itself in a recession in 1999. The Russian crisis, by reducing external demand, doubtless made matters worse, but fewer goods are being exported to Russia (Table 2.7) and its impact should not be overstated.

*Table 2.7    Lithuania and Estonia – geographical distribution of foreign trade*

|  | 1994 | | | | 1998 | | | |
|  | Estonia | | Lithuania | | Estonia | | Lithuania | |
|  | Exports | Imports | Exports | Imports | Exports | Imports | Exports | Imports |
| Euro area | 30.8% | 49.7% | 22.9% | 25.8% | 30.2% | 43.3% | 26.8% | 36.0% |
| Russia | 23.1% | 16.7% | 28.2% | 39.3% | 13.4% | 11.1% | 19.7% | 21.1% |

*Sources*:   Statistical Office of Estonia and Kohronen (1999), www.stat.ee/

## Bulgaria: Doomed to Stagnation?

Unlike Estonia, Bulgaria does not appear to have embarked on a process of growth facilitated by the inflow of foreign currency. And yet, the objectives of monetary and financial stabilization have been attained: inflation fell to 1 per cent[5] at the end of 1998 and interest rates have dropped back to moderate levels.

The Bulgarian monetary authorities are today addressing the conditions required for the recovery of the national economy. But their analysis fails to establish clearly the connection between the conditions of domestic financing of production and stagnation of activity. Initially, the scarcity of new commercial credits in the non-financial sector was seen as a positive factor illustrating the sharp reduction of the subsidies implicit in loss-making activities and the new concern for bank solvency. Compared to other economies in a state of transition, Bulgaria was notable for the business sector's greater reliance on financing by bank credit. Arguments of a more theoretical tenor were then advanced in an effort to explain the persistent slowing down of domestic credit (Nenovsky and Hristov, 1999). Such arguments are based on analyses in terms of credit rationing based on asymmetrical information. They reach the conclusion that, owing to the distortions brought about by previous credit policies, the Bulgarian banking sector still lacks the necessary experience and skill in efficient lending practices. Lacking proper expertise in evaluating and monitoring projects, and in collecting and processing information on borrower solvency, banks are obliged to operate in a context of uncertainty and marked by the problems of moral hazard and adverse selection.

These analyses have the merit of emphasizing the uncertainty characterizing the contractual relationship between lender and borrower. They also bring out the need for the rapid development of financial markets in these economies. But they mask an essential factor explaining the low credit dynamics of Bulgarian banks: the liquidity constraint imposed upon them, in compliance with the logic of the CBA. Bulgarian banks are not particularly outward looking and we note that the monetary base, supplied by foreign assets, is not really increasing and that credit expansion is still very modest (Figure 2.1). The latter represents only 10 per cent of GDP, as in Albania (Table 2.8). In the absence of the ability to generate a current account surplus – exports remain subdued while imports are on the increase – Bulgarian growth remains dependent on major injections from foreign investors, currently showing a certain reluctance despite the restoration of monetary and financial stability.

Although Bulgaria was relatively unaffected by the Russian crisis – Russia accounts for only 5 per cent of Bulgaria's exports – exports and activity suffered in 1999–2000 because of the Kosovo crisis. However, the country's bargaining position with western creditors may have been strengthened as a result of its cooperation during and after the conflict with occidental countries.

**Lithuania. Rules With Discretion?**

The Lithuanian currency board functioned well during the first six months of its existence, encouraging the influx of foreign capital until the end of 1994. But the external situation then rapidly worsened due to the pronounced appre-

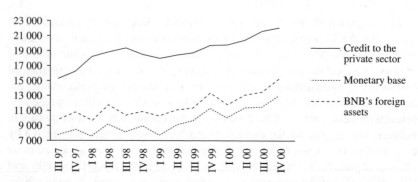

*Figure 2.1    Bulgaria – BNB's foreign assets, monetary base and credit to the private sector (million leva)*

ciation, in real terms, of the litas. The suddenness of this reversal may be attributed to the rise in value of the dollar – causing loss of competitiveness – but most of all to a lack of credibility and firm commitment on the part of the Lithuanian government in favor of the CBA (Camard, 1996). The speculative attacks unleashed in December 1994 were fuelled by incessant rumors of devaluation and a reshaping of issuing rules. Outflows of capital gathered momentum and interest rates rocketed. Successive banking crises led to the closure of major financial institutions. Moreover, the inflows of FDI remained low until 1996, not exceeding $41 per inhabitant.

The election to the office of President of the Republic of Valdas Adamkus, who has been living in the United States for 40 years, has breathed fresh life into the process of liberalization and has acted as a catalyst for the inflows of FDI. One of the new President's objectives is to 'place the Lithuanian economy in private hands'. FDI inflows, hitherto mostly from the United States – Motorola, Lancaster Steel Co, Philip Morris and so on – have diversified and grown, increasing fivefold between 1996 and 1999 and even exceeding in volume the FDI destined for Estonia. Even so, the cumulated inflows per inhabitant since 1989 remain low – $344 per capita for Lithuania; $695 per capita for Estonia.

The jolts inflicted by the Russian crisis have caused short term capital to flee, penalizing the banks in the process. The impact of reduced exports to Russia has been higher than in Estonia. Lithuania has also been hit by knock-on effects from economic problems in two other large CIS countries: Belarus and Ukraine (Korhonen, 1999). At the same time, Lithuania's external competitiveness suffered from the peg of the litas to the strong US dollar. So, for the first time since 1994, Lithuania found itself in a deep recession in 1999 (Table 2.8).

*Table 2.8   Lithuania – main indicators*

|  | 1994 | 1995 | 1996 | 1997 | 1998 | 1999 | 2000 |
|---|---|---|---|---|---|---|---|
| Real growth of GDP (%) | –9.8 | 3.3 | 4.7 | 7.3 | 5.1 | –4.2 | 2.7 |
| Consumer price index (%) | 45.0 | 35.5 | 13.1 | 8.4 | 2.4 | 0.3 | 1.1 |
| Current account balance (% GDP) | –2.1 | –10.2 | –11.4 | –10.2 | –12.1 | –10.8 | –6.9 |
| Credit to private sector growth (%) | – | 23.0 | –4.4 | 18.9 | 16.9 | 11.8 | –4.0 |
| Foreign direct investments inflows (million US$) | – | 72.6 | 152. | 354.5 | 925.5 | 486.5 | – |
| Unemployment rate (%) | 4.5 | 6.1 | 6.2 | 6.7 | 6.9 | 10.0 | 11.8 |

*Sources*:   BOL, BOFIT

## Bosnia and Herzegovina: Monetary Stability and Aborted Reconstruction

Confidence in the currency was swiftly restored with the three communities making up Bosnia and Herzegovina – Bosnian Muslims, Serbs and Croats – despite a certain reluctance on the part of the Croat and Serb communities.[6] The new banknotes, which have been carefully devised, are gradually taking the place of the three main units of account and payment used during the civil war – the Yugoslav dinar, the Croat kuna and the deutschmark.

Despite a relative favorable monetary framework – inflation below 4 per cent, the wiping out of two-thirds of the public debt by the Club de Paris, and foreign aid for reconstruction to the tune of $1.25 billion – growth has signally failed to materialize. Export receipts currently cover only about 20 per cent of import payments. The current rates of economic growth and of imports are only being sustained by the very high levels of official capital, mainly from some foreign donations coming into the country. Today the slowdown in official capital flows has started. The need to attract private direct investment is very clear. But the environment in Bosnia and Herzegovina is still far from an attractive and supportive one for private investment (Nicholl, 2000).

The banking system is still weak and fragmented[7] and it does not play a significant role in the economy (Table 2.9). Even before the Kosovo conflict, the governor of the CBBH was forced to admit to the IMF that, although the CBA had succeeded in restoring confidence in the currency, economic growth was

Table 2.9   *Bosnia and Herzegovina – credit to private industrial enterprises (millions KM)*

|  | 31.12.1999 | 30.09.2000 | 31.12.2000 |
|---|---|---|---|
| Short term credit | 0.549 | 0.519 | 0.483 |
| Long term credit | 0.901 | 0.494 | 0.395 |

*Source*:   CBBH

well below forecast levels in a context of generalized unemployment (Kurtovic, 1998: 71).

The rare signs of economic recovery concern the reconstruction of buildings, transport systems and energy distribution. Emerging businesses for the most part originate in the Croat community, which is in a position to call upon capital from neighboring Croatia. The partly failed installation of a Skoda automobile assembly line in August 1998 shows how hard it is to find opportunities not only on the local market – characterized by low purchasing power – but also on the export market – characterized by a lack of competitiveness.

However, the convertible marka is henceworth fixed against the currency of 12 European countries, which include most of BiH's trading partners. This should be good for both exporters to and importers from those markets as it eliminates exchange rate risk from that trade. An added benefit is the reality that before the euro, the CBBH was limited to the choice of where to invest its foreign reserves. Under the CBA rules, the CBBH could only place those reserves in German banks. Henceworth with the euro, CBBH has a choice of banks in 12 euro countries.

## ADJUSTMENTS AND DISTORTION OF THE CBA

In order to make up for the central banking deficiency, the banking system is developing special strategies, and the authorities are seeking to imbue the system with a greater degree of flexibility.

### Remedies to the Absence of a Lender of Last Resort

In the face of the CBA constraints, the financial sector has developed of its own volition towards increased concentration and extraversion.

1.   Banks in difficulty are going to the wall or, more often, are being bought up by other banks. The State is encouraging mergers as a means of building

solid banking groups. For example, the Bosnian Federation Banking Agency closed insolvent banks and encouraged small but solvent banks to merge. As a consequence, the number of banks licensed in the Federation has dropped from 55 to 42 over 2000.

2.  This trend towards concentration is mostly fuelled by an increased foreign share in the capital of the major banks. This tendency accelerates in times of banking crisis. It concerns above all Estonia and, more marginally, Lithuania: Swedish and Finnish banks in search of new markets look upon the two Baltic States which are also becoming a stepping stone to Russia. Thus, having forsaken the central banking prerogatives of their monetary institution, the CBA economies find themselves obliged to entrust their banking system to foreign investors.

3.  The banks are opening up to the outside world so that they can, to all intents and purposes, operate without a national LOLR. In the case of pressure on banks' liquidity, the internationalized banks can easily and quickly obtain foreign currency, which they can then present to the board in order to ease their domestic liquidity position. This mechanism is reminiscent of the co-lonial CBAs in which the local banks were in most cases branches of London banks to whom they turned for refinancing in times of need. The Estonian banking system is the most advanced in the openness process: the chief refinancing procedures are now carried out with Scandinavian and Finnish interbank markets. Conversely, the Bulgarian and Bosnian banks are finding it more difficult to look outwards.

In addition to these individual strategies adopted by commercial banks, the authorities have endeavored to introduce particularly strict prudential regulation and implementation of banking supervision designed to guarantee the stability of the financial system. They hope that an adequate adaptation of the prudential framework can markedly limit interest rate volatility and increase the resilience of financial sector, thereby fully or partially compensating for the lack of an official safety net (Ghosh et al., 2000: 296):

1.  Level of *reserve requirements* are very high – closer to 10 per cent of de-posits. Under a CBA, banks' reserve requirements are more a prudential tool than a monetary policy instrument. But they can only serve as a liquid-ity buffer if they can be 'averaged' during the holding period (month).

2.  *Liquid assets requirements* complement reserve requirements. Minimum limits for liquid assets and the types of permissible assets allowed to fulfil these requirements are specified.

3.  *Open position limits for the anchor currency* are increased or eliminated, which encourages banks to maintain high liquid balances in the anchor currency.

4.  *Capital adequacy rules* are often more stringent than the minimum called for under the Basle standard in order to provide additional safeguards and reassurance to the public. In Lithuania, the capital adequacy ratio was initially set at 13 per cent but was lowered to 10 per cent in 1997.
5.  Because losses of one bank could trigger a global deposit run, *deposits insurance schemes* which protect depositors may strengthen confidence and avoid bank runs. These deposits protection also preserve the authority to bail out failed banks. For instance, the Deposit Protection Law was approved in Lithuania just after the banking crisis of 1995. In Bosnia and Herzegovina, a Deposit Insurance Agency has just been formed in order to re-establish citizens' confidence in the banking sector.

So, as mentioned by Dornbusch and Giavazzi (1999: 30): 'A way to accomplish financial credibility is to require that banks have offshore guarantees [of their liabilities by high-grade foreign financial institutions]. It amounts to privatizing both the lender of last resort and the supervisory function'.

### The Absolute Necessity of a Lender of Last Resort

This spontaneous development and these prudential arrangements cannot, however, altogether make up for the lack of a lender of last resort (Balino, 1997: 23). Indeed, how could it be different with a scheme based on a fractional reserve banking system and in a situation where shocks cannot be predicted? Moreover this tighter prudential control causes negative effects on financial sector profitability. Last of all, spontaneous internationalization of banks is fraught with difficulty as in Bulgaria and Bosnia and Herzegovina. However three complementary avenues remain to be considered:

1.  The first is the temporary suspension of payments policy suggested by Wallace (1990). Liquidity shocks should be confronted with partial suspension of payments rather than with a LOLR: financial intermediaries should be allowed not to fully honor deposits withdrawals to face bank runs. It has never been applied in the economies under review here. In point of fact, it implies a discretionary act on the part of the authorities, counter to the spirit of the CBA, and would increase public suspicion of the banking system. Moreover, it does not solve the question of bank refinancing in normal times.
2.  The second solution consists in trying to find an external agent capable of taking on the function of the LOLR. This brings us up against the problem of the international LOLR. In the wake of the liquidity crisis of 1995, Argentina attempted to follow this course of action, but the Federal Reserve Board refused to institutionalize a relation of this kind, and it is difficult to

see the IMF adopting such a role today. An alternative approach was for Argentina's authorities to negotiate standby lines of credit with foreign commercial banks available in return for a commitment fee (Eichengreen, 1999: 64). Such facilities – $6.1 million in the Argentinean case – could provide additional resources to insure against liquidity shocks.

3. The third option consists in gathering a foreign exchange reserve surplus, in other words holding foreign assets whose value exceeds 100 per cent of the monetary base, and using part of the excess amount for issue when the need arises. This is only a partial distortion of the CBA in the sense that the board may assume the function of lender of last resort without contravening the 100 per cent reserve rule. In Bulgaria, for example, the funds of the 'excess coverage' are kept as the Banking Department's deposits with the *Issue Department* (figure 2), and may be used to grant collateralized loans to commercial banks in the case of an acute liquidity crisis.

### The Difficult Restoration of Discretionary Margins

Unlike the first two solutions, this latter procedure is applicable in European CBAs. However, while it is true that the full backing rule is maintained, the procedure opens the way to the restoration of a kind of discretionary power, thereby breaking the taboo of non-intervention.

In short, the CBAs are gradually being 'adapted' in order to soften the effects of financing and adjustment constraints. European CBAs depart from the mechanical operation of the CBA by various subterfuges instruments. Roubini (1998) called 'cheating' this strategy elaborated to have market discretionary instruments influencing the money supply.

1. Example 1. For instance, in 1993, the Bank of Estonia was allowed not to back all of its liabilities with foreign assets. Since, the BOE has not been required to back its certificates of deposits (CDs) issued to banks. The liquidity of these CDs is guaranteed: the BOE stand ready to buy them back and to enter into repurchase agreements with banks. However, during turbulent times, the use of CDs has always been modest (Lepik, 2000).

2. Example 2. In Bulgaria, the BNB may marginally provide Lombard credit at a penalty rate against collateral of government securities. Moreover, government fiscal reserves are included in the liabilities of the BNB's Issue Department, i.e. covered with international reserves (Table 2.2). This inclusion involves a specific channel of 'quasi-monetary policy' transmission (Nenovsky and Hristov, 1999). Income and expense policies in combination with structural and privatization policies in the period of the transition impact directly reserve money and money supply. Therefore the government is capable of executing discretion, integrating fiscal and 'quasi-monetary

policy' into a syncretic whole. In these circumstances, fiscal policy approximated with fiscal reserve dynamics in the balance sheet of the Issue Department may offset shocks and help smooth reserve money and interest fluctuations.

3.    Example 3. Bulgaria and Lithuania calculate international assets for backing without taking into account central banks' long term external obligations, mainly to the IMF.

This gradual relaxing of CBA rigidity is reminiscent of how monetary systems spontaneously developed under the gold standard. It seems that the 'rules of the game' are fated to be transgressed with the CBA, just as they were with the gold standard. In reality, however, there is much less room for manoeuvre than in the case of the gold standard. In the case of cover surplus, intervention is limited in quantitative terms by the backing rule. These excess foreign reserves are essentially the result of revenue from seigniorage – interest paid on invested foreign reserve assets – donations or long-term resources at preferential rates granted by international institutions. Thus, unlike the special situation pertaining in Hong Kong's CBA, leverage is far too short in smaller economies like Bulgaria or Bosnia and Herzegovina. The only remaining instrument – the required reserves rate – offers only limited scope for manoeuvre in the event of strong pressure on liquidity.

In this state of affairs, the restoration of a limited form of discretionary power may turn out to be insufficient, in which case the only remaining solution is to break with the backing rule, in other words to leave the CBA.

**The Awkward Question of Withdrawal From the CBA**

The withdrawal process may be programmed, as was the case with Lithuania which, in 1997, adopted the Program on Monetary Policy for the period 1997–9. The strategy for exit was based on a gradual approach (Niaura, 1998). At the first stage, new instruments of monetary policy had to be implemented, under the CBA, to help to regulate more effectively the liquidity of the banking system. At the second stage, CBA had to be reformed further with the intention to restore the flexibility of monetary policy, but without affecting the peg to the US dollar. During the third stage – not before 1999 – the policy of linking the litas more closely to the currencies of EU had to start: first with a currency basket comprising the dollar and the ECU; afterwards with the ECU (euro) only. The peg to the euro was needed for realignment to EU monetary rules and was called for by exporters, who complained they were hurt by a strong dollar. In spite of the decision of the repeg to a basket in 1999, the Russian crisis and uncertainties in emerging countries caused the shift to be put off until 2001. To limit speculation about a simultaneous devaluation of the litas, the BOL has proposed that the Law on the Credibility of the Litas be amended to prohibit a devaluation with the repeg. The peg to the dollar had been maintained during these several years of hesitation. Finally, the BOL announced in January 2001 that the litas would be pegged directly to the euro in 2002 but the CBA is officially maintained (BOFIT, 2001).

The difficulties encountered in applying this measure show that the main danger in the exit operation is linked to the uncertainty surrounding the transfer of the previous system's credibility – based on the constitutional commitment and the monetary rules locked into the CBA – to the new system – a central bank charged with the mission of defining and implementing a monetary policy.

## EUROIZATION VS. EU/EMU ACCESSION PERSPECTIVE

Returning to a central banking system, with or without flexible exchange rates, is not the only way of withdrawing from the CBA. Two other solutions may be envisaged: (1) official and unilateral 'dollarization', that is to say the adoption of a foreign currency without the approval of the country issuing the said currency; or (2) monetary union. Although dollarization – or more exactly euroization in European cases – remains an option, it does not constitute a natural means of withdrawal. In the wake of the decision to open up the EU to the Central and Eastern European Countries (CEECs), launched in Copenhagen in 1993, the second solution appears far more likely.

The question of the European CBAs that, at the outset, met the requirements for the transition towards the market economy and macroeconomic stabilization, assumes a new dimension in the context of problems linked to the expansion of the EU towards the CEECs.

### Euroization

A debate was recently conducted in Bulgaria on the possibility of total euroization. *Project Euro 2000*, drawn up in 1998 with the backing of certain economists from the BNB, recommended the introduction of the euro as a legal tender as soon as possible, even before the country became a member of the EU (Nenovsky et al., 1999). This irreversible unification would underpin once and for all the credibility of Bulgaria in a way that the present currency board, by virtue of its operational complexities, is unable to do. To those who say that such a step would require the prior agreement of the European authorities, the pro-euroization lobby replies: (1) that this unilateral undertaking would not in any way amount to a commitment on the part of the ECB; (2) that Romano Prodi himself has argued in favor of euroization in the southeastern European economies.

It should, however, be remembered that this opinion by the European Commission was pronounced in 1999, the year of the Kosovo conflict. Besides, such a strategy is fraught with danger. It involves: (1) losing any remaining room to manoeuvre – reduced but necessary nonetheless – of the present CBA; (2) the loss of income derived from seigniorage; and (3) the risk of compromising a future adherence to the EU and the EMU. Euroization would constitute a premature but above all incomplete adherence to monetary union. Despite the euro, the BNB would enjoy neither voting rights within the ECB nor the rights and instruments of the central banks of the EU economies. In such circumstances, we may well query the advantages to be gained from this strategy of 'surrogate implantation of the euro' (Avramov, 2000).

While the question of anticipated adoption of the euro does not really arise in the case of CBA countries in the process of negotiating with the EU, the situation is different for Bosnia and Herzegovina and especially for the Balkan entities where the deutschmark has been established as legal tender. The question of the monetary future of Kosovo, Montenegro and even Serbia remains very much alive.

**The Long Road to EMU**

There are three steps involved in the european monetary integration: (1) EU membership; (2) participation in ERM2;[8] and (3) adoption of the euro – EMU membership.

The maintenance of the CBA in no way contradicts the three series of criteria to be met for entry into the EU – the existence of democratic institutions, the functioning of a market economy and the ability to shoulder the *acquis communautaire*, i.e. all the standards and directives shaping the operation of the EU. While the question of the CBA's compatibility with participation in ERM2 has yet to be resolved, some CBA aspects are already compatible with the basic requirements of the transitional phase:

1. Monetary financing of government deficits is prohibited;
2. Access of public authorities to the financial institutions is forbidden;
3. More generally, independence of central bank is admitted/effective;
4. Exchange rates are not flexible;
5. Euro is the anchor – Lithuania excepted;
6. Macroeconomic policy discipline is well established. EU membership will force the authorities to accelerate reforms and address remaining macroeconomic imbalances. It will reinforce the commercial links between the EU countries and these economies: it means a large degree of shock correlation and business cycle synchronization and a limitation of the problem of asymmetric shocks (Gulde et al., 2000).

But on the other hand, operational, nominal and real convergence with the euro area during the second step face the following problems:

1. The *anchor currency problem*. Euro is the common currency. Obviously, Lithuanian CBA will have to switch from the dollar to the euro as anchor currency before EU membership;

2. The *interdependence problem*. A new entrant will need to avoid choosing an appreciated central rate that would undermine competitiveness. One problem is that entry rates will not be market determined and could be inadequate;

3. The *volatility problem*. With the convergence process, the forex market fortunes of each of the new entrants will be increasingly intertwined. It may be a time of extreme volatility in capital flows and interest rates in countries with CBAs (Keller, 2000);

4. *CBA-compatibility with the Statute of the European System of Central Banks (ESCB)*. New members shall ensure that their national legislation, including the statutes of the central bank, is compatible with the Treaty and the Statute of the ESCB. A ESCB membership supposes in particular the performance of open market and credit operations, a set of specific eligible instruments, a particular scope of allowed monetary policy, which contradicts the rules of the CBA. Actually, a *stricto sensu* reading of the requirements allows the following flexible interpretation: only the presence of unacceptable discretionary instruments should be incompatible ... but not necessarily the absence of acceptable ones as in the CBA case (Avramov, 2000);

5. *CBA compatibility with the ERM2*. A main issue is to reconcile absolute fixed exchange rates of the CBA with the relative flexible parameters of the transitional exchange rate mechanism. Once again, a solution should be obtained thanks to a broad interpretation of requirements. For example, Estonian authorities proposed to agree '0 per cent fluctuation band' for CBA countries instead of the standard ± 15 per cent one.

In order to erase ambiguity, the ECB recently expressed a position that marks a substantial progress. Vice President Noyer for the first time made official the possibility of convergence to CBAs.[9] All in all, the justification for allowing CBAs into ERM2 appears strong. There are too many risks in abandoning a CBA during the EU accession process or under ERM2. This strategy would amount to returning to monetary authorities and to the government the ability to conduct monetary and exchange rate policies – which they resigned when adopting the CBA – and then to deprive them again of this ability on joining the euro. This strategy would be not only inconsistent but also perilous since the economies involved should provide evidence of their central banking skills during the ERM2 phase.

However, the success of this second step, within the framework of the CBA, will be dependent on the continuation of their current struggle for withstanding the CBA's rigidity, with more labor market flexibility, conservative financial stance and foreign borrowing policies, cautious external debt management, and a sounder banking system (Keller, 2000; Gulde et al., 2000).

### Eviction Effects

The Berlin European Council (March 1999) ratified the EU's action program for the years 2000–6. With regard to the enlargement of the Union to include CEECs, Agenda 2000 – completed by the Nice Treaty – makes a distinction between two waves: only Estonia, Hungary, Poland, the Czech Republic and Slovenia – plus Cyprus – would be included in the first wave, the others being excluded for the time being. As a matter of fact, this distinction, reflecting more the *potential* for future integration rather than an already-acquired convergence, is likely to prove self-fulfilling. Pegging a currency to the euro does not in itself guarantee actual convergence, i.e. a narrowing of the gap in living standards. To set the process in motion there must first of all be 'catch-up'. But this dynamic cannot be launched unless these economies have at their disposal the funding required to transform and modernize production capacity and infrastructures. Since the middle years of the 1990s, there has been a complementarity of private and official capital flows. Private investments have concentrated, along with official flows, in the most dynamic countries which today belong to the first wave of countries eligible for EU membership. In the long run, adhesion to the EU of the better-placed economies could aggravate internal divergences, with the 'ins' keeping the others out. It therefore comes as no surprise to see that, of the CBA economies, only Estonia, i.e. the country benefiting most from long-term influxes of capital, belongs to the first wave mentioned above. In stark contrast, the Bulgarian and Bosnian[10] economies are likely to be doomed to stagnation, on the margin of the EU, despite the monetary stability contributed by the CBA.

## CONCLUSIONS AND LESSONS FOR THE AMERICAS

Several lessons may be drawn from the experiences of the CBAs in Europe:

1.  Before opting for a CBA, it is important to assess both the requirements and consequences of abandoning central banking for the sake of stability and credibility. The CBAs illustrate the advantages and disadvantages of this strategy involving central banking apostasy and exchange rate freeze.
    *   Advantages:
        –   radical stabilization of inflation;

     – guarantee of convertibility;
     – restoration of confidence in the currency;
     – introduction of a macroeconomic 'discipline' driving out any inflationary or fiscal drift.
- Disadvantages:
     – restriction, even cancellation, of the action of the LOLR, hence banking vulnerability;
     – introduction of a credit dynamic depending on foreign currency flows;
     – prevention of an active monetary policy to stabilize the economy and of any intervention on the exchange rate; hence extreme vulnerability to external shocks, which necessitates a painful adjustment for the real sector and employment;
     – limited protection against speculative attacks.

2. The choice of anchor currency is of crucial importance, for this will dictate the impact of exogenous shocks. The choice of a basket of currencies limits the effects of exchange rate volatility. However, compared to a single CBA, it is a source of confusion since it calls for active management of the foreign currency reserves in order to ensure the backing rule. The peg of the currency to the natural economic integration zone is a better strategy, but it has to be distinguishable in the long as well as the short run. With hindsight, we can see that Estonia made the right choice back in 1992. An initial project provided for the Swedish kronor as the reference currency. In opting for Europe's pivotal currency, Estonia avoided the pitfall of being pegged to another currency that was exposed to speculative attacks in 1992–3. In contrast, Lithuania's choice of the dollar appears to have been ill-advised. The country is today paying the price for the dollar's high level, in terms of its inevitable commercial rapprochement with the euro area and the difficulties encountered in switching to the euro.

3. The loosening of the rules fixed at the outset has a devastating effect on credibility. The introduction of the CBA includes the following dilemma. Either very firm engagements are made at the outset in order to reap the benefit of the credibility effect; but in this case the CBA constraints are felt with greater intensity; the temptation to introduce subsequent flexibility is then high, but this kind of betrayal provokes a credibility crisis. Or the opposite path, i.e. with very limited commitments, is adopted, but in this case the credibility-effect is virtually nil right from the start.[11]

4. An awareness of the inevitable constraints from the CBA is of vital importance. Otherwise, the CBA may turn out to be a trap from which it is difficult to break free. The difficulty of reverting to a central banking system is well illustrated by Lithuania's failure to manage its withdrawal from the CBA. The only possible ways out seems to be euroization or monetary union.

5.  In the context of Europe, the creation of the single European currency and the enlargement of the EU seem to offer a favorable way out. But if it is to serve as an instrument of European integration, the CBA nonetheless needs to be accompanied with considerable inflows of capital. The fact is that the strict issuing rules of the CBA subject the domestic credit dynamic to influxes of foreign currency and/or the extraversion of the banking system. If this is not the case, the CBA is not playing its role as a catalyst and, on the contrary, runs the risk of compromising rapid integration by slowing down the process of real convergence. Monetary stability resulting from the CBA is not enough: it has to be buttressed by major financial commitments on the part of the EU.

On the strength of these conclusions, we may legitimately voice doubts as to the future of the Argentinean CBA. Here, the constraints have plunged Argentina into a recession from which it is having the utmost difficulty in extricating itself. The various adjustments made to the initial CBA – the lowering of the CBA's backing to 66 per cent after the Tequila effect by 1995, the perspective of a switch of the peg from US dollar to a currency basket made up in equal parts of dollars and euros – have proved unequal to the task and have damaged the country's credibility.

In order to leave the CBA definitively, Argentina can choose between, on the one hand, integral and official dollarization and, on the other hand, monetary union. If the choice is dollarization, certain agreements will have to be reached with the US authorities, as was the case with Ecuador. This can in no way be considered as a monetary union as monetary power will not be shared and will remain exclusively in the hands of the United States. Withdrawal by means of monetary union with the United States is therefore not a serious option, indeed it has created little enthusiasm. On the other hand, monetary union within the framework of Mercosur is conceivable and has in fact already been proposed. As in Europe, monetary union would make it possible to exit from the CBA honorably. Unlike its European counterparts, however, Argentina is confronted with a problem of major proportions: the monetary union which the country would seek to join does not actually exist yet. And for this union to become reality, Brazil and Argentina would first have to agree on the project and define convergent monetary strategies.

## NOTES

1.  By 2002, the Law on the CBBH was amended to substitute the euro for the deutschmark.
2.  For a critical view of credibility models, see Arestis and Sawyer (1998), in particular papers by Grabel and Bain.
3.  To those who regret the replacement of discretionary powers by a rigid set of rules, Dornbusch

and Giavazzi (1999: 27) reply: 'That is an old-fashioned objection that does not hold up easily to modern scrutiny. Rules-based central banking is in; discretion has been discredited in the inflationary experience of the 1970s in industrial countries, and throughout the emerging market world in the past decade. Flexibility is desirable, but you can only afford it if your central bank is the Fed or the Buba'.

4. Not all post-Keynesians agree on the level of central bank accommodation. See the horizontalism vs. structuralism debate (Rochon, 1999: 155–201).

5. Despite a CPI forecast of 10 per cent for the year 2000.

6. As the Governor of the CBBH notified: 'The convertible marka is the only "domestic" currency. It is developing well and it is used all over the country, but we still have a long way to go, particularly in Herzegovina, before the convertible marka can be described as the dominant currency in the whole country' (Nicholl, 1999).

7. Six years after Dayton, the Bosnian financial system is still divided into two or even three relatively distinct systems. Not one of the 42 so-called commercial banks yet operates over the whole country.

8. ERM2 is based on a fixed but adjustable peg to the euro. In order to avoid significant misalignments, realignments shall be conducted in a timely fashion, with a standard fluctuation of ±15 per cent around the central rate of participants countries.

9. 'Accession countries which have operated a euro-based CBA deemed to be sustainable might not be required to go through a double regime shift in their strategies to adopt the euro. Thus such countries may participate in ERM2 with a CBA as a unilateral commitment augmenting the discipline within ERM2. However, it should be clearly understood that a common accord would have to be reached on the central parity against the euro' (Noyer, 2000).

10. Negotiations concerning Bosnia and Herzegovina's membership of the EU have not really got under way. But the CBBH still hopes that the project will materialize one day thanks to the CBA.

11. See for instance the negative experience of Turkey's quasi-CBA in 1999–2000.

# REFERENCES

Arestis, P. and Sawyer, M.C. (eds) 1998. *Political Economy of Central Banking.* Cheltenham: Edward Elgar.

Avramov, R. 2000. Exit Strategies from Currency Board Arrangements, *Seminar on Currency Boards. Experience and Prospects.* Eesti Pank, Tallinn, 5–6 May.

Balino, T. et al. 1997. Currency Board Arrangements: Issues and Experiences. *IMF Occasional Paper* 151.

Barro, R. and Gordon, D.B. 1983. Rules, Discretion, and Reputation in a Model of Monetary Policy, *Journal of Monetary Economics* 12.2: 101–21.

Barro, R. 1998. What Might Save Russia: Tying the Ruble to the Dollar. *Business Week.* 28 September: 24.

BOFIT. 2001. Estonia, Lithuania, Latvia. *Baltic Economies. The Quarter in Review* 1/01.

Boone, P., Breach, A. and Johnston, A. 1998. Institutions and Prospects for a Currency Board in Russia: Perspectives on a Deepening Crisis. *Post-Soviet Geography and Economics* 39.7: 371–8.

Camard, W. 1996. Discretion with Rules? Lessons from the Currency Board Arrangement in Lithuania, *IMF Paper on Policy Analysis and Assessment* 96/1.

Davidson, P. 2000. Is a Plumber or a New Financial Architect Needed to End Global International Liquidity Problems? *World Development*, June.

Dornbusch, R. and Giavazzi, F. 1999. Hard Currency and Sound Credit: A Financial Agenda for Central Europe, *EIB Papers* 4.2: 24–32.

Eichengreen, B. 1999. *Toward a New International Financial System*. Washington: Institute for International Economics.

Fleming, A., Chu, L. and Bakker, M.R. 1997. Banking Crises in the Baltics, *Finance and Development* 34.1: 42–5.

Frenkel, J.A. 1999. The International Financial Architecture, *The Brookings Institution Policy Brief* 51.

Friedman, M. and Schwartz, A.J. (1963), *A Monetary History of the United States, 1867–1960*, Princeton, NJ: Princeton University Press.

Ghosh, A.R., Gulde, A.-M. and Wolf, H.C. 1998. Currency Boards: The Ultimate Fix?, *IMF Working Paper* 98/8.

Ghosh, A.R., Gulde, A.-M. and Wolf, H.C. 2000. Currency Boards: More than a Quick Fix?, *Economic Policy*, October: 269–335.

Gulde, A.M. 1999. The Role of the Currency Board in Bulgaria's Stabilization, *IMF Policy Discussion Paper* 99/3.

Gulde, A.M., Kahkonen, J. and Keller, P. 2000. Pros and Cons of Currency Board Arrangements in the Lead-up to EU Accession and Participation in the Euro Zone, *IMF Policy Discussion Paper* 00/1.

Hanke, S.H. 1998. The Case for a Russian Currency Board System, *Foreign Policy Briefing* 49.

Hanke, S.H., Jonung, L. and Schuler, K. 1993. *Russian Currency and Finance. A Currency Board Approach to Reform*. London: Routledge.

Keller, P.M. 2000. Recent Experience with Currency Boards and Fixed Exchange Rates in the Baltic Countries and Bulgaria and Some Lessons for the Future, *Seminar on Currency Boards. Experience and Prospects*. Eesti Pank, Tallinn, 5–6 May.

Korhonen, I. 1999. The Effect of Russian Crisis on the Baltic Countries, *Baltic Economies. The Quarter in Review*, 8 February.

Kurtovic, M. 1998. In *Summary Proceedings of the Fifty-third Annual Meeting of the Board of Governors*, IMF.

Kydland, F.E. and Prescott, E.C. 1977. Rules rather than Discretion: The Inconsistency of Optimal Plans, *Journal of Political Economy* 85.3: 473–92.

Lepik, I. 1999. Basic Features of the Estonian Currency Board: Convertibility and Liquidity Management, *International Workshop on Currency Boards: Convertibility, Liquidity Management and Exit*. Hong Kong Baptist University, 9 October.

Lepik, I. 2000. Evolution of Monetary Operational Framework and Challenges Ahead (Estonia), *Seminar on Currency Boards. Experience and Prospects*. Eesti Pank, Tallinn, 5–6 May.

Lewis, M.K. and Sevi, Z. 2001. The Political Economy of Currency Boards in the Balkans, *MOCT-MOST: Economic Policy in Transitional Economies* 1.

Nenovsky, N. and Hristov, K. 1999. Monetary Policy under the Currency Board: The Case of Bulgaria, *International Workshop on Currency Boards: Convertibility, Liquidity Management and Exit*. Hong Kong Baptist University, 9 October.

Nenovsky, N., Hristov, K. and Petrov, B. 1999. Transition from Lev to Euro. Early Step to the EU. Available at www.capital.bg.

Niaura, J. 1998. The Experience of Lithuania in Adopting and then Exiting from the Currency Board System, *International Conference on Exchange Rate Stability and Currency Board Economics*. Hong Kong, 28–9 November.

Nicholl, P. 1999. Bosnia & Herzegovina and the Euro, *European Commission Conference on the Effect of the Euro on Third Countries*. Sarajevo: CBBH.

Nicholl, P. 2000. Speech Notes, *Round Table Discussion on Direct Foreign Investment in BiH*. The BiH Chamber of Commerce, Sarajevo, 8 February.

Noyer, C. 2000. ECB Official Statement to the Press, 13 April.

Ponsot, J.F. 2001. Parité fixe et règle de convertibilité monétaire. L'impact d'un 'currency board' sur la croissance. In *La croissance économique dans le long terme*, ed. C. Diebolt. Paris: L'Harmattan (Fortcoming).

Rochon, L.-P. 1999. *Credit, Money and Production: An Alternative Post-Keynesian Approach*. Cheltenham: Edward Elgar.

Roubini, N. 1998. The Case against Currency Boards: Debunking 10 Myths about the Benefits of Currency Boards, *www.stern.nyu.edu*.

Sorg, M. and Vensel, V. 2001. Banking System Development under the Estonian Currency Board Arrangement, *The 51st International Atlantic Economic Conference*. Athens, 13–20 March.

Tsang, S.K. 1999. Legal Frameworks of Currency Boards Regimes, *HKMA Quaterly Bulletin* 8: 50–63.

Wallace, N. 1990. A Banking Model in which Partial Suspension is Best, *Quaterly Review of the Federal Reserve Bank of Minneapolis*, Fall: 11–23.

## APPENDIX

*Table A2.1 Estonia – FDI (million kroons)*

|           | 1993   | 1994   | 1995   | 1996   | 1997    | 1998   | 1999    | 2000    |
|-----------|--------|--------|--------|--------|---------|--------|---------|---------|
| (Net)     | 2070.8 | 2789.4 | 2281.8 | 1329.9 | 1781.2  | 7989.7 | 3208.2  | 4140.9  |
| Inflow    | 2152.9 | 2819.2 | 2312.9 | 1814.4 | 3694.1  | 8071.4 | 4448.0  | 6807.3  |
| Outflow   | −82.1  | −29.8  | −29.1  | −484.5 | −1912.9 | −81.7  | −1239.8 | −2666.4 |

*Source*: IMF

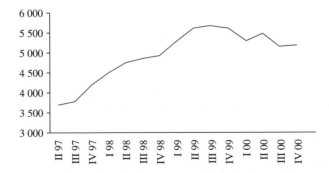

*Figure A2.1 Lithuania – credit to the private sector (million litai)*

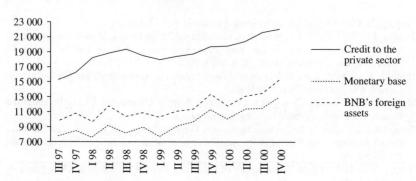

*Figure A2.2    Bulgaria – BNB's foreign assets, monetary base and credit to
the private sector (million leva)*

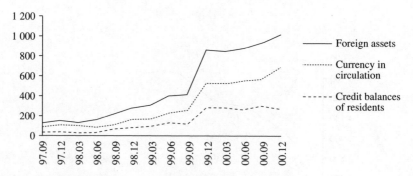

*Sources*:   BOL, IMF, CBBH

*Figure A2.3    Bosnia and Herzegovina – CBBH: foreign assets and monetary
liabilities (million KM)*

# 3. The lessons of the European Monetary Union

## Alain Parguez

### INTRODUCTION

According to the advice and consent of experts and columnists, the European Monetary Union (EMU) is one of the most stunning achievements of the late twentieth century that must deeply shape the economy of the twenty-first century. Europeans were the first to discover that objective market laws impose the substitutions of supra-national regions for erstwhile nation-bounded economies. They were shrewd enough to understand that to abide by market determinism they had to substitute a supra-national currency for ancient domestic currencies. The proof of their unbridled commitment to economic determinism is that as soon as they understood what they wanted to do they did it by engineering the set of institutions which constitutes the conditions of existence for monetary union. The success of the new currency must convince everyone that Europeans rightly integrated the requirements of the market.

The EMU is henceforth the laboratory experiment of social engineering that must be successfully repeated everywhere, at least in America and Asia. As shown by Parguez et al. (2003), however it is not obvious that the result of the experiment must be the same everywhere for quite logical reasons. In Europe, the experiment led to the creation of a composite currency reflecting the real strength of the relative equilibrium in national economics. None of the existing currencies could achieve the status of a regional currency as the ultimate result of the quasi-tâtonnement process (ibid.) culminating in monetary union. Political constraints aside the solution must be the same in Asia when Japan, China, South-East Asian countries start the experiment. Neither the Yen nor the Chinese Yuan will be the equilibrium solution when an Asian monetary union is created in the distant future. In America, on the other hand, whatever the scale of the experiment the sole equilibrium solution will be to choose the US dollar as the regional currency. So incommensurate is the size of the US economy relative to the economies of Canada, Mexico and South America that the very quasi-tâtonnement process leads inevitably to the US dollar. Wishing for a European solution to an American monetary union on the grounds of the underlying economics of the EMU contradicts its core principles. Dollarization fits the EMU norm as long as it is sustained by the same set of institutions to which all members of the Union, including the USA, must abide (ibid.). Herein is the explanation of the failure of ongoing experiments in dollarization for anyone who believes in the EMU as the benchmark of a genuine monetary union – since they are not supported by any kind of supra-national institution they do not entail any kind of commitment for the USA. Pseudo-dollarized countries are now, like the state of Mississippi, bereft of federal transfers; a situation that cannot be deemed the optimal solution of an equilibrium process.

In any case, EMU is a cogent experiment for America (and Asia) if three conditions are met:

1.  It must have been undertaken independently of a long-run historical process. Once upon a time, Europeans had a vision of the market will and they acted on it immediately.
2.  It is independent of any subjective preference for a specific economic and social doctrine.
3.  It must be a convincing success, which precludes any doubt over its future.

None of those conditions is met, which explains why the EMU is not the best example of monetary union for these regions to follow. Condition 1 does not hold because monetary union was the last stage of a European plan which started a very long time ago, in the late 1930s and early 1940s. Architects of this plan wished, in the long run, to build a New European Order, some third way relative to the two models they loathed, the Soviet-style statism and collectivist model on one side, and the US-style model of unfettered capitalism on the other side. The new order ultimately had to be rooted in a new single currency so sound that it is the modern form of the gold standard. Condition 2 cannot be met because the EMU is explicitly enshrined into an a-priori vision of economics, what is deemed the European techno-classical school (Parguez 2000). The euro was born as a conservative quasi-gold currency enforcing a dramatic set of constraints to any degree of freedom in the economic and social policy of member states. The euro has therefore been created as a pure stateless currency and therefore a fragile one which has not been met and it is still impossible to foresee when it will fulfill its supporting vision by successfully competing with the US dollar.

# EMU AS THE ACHIEVEMENT OF A LONG-RUN HISTORICAL PROCESS

According to the story told by European technocrats and politicians, EMU was born suddenly in the late 1980s. They were desperately in search of a vision which would rejuvenate the faith of Europeans and they thought that a single currency was the best solution. This conventional story encapsulates the claim that European unification did not logically imply monetary union, which means that monetary union had never been the ultimate consequence of the earlier steps towards the European Union. If that story were true, one would be obliged to wonder at the speed of monetary union. In the very short span of ten years, what had been a last resort expedient was turned into a full re-engineering of Europe and the euro was officially born.

This story contradicts history! It was told to hide the true nature of EMU because the European elite was aware of the necessity of preventing any debate on the economic content of the Treaty of Maastricht (1992). The truth is that as soon as the vision of a future New European Order was born within what can be deemed the Techno-Classical European (TCE) group (ibid.), it explicitly enshrined a quasi-gold single European currency as its ultimate achievement. All those sharing the European vision of a perfect New Order had been trained in Austrian economics, especially in the general theory of money spelled out by Carl Menger (1892), in which money and the state were natural adversaries. Menger's theory ensconced three major propositions:

1.  Given a perfectly integrated transaction space, money evolves out of the spontaneous market process without any kind of exogenous intervention. There is only one commodity individual transactions have to choose as the medium of exchange because by doing so they maximize their wealth (or minimize their transaction costs).
2.  Money exists as a commodity because it has a constant objective intrinsic value, which requires that prices expressed in this commodity are constant over time. Permanent zero inflation is an existence condition of money.
3.  Since the state plays no part in monetizing the economy, money must always be protected from the state and therefore from politics. To enhance its power the state must debase the value of money by generating inflation.

From Menger's theory stemmed three major propositions that became the core of the New European Order:

1.  Since Europe must be a perfectly supra-national Mengerian space, only one currency must exist as the single European currency. Europeans of the first generation, such as of François Perroux and Jacques Rueff[1] had therefore

invented the so-called optimal currency area principle (Parguez, 2000). (It is inaccurate to ascribe to Mundell any crucial influence on the birth of the euro).

2.  This European money exists as long as prices denominated in euros are stable. Permanent price stability must be maintained by protecting the currency against political intervention. Europeans believed in the necessity of a supra-national sovereign system of Central Banks whose sole mission must be absolute price stability.

3.  This system must be supported by a stringent set of institutional rules forcing member states to abide slavishly to the zero inflation principle (the theory of value).

Proposition 3 reveals the technocratic ideology of Europeans who scorned democracy and its inbred tendency to socialism so much that they planned the scientific engineering of society that would permanently enforce economic laws on spontaneously irrational individuals. Because of their Austrian training, the Europeans shared an ultra-classical faith in the scarcity principle as the prerequisite for invariance in the value of money. Money has to be scarce which explains why it has to be exogenous. Indeed it must be scarcer than gold. Scarcity rules as long as the *ex-ante* saving constraint is absolute, hence it has been the cornerstone of the theory of value for Europeans since the start. Member states must be deprived of the possibility of harming the scarcity principle by excess spending. Europeans agreed on the necessity of freezing fiscal policy by imposing, as a minimum, permanent zero public deficits attained by a mix of spending squeezes and tax hikes. They have not opposed high taxation when the tax burden falls on spendthrift individuals who are the wage and salary earners.

## UNFOLDING THE EUROPEAN PLAN TOWARDS EMU

Both in France and Germany in the late 1930s and early 1940s some members of the TCE were so obsessed by the threat of the American economy and society that they wanted to accelerate the pace of history. It is now well documented (Smith and Stirk, 1990) that a blueprint of a treaty of monetary union had been drafted in 1942 by the German finance minister, Walter Funk, and submitted to the then finance minister of the Vichy Regime. The Funk plan is the true ancestor of the European Treaties of Maastricht and Amsterdam. In the prospect of a German victory, there would be a New Order supported by a single currency, an independent central bank achieving price stability, and fiscal rules imposing fiscal soundness (or responsibility). The Funk Plan won the support of many Vichy technocrats while it was endorsed by those technocrats of the Nazi regime who feared the inbred profligacy of the Nazi leadership.[2]

The course of history vindicated those who thought both in France and in Germany that it was too early to create a monetary union. Mengerian propositions had convinced them that monetary union should process step by step. Their evolutionary view prevailed from the aftermath of the Second World War onwards. The first logical step imposed the building of a Mengerian European transaction space encompassing both free trade and perfect competition and institutions supporting the targeted economic order. The 'real' stage led to the European Common Market (1957) and later (1985) to the European Union by virtue of the so-called single Act deepening the transaction space in terms of commitment to market laws and economic order. The 'monetary' stage started in 1979 with the European Monetary System imposing very narrow bands on the fluctuations of relative exchange rates between European currencies. Overlapping of 'real' and 'monetary' stages could be justified on Mengerian grounds.

*Table 3.1    Debates over the New European Order*

| 1 | 2 | 3 |
| --- | --- | --- |
| Inception of the plan | Generation of the real | Generation of the |
| Early debates | transaction space | single currency |
| Late 1930s | Early 1950s | |
| Early 1950s | Mid-1980s | |
| | | |
| 1979 | 1992 | 1999 |
| EMS | Treaty of the Euro | Official birth of single |
| Maastricht Treaty | | currency |

On the one hand, by the end of the 1970s there had been so much progress towards European integration that the time was right for a first step toward monetary union. On the other hand, harsh constraints on exchange rates accelerated the pace of integration by removing the destabilizing impact of exchange rates fluctuations over relative prices. In the long run the EMU was to prevent member states from using exchange rates as an adjustment mechanism to support unsound policies. Integration would operate as some tâtonnement process leading to the full equilibrium relative values of the currencies in the wake of a progressive narrowing of the fluctuation bands. Some 20 years after its inception, it would be possible to determine the exact composition of the new currency by relying on the solutions of the long-run Mengerian process. The euro was born in 1999, seven years after the Treaty of Maastricht. In 1999, the time was ripe to know the equilibrium composition of the single currency; seven more years were required for the tâtonnement process, of which the pace has been accelerated by the so-called 'converging norms'. In retrospect, at least 60 years have elapsed since the early debates over the New European Order, as shown in Table 3.1.

Ultimately the EMU enshrines a form of genuine conservative economics which is its condition of existence. The actual nature of the EMU is revealed by the Treaties of Maastricht and Amsterdam (which includes the famous Growth and Stability Pact). It abides by the vision of economic order spelled out by the French–German techno-classical school,[3] which precludes any conciliation with post-Keynesian economics.

## THE EFFECTIVE NATURE OF THE EURO: A MENGERIAN STATELESS CURRENCY

### A Very Fragile Currency

At first glance, the financial structure of Euroland could be compared with the supporting structure of the US dollar. There is a unique and fully independent Central Bank, the European Central Bank (ECB), endowed with supreme stewardship over the currency like the Federal Reserve System. As shown by Steiger (2004) this widespread interpretation is wrong. The ECB is not at all a genuine Central Bank, it enjoys none of the functions of the FRS and it is devoid of all the characteristics of Central Banks:

1.  It cannot issue notes denominated in euros, which is proven by a careful study of its balance sheet. Notes are only issued by the Domestic Central Banks (DCBs). To maintain the illusion of a true Central Bank, a share of those notes is 'statistically allocated' (Steiger, 2004) to the ECB and 'appears' in its side (one-thirteenth of the issue of notes).
2.  It does not hold public or private debts on its assets side, which could be used for open market interventions. The DCB alone holds public and private debts as assets.
3.  Logically, it cannot alone act as a lender of last resort to commercial banks.

It means that the actual 'monetary stewardship' has been bestowed on the so-called Council of Governors of the European Central Banks System whose members are all presidents of DCBs (12 today, many more soon) plus six representatives of the ECB (they are just a minority). Contrary to what is usually believed, it is a perfectly decentralized structure: a Central Bank oligarchy. The ECB as such has not the least authority over DCBs which must act collectively. Each of them is independent of the respective domestic state.

From this description of the ECB stems a logical conclusion: monetary policy is the sole responsibility of the Council of Governors and it is implemented by DCBs and not by the ECB. Its explicit mandate is to maintain the value of the currency by imposing price stability. According to Paragraph 2 of the Treaty of Maastricht the Council of Government (COG) should also sustain growth and therefore employment without jeopardizing its 'primary' goal, zero inflation. The COG was left to decide how the secondary mission could be reconciled with its primary and fundamental mission. It solved the problem by rewriting Paragraph 2 when it declared that its unique mission was 'to maintain price stability and in this way to contribute to the achievement of the objective of the community' (ECB bulletin, October 2000). As shown by Bibow (2001) by excluding the very possibility of a trade-off, the COG has freed itself of concerns with the level of employment. It is much more in line with the hard-line version of classical economics than the Federal Reserve (ibid.) since it postulates that full employment can only be attainded in the long run as a reward of price stability.

In line with the TCE School theory of inflation the Treaty of Maastricht endorsed a quantity theory-led monetary policy. According to Paragraph 18 of the protocol relative to the COG, it has to fight inflation by the control of monetary aggregates, using open-market interventions, required reserves or any other relevant instruments (Parguez, 2000). The COG would have absolute control over monetary aggregates, which is a strong version of the exogeneity-of-money claim, regardless of the true role of banks. European monetary policy would be implemented quite differently from the Federal Reserve's monetary policy which renounced a long time ago the direct control of monetary aggregates. The COG rewrote its charter again by deciding to control indirectly the relevant monetary aggregate through the direct control of short-term interest rates (ECB bulletin, October 2000). In the neo-Rueffian stance, the COG monetary policy should proceed as follows according to the following table.

It explains why the COG has been led to rely on the strong version of the natural rate of employment. Unemployment cannot fall below the level which is allowed by the real growth rate consistent with the equilibrium level of M3. As soon as unemployment falls below its equilibrium threshold, inflation starts by wage hikes revealing the excess supply of 'money'. Complying with Rueff's erstwhile theory, the COG believes that genuine price stability exists when nobody expects (or bets on) inflation. The significant level of unemployment is the level beyond which there is no expected inflation; it can be deemed the Non Accelerating Inflation Rate of Unemployment (NAIRU). A true policy of zero inflation is so painful that it can only be imposed by a sovereign central bank free of any kind of political intervention. Architects of the EMU have been taught this hard lesson by their old masters. Herein is the explanation of the greater status of the ECB relative to the Federal Reserve of Allan Greenspan, which aims for full employment (Bibow, 2001).

*Table 3.2    Phases of monetary policy*

| 1 | 2 | 3 | 4 | 5 |
|---|---|---|---|---|
| Price stability required → | Equilibrium growth required → (potential growth rate) | Excess expected → relative to the potential rate | Goal of M3* ↓ Squeeze of aggregate demand → by interest rate hike | Growth of M3 |

*Note*:    M3 is the equilibrium level.

The COG is totally independent of both member states and European institutions, including the Council of Ministers, the Commission and the European Parliament. None of these institutions can issue advice or recommendations to the COG, nor therefore to former national Domestic Central Banks when they interfere with its mandate. According to COG interpretation, independence means that it has to increase interest rates if it fears expected inflation, even if those hikes are fiercely opposed by a unanimous council of ministers. For some supporters of the EMU, the situation has improved relative to the time when an inflation-obsessed Bundesbank ruled over the European Union through the EMS. They used to refer to Paragraph 10 of the ECB protocol giving an equal voting right within the Council of Governors to all presidents of national central banks. EMU would have instated a monetary democracy under the guise of a sovereign ECB of which the policy could therefore be reshaped to support full employment. It is a dream that contradicts the very character of the EMU which is a perfect oligarchy of Central Banks.

Independence has been bestowed on the ECBS to get rid forever of political noises within the technocratic realm of monetary policy. It would be absurd to believe that the Council of Governors is the Trojan horse of democracy. There has been no trade-off between monetary sovereignty and monetary democracy, and herein is another lesson for advocates of monetary union outside Europe. So decentralized is the supporting structure of the euro, that imposing a common monetary policy of scarcity is not enough.

## An Effort to Protect the Currency by Permanent Squeeze of Aggregate Demand

Since the start, TCE economists have spelled out what Rueff for instance deemed the most fundamental theorem of economics: state deficits are the last resort cause of inflation because they allow the state to steal a share of the real *ex-ante* saving fund by issuing valueless money or false rights.

Inflation should therefore proceed as follows:

State deficit → Excess creation of state money → Drop in the value of money inflation → Excess demand → Wage hikes

Herein is the crowding out principle since the state deficit determines an automatic decrease in private investment through the saving leakage. As far back as the early 1940s TCE economists had derived three general principles from their theory of inflation:

1. The state must be deprived of its power to create money.
2. Deficits must be forbidden both in the long run and in the short run, which excludes a contra-cyclical fiscal policy.
3. The state must raise a surplus, which is an automatic increase in the saving fund.

Those rules form the conditions of existence for the sound currency they wished to create. They could be implemented in a future monetary union because of the absence of political constraints on economic policy resulting from its stateless nature.

These three principles have been carefully implemented in the EMU by the Treaties of Maastricht and Amsterdam, which function as a legal or rather constitutional enforcement of classical economics. They were enshrined in the proposed European Constitution. Fiscal policy of member states is constrained by four rules:

1. The ECB is forbidden to create money at the request of member states and European institutions; this means that all Domestic Central Banks are prohibited from creating money for their former respective states. The prohibition aims at depriving member states of their former monetary power, which is principle 1 of the TCE agenda.

   According to the conventional interpretation, the prohibition first means that the state cannot 'monetize' its deficit by the direct acquisition of new bonds by the Domestic Central Bank. It is much more demanding because it must be interpreted in the context of modern theory of public finance.

The general law of circulation applies to private agents and to the state. Nobody can spend now an income that will be earned in the future as the consequence of initial expenditures. The state cannot finance its outlays (they are part of the flux phase of the monetary circuit) by its tax revenue since taxes will be raised on future private sector income which, for a large share, depends on initial state outlays (taxes are part of the reflux phase of the monetary circuit). Taxes withdraw income from the private sector to the state and as soon as they are collected tax liabilities of the private sector are extinguished, which destroys an equal amount of money.

The state is therefore obliged to finance its expenditures by the creation of money, which should be undertaken by the state, directly by the Treasury, or by the state banking branch, the Central Bank. State money creation is still the rule in federal finance of the USA where it is operated through the accounting relationship between the Treasury and the Federal Reserve System.

Since state money creation is now impossible within the EMU, member states are obliged to finance their initial outlays by the creation of money operated by private banks. This privatization of public finance is emphasized by the ECB according to which a major aspect of monetary policy is that states finance their expenditures through their accounting relationship with commercial banks (Bibow 2001, ECB bulletin, October 2000).

State outlays have to meet the ECB's monetary target. Excessive state outlays relative to the M3* target lead the ECB to foresee inflation that it must curb by an interest hike that will increase the public debt burden. The prohibition is a cornucopia for commercial banks since the state now has to pay interest on the money it needs whereas before it was interest-free. Since European monetary policy relies on a given aggregate supply of money, the prohibition could lead to a crowding out of the private sector. It should be prevented by a permanent constraint on outlays (ECB bulletin October 2000), which has already been recommended by the Growth and Stability Pact.

2.   Contrary to widespread opinion, the strait-jacket is much more demanding than the 3 per cent limit on the deficit to GDP ratio. Whatever the required rate of growth of state outlays, it must never run a deficit if it is to abide by the Growth and Stability Pact. The initial formulation included in the Treaty of Amsterdam was that the state has at least to balance its budget over the 'medium term'.

In line with the general preamble of the pact, the 3 per cent rule has been interpreted by the Commission and the ECB as at least imposing a permanent balanced budget, 'Medium' only refers to the time required to suppress the deficit, two or three years after the official birth of the euro. No distinction is now made between structural and cyclical deficits. The destabilizing impact of public finance on the currency cannot be offset if anti-cyclical policy is allowed.

According to the pact, member states must go farther than balanced budgets; they must target a fiscal surplus that must be permanent according to subsequent interpretation. Fiscal surpluses are praised on pure Rueffian terms by the ECB and European technocrats, since they are a net addition to the aggregate *ex-ante* savings fund. The EMU turns so-called 'Clintonomics' into a permanent and compulsory policy. Like the former Clintonomics, Euro-economics cannot understand that a state surplus generates an equal deficit in the private sector. It cannot escape from the straight-jacket of its underlying classical economics (principles 2 and 3 above).

Some staunch supporters of the Growth and Stability Pact want to restore the cyclical interpretation of fiscal deficits. The budget should be balanced 'over the cycle'. Since the cycle is defined in relation to the neoclassical long-run optimal growth trend, the cyclical interpretation just makes the fiscal rules more restrictive.

3.  According to the Treaty of Maastricht, public debt must never exceed 60 per cent of GDP. According to the Growth and Stability Pact, member states must still do better and reach a lower level of indebtedness. Minimizing the public debt is now on the agenda: it fits the surplus norm. Surpluses can only be spent on repaying debt and therefore state saving is automatically recycled into net private saving. Herein is the ultimate explanation of ECB emphasis on surpluses: debt targets are met by surplus targets which are themselves met either by outlay cuts, cuts or tax hikes on households with low propensity to save or both. This so-called 'virtuous' cumulative policy of restraint is the last resort benchmark of the inbred classical nature of EMU.

    Principles 2 and 3 are monitored by the Council of Governors and the European Commission. Both can send recommendations to member states that do not comply with the rules. If a guilty state refuses to amend its policy, it can be indicted before the Council of Ministers on the advice of the Commission and the ECB. Assuming that it persists to ignore the rules, the Council can raise on the culprit a fine equal to 0.5 per cent of the GDP per year of excess deficit. Herein is the cornerstone of the demise of the state as sovereign entity with the power to choose the course of its policy.

4.  EMU requires a deep long-run program of structural adjustment to remove obstacles to market laws. 'Structural rigidities' can hold at bay monetary policy because they freeze the wage–price adjustment sustaining the value of the currency. Excruciating unemployment hikes would be required to curb real wages and adjust them to real long-run productivity. The efficiency of monetary policy requires that all factors of structural rigidity can be

removed with EMU. The Growth and Stability Pact is straightforward: greater obstacles to monetary policy lie in the labor market. Its built-in rigidity is the sole cause of high levels of unemployment, which are therefore independent of aggregate demand. So rigid should be the real wages structure that the Council of Governors must aim at very high levels of unemployment to attain its price stability mandate. The 'structural rigidity' postulate is the underlying rationale of ECB proposition according to which full employment cannot be an independent goal of monetary policy. It is addressed by the Growth and Stability Pact and subsequently interpreted in a very extensive way by the ECB. Perfect flexibility of the labor market is to be attained by an agenda that the first generation of TCE economists would have keenly embraced. It is indeed quite impossible to go farther in the fight against post-Keynesian economics since the flexibility agenda includes:

- The substitution of workforce programs for welfare programs in order to force an increase in the supply of labor.
- The decrease in real minimum incomes to increase incentives to work.
- The increase in the power of firms to fire workers when their profits fall, which requires weaker or more market-oriented unions.
- A long-run fall in real labor costs paid by firms, in terms of social contributions, in order to allow an increase in their demand for labor.

## THE DUBIOUS PERFORMANCE OF EMU: AN UNCERTAIN FUTURE

An experiment is successful when its outcome fits what had been expected by those who undertook it. When Europeans started their experiment of monetary union, they expected to achieve a quasi-gold currency which would overthrow the US dollar as the soundest currency. They expected that, after an initial depreciation of the dollar relative to the euro, exchange rates will remain perfectly stable in the long run, which would prove that the new currency was perfectly protected, like gold, against the forces of speculation.

What happened was the triumph of speculation. In the first phase (from the start until 2002), the euro fell relative to the dollar even in the wake of the US economy slowing down and the collapse of the US stock market, and the so-called fundamentals were ignored. In the second phase, there was a dramatic reversal of speculative spirits. The euro started to rise relative to the dollar even in the wake of the ongoing stagnation of the Euroland real economy while growth accelerated again in the US economy. The more the Euroland economy weakens relative to the US economy, the more speculation pushes the euro appreciate.

What could explain the speculative nature of euro but the very intrinsic nature of the EMU? Born without a robust institutional and harmonizing supporting structure, the euro is a currency deprived of any extrinsic value. Following the Theory of the Monetary Circuit it must be deemed a currency of which the exchange rate relative to true currencies is quite 'non-determined' (arbitrary). The prerequisites for a sound currency contradict the very nature of the new monetary union.

1. There should be a unique and genuine European Central Bank enjoying all the functions of true Central Banks. The oligarchy of Central Banks should be replaced by a European Federal Reserve System.
2. In the like of the FRS the new ECB should be connected to a unique European Treasury which would require a true European Budget and therefore a European Federal State (whatever the legal term taking care of domestic rhetorical concerns): Henceforth the prohibition should disappear; there would be again a genuine fiscal policy supporting the currency, endowing it with a determined value by targeting full employment.

Since the start, the sole anchor of the currency has been the strait-jacket imposed on domestic states. Whatever they say to their electorates, governments never stop applying the constraints. This is the sole explanation, shown by Parguez et al. (2003), of the relatively poor performance of the Euroland economy. It is enough to explain the speculative fluctuations of the exchange rate:

- In the first phase the relative by greater fall in profits within Euroland reflected a relatively higher depreciation of assets. It convinced all rational speculators of the fall in the relative value of the currency.
- In the second phase the same rationale led speculators to believe the strait-jacket to be unsustainable. They bet on a reversal of policies and therefore on a change in the structures of Euroland. Now that assets were under-valued, it was time to acquire assets denominated in euro, as sooner or later their value would rise.

It is indeed impossible to know now if those bets are justified. Speculation could turn again if the required reforms are not implemented.

## CONCLUSION: THE LESSONS OF THE EMU

None of the conditions for a convincing experiment is therefore met. The EMU has been the outcome of a very long-run historical process initiated by the planned vision of a European Order. Some 60 years were required to unfold the plan and reach its ultimate phase. Such a plan does not exist in North America; a society obsessed by the short run is not sustained by the same vision of the distant far future. The EMU is rooted in a commitment to a specific economic order enshrined in a specific general theory of economics. This conservative and ultra-classical economics sustained a political vision, an institutional order shifting power far away from the people. The EMU is not a convincing success, the experiment has failed on its own terms and its future is uncertain.

Since the EMU is the only model of the monetary union, a sole lesson can be learned from its existence. There is not the least reason to create a monetary union in North America unless one dreams of engineering the perfect conservative society which is the ultimate purpose of the EMU!

## NOTES

1.  Most were indeed French economists of Austrian training. For their contribution, one could read Perroux and Rueff, the latter being a life-long adversary of Keynes and played a leading role in the generalization of Menger's theory into a general theory of money. He scarred a democracy like all other TCEs.
2.  New studies of Nazi Germany unravel the myth of a unified vision of the economy. In 1942 orthodox economics had still many supporters who feared cumulative inflation in the post-war period, assuming a German victory. Keynesian economics had very few supporters within the international regime establishment.
3.  In the post-war period, German economics was the realm of the 'Social Market School' a twin of the economics of Rueff. It believed that the market has to be protected by an order suppressing any degree of freedom in politics.
4.  The policies of squeeze started very early in phase I of Table 3.1. They had to adjust exchange rates to their equilibrium level fitting the EMS. Contrary to what is told, the Mitterrand regime did not contradict the rule. It is well documented (Parguez, 1998) that the so-called Keynesian profligacy of the early years never existed.

## REFERENCES

Bibow, J. (2001), 'Easy money though the back door: the market v. the ECB,' preliminary draft, prepared for presentation at Annual conference of the Eastern Economic Association, New York, 23–5 February, processed.

EBC Bulletin (2000), February.

Menger, C. (1892), 'On the origin of money,' *Economic Journal*, **2** (6), 230–55.

Parguez, A. (1998), 'The Role of Austerity in France,' in J. Halevi and J.-M. Fontaine (eds), *Restoring Demand in the World Economy*, Cheltenham, UK and Northampton, MA, USA: Edward Elgar.

Parguez, A. (2000), 'For whom tolls the monetary union,' paper prepared for the Conference on Monetary Union, University of Ottawa, Ottawa, 10–11 October, processed.

Parguez, A., M. Seccareccia and C. Gnos (2003), 'The theory and practice of European monetary integration: lessons for North America,' in M. Seccareccia and L.P. Rochon (eds), *Dollarization: Lessons from Europe and the Americas*, London: Routledge.

Smith, M. and P. Stirk (eds) (1990), *Making the new Europe: European unity and the Second World War*, London: Pinter Publishers.

Steiger, G. (2004), 'Which lender of last resort for the euro,' forthcoming in V. Chick (ed.) *The Challenge of Endogenous Money: Theory and Policy*, London: Palgrave.

PART 2

Dollarization in North America?

# 4. Does NAFTA move North America towards a common currency area?

## William C. Gruben and Jahyeong Koo

## INTRODUCTION

Following the inception of the North American Free Trade Agreement on 1 January 1994, the idea of a common currency area that includes the three nations of NAFTA has received much public attention. This should not be surprising. When someone borrows from abroad, devaluation risk may be factored into the borrowing cost when the lenders' country and the borrowers' country do not use the same currency – sometimes even if the loan is denominated in the lender's currency. The United States is a significant source of credit for Mexican firms and for Mexico's central government. Moreover, Powell and Sturzenegger (2003) find evidence that in Latin America, greater currency risk causes greater country or debt risk.

Second, countries that give up their currency are surrendering a measure of monetary policy independence. One benefit is that when countries with problematic inflation histories commence sharing a currency with a country with a good inflation history, the former countries no longer have central banks that created those bad histories. To the extent that the national central bank with a good record in inflation control influences the new currency arrangements of the problem history countries, market anticipations of inflation will ebb. The new expectations affect credit costs, credit availability and, in particular, the availability of longer term credit.[1]

Third, sharing a currency lowers the transaction costs of international commerce in goods and services between the sharing countries. When countries trade a great deal with each other, sharing a currency can increase the efficiency gains due to trade.[2]

Fourth, as Mundell (1973) argues, a national currency is not a reserve for the nation overall, except to the extent that it can be marketed abroad. This argument is seen as applicable even though the same currency is a reserve for an individual within the nation. That is, 'what is a hard asset for the individual may not be a hard asset for a single country' (Mundell, 1973: 114). To the extent that a local currency is backed by an internationally acceptable medium of exchange, the reserve for contingencies is greater. The extreme occurs when a country uses a foreign currency as its circulating medium and the currency is an internationally acceptable medium of exchange.

## CURRENCY AREA OPTIMALITY: WHY ANALYSTS ARE CONCERNED ABOUT IT

Although political considerations sometimes dominate other concerns when countries decide whether or not to establish common currency areas, international economic interrelationships can play an important role in determining the viability of a currency area. This chapter focuses on the international economic relations that make a currency area consistent or not with the monetary policy that a prospective area's members would likely think is in each of their individual interests.

Using standard approaches to gauging how consistent one North American country's optimum monetary policy might be with that of the other two, we attempt to measure changes in the degree of currency union optimality during periods before and after NAFTA. Dollarization is one approach to the development of a common currency area, and our results could be functional in considering the policy validity of dollarization. In this chapter, however, our focus will be broader, addressing factors associated with changes in the optimality or at least viability of a North American currency area in general.

A set of countries fulfills the standard conditions for currency area optimality if fixing the exchange rate between each pair of countries does not impose any real costs on either of the countries. If factors are completely mobile, or if prices or wages are perfectly flexible, this condition is met. In this context, when investigating currency area optimality, the chief interest has been how closely correlated are the candidate countries' business cycles. When business cycles are perfectly synchronized among a group of countries, an identical monetary policy may also be optimal for all of them.

Conversely, if a slowing and deflating economy merits looser monetary policy than an economy with accelerating inflation, binding capacity constraints and above-trend growth, then those two countries are unlikely to agree on monetary policy. The two countries almost certainly do not form an optimal currency area.

Historically, the principal concerns of economists curious about the viability of a currency area have been more complicated than the simple similar business cycle story we have been telling so far, but not very much more. These concerns about countries considering (or at least being considered by some for) monetary union include the following (Frankel and Rose, 1998): (1) the extent of trade between the countries in question; (2) the similarity of their shocks and cycles;

(3) the degree of labor mobility between them; and (4) the system of risk sharing, typically through fiscal transfers.

## WHY NAFTA MAKES THE IDEA OF CURRENCY SHARING MORE INTERESTING TO SOME PEOPLE

From this list it may be easily seen not only why the extent of trade and the viability of a currency area could be closely related but why the onset of the North American Free Trade Agreement might have triggered interest in a currency area for North America. Some expected results of currency sharing for some countries – including lower interest rates, greater credit availability and lower inflation – are always attractive but we would not expect that NAFTA would make them any more attractive per se. However, an increase in trade between two countries means an increase in the cost savings that would derive from sharing a currency. The shared currency-related savings that would increase with trade include savings in transaction costs and reductions in risks associated with holding different currencies – such as devaluation risk.

However, other costs resulting from the formation of a currency union in the wake of NAFTA could more than offset the benefits of these savings. Offsetting difficulties could arise if post-NAFTA trading relations turned out to be so specialized that the business cycles in the three participating countries were not synchronous. The less business cycle synchronicity, the more inappropriate a common currency area's monetary policy will be for some members and accordingly the more stress on the currency union itself. Frankel and Rose (1998) argue that, given sufficiently large supply shocks, specialization reduces international income correlation and therefore currency area optimality. Eichengreen (1992), Kenen (1969) and Krugman (1993) all suggest that increases in trade lead to greater country-by-country specialization. If NAFTA has been the result of increased trade between North American countries – and certainly this allegation is still under debate – it is possible that the agreement itself could have resulted in less business cycle synchronization.[3]

This issue might be construed as having particular resonance in the context of NAFTA. NAFTA is seen by some as a classic case of 'the establishment of free trade between a number of countries with the aim of securing the benefits of international specialization' (Pass, Lowes and Davies, 2000, p. 537). Frankel and Rose (1998) note that if most trade between two countries is inter-industry, increases in trade are tantamount to increases in specialization. In contrast if intra-industry trade dominates commerce between two countries, then the synchronicity of their business cycles increases when their trade grows.

In fact, intra-industry trade may be particularly important for NAFTA countries. Gonzalez and Velez (1993) show that – for US–Mexico trade in 1990, prior to NAFTA – intra-industry trade occupied a much more significant share of total trade than it did in bilateral trade between France, Italy and Germany in 1959 (prior to the formation of the European Union). Moreover, Gonzalez and Velez (1995) show that as of 1991, intra-industry trade as a share of total US–Mexico bilateral trade exceeded the intra-industry share of bilateral trade between the United States and Argentina, Brazil, Chile, Colombia, Paraguay, Uruguay or Venezuela.

## ENDOGENOUS CURRENCY AREA OPTIMALITY

Despite our erstwhile allegations of the relevance of our approach to considering the validity of a common currency area for North America, and the very traditional character of our considerations, the narrative of this chapter is in some ways out of the mainstream of the current optimal currency area literature. Indeed, some of this current mainstream literature may be seen as trivializing our examination approach and goals.

Specifically, some of the most significant papers on the subject hold that currency area optimality is endogenous in any case. From this literature, it could be concluded that under some circumstances nations contemplating sharing a currency need not fret over business cycle synchronicity. The reason is, if two countries increase their trade through trade liberalization, it may be that business cycle synchronicity will begin to occur soon enough in any case.

Despite the caveats mentioned above in Frankel and Rose (1998), for example, the thrust of their work is that currency area optimality is endogenous – that we can affect optimality by policy. In particular, we may often expect increased trade to result in business cycle synchronicity. In such a case, perhaps the greatest contribution to increasing the viability of a currency union is to establish a free trade agreement first.

Completing the circle of trade, common currencies, and business cycle synchronicity, Rose (2000) offers evidence to suggest that trade liberalization itself may need not be a significant prerequisite to the establishment of currency area optimality, inasmuch as the simple establishment of a common currency area can triple trade between two countries, other things being equal. If increased trade creates business cycle synchronicity and if a common currency area triples trade between two countries, it is possible that all that is necessary to establish the business cycle synchronicity that has concerned optimal currency area scholars of past generations is to set up a common currency area in the first place. Why, then, even inquire into business cycle synchronicity questions for North America?[4]

Despite the compelling results of Frankel and Rose (1998), there is much evidence that this circle can be broken. There has been plenty of recent evidence to suggest that at least hard currency pegs – to say nothing of what had been presented as closely managed bands – need not always engender sufficient trade to create currency area optimality. The case of Argentina's currency board, for example, in which both the Argentine peso and the US dollar were legal tender for all payments except wages and taxes, never resulted in substantive business cycle synchronicity between Argentina and the United States, even though the program existed for a decade. The same could be said for Brazilian and US business-cycle synchronization under Brazil's less restrictive Real Plan (1994–9).

Moreover, despite the enormous historic importance to Mexico of its trade with the United States, and despite the enormous historic importance to the United States of its trade with Mexico, most of recent history had suggested that their business cycles have not been at all synchronous. Our presentation is not the only recent effort to address questions about currency area optimality in the three NAFTA countries, and certainly other work in the field has suggested little basis at all for currency optimality in North America. Michelis and Paraskevopoulos (1999), for example, use cointegration analysis to examine synchronicity between the United States, Canada and Mexico. They find that a currency area is feasible between the United States and Canada, but not for the other trading partners.[5]

Similarly, publishing two months after the inception of NAFTA, Bayoumi and Eichengreen (1994) find a negative correlation of supply shocks to Mexico with those of the industrial regions of the United States. Accordingly they argue that the costs of a North American monetary union – in which Mexico would be unable to make exchange rate adjustments to accommodate these shock asymmetries – are too high to permit a North American currency union. Even though NAFTA will result in increased trade between Mexico and the United States, and even though Bayoumi and Eichengreen (1994) are clear in pointing out that increased trade results in greater cyclical synchronicity, they argue that these trade increases are not likely to overcome these shocks asymmetries 'even in the very long run ...' (p. 126).

## NAFTA AND CURRENCY AREA OPTIMALITY?

The problem with most approaches to measuring currency area optimality, including the cointegration approach used by Michelis and Paraskevopolous, is that they require a very large number of observations. The relatively short time even now since the inception of NAFTA in 1994 means that not many post-NAFTA observations are available. However, the work of Frankel and Rose (1998) suggests the possibility that NAFTA – an event whose inception did not occur very many annual observations ago – might have brought its members closer to currency area optimality.

Certainly there is no reason to be certain that NAFTA could cause such a change. Bayoumi and Eichengreen (1994) did not perceive a future likely to offset what their pre-NAFTA findings suggested. Moreover, the United States and Mexico have long been important trading partners and Michelis and Paraskevopolous (1999) did not see currency area optimality between them. Indeed, that finding was one of the reasons why Michelis and Paraskevopolous argued that there is not yet a synchronistic basis for a North American Monetary Union.

However while Michelis and Paraskevopolous (1999) did not find a longer run basis for a common currency area between Mexico and the United States, and Bayoumi and Eichengreen (1994) did not expect one either, increases in trade between the Mexico and the United States were easily the largest increases in bilateral trade amongst NAFTA countries. Indeed from the 1994 inception of NAFTA until Mexico and the United States fell into recession in 2000–2001, Mexican–US trade increased at an average of 20 per cent per year. Since NAFTA, Mexico has surpassed Japan as the United States' second largest trading partner.

In sum, longer-run models suggest that US–Mexico economic fluctuations are inconsistent with currency area optimality but these longer-run models cannot conveniently separate events as recent as those since NAFTA from those before. They cannot easily identify the presence of some break point that may have caused the business cycle to become more synchronous, whether due to NAFTA, GATT or some other phenomenon.

Even to offer anecdotal statistics as to changes in business cycle synchronicity, it would be useful to have a longer time period than is in fact available since North American business cycles were clearly inconsistent with each other. In order to ask if statistical anecdotes might offer evidence that might be consistent with Frankel and Rose's (1998) work for other countries, rather than with Michelis and Paraskevopolous's (1999) longer-run model for the NAFTA countries, or with the experience of Argentina over the ten-year run of its Convertibility Plan, we resolved to create three measures of business cycles for each of the three NAFTA countries and examine whether or not there seemed to be an increase in correlation of these business cycles in the wake of NAFTA. Here, of course, we define an increase in correlation of business cycles as an increase in business cycle synchronicity.

In terms of a general approach to defining a business cycle, we follow Lucas (1977) and the majority of the macroeconomic literature and define the business cycle in terms of fluctuations around a trend.[6] The particular fluctuation around trend that we have in mind is fluctuation of each country's gross domestic product around its real gross domestic product trend. Having defined a business cycle in terms of gross domestic product fluctuations around some definition of a trend gross domestic product, we then had to determine what a trend was. Although every version of a business cycle that we use is a deviation from some measure or other of a long-term economic trend, each of our gross domestic product business cycles represents a deviation from a different definition of a gross domestic product trend. To facilitate measurement of trend for a protracted period of economic history we use annual data, since the Mexican measure of gross domestic product more often than annually is a relatively new event.

Moving from the least to the most complicated or refined, the three bases we use for constructing a cycle are:[7] (1) a random walk; (2) a quadratic trend; and (3) a Hodrick and Prescott filter.[8]

Having constructed cycles as deviations from these trends, we then determined periods over which we would measure correlations among pairs of NAFTA countries. Since our post-NAFTA data were only for the nine-year period 1994–2002, we resolved to estimate nine-year correlation periods to estimate business cycle synchronicity and to characterize changes in this synchronicity. To characterize changes in business cycle synchronicity visually we present four nine-year periods, 1967–75, 1976–84, 1985–93, and 1994–2002. Business cycle correlations (again, here, correlations of deviations from trend for each pair of NAFTA countries) are presented in Figure 4.1 (Mexican–US business cycle correlations by each of the three definitions of a cycle), Figure 4.2 (Canadian–US business cycle correlations by each of the three definitions of a cycle) and Figure 4.3 (Canadian–Mexican business cycle correlations by each of the three definitions of a cycle).

Figure 4.1 depicts Mexican–US business cycle correlations for the post-NAFTA period 1994–2002 and for three pre-NAFTA nine-year periods. It is easy to see why a longer run model, such as that of Michelis and Paraskevo-

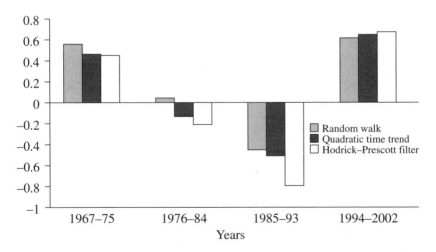

*Figure 4.1    Correlation of Mexican and US business cycles before and after NAFTA*

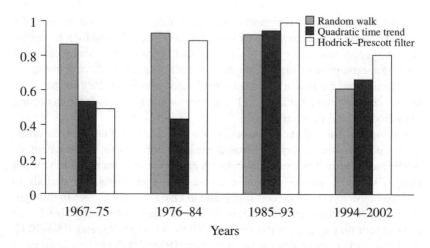

*Figure 4.2    Correlation of Canadian and US business cycles before and after NAFTA*

polous (1999) would not offer evidence of synchronicity between Mexican and US business activity. Indeed, for the three nine-year pre-NAFTA periods – that is, 1967–75, 1976–84, and 1985–93 – five out of the nine (three for each of the three nine-year pre-NAFTA periods) business cycle measures show negative correlations. Of the remaining four correlations, only one (random walk for 1967–75) is greater than 0.50.

The NAFTA nine-year results, however, are markedly different, with correlations of +0.61 +0.64 and +0.66 respectively. Obviously, none of these three measures of correlation comes close to reaching the perfect degree of 1.000. However, the transformation of business cycle correlations from persistently negatively correlated (in case of the 1985–93 period) or from weakly correlated in either direction (1976–84) or from weakly or moderately positive (1967–75) to the 1994–2002 correlations suggests that up to now, post-NAFTA business cycle relations may be different.

Moreover, a significant portion of the trade increase may be attributed to other less permanent factors than NAFTA, particularly the Mexican devaluation of December 1994. If devaluation led to lower wage costs in dollar terms in Mexico, and a resulting shift in US trade-related economic activity to Mexico from regions that did not devalue, a shift in the other direction could occur whenever Mexican wages ultimately adjusted back to where they had been in real dollar terms. To complicate this analysis, however, note that Mexico also had megadevaluations in 1976, 1982 and 1986. These devaluations did not result in trade increases sufficient to result in the high business cycle synchronicity between the two countries that materialized post-NAFTA.

For the post-NAFTA period, what these results suggest is (1) owing to trade growth that may or may not be due to NAFTA, an increase may have taken place in some measures of currency area optimality between Mexico and the United States and (2) more sophisticated but degrees-of-freedom-hungry modeling procedures would have been less likely to pick up the transition.[9]

Figure 4.2 presents business cycle correlations like those in Figure 4.1, but for Canadian–US business cycle correlations. Unlike Mexican–US business cycle correlations, which only became large in the wake of NAFTA, Canadian–US synchronicity is virtually always high in these charts.[10] We would in any case not expect NAFTA to result in a sudden change between Canadian and US business cycle synchronicity. NAFTA did not result in the sorts of large increases in trade that occurred post-NAFTA between the United States and Mexico. The United States and Canada had already entered into a free trade agreement five years before the inception of NAFTA. Also, rather than moving from our third largest trading partner to our second largest trading partner, as Mexico did post-NAFTA, Canada remained our largest trading partner during the entire period and well before.

Currency area optimality between Canada and the United States has long been argued. The originator of optimal currency area theory, Robert Mundell (1961), posited that there was a sense in which Eastern Canada and the Eastern United States comprised one logical currency area and that Western Canada and the Western United States comprised another. Commenting on this argument, Bayoumi and Eichengreen (1994) note that 'since there was no prospect of the United States splitting into several district currency zones, the implication was that the two countries might as well be combined into a single currency area' (p. 126). Recall also that Michelis and Paraskevopolous's (1999) results found in favor of currency area optimality for Canada and the United States even though they did not find for currency area optimality between either country and Mexico.

Figure 4.3, Canadian–Mexican business cycle correlation, offers less consistently significantly positive post-NAFTA synchronicity estimates than either Mexico–US or Canada–US, but the highest correlation coefficient of the entire post-NAFTA series is that of the quadratic time trend for Canada, Mexico. Thus, while the Mexican–US post-NAFTA correlations were +0.61 +0.64 and +0.66 for the random walk, quadratic time trend and Hodrick–Prescott filter respectively, the Canadian–Mexican post-NAFTA correlations were 0.12, 0.87 and 0.39 respectively. Even so, taking together the three categories of estimates post-NAFTA clearly suggests that there has been an at least transitory turnaround in the negative business cycle correlations for the nine-year period 1985–93.

In a sense the relatively weak performance of Canadian–Mexican synchronicity (aside from the quadratic function outlier) may not be surprising considering

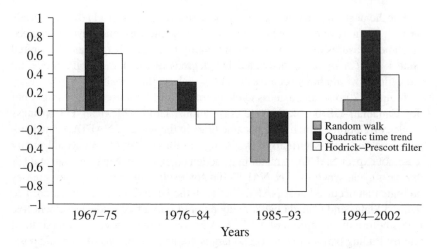

*Figure 4.3    Correlation of Canadian and Mexican business cycles before and after NAFTA*

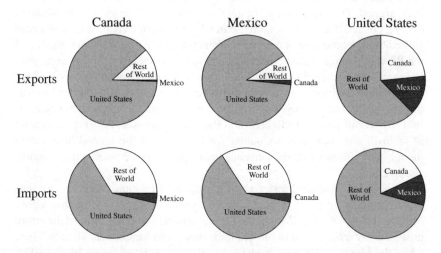

*Figure 4.4    Exports and Imports*

the low level of trade that has traditionally characterized these two countries and that continues to characterize them post-NAFTA.

Figure 4.4 depicts the share of each NAFTA country's total trade that is represented by each other NAFTA country. Export shares appear on the first row, while import shares appear on the second row. Note that 1 per cent of Canada's exports go to Mexico while 88 per cent of Canada's exports go to the United

States. Similarly 2 per cent of Mexico's exports go to Canada, while 89 per cent of Mexico's exports go to the United States. Moreover, this signifies that Mexico's exports to the United States constitute 22 per cent of Mexican GDP while Mexican exports to Canada represent 0.4 per cent of Mexican GDP. The import side of the each nation's trade statistics also shows that Canadian–Mexican trade remains very small. Indeed, such correlation as has lately appeared between Canada's and Mexico's business cycles may be suspected to result from the importance of the United States as a trading partner to each. That is, to the extent that Canada and Mexico's business cycles are any more synchronous than before, they may be so largely because Mexico's business cycle is more synchronous with the US business cycle, while Canada's business cycle has long been synchronous with the US business cycle.

With respect to opportunities for transmission of business cycles through trade, it should also be noted that while 89 per cent of Mexican exports go to the United States, only 14 per cent of US exports go to Mexico. The share of US GDP represented by US exports to Mexico moreover is 0.9 per cent compared, as noted above, with Mexican exports to the United States representing 22 per cent of Mexican GDP. The United States does not trade very much as a share of GDP in any case, much less than Canada or Mexico.

## CONCLUSION

While a nine-year period is still not enough to separate with conclusiveness the transitory from the permanent changes in business cycle correlations that may have occurred in the wake of NAFTA, it is clear that some change in business cycle synchronicity has occurred between Mexico and the United States. A similar, but less pronounced, change might have occurred in between Canada and Mexico at least in comparison with the two previous nine-year periods. It would be hard altogether to determine why this latter change has occurred, but certainly the annual increases in trade of roughly 20 per cent between Mexico and the United States during the late 1990s must be an important part not only of the explanation for Mexico–US synchronicity but, for reasons, discussed above, for increases in Canada–Mexico synchronicity.

What is striking about these results is how strongly they contradict the conclusions of Bayoumi and Eichengreen (1994), which do not directly account for actual post-NAFTA trade increases, as well as the conclusions of Michelis and Paraskevopolous (1999), who do account for NAFTA but only as a small part of a much larger total sample that swamps NAFTA. Our results are only anecdotal statistics, in a sense. However, we hope we have offered enough alternative choices for cyclical definition and determination to suggest that, at least for now, a positive move towards currency-sharing opportunities has occurred.

# NOTES

1. For a further development of these notions see the Joint Economic Committee (2000) and for a more skeptical view see Sims (1999). The degree of surrender can vary considerably, depending on the nature of the currency area agreement. Under the European system, every country participating in the euro system has a representative on the European Central Bank, so that no nation that participates can be said to surrender independence utterly. In the case of countries that share a currency in the absence of European-style policy-sharing agreements – as in Panama's and Ecuador's use of the US dollar – surrender of monetary independence is of course complete. An important detail here is that, while Mexico endured significantly higher inflation rates than the United States for protracted periods during the last 50 years, Mexico's current inflation-targeting regime has brought price increase to extremely low rates and has resulted in low interest rates as well although not as low interest rates as in the United States. As of this writing Mexico has lately experienced fairly high rates of monetary aggregate growth along with the persistently low inflation. Mexicans have increased their demand for Mexican money as they become more confident in it as a store of value. Nevertheless, Mexico's interest rates on long-term (20–year) bonds are several hundred basis paints higher (that is, several percentage points higher) than interest rates in the United States on a 30–year mortgage.

2. One would not want to make too much of this as a principal reason for North American currency sharing. Emerson et al. (1992) estimate that the adoption of the European Monetary Unit would mount to total transactions cost savings about 0.3 to 0.4 per cent of GDP per annum for members.

3. Garcés Diaz (2001), for example, presents a computable general equilibrium model to suggest that while trade between the United States and Mexico has increased enormously, the expansion is the result of Mexico's entry into the GATT.

4. One reason not discussed in the body of the paper involves Walsh's (2000) questions about the validity of Rose's findings. Walsh complains that in a very large number of cases, entities that Rose claims are separate countries sharing a common currency are actually parts of the same country, causing Rose to attribute trade affects to common currencies that might actually result from common political systems or, at the least, intimate political alliances. Examples that Walsh offers include the Falkland Islands, the Isle of Man and the Channel Islands (all closely linked politically to the United Kingdom), Niue, the Cook Islands, Pitcairn Island and Tokelau (linked to New Zealand) and Puerto Rico and Guam. These last two of course are protectorates of the United States or, as in a song in the musical *West Side Story*, 'Nobody knows in America Puerto Rico's in America.' The other problem Walsh points out is that, because Rose measures trade in dollar values, exchange rate movements can play strong and misleading roles in his results. Since Rose makes much of his results on Ireland, it is particularly interesting to see Walsh's discussion of the misleading aspects of the Irish case in this context.

5. It should be noted that the cointegration tests of economic fluctuations in two countries may not tell us as much as we would want to know about their business cycles. Cointegration is properly applied to test for the presence of a common trend whereas a business cycle represents not the trend, but the deviation from it.

6. Even though this definition is more commonly used than any other in modern macroeconomics, the widely attended National Bureau of Economic Research definition of a business cycle differs markedly. The latter definition, which follows the work of Arthur Burns and Wesley Clair Mitchell (1946) involves absolute declines in economic activity rather than the deviations-from-trend approach we use.

7. Note that we do not use the BP or band-pass filter popularized by Baxter and King (1995) and have chosen to apply trend estimation procedures that are less highly regarded in the literature. We have not used the band-pass filter because it does not allow the use of the last three or first three observations to define the trend and, accordingly, to define a business cycle. One of our principal concerns in this measurement process is examining whether or not the post-NAFTA correlation between business cycles is measurably greater than the pre-NAFTA correlation.

That is, we want to know if NAFTA has brought the North American countries closer to currency area optimality. Using the band-pass filter effectively means sacrificing three of the nine annual observations available from the post NAFTA period. Although the band pass filter may offer a superior measure of trends, we felt the sacrifice of observations was too great and hoped that the observations from three full-period business cycle measures would dominate one half-post-NAFTA business cycle measured with the band-pass.

8. Disadvantages of the HP filter include unusual behavior of the isolated cyclical components near the end of the sample period and the problematic requirement of choosing the smoothing parameter, $\lambda$. The Hodrick-Prescott filter defines the cyclical component $y_t^c$ of a time series $y_t$ as $y_t^c = ((\lambda(1 - L)^2(1 - L^{-1})^2)/(1 + \lambda(1 - L)^2(1 - L^{-1})^2))y_t$ where L represents the lag operator.

9. It could be argued that the change in Mexico–US business cycle correlations during the post-NAFTA period might not be associated with trade increases or NAFTA, but might be a peculiar political business cycle artifact of the coincidence of US and Mexican presidential elections in 2000. Such a coincidence, after all, only occurs every 12 years. It should be noted however that the last pre-NAFTA nine-year period (see Figure 4.1) leading up to such a coincidence was 1976–84 and obviously strongly positive correlation between business cycles did not occur then. Moreover, breaking up business cycle examination periods by other durations gets the same post-NAFTA anomalies as the nine-year breakdowns. To contrast with the four nine-year periods presented in Chart I, note below, the US–Mexico business cycle correlations (annual GDP by each of the three definitions we use) for five five-year periods.

|  | 1975–9 | 1980–84 | 1985–9 | 1990–94 | 1995–9 |
|---|---|---|---|---|---|
| Random Walk | 0.007 | –0.077 | 0.144 | –0.133 | 0.916 |
| Quadratic | 0.685 | –0.706 | –0.742 | –0.368 | 0.927 |
| Hodrick-Prescott | 0.255 | 0.224 | –0.462 | –0.678 | 0.934 |

10. Note that the lowest correlation on Figure 4.2 is the random walk correlation post NAFTA, a value of 0.484. The other two estimates for the post NAFTA period are 0.993 (quadratic time trend) and 0.926 (Hodrick–Prescott filter).

# REFERENCES

Baxter, Marianne and Robert G. King (1995), 'Measuring business cycles: approximate band pass filters for economic time series,' NBER working paper no. 5022.

Bayoumi, Tamim and Barry Eichengreen (1994), 'Monetary and exchange rate arrangements for the North American Free Trade Area,' *Journal of Development Economics*, **43**, (March) pp. 125–65.

Burns, Arthur and Wesley C. Mitchell (1946), *Measuring Business Cycles*, New York: National Bureau of Economic Research.

Eichengreen, Barry (1992), 'Should the Maastricht Treaty be Saved?', Princeton Studies in International Finance, no. 74, International Finance Section, Princeton University, December.

Emerson, Michael, Daniel Gros, Alexander Italianer, Jean Pisani-Ferry and Horst Reichenbach (1992), *One Market, One Money: An Evaluation of the Potential Benefits and Costs of Forming an Economic and Monetary Union*, New York: Oxford University Press.

Gonzalez, Jorge and Alejandro Velez (1993), 'An empirical estimation of the level of intra-industry trade between Mexico and the United States,' in K. Fatemi (ed.), *North*

*American Free Trade Agreement: Opportunities and Challenges*, London: MacMillan Press.

Gonzalez, Jorge and Alejandro Velez (1995) 'Intra-industry trade between the United States and the major Latin American countries: measurement and implications for free trade in the Americas,' *International Trade Journal*, **9** (4), (Winter).

Frankel, Jeffrey A. and Andrew K. Rose (1998), 'The endogeneity of the optimal currency area criteria,' *Economic Journal*, **108** (July), 1009–25.

Garcés-Diaz, Daniel (2001), 'Was NAFTA behind the Mexican export boom: 1994–2000?,' Banco de México, February.

Hodrick, Robert J. and Edward C. Prescott (1997), 'Postwar US business cycles: an empirical investigation,' *Journal of Money, Credit and Banking*, **29** (1), (February) 1–16.

Joint Economic Committee (2000), 'Basics of dollarization,' United States Senate Joint Economic Committee.

Kenen, Peter (1969) 'The theory of optimum currency areas: an eclectic view,' in R. Mundell and A. Swoboda (eds), *Monetary Problems in the International Economy*, Chicago: University of Chicago Press.

Krugman, Paul (1993), 'Lessons of Massachusetts for EMU,' in G. Giavazzi and F. Torres (eds), *The Transition to Economic and Monetary Union in Europe*, New York: Cambridge University Press, 241–61.

Lucas, Robert (1977), 'Understanding business cycles,' Carnegie-Rochester Conference on Public Policy.

Michelis, Leo and Chris Paraskevopoulos (1999), 'Prospects of a monetary union in North America,' Ryerson Polytechnic University and York University, Toronto, paper presented at the January 1999 meetings of the Allied Social Sciences Association.

Mundell, Robert (1961), 'A theory of optimum currency areas,' *American Economic Review*, **51**, 657–65.

Mundell, Robert (1973), 'Uncommon arguments for common currencies,' in Harry G. Johnson and Alexander K. Swoboda, (eds), *The Economics of Common Currencies: Proceedings of the Madrid Conference on Optimum Currency Areas*, New York: Allen and Unwin, 114–32.

Pass, C., B. Lowes and L. Davies (2000), *Collins Dictionary of Economics*, 3rd edn, New York: HarperCollins.

Powell, Andrew and Federico Sturzenegger (2003), 'Dollarization: the link between devaluation and default risk,' in Eduardo Levy-Yeyati and Federico Sturzenegger (eds) *Dollarization: Debates and Policy Alternatives*, Cambridge, MA: MIT Press, 201–36.

Rose, Andrew K. (2000), 'One money, one market: estimating the effect of common currencies on trade,' NBER Working Paper No. 7432.

Sims, Christopher A. (1999), 'Fiscal consequences for Mexico of adopting the dollar,' Princeton University, paper presented at the December 1999 Instituto Tecnologico Autonomo de Mexico conference on Optimal Monetary Institutions for Mexico.

Walsh, Brendan (2000), 'Currency unions and trade: a skeptical note,' Department of Economics, National University of Ireland, University College, Dublin 4.

# 5. Dollarization and illegal immigration: implications for NAFTA

**Susan Pozo**

## INTRODUCTION

When economists were asked to predict the impact of NAFTA on illegal immigration from Mexico to the USA, there were two opposing responses. Some argued that illegal immigration would increase, while others argued instead that illegal immigration would decrease.[1] The former argued that restructuring the Mexican economy in response to trade liberalization would raise the Mexican unemployment rate and increase US/Mexican wage differentials. The incentive to migrate would thereby increase. In addition closer economic ties forged by the treaty would increase trade between Mexico and the USA. The increased flow of goods across the border would make for more camouflage opportunities for undocumented immigrants. The probability of detection would be lowered increasing the success of illegal border crossings and hence raising the total level of illegal immigration.

Others argued, to the contrary, that illegal immigration would be decreased. A standard trade model (say the Heckscher–Ohlin model) would argue that given the relative abundance of capital in the USA and the relative abundance of labor in Mexico, specialization along the lines of comparative advantage would cause Mexican wages to rise, while US wages would fall. The incentive for Mexican workers to migrate to the USA would thereby fall, reducing the level of illegal immigration. In effect, trade would substitute for migration.

Still others argued that NAFTA was unlikely to have any effect on illegal immigration. Markusen and Zahniser (1997), for example, present several trade models that suggest that NAFTA does not effect the relative wages of US or Mexican unskilled labor, thereby eliminating the main channel by which trade integration affects migration.

In this chapter I would like to reconsider the impact of increased economic integration on illegal immigration, but from a different angle. Specifically, I would like to ask, what impact might monetary integration have on the illegal flow of workers across the border? Given current discussions about monetary integration, what impact would its adoption have on the politically sensitive issue of illegal immigration? My intention is not to pass judgement on illegal immigration or dollarization. My objective is simply to measure how economic policy, in the form of dollarization, may influence the flow of persons across the border.

At this juncture, let me note that my discussion and subsequent empirical analysis relates only to the specific case of US/Mexican migratory flows. This 'case study' may provide some insights into the effect of monetary integration on migratory flows between countries at disparate levels of development.


## MEASURING ILLEGAL IMMIGRATION

How much illegal immigration does the United States experience?[2] Before answering the question, one needs to distinguish between the stock of illegal immigrants and the flow of illegal immigrants. A common measure of illegal immigration is obtained by comparing the number of immigrants counted in the decennial census with the reported number of legal immigrants. But this number is inaccurate for a variety of reasons. We err when counting the 'known' quantity of legal immigrants because we lack information on deaths of immigrants and on return migration. We also err in the accounting of immigrants in the decennial census because there is likely an undercount of immigrants (both illegal and legal). In addition, the relative undercount of legal and illegal immigrants probably differs.

But even if we could obtain an accurate count of the stock of illegal immigrants, the decennial census only provides us with information at 10-year intervals – a time frequency too low to uncover the effects of dollarization on illegal international labor flows.

In practice estimates of the flow of illegal immigration into the United States are usually based on the Immigration and Naturalization Service's (INS) (1998) series of apprehensions of illegal immigrants. Such a series may serve as a proxy for the changing flow of illegal immigration. We might reason that the greater the number of apprehensions, the greater the number of individuals successfully crossing the border and hence the greater the level of illegal immigration. Several problems remain with such a series, however, which at best represents only the 'tip of the iceberg'. First, for each individual apprehended many more illegal immigrants may be undetected and we do not know whether the relative proportions are constant. Second, there are a considerable number of 'commuters' who frequently cross the border. Should these individual be apprehended several times in one year, do we treat the multiple apprehensions as several potential illegal immigrants, or as one? The third problem that exists is with respect to the narrowness of the question at hand – what would be the impact of *Mexican* dollarization on illegal immigration of *Mexican* nationals into the USA? Not all

INS apprehensions are of Mexican nationals. Nonetheless, these data are probably the best available on the flow of undocumented persons of Mexican origin into the USA. The INS reports that in 1998, 1.6 million out of a total of 1.62 million deportable aliens – that is 96 per cent – were Mexican nationals.

Using apprehension data to get a handle on Mexican illegal immigration into the USA has been undertaken by Hanson and Spilimbergo (1999). We follow their methodology and note that apprehensions of undocumented immigrants at time $t$ ($APP_t$) can be expressed as follows:

$$APP_t = P(HOURS_t, M_t) * M(X_t). \qquad (5.1)$$

with P representing the probability of getting caught crossing the border. This probability is a function of the level of resources the INS devotes to border patrol (HOURS) and the number of undocumented persons (M) attempting the crossing. The number of undocumented persons who attempt to cross, in turn, depends on a vector of economic variables that affects migration ($X_t$). By substituting $M(X_t)$ into $P(HOURS_t, M_t)$, we obtain a reduced form equation as follows:

$$APP_t = M (HOURS_t, X_t). \qquad (5.2)$$

Later we discuss the specific vector of variables $X_t$ that belong in the equation we ultimately estimate.

## MEASURING DOLLARIZATION

I am not the first to ask the question of the impact of dollarization on illegal immigration. Borjas and Fisher (2001) present a model for Mexican/US illegal immigration and empirically test it. They assume that illegal immigration takes place to take advantage of wage differentials and they concentrate on the impact that different exchange-rate regimes would have on the responsiveness of illegal immigrants to changes in real Mexican and US wages. They compare the elasticity of illegal immigration to wages movements during periods when Mexico has had in place a system of fixed nominal exchange rates, with periods when Mexico has allowed the nominal exchange rate to be market-determined. They associate a fixed nominal exchange regime with dollarization and arrive at two conclusions. One conclusion is that shocks to the labor market would be greater under dollarization. Their second finding is that the elasticity of migration to changes in the wage differential would rise with dollarization. That is, the level of illegal immigration would be more responsive to wage differentials. This result in conjunction with the greater magnitude of shocks that would take place under dollarization has them conclude that illegal immigration would be more volatile under dollarization.

I use a different approach to get at the issue of dollarization and illegal immigration. I reason that dollarization implies more than fixing the nominal exchange rate. It means accepting a common monetary policy, which would imply that Mexico's *real* exchange rate (rather than nominal exchange rate) would be stabilized. Of course, dollarization means that the nominal exchange rate is fixed, but more importantly it implies that Mexican prices relative to US prices will remain stable. Hence, I propose an alternative methodology to that of comparing fixed nominal exchange regimes with flexible nominal exchange regimes in order to uncover what might be the impact of dollarization on illegal immigration. I propose to assess the impact of dollarization on illegal immigration by assessing the effects of variations in the smoothness of the real exchange rate on immigration.

To back my point that it may be misguided to focus on nominal exchange rate regimes, refer to Figure 5.1.

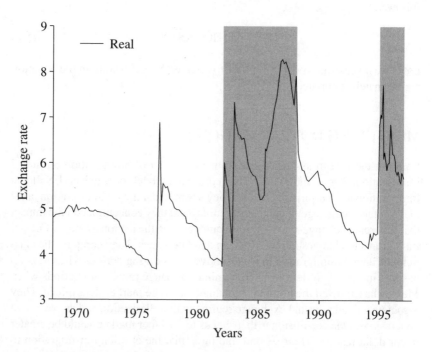

*Note*:   Shaded areas correspond to flexible exchange regime periods

*Figure 5.1    Real peso/dollar exchange rate*

The monthly real peso/dollar exchange rate is plotted from 1968 to 1996. According to Borjas and Fisher (2001) the periods February 1982 to March 1988 and January 1995 to December 1996 correspond to flexible exchange regimes periods. In Figure 5.1 I have shaded the two flexible nominal exchange regime periods 1982:02 to 1988:03 and 1995:01 to 1996:12. Examination of this plot reveals that fixed nominal exchange regime periods do not result in stable real exchange rates. Fixed nominal exchange regime periods do not exempt countries from real exchange-rate volatility. We see dramatic movements in the real exchange rate series both during flexible and during the fixed exchange regime periods.

I argue that we can expect dollarization to result in more stable real exchange rates. To back this point I resort to the empirical findings of Abdel-Kader and Balan (2001). Using a panel of 33 European and Latin American countries, they find that dollarization reduces the volatility of the real exchange rate. They use monthly data from 1995 through 1999 and measure dollarization and variations in dollarization using the so-called 'dollarization ratio' – the ratio of foreign currency deposits to M2. The volatility of the real exchange rate is regressed on the dollarization rate. Using a random effects estimator, they find that countries that experience greater levels of dollarization (as measured by the dollarization ratio) experience lower volatility in the real exchange rate. This is true whether or not the panel includes as control variables the volatility of the inflation differential (to account for other variables or noise that might explain real exchange rate variability). I take this as empirical support for my intuition that full dollarization will stabilize the real exchange rate.[3]

Hence in this chapter we attempt to answer the question, what impact will dollarization have on illegal immigration, by uncovering the effect of the smoothness of the real exchange rate on illegal immigration. We estimate an equation with our proxy of illegal immigration as the dependent variable and volatility of the real exchange rate as an explanatory variable. But to obtain unbiased estimates of the effect of exchange-rate volatility on immigration, we need to determine what other factors may explain illegal immigration into the USA. That is, we need a complete specification for the determination of illegal immigration.

## DETERMINANTS OF ILLEGAL IMMIGRATION INTO THE USA

To get a handle on the level of illegal immigration from Mexico to the USA most would include as explanatory variables the Mexican real wage and the US real wage. These variables are included in the model of illegal immigration proposed by Hanson and Spilimbergo (1999) and by Borjas and Fisher (2001).

Increases in the Mexican real wage should deter illegal immigration into the USA, while increases in the US real wage should increase the incentive of Mexican workers to migrate to the USA. In general, the data confirm these effects on the level of illegal immigration into the USA.

In this chapter we use a monthly index of average nominal hourly wage of production labor in manufacturing in Mexico to measure Mexican wages. This series was obtained by Hanson and Spilimbergo (1999). We deflate the series using the Mexican CPI (obtained from IMF *Statistics*, various years) and display a plot of the Mexican real wage in Figure 5.2.

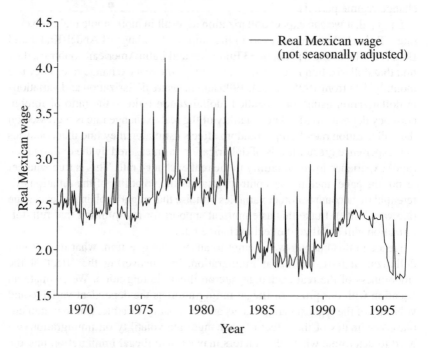

*Figure 5.2    Real Mexican wage*

The series exhibits a considerable amount of seasonality due to bonuses that significantly increase hourly earnings during December.[4]

To obtain a better overall view of the pattern in Mexican wages a deseasonalized series was obtained by estimating the following equation.

$$\text{RWAGESMEX} = \alpha_1\text{JAN} + \alpha_2\text{FEB} + \ldots + \alpha_{12}\text{DEC} + \mu_t. \qquad (5.3)$$

The residuals from this regression, correspond to a simple deseasonalized real wage series.[5] These are plotted in Figure 5.3 and, as with the plot of the real

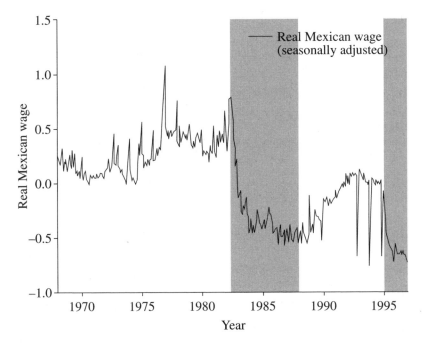

*Note*: Shaded areas correspond to flexible exchange regime periods

*Figure 5.3    Real Mexian wage (seasonally adjusted)*

exchange rate, I have shaded the areas corresponding to flexible exchange regimes.

It is apparent from this plot that there is a 'structural shift' in the behavior of the real Mexican wage series each time the Mexican economy moves from fixed to flexible nominal exchange regimes. Also apparent is that the 'smoothness' of the wage series does changes in character. The 'spikes' in the series appear somewhat less pronounced during the flexible regime periods. Nonetheless the series continues to display considerable volatility both during fixed and flexible exchange regimes.

To get a comparable 'feel' for how US real wages have behaved over the sample period, we use an analogous procedure and plot the deseasonalized real US wage series in Figure 5.4.

There appears to have been some growth in real wages during the 1970s, stabilization of real wages in the early 1980s and a decline in real wages in the later 1980s and in the 1990s.

Another variable that potentially affects the level of illegal immigration is the real exchange rate. The real exchange rate between the peso and the dollar

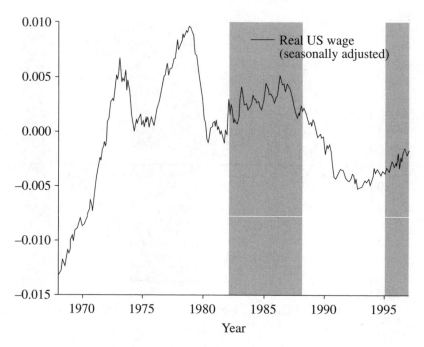

*Figure 5.4    Real US wage (seasonally adjusted)*

measures the relative cost of living and visiting the USA for a Mexican resident. There is a great deal of 'fluidity' in living arrangements by individuals, particularly in the border areas. Many persons not necessarily attached to the labor market make frequent crossings to visit and remain for extended periods of time with family and friends on the other side. Some workers live in Mexico while working in the USA, while others work in Mexico, but make frequent visits to the USA. That is, not all border crossings are motivated by relative wages. Visiting family and friends north and south of the border is an important source of flows across the border. Hence, we need to also account for this other source of border crossings. We obtain the real exchange rate as: REAL = [$E_{peso/\$}$ CPIUS] / CPIMEX. As REAL rises, the real peso depreciates, so it becomes more costly to travel to the USA, (accommodations and other travel services would become more costly). We would expect that real depreciation will reduce the number of illegal border crossings from south to north. This is analogous to service and good imports falling (rising) when the local currency depreciates (appreciates). Descriptive statistics for this and all of the series discussed are presented in Table 5.1.

*Table 5.1  Descriptive statistic for non-seasonal series*

|  | APP | HOURS | REAL MEXICAN WAGE | REAL US WAGE | REAL | VOLREAL |
|---|---|---|---|---|---|---|
| Mean | 43099 | 182040 | 2.40 | 0.14 | 5.23 | 0.0033 |
| Median | 42746 | 174155 | 2.41 | 0.14 | 4.97 | 0.0001 |
| Max. | 129612 | 386966 | 4.15 | 0.16 | 8.29 | 0.0436 |
| Min. | 1555 | 68460 | 1.68 | 0.13 | 3.67 | 0.0000 |
| Std. dev. | 26527 | 69931 | 0.41 | 0.01 | 1.05 | 0.0077 |
| Skew | 0.41 | 0.68 | 0.70 | −0.25 | 0.98 | 2.5237 |
| Kurt | 2.73 | 3.38 | 4.42 | 2.04 | 3.59 | 8.8013 |
| Obs | 348 | 348 | 348 | 348 | 348 | 348 |

*Notes*:
The real mexican and US wage series are index numbers derived from different sources and constructed in different ways and hence are not directly comparable to each other.
Sample: 1968:01 1996:12.

## ESTIMATING THE IMPACT OF DOLLARIZATION ON ILLEGAL IMMIGRATION

Now that we have specified the main economic determinants of Mexican illegal immigration into the USA, what remains is to isolate the impact that dollarization has on the illegal immigrant flow. This is easily accomplished now by including as an additional determinant of border crossings, exchange-rate volatility. In this way we can discern whether the 'smoothness' of the real exchange rate has an effect on border crossings into the USA.

The equation estimated is as follows:

$$\text{LAPP} = \alpha + \beta_1 \text{LHOURS} + \beta_2 \text{LRWAGESUS} \tag{5.4}$$
$$+ \beta_3 \text{LRWAGESMEX} + \beta_4 \text{LREAL} + \beta_5 \text{VOLREAL}$$
$$+ \delta_1 T + \delta_2 T^2 + \varphi_1 \text{JAN} + \ldots + \varphi_{11} \text{NOV} + \varepsilon_t$$

The log of monthly apprehensions (LAPP) is posited to depend on the log of US real wages (LRWAGESUS) and the log of Mexican real wages (LRWAGESMEX). Apprehensions, however, will also depend on the level of resources that the INS devotes to border patrol. Hence the inclusion of LHOURS. In addition, we recognize that given the familial ties many have on both sides of the border, crossings are likely to be highly related to the real exchange rate entered in log form (LREAL) which measures the real cost of travelling, purchasing and visiting in the USA. We include time trend variables (T and $T^2$) and monthly dummy variables (JAN to NOV) to account for the seasonal patterns observed in the various series.[6] The primary variable of interest, the volatility of the real exchange rate (VOLREAL) is also included. This is obtained by constructing a time series of the volatility of the real exchange rate by calculating the 12-month moving standard deviation of percentage changes in the monthly real exchange rate.

The results from estimating equation (5.4) are presented in Table 5.1. A preliminary perusal of the results appear promising. As would be expected, when the INS increases its resources devoted to border patrol, apprehensions rise. A rise in the US real wage appears to encourage illegal immigration while a real increase in Mexican wages appears to discourage illegal immigration. As anticipated, real peso depreciation reduces immigration. The time dummies suggests that apprehensions are trending upward and the monthly dummies exhibit the anticipated pattern of illegal immigration (more immigration during US harvest seasons and fewer crossings into the USA over the Christmas holiday season).

The variable of interest, real exchange rate volatility, is significantly different from zero and is positive. Increased volatility of the real exchange rate increases illegal immigration. Hence this regression suggests that dollarization, by smoothing the real exchange rate, will reduce the level of illegal immigration into the USA.

A more critical statistical and economic examination of the results contained in Table 5.2, however, cause me to question the appropriateness of the interpretations I have just outlined.

The diagnostics reveal considerable serial correlation (the Durbin–Watson statistic is 0.36 and the Ljung–Box $Q^2_{(12)} = 281$). The coefficient on US real wages suggests that the elasticity of illegal immigration with respect to US wages is 50; while the elasticity of illegal immigration with respect to Mexican wages is only –0.34. That is, a 1 per cent increase in US real wages increases illegal immigration by 50 per cent while a 1 per cent rise in Mexican real wages reduces illegal immigration by one-third of 1 per cent.

Further diagnostics reveal that LAPP, LHOURS, LWAGESUS, LWAGES-MEX and LREAL are all I(1), that is they are nonstationary containing 1 unit root. We know that nonstationary series in a regression equation can yield spurious results (Granger and Newbold, 1974). In such a case it is necessary to difference the data, obtain stationary series and estimate the regression equation with the stationary series. However, if series are co-integrated, the regression of the differenced stationary series requires an error-correction to capture the long-run equilibrium relation that exist among the co-integrated variables (Engle and Granger, 1987). In other words, the regression results presented in Table 5.2 are potentially unreliable because many of its component series are trending.

*Table 5.2   Estimation of equation (5.4)*

| Variable | Coefficient | Std. Error | t-Statistic | Prob |
|---|---|---|---|---|
| Constant | 12.94201 | 1.816109 | 7.126233 | 0.0000 |
| LHOURS | 0.646458 | 0.092356 | 6.999654 | 0.0000 |
| LRWAGEUS | 5.954760 | 0.552365 | 10.78049 | 0.0000 |
| LRWAGEMEX | −0.372981 | 0.122396 | −3.047328 | 0.0025 |
| LREAL | −0.396989 | 0.084378 | −4.704880 | 0.0000 |
| VOLREAL | 6.925525 | 1.530689 | 4.524449 | 0.0000 |
| T | 0.014715 | 0.000575 | 25.59861 | 0.0000 |
| $T^2$ | −2.02E-05 | 1.88E-06 | −10.76195 | 0.0000 |
| JAN | 0.371942 | 0.063551 | 5.852664 | 0.0000 |
| FEB | 0.503332 | 0.063672 | 7.905082 | 0.0000 |
| MAR | 0.697164 | 0.060589 | 11.50647 | 0.0000 |
| APR | 0.642067 | 0.061203 | 10.49085 | 0.0000 |
| MAY | 0.635562 | 0.059929 | 10.60529 | 0.0000 |
| JUN | 0.560648 | 0.060216 | 9.310695 | 0.0000 |
| JUL | 0.611043 | 0.058964 | 10.36298 | 0.0000 |
| AUG | 0.613210 | 0.059904 | 10.23657 | 0.0000 |
| SEP | 0.426313 | 0.059737 | 7.136450 | 0.0000 |
| OCT | 0.273088 | 0.059853 | 4.562651 | 0.0000 |
| NOV | 0.080706 | 0.059264 | 1.361790 | 0.1742 |
| | | | | |
| R-squared | 0.960715 | Mean dependent var | | 10.37450 |
| Adjusted R-squared | 0.958566 | S.D. dependent var | | 0.913632 |
| S.E. of regression | 0.185973 | Akaike info criterion | −3.311258 | |
| Sum squared resid | 11.37877 | Schwarz criterion | | −3.100936 |
| Log likelihood | 101.3682 | F-statistic | | 446.9868 |
| Durbin–Watson stat | 0.381639 | Prob(F-statistic) | | 0.000000 |
| $Q^2_{(12)}$ | 281.34 | | | |

*Notes*:   Sample: 1968:01; 1996:12; included observations: 348.

Below we re-estimate the relationship at hand and take into consideration the appropriate statistical issues.

We test for co-integration among the series within the framework established by Johansen (1991). The co-integration test was performed using those series that are integrated of the same order, that is LAPP, LHOURS, LRWAGESUS, LRWAGESMEX and LREAL. The results from the cointegration test indicates the existence of one cointegrating vector. A long-run equilibrium relationship exists among LAPP, LHOURS, LRWAGESUS, LRWAGESMEX and LREAL. This implies that an OLS model of the log of apprehensions estimated using the differenced series of LHOURS, LRWAGESUS, LRWAGESMEX, LREAL (so as to remove the unit roots) and the non-differenced VOLREAL is not appropriate. We need to account for the long-run equilibrium relationship (that was purged with the differencing) by including an error correction term.

We employ the Engle–Granger (1987) two-step procedure by estimating the following error-correction model:

$$\delta(LAPP_t) = \alpha + \beta_1\delta(LHOURS_t) + \beta_2\delta(LRWAGESUS_t) + \qquad (5.5)$$
$$\beta_3\delta(LRWAGESMEX_t) + \beta_4\delta(LREAL_t)$$
$$+ \beta_5VOLREAL_t + \varphi_1JAN + \ldots + \varphi_{11}NOV + > \mu_{t-1} + \varepsilon_t$$

The $\mu_{t-1}$ are the lagged OLS residuals from the estimation of the long-run relationship corresponding to the first step regression in the Engle–Granger (1987) two-step estimation procedure. The OLS residuals were obtained from the regression of LAPP on a constant, LHOURS, LRWAGESUS, LRWAGESMEX and LREAL. The behavior of these variables in the long-run is captured by the coefficient on the error correction term.

The results of estimating equation (5.5) are presented in Table 5.3.

The coefficient on $\mu_{t-1}$ is statistically different from zero, reaffirming the existence of a long-run equilibrium relationship among the five cointegrated variables.

The short-run impacts of the economic variable on LAPP can be discerned from the coefficient estimates in Table 5.3. We find that border patrol resources increase apprehension in the short run (as they do in the long run.) It is interesting that in the short run increases in the real US wage do not appear to prompt illegal immigration (though in the long run a relationships does exist). We find that the volatility of the real exchange rate contributes to illegal immigration, suggesting that dollarization could result in less illegal immigration.[7]

In all, what do these results suggest? We see that given the statistical properties of these series, there is a confounding of short-run and long-run relationships. But we are able to disentangle these using the Engle–Granger two-step procedure. It appears that illegal immigration is affected in the long run by relative real wages, by the level of the real exchange rate and by border

*Table 5.3   Estimation of error-correction equation (5.5)*

| Variable | Coefficient | Std. Error | *t*-Statistic | Prob. |
|---|---|---|---|---|
| Constant | −0.134687 | 0.037497 | −3.591896 | 0.0004 |
| δLHOURS | 0.492489 | 0.086236 | 5.710951 | 0.0000 |
| δLRWAGEU | −0.215530 | 1.595957 | −0.135048 | 0.8927 |
| δLRWAGEM | −0.169253 | 0.114109 | −1.483261 | 0.1390 |
| VOLREAL | 1.534813 | 0.779086 | 1.970018 | 0.0497 |
| δLREAL | −0.166698 | 0.102024 | −1.633912 | 0.1032 |
| $\mu_{t-1}$ | −0.073357 | 0.018625 | −3.938736 | 0.0001 |
| JAN | 0.542432 | 0.076156 | 7.122612 | 0.0000 |
| FEB | 0.212898 | 0.046238 | 4.604417 | 0.0000 |
| MAR | 0.339491 | 0.038586 | 8.798393 | 0.0000 |
| APR | 0.108928 | 0.043563 | 2.500497 | 0.0129 |
| MAY | 0.150725 | 0.040654 | 3.707523 | 0.0002 |
| JUN | 0.060760 | 0.044392 | 1.368704 | 0.1720 |
| JUL | 0.220965 | 0.040460 | 5.461276 | 0.0000 |
| AUG | 0.141197 | 0.045350 | 3.113516 | 0.0020 |
| SEP | 0.005986 | 0.041995 | 0.142536 | 0.8867 |
| OCT | −0.028015 | 0.043466 | −0.644524 | 0.5197 |
| NOV | −0.096055 | 0.043337 | −2.216466 | 0.0273 |
| | | | | |
| R-squared | 0.782125 | Mean dependent var | | 0.009397 |
| Adjusted R-squared | 0.770867 | S.D. dependent var | | 0.224655 |
| S.E. of regression | 0.107538 | Akaike info criterion | −4.409350 | |
| Sum squared resid | 3.804666 | Schwarz criterion | | −4.209673 |
| Log likelihood | 290.650 | F-statistic | | 69.47309 |
| Durbin–Watson stat | 1.928262 | Prob(F-statistic) | | 0.000000 |
| $Q^2_{(12)}$ | 8.3 | | | |

*Notes*:   Dependent variable is )(LAPP$_t$); Sample(adjusted): 1968:02; 1996:12; Included observations: 347 after adjusting endpoints.

patrol resources. In the short run a different set of variables explains apprehensions, with border patrol resources and the volatility of the real exchange rate playing prominent roles. In all, this seems plausible. Migrants make decisions regarding immigration based on long-run trends in variables such as those contained in relative real wages. Decisions to migrate take time to coalesce in many circumstances. On the other hand, other variables can prompt migration in the short run as in the case of real exchange-rate volatility. Short-run variables may be considered push factors, more easily and more rapidly explaining flows. The long-run pull factors such as US real wages also affect immigration, but they take longer to do their work.

## CONCLUDING REMARKS

In this chapter we have attempted to discern the impact that dollarization might have on the flow of illegal immigrants into the USA from Mexico. The conclusions derived are based on two major premises; (1) that the adjusted apprehension data is a reasonable estimate of illegal immigration into the USA from Mexico, (2) that dollarization will result in greater stability in relative prices between Mexico and the USA.

If these premises are reasonable ones, these results suggest that dollarization could result in a reduction in the level of illegal immigration from Mexico to the USA, all other things equal. If dollarization results in more volatile real exchange rates, our conclusions would need to be reversed. And, if all other things are not equal, if dollarization impacts the relative wages of Mexican and US workers, then our conclusions would need to be modified to reflect that additional effect. Nonetheless, our econometric results suggest that there is no 'long-run equilibrium relationship' between the volatility of the real exchange rate and the other variables we reasoned would affect illegal immigration (VOL-REAL is not cointegrated with the other variables in our model). Hence, these results provide reasonable evidence that illegal immigration could be reduced under dollarization.

## DATA APPENDIX[8]

1. Apprehensions: from Hanson and Spilimbergo (1999). Linewatch apprehensions include apprehensions at the borders and at other international ports of entry.
2. Linewatch hours: from Hanson and Spilimbergo (1999). Number of person hours spent patrolling the border and other international ports of entry.
3. Mexican wage: from Hanson and Spilimbergo (1999). Monthly index of average nominal hourly wages in manufacturing.
4. US wage: from Borjas and Fisher (2001). Nominal hourly wages in the manufacturing sector.

5. Mexican CPI: from *International Financial Statistics*. Monthly.
6. US CPI: from *International Financial Statistics*. Monthly.
7. Nominal Peso/US dollar exchange rate: From *International Financial Statistics*. Monthly.

## NOTES

1. See Smith (1997) and Cornelius and Martin (1993) for a review of contrasting arguments.
2. See Bean et al. (1990) for an overview of the evidence on illegal immigration from Mexico to the USA.
3. The Abdel-Kader and Balan paper is more properly testing the impact of partial dollarization while here we are concerned with the possibility of full dollarization. It is possible that full dollarization could result in a different effect on the real exchange rate than partial dollarization. Also note that this chapter does not distinguish between dollarization and the adoption of a common currency that would be managed jointly by treaty members.
4. Workers who have remained with their employer for at least one year get a bonus in December which effectively doubles their hourly wages in December (Hanson and Spilimbergo, 1999).
5. Some argue that this is an inappropriate way to deseasonalize data and would suggest resorting to one of the deseasonalization procedures such as X-11. I also ran the series through X-11 and it resulted in a series very similar to the series depicted in Figure 5.3.
6. Instead of deseasonalizing each individual series, we allow the seasonal dummies to account for the seasonality in all the data series.
7. Since the dependent variable is the *change* in log of apprehensions, the pattern on the monthly dummy variables differs from what we observe in the level equation discussed earlier.
8. I am grateful to Eric O'N. Fisher for providing me with the following series: Apprehensions, Linewatch hours, Mexican wages, US wages.

## REFERENCES

Abdel-Kader, Khaled and Alex Balan (2001), 'The impact of dollarization on the volatility of nominal and real exchange rates,' unpublished manuscript, Western Michigan University, April.

Bean, Frank D., Barry Edmonston and Jeffrey S. Passel (eds) (1990), *Undocumented Migration to the United States: IRCA and the Experience of the 1980s*, Washington, DC: Urban Institute.

Borjas, George J. and Eric O'N. Fisher (2001), 'Dollarization and the Mexican labor market,' *Journal of Money Credit and Banking*, **33** (2) Part. 2, 2 May, 626–47.

Cornelius, Wayne A. and Philip L. Martin (1993), 'The uncertain connection: free trade and rural Mexican migration to the United States,' *International Migration Review*, **27**, Fall 1993, 484–512.

Engle, Robert F. and C.W.J. Granger (1987), 'Co-Integration and error correction: representation, estimation and testing,' *Econometrica*, **55**, 251–76.

Granger, C.W.J. and P. Newbold (1974), 'Spurious regressions in econometrics,' *Journal of Econometrics*, **26**, p. 39–56.

Hanson, Gordon H. and Antonio Spilimbergo (1999), 'Illegal immigration, border enforcement, and relative wages: evidence from apprehensions at the U.S.-Mexico border,' *American Economic Review*, December, 1337–57.

International Monetary Fund, *International Financial Statistics*.

Johansen, Soren (1991), 'Estimation and hypothesis testing of cointegration vectors in Gaussian vector autoregressive models,' *Econometrica*, **59**, 1551–80.

Markusen, James R. and Stephen Zahniser (1997), 'Liberalization and incentives for labor migration: theory with application to NAFTA,' NBER working paper no. 6232, October.

Smith, Peter H. (1997), 'NAFTA and Mexican Migration,' in Frank D. Bean, Rodolfo O. de la Garza, Bryan R. Roberts and Sidney Weintraub (eds), *At the Crossroads: Mexican Migration and U.S. Policy*, Lanham: Rowman & Littlefield Publishers.

U.S. Immigration and Naturalization Service (1998), *Statistical Yearbook of the Immigration and Naturalization Service*.

# 6. Is the Canadian dollar destined to disappear? A critical perspective

**Mario Seccareccia**

## INTRODUCTION

By a vote of 175 to 67, in March 1999, Canada's House of Commons rejected a motion to study the creation of a North American monetary union and, thereby, eventually scrap the Canadian dollar. To my knowledge, this was the first time in almost 150 years since the adoption of the Canadian dollar in 1854 that such an idea had been entertained by the Canadian parliament (see Powell, 1999). Although the Bloc Québécois, a party that advocates Quebec's secession from the Canadian federation, had introduced the motion, primarily conservative members of parliament had supported the proposal. As expected, however, the governing Liberal Party together with the social-democratic New Democratic Party easily defeated the motion.

Not unlike the debate during the late 1980s over the Canadian–US Free Trade Agreement (FTA), a sharp cleavage emerged politically in Canada. The traditional Left and Centre of the political spectrum was unanimously opposed to the notion of abandoning Canada's national currency. On the other hand, the political Right, the Tories and the then Canadian Alliance, together with the Quebec sovereignists (who tend broadly to be situated to the left of the Canadian political spectrum) showed interest in forging stronger institutional links with the United States and entertaining the idea of a common currency. This was so despite the fact that the Bloc and the conservative members of Canada's parliament had widely different long-term political interests in supporting such policy of increased North American monetary integration. For instance, the Quebec *indépendantistes* viewed monetary union largely as a way of eliminating one more obstacle on the road towards political independence for Quebec; while the Canadian Right saw it as one additional opportunity to curtail the power of the state and further dismantle the Canadian welfare state.

During debate in the Canadian parliament, proponents of greater monetary integration did not, however, put forth such stark political concerns. The advocates of greater monetary integration with the United States shrewdly presented their view by articulating some of the arguments that are now quite familiar to economists well-versed in Mundellian economic logic. In particular, Mundell's prognostication of an evolutionary trend towards some sort of tripolar world, with the emergence of a set of G-3 currency blocs based on the euro, the yen and the US dollar (see Mundell, 2000c), echoed in the halls of Canada's House of Commons. Given the underlying tendency in favour of international currency blocs, supporters of dollarization argued that government refusal to recognize this historical process towards monetary integration would place Canada in an unfavourable competitive position internationally and would impose severe costs on the Canadian economy. Courchene and Harris (1999, pp. 3–4) have, inter alia, summarily stated the political justification for this position to join a North American monetary bandwagon in a paper in support of the establishment of a North American Monetary Union (NAMU):

> While a NAMU is not in the immediate horizon, there is nonetheless an urgent need to place the currency union issue on the public policy agenda. Policy developments within the NAFTA and elsewhere in the Americas appear to be moving quickly in the direction of dollarization. Since widespread dollarization could preclude the emergence of a NAMU by reducing the advantages the United States would garner from it and since ... a NAMU would be preferable to dollarization from a Canadian perspective, Canada must become engaged on this issue with its NAFTA and hemispheric partners – and sooner rather than later.

Greater monetary integration would supposedly bring forth significant benefits in the form of lower transaction costs, low inflation, higher output and greater economic stability. However, it is primarily the fear of being 'left out' of a fast accelerating train of North American monetary integration that was being sold politically by those partial to the Mundellian logic.

It would appear that historically this bandwagon effect was also the principal political factor behind much of European monetary integration and that Mundellian analysis, based on the theory of optimum currency areas (OCA), was at best used only as a rhetorical device by the advocates of greater integration. For example, the establishment of the European Monetary System (EMS) – a pegged exchange rate system tied to the German mark – followed a bandwagon logic of development whereby fear of missing the European 'train' pushed the recalcitrant Italian and British authorities ultimately to join the EMS. To quote Gruber (1999, p. 4),

> So what ... prompted the Italians (in 1979) and the British (in 1990) to reinquish their monetary autonomy? The answer, in a word, is power – specifically ... the 'go-it-alone power' exercised by the EMS regime's French and German beneficiaries.

Hence, defying OCA logic, according to Gruber (1999), at least two of the EMS's largest signatories would have much preferred the pre-EMS system of floating exchange rates. Yet, fearing the political damages that non-entry entailed (see Dyson and Featherstone, 1999, p. 474), the political authorities in Italy, and later in the United Kingdom, finally succumbed to the bandwagon pressures of greater monetary integration. They joined, therefore, even though this would entail, as was the case especially for Italy, lower economic performance than during the pre-EMS era. It is of interest to note that Mundell (1997, p. 215) himself has, in more recent times, defended the politics of being 'left out' as the basis for the United Kingdom's eventual full-fledged entry into the euro fold in the near future.

Much as in Europe, and as history of monetary unions elsewhere broadly demonstrates (see Bordo and Jonung, 1999), it may be said that North America's monetary trajectory over the coming decade will not be based on any underlying economic logic that ensues from the application of Mundellian theory of OCA but on the power politics that will ultimately be played out institutionally in the respective NAFTA countries. As Keynes once affirmed, political leaders may become persuaded by, and indeed become enslaved to, economic ideas of some academic scribbler of long ago but only if they serve as a rhetorical tool to further the leaders' specific political ends. This is not to deny the persuasive power of specific economic theories. In the struggle over public opinion, it is exactly the power of such ideas in shaping opinion, and therefore in remoulding the political *status quo*, that matters. However, as was the case with European monetary unification, it is not on the basis of OCA economic determinism that greater monetary integration will be sold to the Canadian public but primarily on the fears of being 'left out' of some supposed accelerating NAMU train.

The politics and rhetoric notwithstanding, it has been precisely OCA deterministic logic that is generally espoused by those supportive of greater monetary integration in North America. Hence, the purpose of this paper is to analyse critically the basic arguments put forth in Canada by the defenders of Mundellian theory and to evaluate their relevance. To do this, I shall first seek to describe the shaky ground upon which this theory is based. This will then be followed by a broad critical analysis of the presumed economic benefits from greater monetary integration that OCA theory predicts.

## MUNDELLIAN THEORY OF OPTIMUM CURRENCY AREAS: A CRITICAL ANALYSIS

As pointed out by Goodhart (1998) and Parguez (2000), the dominant OCA paradigm is the lineal descendent of a long tradition in monetary theory on the nature and evolution of money that was perhaps best formulated by Carl Menger at the end of the nineteenth century. However, its historical origin is to be found in medieval times and is sometimes referred to as the *théorie marchandise* – the commodity or metalist theory of money (see Seccareccia, 1999). For this group of theorists, money should best be conceived as a specific commodity evolving from a barter system and which is eventually adopted via the spontaneous action of private agents seeking to minimize transactions costs. How, Menger (1892) asked, can a barter exchange system in which economic agents face the problem of the double coincidence of wants slowly evolve into a monetary economy? The solution which remains at the core of neoclassical monetary orthodoxy is that, in a given spacial and temporal transactions space, there will emerge a commodity whose objective characteristics in terms of degree of 'saleableness (*Absatzfähigkeit*)' (i.e. the degree to which economic agents are able to dispose of such a commodity to acquire other less 'saleable' goods) are such as to be conferred the role of medium of exchange. Because of their intrinsic characteristics of fungibility, divisibility, durability and portability, Menger (1892) argued that this is why historically precious metals emerged as acceptable media of exchange both in local and in international markets without the intervention of the state. 'Money', Menger (1892, p. 255) wrote, 'has not been generated by law. In its origin it is a social [*i.e.*, market], and not a state-institution. ... [state recognition and state regulation] have not first made money of the precious metals, but have only perfected them in their function as money.' Moreover, given the monetary commodity's supply constraints, banks play no role in monetary creation since they are conceived only as intermediaries in their capacity to transfer a scarce monetary resource from savers to investors. Commercial bank deposits, and even central bank notes, appear, therefore, simply as 'surrogates' for commodity money (Realfonzo 1998, chapter 2).

In opposition to this commodity view of money, there exists perhaps an even older approach. This latter tradition ties the existence of money to the role of the state both as the ultimate purveyor of liquidity and as the legal authority that bestows on a commodity its status as legal tender money within an institutional structure defined by the state (see Innes, 1913). This approach has been dubbed the *théorie signe* or simply the Chartalist theory of money (Wray, 1998; Mosler and Forstater, 1999). Unlike Mengerian theory that considers money as the spontaneous outcome of a market process whose intrinsic characteristics ultimately qualify it as being money, Chartalist theory views money as a creature of the state and highlights the link between the existence and creation of money to the fiscal needs of the political authorities. The existence of a national currency (i.e. a token chosen by the state to command societal resources) is thus inseparable from the question of political sovereignty and from the state's prerogative to enforce tax payments within a precise geographical domain. In more advanced monetary economies in which has evolved a system of banking institutions that can create 'inside' money *ex nihilo* (always denominated in the state's unit of account) via bank credit advances, both the legal existence of such institutions and the possible fulfilment of their liquidity needs (such as during times of crisis) still would very much depend ultimately on the actions of the state (Parguez and Seccareccia, 2000).

Mengerian analysis permeates much of neoclassical monetary theory, but its empirical applicability is, to say the least, very weak. Historically, there are many examples of how strong and stable monetary systems are often associated with strong and stable governments; while monetary debasement and flight from money have characterized a crumbling state authority. On the other hand, it would be difficult to find examples of currencies (even in their purest commodity forms) evolving 'spontaneously' from barter without either the hidden or overt accompanying hand of the state. As argued by Goodhart (1998), despite Mengerian theory's lack of realism and its incapacity to explain the actual origin and general historical evolution of money, it is upon this latter conceptual *toile de fond* that Mundellian OCA theory has been grafted.

Mundellian OCA theory extends to international monetary relations similar Mengerian analytics to that pertaining to a national economic space. In particular, OCA theory rests primarily on the Mengerian concern with minimizing transactions costs. Since it is postulated that transactions costs rise exponentially with the number of currencies in circulation, money would slowly lose its traditional functions of unit of account and medium of exchange as the number of currencies increases within a given international economic space. Mundell (1961, p. 662) writes:

> Any given money qua numeraire or unit of account fulfils this function less adequately if the prices of foreign goods are expressed in terms of foreign currency and must then be translated into domestic currency prices. Similarly, money in its role of medium of exchange is less useful if there are many currencies; although the costs of currency conversion are always present, they loom exceptionally large under convertibility or flexible exchange rates. (Indeed, in a hypothetical world in which the number of currencies equaled the number of commodities, the usefulness of money in its role of unit of account and medium of exchange would disappear, and trade might just as well be conducted in terms of pure barter).

On this basis, it would ensue tautologically that the optimum currency area would be the world as a whole with the existence of either a single world currency or a system of national currencies firmly locked together via fixed exchange rates, such as under the gold standard. However, as much as the prospect of a single world currency may be appealing to Mundell (2000a), because of asymmetric shocks to various regions internationally, regional differences in the structure of production, obstacles to factor mobility, and the extent of automatic stabilizers and/or interregional transfers, for OCA theorists such as Mundell (1961), McKinnon (1963) and Kenen (1969), an OCA cannot be the world but some subset of regional trading blocs.

Hence, as the theory of OCA has been filtered down historically and rendered empirically operational by economists such as Bayoumi and Eichengreen (1994, 1997), and, among many others, Williamson (2000), a list of important criteria has been proposed to determine whether any two regions or countries constitute an OCA and therefore should engage in greater bilateral integration via either a common currency or a pegged exchange rate. Some of the important conditions to be met can be summarized as follows:

1. the two regions or countries should be highly exposed as trading partners with foreign trade constituting a significant share of GDP;
2. real shocks to output in both regions ought to be symmetrical, thereby giving rise to highly correlated business cycles;
3. there should be present a high degree of factor mobility between the two regions; and
4. there should be much institutional and policy convergence.

Empirical work in this area has shown that the theory of OCA can provide a wealth of meaningful information on the degree of economic symbiosis among countries, that is to say, on the extent to which economic integration is associated with monetary integration. However, as emphasized by Goodhart (1995), the predictive power of OCA criteria in explaining existing monetary integration internationally is terribly weak. Even where OCA theory has shown greater success, that is, in explaining why certain countries choose pegged exchange rate regimes to flexible exchange rate systems, the evidence is problematic for OCA theorists. For instance, in a study using the methodology developed by Bayoumi and Eichengreen (1997), Bénassy-Quéré and Lahrèche-Révil (1998) find that while some of the standard OCA criteria, such as the asymmetry of business cycles, can explain exchange-rate volatility and thus the degree to which countries should be anchored to the euro or the US dollar, using their relative OCA index one would infer that currently countries such as Ireland, Spain and the United Kingdom would benefit from pegging their respective currencies to the dollar rather than to the euro! Ironically, using a similar methodology, Bayoumi and Eichengreen (1997, p. 769) found that France, together with the United Kingdom, Denmark, Finland and Norway, were a group of countries for which there was little evidence of exchange rate convergence vis-à-vis Germany, and thus concluded that 'the desire for monetary unification in France is driven by political rather than economic considerations'. From this, one may conclude that even explaining why economies such as France have bound themselves to fixed exchange rate systems has been a significant problem for OCA theorists.

If such conflicting evidence is not enough to question the usefulness of the OCA approach, paradoxically, where OCA theory is least effective is in the domain for which it was originally most intended, i.e. the field of common currencies. As pointed out by, among others, McKinnon (2000), in Mundell's (1961) original work, his theory sought to offer insights as to why optimal currency areas ought to be smaller rather than larger. Both in Mundell's original Canada–USA example and in most of the work patterned on OCA theory, such as that of Bayoumi and Eichengreen (1994), it would suggest that, when OCA criteria are applied to a common currency area such as the United States or Canada, the east and the west of the North American continent face supply disturbances that tend to be negatively correlated geographically. Hence, because of such strong regionally asymmetric shocks, *ceteris paribus*, OCA theory would recommend common currency areas that would more easily dissect the North American continent east–west rather than north–south, but would hardly advise in favour of a single North American currency! Hence, in large multi-regional blocs such as Canada, the United States and even the current EMU, OCA theory would support that currencies be reorganized on a regional basis for overall welfare enhancement. The theory does not automatically predict, therefore, that a larger monetary bloc is preferred to a smaller currency union. In fact, it is primarily for this reason that Mundell himself was very careful in his seminal article about the practical application of his theory. For instance, Mundell (1961, p. 661) concludes:

> In the real world, of course, currencies are mainly an expression of national sovereignty, so that actual currency reorganization would be feasible only if it were accompanied by profound political changes. The concept of an optimal currency area therefore has direct practical applicability only in areas where political organization is in a state of flux, such as in ex-colonial areas and in Western Europe.

In the final analysis, therefore, what really matters in explaining the actual history and existing structures of currency unions are broad political preferences and evolving political institutions and not *ex ante* economic rationalizing based on Mengerian transactions cost minimization. Hence, despite the high degree of economic integration between two regions, such as Canada and the United States, as Buiter (1999) has argued, without some form of political union to ensure an acceptable degree of accountability of a North American central bank, a NAMU would lack political legitimacy and would very quickly unravel.

While Mundell has been described as the chief architect or 'father of the euro' (Salvatore, 2000, p. 305) and has undeniably been one of its leading advocates, the irrelevance of OCA theory perhaps is most evident in explaining the creation of the European Economic and Monetary Union (EMU) itself. Despite the official rhetoric to the contrary, as pointed out by numerous advocates of the OCA approach, Mundellian theory cannot justify the formation of the EMU (see, among others, Feldstein, 2000). Indeed, while depending on the precise empirical methodology, one can conceivably make a case for a 'small EMU' centered around Germany, which could include some of the adjacent Benelux countries, one can hardly find any strong economic rationale for EMU's existence based on OCA theory. Even with the presence of common market arrangements spanning a few decades, many of the major EMU members are economically less integrated today than, say, Canada is with the United States (see Courchene, 1998), and thus the case for welfare enhancement on the basis of OCA theory is not a very strong one. This, therefore, had brought supporters of the OCA approach, such as Eichengreen and Frieden (1994, p. 9), to conclude that 'uncertainty about the empirical magnitude of every one of the [OCA calculated] benefits and costs suggests the absence of a clear economic case in favour of EMU'. A similar blunt judgement on the EMU project is passed by Willett (2000, pp. 383–4) when the author describes the actual process of European monetary unification:

> The leaders of the political push for EMU seemed totally unaware of the considerations emphasized by economists in the theory of optimum currency areas. They stressed [OCA] economic benefits as a sales technique, but it was clear that their basic objective was political, and discussion of EMU quickly took on all the signs of ideological debate. ... A particularly dangerous oversight of the European political elite was to ignore the warnings of the OCA theory that the sign of the net economic costs–benefits equation of monetary union can vary across countries. Some countries would have net benefits, others net costs. ... It may be welfare enhancing for a 'core' group of members, but clearly not for the full set of EU members.

Yet, when Mundell (2000b) and OCA proponents of North American monetary integration defend the prospects for a NAMU in this hemisphere, it is usually done on the basis of the success of the 'euro revolution' exactly because of its Paretian welfare-improving implications in accordance with OCA theory (see Courchene, 1998; Courchene and Harris, 1999; and Grubel, 1999).

Even though OCA supporters do not fully agree on the precise significance of the EMU and on whether OCA is of limited usefulness to the understanding of actual currency areas, beginning with Mundell himself a number of economists partial to OCA theory have argued in favour of a NAMU for exactly the cornucopia of benefits that would result from its creation. In the following section, some of the specific arguments that have been put forth by these proponents of greater North American integration for either pegged exchange rates or the eventual elimination of the Canadian dollar (and the Mexican peso) will be discussed and critically evaluated.

## THE BENEFITS OF MONETARY INTEGRATION: SHOULD CANADA BECOME THE THIRTEENTH FEDERAL RESERVE DISTRICT OF A NORTH AMERICAN MONETARY UNION?

The launching of the euro in January 1999 may be considered a truly extraordinary event in monetary history. In fulfilling somewhat the Mengerian dream (see Parguez, 2000), for the first time historically a group of 11 countries scrapped their national currencies and adopted a single currency. In the process, the EMU seemingly shattered the long-established link between money and the state by divorcing monetary policy (via an independent, supra-national and largely unaccountable ECB) from fiscal policy (to be pursued by national governments within the constraining framework of the Maastricht Treaty and the Amsterdam Stability and Growth Pact). Since the advent of the euro, there has been a proliferation of papers promoting the virtues of the EMU and its institutional adaptation to the North American continent.

In Canada, we are told by its most ardent supporters, such as Courchene (1998), Courchene and Harris (1999) and Grubel (1999), that Canada is no longer a viable OCA and that the economic benefits of greater monetary integration on the basis of the EMU blueprint are many and the costs are very few, the latter being usually associated with intangible political costs relating to the loss of national sovereignty. For instance, Courchene (1998, p. 20) concludes that:

> Canada is no longer an optimal currency area in terms of maintaining a stand-alone, freely-fluctuating currency. On grounds both of transactions certainty and accommodating asymmetric shocks and of pervasive forces triggering North American monetary integration, the optimal currency area for Canada involves the US currency area as well.

But what exactly are these presumed benefits of a NAMU?

### Efficiency Gains in the Form of Reduced Transactions Costs

The first of these benefits pertains to what traditionally has been the central proposition of OCA theory. This has to do with the existence of Mengerian static gains accruing to economic agents from minimizing transactions costs because of the elimination of currency transactions between two countries. Many of the studies in support of European monetary unification made much of these potential gains and the argument may be dubbed the 'tourist' perspective on monetary union, as it was perhaps most dramatized by Emerson et al. (1992, p. 66) when calculating the currency transaction losses in a hypothetical round-trip through ten countries in Europe. If, with a common currency, one were to eliminate all the foreign exchange dealings between Canada and the United

States, the economic gain would comprise the direct savings to the public engaged in cross-border transactions. These savings would represent essentially the loss of net financial revenues of banks and other foreign exchange dealers pertaining to the elimination of the bid-ask spread of the pre-NAMU partner's foreign currency. Because of the net revenue loss, the savings to the public could be measured by the proportion that the foreign exchange departments of banks and other firms would shrink owing to the elimination of a large portion of the public's foreign exchange needs. For instance, Grubel (1999) provides a casual estimate for the NAMU countries as a whole at about 0.1 per cent of national income – a figure that seemed perhaps more reasonable than the estimate of 0.4 per cent of GDP found in European studies following the Delors Report (Grubel, 1999, p. 9).

Given the weight that reduced transactions cost holds in the OCA arsenal of arguments in favour of greater monetary integration, it is somewhat surprising that we are only talking about a 0.1 (or even a 0.4) per cent average annual efficiency gain from dollarization for Canada! While such welfare gain may not appear to be so substantial in size, in present value terms it would loom much larger. However, regardless of its estimated magnitude, such postulated gain is in fact highly illusive. Firstly, as pointed out by Arestis and Sawyer (1999) with respect to the euro, when these Mengerian welfare benefits are balanced against the costs of transition to a single currency, in present value terms the estimated *net* benefits tend largely to disappear. For instance, in referring to these estimated benefits, even in official reports such as that of Currie (1997, p. 6), it is stated quite candidly that 'The likely amounts [of the estimated benefits] are not however very large, and once the one-off costs of converting to the euro are taken into account as well, the net transactions savings do not provide a strong reason for moving to the euro'.

Secondly, and perhaps even more importantly, when a new common currency is adopted (as was the case with the euro in January 1999), naturally the effect would be to wipe out the bid-ask spread from which financial institutions can make a profit and, therefore, to reduce the direct cost for those engaged in such foreign exchange transactions. Yet, this ought not mean that these financial institutions would naively sit back to see their net revenues fall! Indeed, much of OCA theory is based on a view of the monetary system that largely abstracts from an analysis of the role of commercial banks. As profit maximizing institutions holding a certain degree of local monopoly, it would be much more realistic to assume that they would be attempting to maintain their overall bank revenues, for example, by charging service fees for related activities. This is basically what happened in Europe as of January 1999, when, in order to recoup some of their losses arising from the elimination of the foreign exchange spread, banks began opportunistically to charge user fees to citizens of the EMU countries seeking, for instance, to cash their travelers' cheques. It is most probably for this reason that the European Commission (1999, p. 3) kept warning the public after the launching of the euro that banks could not take advantage of the transition by charging the public for even the conversion of their national currencies into the euro! Hence, the disappearance of one type of transaction costs seems merely to have triggered a compensating increase of alternative bank charges faced by the European public under a common currency arrangement. Unless one can show why the share of net revenues of financial institutions ought to fall under NAMU, the argument in favour of efficiency gains because of reduced transactions cost is terribly misleading. If the share of net bank revenues out of GDP would essentially remain unchanged between the pre- and post-NAMU period, this would result in a possible redistribution among economic agents of the burden of transacting within the enlarged currency space but *not* necessarily in a reduction of overall transactions cost to the community at large.

**Efficiency Gains in the Form of Higher Productivity**

A second argument that has been promoted by those in favour of alternative currency arrangements for North America focuses, in this case, not on the presumed efficiency gains pertaining to lower transactions costs, but on the enhanced economic efficiency or increased productivity that would be forthcoming from greater monetary integration. Following the research findings of McCallum (1998, 1999) who had looked at productivity growth in the Canadian manufacturing sector since 1977, there was found to be a strong statistical correlation between the Canada/US exchange rate (lagged two years) and manufacturing productivity growth. From these findings, which have been further reinforced by anecdotal evidence in the Canadian media about the 'lazy' manufacturing sector being favoured by the declining exchange rate, advocates of greater monetary integration with the United States have suggested that there is a causal link between the falling Canadian dollar and low productivity growth.

The idea is quite simple and it is based on the premise that a floating Canadian dollar since the 1970s has had a long-term negative effect on Canada's competitiveness. While there is a short-term gain associated with a floating exchange rate in amortizing external shocks to the Canadian economy, the long-term impact of a falling dollar on productivity growth in the export sector would supposedly be negative. The argument is appealing and has been marketed a great deal by advocates of pegged exchange rates and greater monetary integration, such as Courchene (1998) and Courchene and Harris (1999). As Laidler (1999a, p. 8) notes, however, the evidence is highly circumstantial.

As is displayed in Table 6.1, it is true that when the Canadian dollar was pegged to the US dollar between 1962 and 1970 (and even during the 1950s

*Table 6.1* *Real GDP per capita and per employed person: average annual percentage change, 1960–98*

| | 1960–79 | 1980–98 | Percentage decline in growth rate |
|---|---|---|---|
| Real gross domestic product per capita | | | |
| Austria | 3.8 | 2.2 | 42.1 |
| Belgium | 3.7 | 2.1 | 43.2 |
| Canada | 3.1 | 1.6 | 48.4 |
| Fmr W. Germany | 3.1 | 1.8 | 41.9 |
| France | 3.6 | 1.4 | 61.1 |
| Italy | 3.9 | 1.9 | 51.3 |
| Japan | 6.1 | 2.6 | 57.4 |
| United Kingdom | 2.2 | 2.1 | 4.5 |
| United States | 2.7 | 2.2 | 18.5 |
| | | | |
| Real gross domestic product per employed person | | | |
| Austria | 4.1 | 2.4 | 41.5 |
| Belgium | 3.7 | 2.1 | 43.2 |
| Canada | 1.8 | 1.4 | 22.2 |
| Fmr W. Germany | 3.5 | 2.1 | 40.0 |
| France | 3.9 | 1.7 | 56.4 |
| Italy | – | 2.2 | – |
| Japan | 6.1 | 2.2 | 63.9 |
| United Kingdom | 2.4 | 1.9 | 20.8 |
| United States | 1.8 | 1.6 | 11.1 |

*Source*: US Bureau of Labor Statistics and Statistics Canada.

and the early 1970s under a floating regime – an era in which the Canadian dollar generally showed much greater stability) this was indeed associated with a period of somewhat higher productivity growth both for the manufacturing sector and for the business sector as a whole. However, as Table 6.1 shows, when looking at output per person employed since 1960, Canada showed a mild decline *comparable* to that of the USA and the UK between the 1960–79 period and the 1980–98 period – thus questioning the significance of the depreciating Canadian dollar in impacting on overall productivity growth. In fact, further econometric work undertaken by Dupuis and Tessier (2000) at the Bank of Canada found that McCallum's (1998, 1999) original bivariate system was highly problematic because of specification error and that a more comprehensive multi-variate analysis found that manufacturing productivity growth and the Canada–US exchange rate to be statistically unrelated variables.

Perhaps, of further annoyance to those supportive of the 'lazy manufacturer' hypothesis: if exchange rate fixity is of such crucial importance to productivity growth, why is it that the European countries who joined the EMS and subsequently the EMU during the post-1979 period faced an even sharper drop in productivity growth? Indeed, (as shown in Table 6.1) even such small open economies as Austria and Belgium which are probably in a similar relation vis-à-vis the core countries of the EMU (France and Germany) as Canada is with the USA, their growth rates of labour productivity (as measured by real GDP per employed person) and growth in their standards of living (as measured by real GDP per capita) all plummeted during the post-1979 period, even though, unlike Canada, they had been pegging their exchange rates within the EMS throughout this period. Stability in the exchange rate did not seem to provide much protection against an even sharper drop in productivity growth for all those European countries that joined the EMS since 1979! In much the same way, one could legitimately argue that greater monetary integration, in the form of pegged exchange rate or dollarization, with the other NAFTA partners could hardly be expected to be a significant factor in speeding up productivity growth in Canada.

### Gains in the Form of Lower Real Interest Rates

A third argument in the Mundellian defence of greater monetary integration has to do with the dampening effect that monetary unification would have on the level of interest rates in Canada. Once again the hypothesis put forth is a very simple one. While sovereign or default risk has never been a visible concern for foreign holders of Canadian securities, exchange rate risk ought to be a very real concern, especially for long-term bondholders because of the risk of exchange rate depreciation. It would ensue, therefore, that, because of the weight of risk-averse bondholders, the greater the volatility in the exchange rate, the higher ought to be the real interest rate spread between Canada and the USA. Moreover, as it has been argued by many EMU observers, since greater monetary integration leads to the further deepening of financial markets (see, *inter alia*, Eichengreen, 2000), this would probably have a further desirable negative impact on domestic interest rates in both countries. Consequently, if these factors are at all important in the determination of interest rates, one ought to find a significant long-term association between exchange rate stability/volatility and the real interest rate spread on long-term bonds across countries.

Figure 6.2 presents data on both the nominal and real interest rate spread on long-term government bonds (10 years and over) between Canada and the USA.

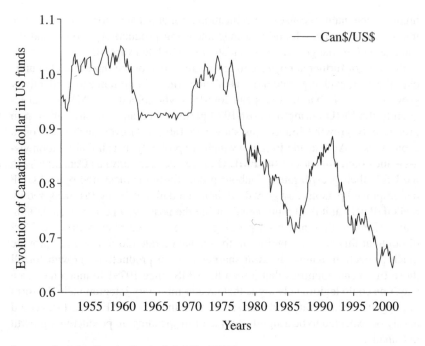

*Source*:   Statistics Canada, Cansim Label No. B3400.

*Figure 6.1    Evolution of Canadian dollar in US funds (1950–2001, monthly*
*observations)*

Casual observation surely would not lead one to conclude any significant decline
for the 1962–70 period during which Canada had pegged its currency to the US
dollar. Indeed, while both the nominal and real interest rate spread remained
relatively stable during the first half of the 1960s, by the latter half of the decade
there was a significant *upward* movement. Moreover, evidence from our graphs
does not suggest that greater exchange rate stability is necessarily associated
with lower spreads. As can be inferred from Figure 6.1, even during the decades
when Canada had floated its exchange rate (as during the 1950s and 1970s), the
Canada–US exchange rate showed a high degree of stability (when compared
with the decades of the 1980s and 1990s). For instance, when measuring the
variability in terms of standard deviation, data in Figure 6.1 exhibit a standard
deviation for the 1980–2001 period over twelve times that for the period from
1950–79. Did this greater volatility lead to a steep rise in the real interest spread
between Canada and the United States for the post-1980 period? The data from
Figure 6.2 shows no such sharp increase on average. For instance, the mean
value in the real interest rate spread for the period 1950–79 went from 0.93

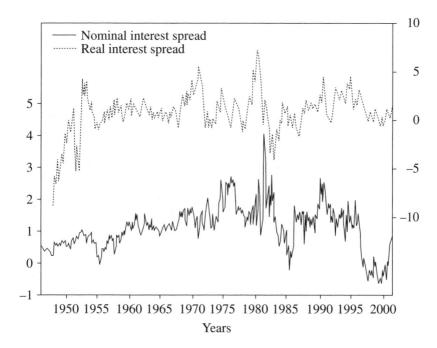

*Source*: Statistics Canada, Label Nos.: B14013, B54403, D139136, P 100000.

*Figure 6.2* *Canada–US nominal and real interest rate spread, 1946–2001 (Canada and US long-term government bonds, 10 years and over) (monthly observations)*

percentage point spread to 1.01 percentage point for the 1980–2001 period. While this was not an insignificant increase, it would be difficult to attribute most of this rise to the greater volatility in the exchange rate rather than to the relatively more restrictive monetary policy stance of the Bank of Canada during the 1980s and first half of the 1990s in fighting inflation (see Seccareccia 1998).

Indeed, empirical evidence in a related study explaining long-term interest rates in Canada (see Seccareccia and Lavoie, 2001) found that movements in the central bank-controlled variables, such as the overnight rate, were of crucial importance in explaining the movement of long-term interest rates, thereby emphasizing the difference in the respective monetary policy positions in explaining the slight widening of the Canada–US interest rate differential since 1980.

A similar argument can be made with respect to the European experience with monetary integration. With the breakdown of the Bretton Woods system

during the early 1970s, European countries did attempt under follow-up agreements to the Werner Report of 1970 to establish a structure of exchange rates,
often referred to as the European 'snake', but which led to extremely loose and
fluid relations during the 1970s until the creation of the EMS in 1979 (see Apel,
1998, chapter 1). Hence, the 1970s was a period during which some of the major
players of what ultimately has become the EMU, such as Italy and even France,
experimented with much greater flexibility in their exchange rate system, especially subsequent to the first oil price shock in 1973. Theory would thus suggest
that elimination of some of the exchange rate volatility would have led to lower
interest rates in Europe with respect to some benchmark interest rate. To evaluate
whether this led to a widening of interest rate spreads, a comparison was done
by looking at the difference between, on the one hand, the average real rates of
the original core countries of the Exchange Rate Mechanism (ERM) of the EMS
(France, Italy, the Federal Republic of Germany, and the Benelux countries)
and the benchmark US real rates on the other. The data displayed in Figure 6.3
was based on a simple averaging of the real rates of the five core countries (with
the exclusion of Luxembourg) for the period between 1965 and 1999. While
undoubtedly many factors would have had an impact on the interest rate spread,
it would be difficult to conclude from the chart that greater monetary integration
in Europe led to a narrowing of the interest rate spread vis-à-vis the United
States. For instance, the graph shows that the spread fell significantly during a
good portion of the 1970s, only to rise during the late seventies and then fall
sharply and rise again from the early 1980s to mid-1990s. Interestingly, when
comparing the evolution for the European countries (in Figure 6.3) to the Canada–US real interest rate spread (previously in Figure 6.2), a close analysis
would confirm that their pattern is conspicuously similar (even though these
countries were under very different exchange rate regimes).

Once again, one can infer from this that, at least from simple graphical analysis, evidence to support the views of Grubel (1999) and others as to the beneficial
effects of eliminating nominal exchange rate variability on long-term interest
rates is extremely weak if non-existent. This is not to argue that exchange risk
is of little importance to long-term bond holders. Rather, as also emphasized by
Seccareccia and Lavoie (2001), market forces are perhaps less important than
the policy actions of the monetary authorities in determining the level of both
short and long-term interest rates and, thus, the interest rate spread between
Canada and the USA.

In an ironic twist, in recent times, some have argued (see Bell, 2000 and
Mosler, 2001) that, if anything, the current structure of the EMU that is so
idealized by the Mengerians because of the clear separation of money from the
state, may have probably created problems of default risk for the member
countries of the EMU. This is because of the lack of liquidity provisions in the
Maastricht Treaty, which currently prohibits national governments to borrow

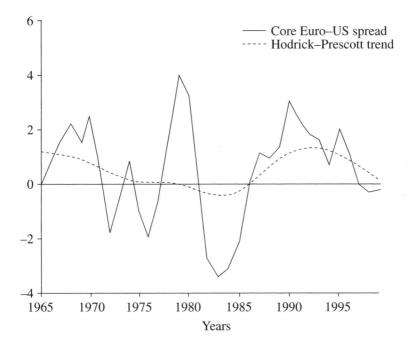

*Source*:   International Monetary Fund (IMF); International Financial Statistics, several issues; Bureau of Labor Statistics (BLS) http://www.bls.gov/.

*Figure 6.3    Evolution of real interest rate spread between core EMS countries and USA; annual data (1965–99)*

from the European Central Bank even in times of financial crisis. Therefore, unlike the customary view that default risk and exchange rate risk are complementary (see Rojas-Suarez, 2000), some have argued that, while exchange rate risk would *de facto* be eliminated under monetary union, the peculiar type of supra-national monetary arrangement along the lines of those existing in Euroland presently may have created more serious problems of default risk if, for instance, a banking crisis were to erupt in any one of the EMU member countries.

**Miscellanea**

In addition to these three important arguments in favour of greater North American monetary integration discussed above, there exists a plethora of other arguments that have traditionally been called upon to support greater monetary integration in North America. Among the other arguments that proponents such as Grubel (1999) have identified traditionally, there is at least one that merits mention here because of its important theoretical ramifications.

We are told that greater monetary integration in the form of pegged exchange rate or outright monetary union will impose the needed discipline on the fiscal authority as exemplified by the current experience of the EMU (see Courchene 1998; p. 18; and Grubel 1999, p. 15). While the theoretical underpinnings of this point of view are quite fluid and founded on questionable economic logic (to be discussed below), where is the evidence that a floating exchange rate leads to fiscal 'indiscipline'? To paraphrase McCallum (2000, p. 8), how can we explain the fact that, despite its floating currency, over a good number of years during the 1990s Canada has been running primary surpluses and is essentially meeting all of the Maastricht criteria? Moreover, as displayed in Figure 6.4 for the period between 1978 and 2000, the evolution of primary balances (as a percentage of GDP) under fixed exchange rates in Europe has not been very different than that under a flexible exchange rate regime in Canada. Unlike

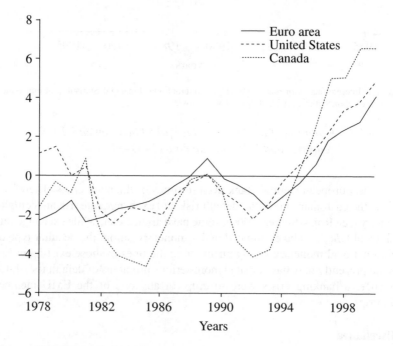

*Source:*   OECD Economic Outlook.

*Figure 6.4*   *General government primary balances surplus (+) or deficit (−)
as a percentage of GDP, Euro Area, United States and Canada,
1978–2000*

Europe, this was achieved in Canada without a major constitutional change to enforce quasi-balanced budgets.

Why then all this concern with fiscal discipline? The reason has to do with the Mundellian underpinnings of the theory of monetary union. In a world of high capital mobility, Mundellian theory as developed during the early 1960s identified fiscal policy as a powerful instrument of macroeconomic stabilization and, therefore, provided at the time strong theoretical support for those favouring activist fiscal intervention. However, under monetary union, such as would be the case under the proposed NAMU, an expansionary fiscal policy, say, to combat unemployment in Canada is widely postulated to have negative externalities on its NAMU partner, the United States (see Carlberg, 1999). This is because, while a fiscal expansion in Canada would raise Canadian domestic income through the usual multiplier effect, the upward pressure that the expansionary fiscal action would place on overall NAMU interest rates would lead to an appreciation of the NAMU dollar and thus to a fall in net exports in both countries. The final outcome of the Canadian fiscal expansion is assumed to be a *relative* rise in Canadian income that would largely be done at the expense of a fall in US income. However, the overall effect on the monetary union would be negative, since it would be associated with higher interest rates (with the usual implications of crowding out investments) in both countries, a higher common currency exchange rate and lower net exports of each member country vis-à-vis the rest of the world. Given this perceived problem of moral hazard pertaining to the behaviour of any member country of a monetary union, strict constitutional rules must be put in place to guarantee fiscal discipline, such as those that have been imposed on the member states of the EMU.

Unfortunately for the member states of the EMU, the imposition of strict rules of fiscal austerity (in accordance with the criteria of the Stability and Growth Pact) has been premised on a highly questionable Mengerian (or neoclassical) theory of money that sees higher interest rates as the unavoidable consequence of a fiscal expansion. If, instead of this questionable neoclassical theoretical framework with its explicit assumption of exogenous money, one were to frame the analysis within the competing Post-Keynesian theory of endogenous money (see Lavoie, 1992; and Rochon, 1999), these negative consequences of an activist fiscal policy cannot be inferred (see Seccareccia and Sharpe, 1994; and Seccareccia and Sood, 2000). On the contrary, within this latter analytical framework, fiscal policy would be a necessary tool to achieve greater economic welfare. As argued by Arestis et al. (2001), the arbitrary 3-per-cent-of-GDP limit on budget deficits seriously impairs the EMU members' ability to absorb macroeconomic shocks and condemns them to rely on the limited monetary policy actions of a highly undemocratic and unrepresentative ECB whose sole responsibility is price stability. Why would the member states of the EMU want to abandon such an important instrument of macroeconomic policy on the basis of a questionable theory of money and to accept as consequence higher long-term rates of unemployment? If the structure of the EMU will lead to increasing problems of unemployment, as predicted, for instance, by Feldstein (1997), how long would national governments last in imposing fiscal austerity domestically? Recently, even some of the strongest supporters of the EMU system (see Fitoussi 2000, p. 20) are beginning to question the current policy mix of the EMU that has (1) given prominence to orthodox monetary policy in favour of price stability, (2) led to the complete abandonment of fiscal policy as a macroeconomic tool, and (3) imparted a deflationary bias on the complete EMU structure.

## CONCLUDING REMARKS

To reply to the question as to whether the Canadian dollar is destined to disappear, it can be said that OCA theory does not offer much of an answer based on its economic/deterministic logic. There are clear political forces at work in Canada, moving in the direction of greater monetary integration with the United States, which has employed Mundellian theory to further its specific political ends. However, as was shown, their arguments have been based on OCA theory that rests on terribly shaky foundations. In addition, the presumed benefits that would accrue to those countries moving in the direction of greater monetary integration are themselves highly uncertain. In particular, we have seen how some of the postulated benefits, in terms of lower transaction costs, increased productivity, lower real interest rates and increased fiscal discipline are neither based on theoretically sound logic nor can they call upon strong empirical support. While the economic arguments are weak, one can never underestimate their capacity to be absorbed by political leaders. Since public opinion is very much conditioned by cataclysmic events, it would probably only take a strong external shock leading to a very sharp drop in the value of the Canadian dollar to move Canadian political opinion inexorably in the direction of greater monetary integration with the United States. Once confidence in a currency is lost, it will be difficult to stop the bandwagon phenomenon from building strength and, so long as it reinforces popular belief, politicians will espouse any argument regardless of its theoretical worth and empirical validity. Hence, depending on the political dynamics, just as in Europe, it is certainly conceivable that the Canadian dollar might disappear. However, as the European experience teaches us, other than for their rhetorical value, it is highly unlikely that OCA arguments based on Mundellian economic/deterministic logic will have any significance in determining such a future outcome.

# REFERENCES

Apel, Emmanuel (1998), *European Monetary Integration, 1958–2002*, London: Routledge.

Arestis, Philip, Kevin McCauley and Malcolm Sawyer (2001), 'The future of the euro: is there an alternative to the stability and growth pact?', *Public Policy Brief No. 63*, Jerome Levy Economics Institute.

Arestis, Philip, and Malcolm Sawyer (1999), 'The deflationary consequences of a single currency', in M. Baimbridge, B. Burkitt, and P. Whyman (eds), *A Single Currency for Europe?*, London: Macmillan, pp. 100–12.

Bayoumi, Tamin and Barry Eichengreen (1994), 'one money or many? analyzing the prospects for monetary unification in various parts of the world', *Princeton Studies in International Finance*, **76** (September).

Bayoumi, Tamin and Barry Eichengreen (1997), 'Ever closer to Heaven? An Optimum-Currency-Area index for European Countries', *European Economic Review, Papers and Proceedings*, **41** (3–5) (April), 761–70.

Bell, Stephanie (2000), 'Common Currency Lessons from Europe: Have Member States Forsaken their Economic Steering Wheels?', Paper Presented at the International Conference on 'The Political Economy of Monetary Integration: Lessons from Europe for Canada', University of Ottawa, Canada (October).

Bénassy-Quéré, Agnès and Amina Lahrèche-Révil (1998), 'Pegging the CEEC's currencies to the euro', Document de travail no. 98-04, Centre d'Études Prospectives et d'Information Internationales, Paris (July).

Bordo, Michael D. and Lars Jonung (1999), 'The future of EMU: what does the history of monetary unions tell us?', NBER Working Paper No. W7365, New York (September).

Buiter, Willem H. (1999), 'The EMU and the NAMU: What is the case for North American monetary union?', discussion paper no. 2181, Centre for Economic Policy Research, London (June).

Carlberg, Michael (1999), *European Monetary Union: Theory, Evidence, and Policy*, New York: Physica-Verlag Heidelberg.

Courchene, Thomas J. (1998), 'Towards a North American Common Currency: An Optimal Currency Analysis', paper presented at the Sixth Bell Canada Papers Conference, Kingston, Ontario (November).

Courchene, Thomas J. and Richard G. Harris (1999), 'From fixing to monetary union: options for North American currency integration', *C.D. Howe Institute Commentary*, **127**, Toronto (June).

Currie, David (1997), *The Pros and Cons of EMU*, London: HM Treasury (July).

Dupuis, David, and David Tessier (2000), 'Une analyse empirique du lien entre la productivité et le taux de change réel Canada–É-U', working paper 2000–22, Bank of Canada (November).

Dyson, Kenneth and Kevin Featherstone (1999), *The Road to Maastricht: Negotiating Economic and Monetary Union*, Oxford: Oxford University Press.

Eichengreen, Barry and Jeffrey Frieden (eds) (1994), *The Political Economy of European Monetary Unification*, Boulder, CO: Westview Press.

Eichengreen, Barry (2000), 'The Euro One Year On', *Journal of Policy Modeling*, **22** (3) (May), 355–68.

Emerson, Michael et al. (1992), *One Market, One Money: An Evaluation of the Potential Benefits and Costs of Forming an Economic and Monetary Union*, Oxford: Oxford University Press.

European Commission (1999), *Frontier-Free Europe* (Monthly Newsletter), Luxembourg: Office of the Official Publications of the European Community (March).

Feldstein, Martin (1997), 'The political economy of the European Economic and Monetary Union: political sources of an economic liability', *Journal of Economic Perspectives*, **11** (4) (Fall), 23–42.

Feldstein, Martin (2000), 'The European Central Bank and the Euro: The First Year', *Journal of Policy Modeling*, 22 (3) (May), 345–54.

Fitoussi, Jean-Paul (2000), *Rapport sur l'état de l'Union européenne 2000*, Paris: Fayard, Presses de Sciences.

Goodhart, Charles (1995), 'The Political Economy of Monetary Union', in Peter B. Kenen (ed.), *Understanding Interdependence: The Macroeconomics of the Open Economy*, Princeton, NJ: Princeton University Press, pp. 450–505.

Goodhart, Charles A.E. (1998), 'The two concepts of money: implications for the analysis of Optimal Currency Areas', *European Journal of Political Economy*, **14**, 407–32.

Grubel, Herbert G. (1999), 'The case for the Amero: The economics and politics of a North American monetary union', *Critical Issues Bulletin*, Vancouver: Fraser Institute (September).

Gruber, Lloyd (1999), 'Interstate Cooperation and the Hidden Face of Power: The Case of European Money', *Harris School Working Paper Series: 99.16*, University of Chicago (September).

Innes, A.M. (1913), 'What Is Money?', *Banking Law Journal*, May, 377–408.

Kenen, Peter B. (1969), 'The theory of Optimum Currency Areas: an eclectic view', in Robert A. Mundell and Alexander K. Swoboda (eds), *Monetary Problems of the International Economy*, Chicago: University of Chicago Press, pp. 41–60.

Laidler, David (1999a), 'The exchange rate regime and Canada's monetary order', *Working Paper 99–7*, Bank of Canada, Ottawa (March).

Laidler, David (1999b), 'What do the fixers want to fix? The Debate about Canada's Exchange Rate Regime', *C.D. Howe Institute Commentary*, Toronto (December).

Lavoie, Marc (1992), *Foundations of Post-Keynesian Economic Analysis*, Aldershot, UK and Brookfield, USA: Edward Elgar.

McCallum, John (1998), 'Drivers of the Canadian Dollar and Policy Implications', *Current Analysis*, Royal Bank of Canada (August).

McCallum, John (1999), 'Seven Issues in the Choice of Exchange Rate Regime in Canada', *Current Analysis*, Royal Bank of Canada (February).

McCallum, John (2000), 'Engaging the debate: costs and benefits of a North American common currency', *Current Analysis*, Royal Bank of Canada (April).

Menger, Carl (1892), 'On the origin of money', *Economic Journal*, **2** (6) (June), 239–55.

McKinnon, Ronald I. (1963), 'Optimum Currency Areas', *American Economic Review*, **53** (4) (September), 717–25.

McKinnon, Ronald I. (2000), 'Mundell, the euro, and the world dollar standard', *Journal of Policy Modeling*, **22** (3) (May), 311–24.

Mosler, Warren (2001), 'Rites of passage', *Mimeograph*, April.

Mosler, Warren and Mathew Forstater (1999), 'A general framework for the analysis of currencies and commodities', in Paul Davidson and Jan Kregel (eds), *Full Employment and Price Stability in a Global Economy*, Cheltenham, UK and Northampton, MA, USA: Edward Elgar, pp. 166–77.

Mundell, Robert A. (1961), 'The Theory of Optimum Currency Areas', *American Economic Review*, **51** (4) (September), 657–65.

Mundell, Robert A. (1997), 'Currency Areas, Common Currencies, and EMU', *American Economic Review, Papers and Proceedings*, **87** (2) (May), 214–16.

Mundell, Robert A. (2000a), 'Currency Areas, Volatility and Intervention', *Journal of Policy Modeling*, **22** (3), (May), 281–99.

Mundell, Robert A. (2000b), 'The Euro Revolution', *National Post*, (13 December).

Mundell, Robert A. (2000c), 'A World Currency?', *National Post*, (16 December).

Parguez, Alain (2000), 'For whom tolls the monetary union: the three lessons of the European Monetary Union', *Mimeograph* , University of Besançon, (January–March).

Parguez, Alain and Mario Seccareccia (2000), 'The credit theory of money: the monetary circuit approach', in John Smithin (ed.), *What is Money?*, London/New York: Routledge, pp. 101–23.

Powell, James (1999), *A History of the Canadian Dollar*, Ottawa: Bank of Canada.

Realfonzo, Riccardo (1998), *Money and Banking, Theory and Debate (1900–1940)*, Cheltenham, UK and Lyme, USA: Edward Elgar.

Rochon, Louis-Philippe (1999), *Credit, Money and Production: An Alternative Post-Keynesian Approach*, Cheltenham, UK and Northampton, MA, USA: Edward Elgar.

Rojas-Suarez, Liliana (2000), 'What exchange rate arrangement works best for Latin America?', *World Economic Affairs*, October.

Salvatore, Dominick (2000), 'Robert Mundell – three brilliant ideas, one nobel', *Journal of Policy Modeling*, **22** (3) (May), 305–309.

Seccareccia, Mario (1998), 'Wicksellian norm, central bank real interest rate targeting and macroeconomic performance', in P. Arestis and M. Sawyer (eds), *The Political Economy of Central Banking*, Cheltenham, UK and Northampton, MA, USA: Edward Elgar, pp. 180–98.

Seccareccia, Mario (1999), 'Money, credit, and finance: history', in Philip A. O'Hara (ed.), *Encyclopedia of Political Economy*, Vol. 2, London/New York: Routledge, pp. 763–6.

Seccareccia, Mario and Marc Lavoie (2001), 'Long-term interest rates, liquidity preference and the limits of central banking', paper presented at a conference on 'The Limits Of Central Banking', West Palm Beach, Florida (March).

Seccareccia, Mario and Andrew Sharpe (1994), 'Canada's Competitiveness: Beyond the Budget Deficit', *Économies et sociétés*, **28** (1/2) (January–February), 275–300.

Seccareccia, Mario and Atul Sood (2000), 'Government Debt Monetization and Inflation: A Somewhat Jaundiced View', in Hassan Bougrine (ed.), *The Economics of Public Spending: Debts, Deficits and Economic Performance*, Cheltenham, UK and Northampton, MA, USA: Edward Elgar, pp. 98–121.

Williamson, John (2000), 'The case for flexibility (in deciding whether to dollarize)', paper presented at a Conference of the North–South Institute on 'To Dollarize or Not to Dollarize: Exchange-Rate Choices for the Western Hemisphere', Ottawa (October).

Willett, Thomas D. (2000), 'Some political economy aspects of EMU', *Journal of Policy Modeling*, **22** (3) (May), 379–89.

Wray, L. Randall (1998), *Understanding Modern Money*, Cheltenham, UK and Lyme, USA: Edward Elgar.

# 7. Float, fix or join? The options for Canadian foreign exchange policy

**Ronald G. Bodkin**

## INTRODUCTION

After accepting this invitation to come speak to you good people on the subject of a choice of a foreign exchange rate regime for Canada, I was suddenly struck with a certain panic. After all, most of you have heard all (or at least most) of the arguments before. I felt a bit like Tommy Manville's tenth wife: I know exactly what is that I am supposed to do. I simply don't know how I am going to make it particularly exciting or even interesting!

At this point, I was hit by a small inspiration. The thought occurred to me that perhaps some humour might alleviate this otherwise very serious subject that has been very much (too much?) in the news recently. I am reminded of the story told by my friend Al Harberger, which I collected during a sabbatical at UCLA in 1989. It seems that two Scotsmen, Ian and Sandy, balloonists, decided to set sail from their native Scotland. As their balloon drifted over the North Sea, following the prevailing easterly winds, fog set in and they couldn't tell where they were. Finally, the fog lifted somewhat and the balloon began a descent towards a park, where, 100 yards below, they spotted two other men walking in the park. Finally, when the balloon came within hailing distance of the men on the ground, Ian decided to chance matters (he had no idea whether the men on the ground spoke English) and called out, 'Hey, you down there! Where are we?'. One of the fellows on the ground began to wave his arms in an excited fashion before crying, 'I know! I know!'. 'All right,' said Ian, 'Where are we?'. The fellow on the ground, obviously a wiseacre, called out, 'You're up in the air in a balloon!'. As if the gods were angry, a sudden fog set in and a sudden up draught removed the balloon far from the hailing distance of the two individuals on the ground. As their balloon drifted away, Ian turned to Sandy and said, 'Sandy, that rascal on the ground must have been an economist!' 'An economist, Ian?', replied Sandy, 'Why do you say that?'. 'For three reasons, Sandy,' Ian replied. 'First, he was so cocksure that he knew the answer. Secondly, he was technically correct; we are up in the air in a balloon. And thirdly and most importantly, now that we have his advice, we're no further ahead than when we started!'

It is hoped that you, the audience, will be somewhat further ahead at the end of this talk, but I do not guarantee it!

Let us begin by defining terms. First, a foreign exchange rate is a price; the price of one country's currency (or that of trading areas, more generally) in terms of another's, (the price of a Canadian dollar in terms of its US counterpart was recently US$ 0.65, or the price of one deutsche mark is [hypothetically] 2½ French francs). A foreign exchange regime is simply a system (strictly speaking, a set of systems) for determining the various foreign exchange rates that economic agents of a particular country will face. For example, if there are 100 foreign currencies in which the agents of a particular economy have financial dealings (trade, investment, or charitable gifts), then 100 foreign exchange rate regimes will be required. Most, if not all, of these foreign exchange rate regimes will be linked together, for example by cross-rates.

Let us now consider, in broad outline, the possible foreign exchange rate regimes that Canada might consider, bearing in mind that the link with the US dollar is the important one as over 80 per cent of our trade and investment links are with the great southern neighbour. A floating rate regime is one in which the market decides (at least in principle) the value of the domestic currency in terms of foreign currencies, and thus the relevant government has no goal (at least no explicit goal) for the international value of the home currency. By contrast, a fixed rate regime is one in which the value of the home currency is locked to the value of at least one external currency or money, by government policy (of course, the 'link' currency might itself float against other external currencies). Finally, a third possibility is that one country (such as Canada) might decide to use another country's currency (such as the US dollar), either unilaterally or as a result of negotiation. In the case of the euro and the European monetary union, the decision to form a monetary union was the result of protracted negotiations. However, in North America (or the Americas generally), 'dollarization' could very well be a unilateral decision; no negotiation with the United States need take place, as it is clearly to the US's advantage to serve as banker to the international community and so capture the associated rents. (The cases of Ecuador or Panama come to mind.) We shall refer to this as the 'join' option.

## FURTHER DISCUSSION OF THE 'FLOAT' REGIME

Recall the definition of a 'floating' regime as one in which the government has no (explicit) goal for the foreign exchange value of the domestic currency. Now in fact we might distinguish between two types of floating regimes: one in which the government absolutely forswears any intervention in the foreign exchange markets of the world and the other in which the authorities may intervene from time to time, if they judge such intervention in the social interest. In the first type of regime, termed a 'pure' floating rate, the monetary authority may not even hold any gold or other foreign exchange reserves, as the pertinent foreign exchange markets are 'turned loose' to do their work. In the second type of regime, which is called a 'managed' or a 'dirty' float (depending upon one's enthusiasm for such a system), the authorities do indeed intervene from time to time to influence the value of the domestic money in the world's foreign exchange markets. Usually such an intervention is undertaken to counteract the effects of speculation that are considered to be destabilizing. Of course, this implies that the foreign exchange authority believes that destabilizing speculation not only exists but is in fact operating in the case under consideration.

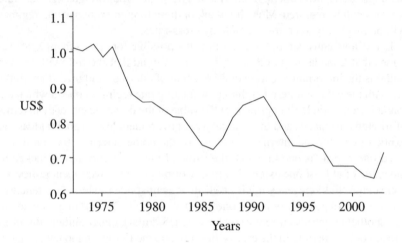

*Source*: Laidler, 1999

*Figure 7.1   US dollar price of one Canadian dollar*

How has the floating regime worked in Canada during the past 30 years? As Figure 7.1 shows, the trend of the Canadian dollar has unquestionably been in the downward direction over this period; only the period of the Crow inflation-fighting period in the late 1980s and very early 1990s, when long-term interest rates rose roughly 400 basis points above their US counterparts, represent a temporary exception to this generalization. Indeed, in the early months of 2001, the US value of a Canadian dollar reached an all-time low of US$ 0.639, well below levels that could be justified on purchasing power parities alone.

In turn, this reminds me of a story that Professor Peter Kenen, the then current President of the Eastern Economic Association, told about himself in his presidential address in New York City February 2000. When Professor Kenen was a graduate student at Harvard, it appears that he decided to sit for a general mathematics examination in lieu of a second foreign language as a doctoral degree requirement, even though he did not consider mathematics one of his major strengths. (Presumably, he made this choice because a second language would have been either a more difficult or else a more time-consuming hurdle.) In any case, the big day came and went, and shortly thereafter the list of successful examinees for the mathematics exam was posted. With some trepidation, future Professor Kenen consulted the list and with delight he noted that his name appeared among those of the successful candidates. 'I passed; I passed!' he cried as he virtually skipped down the hall. But his bubble was duly pricked by the redoubtable Professor Robert Dorfman, who intercepted him to growl, 'You didn't pass, Kenen. We passed you!'

All I should say about this tale is that, in my view, we don't have a floating dollar; we have a sinking dollar! Moreover, as a rational economic agent, I intend to put the bulk of my financial portfolio in US-dollar-denominated securities, at least where tax penalties are not too great, because I fully expect this trend to continue for the rest of my life.

Furthermore, I should suggest that this matters because there is a bit of money illusion among most economic agents, perhaps even professional economists. Two examples which follow will have to suffice.

First, in Canada, we have a two-dollar coin called informally 'the toonie' (similarly to the one-dollar coin which has been nicknamed the 'loony'). However, when the value of the Canadian dollar touched US$ 0.639, the value of this coin in US money was little more than a dollar bill and an American quarter. At the time, some wags in Canada suggested renaming the toonie 'the Georgie' (after US President George Washington, whose portrait appears on the US one-dollar bill).

The second example is closer to home. At my home university, the University of Ottawa, the standard ceiling salary for a full professor is currently $112 500 annually (Canadian, of course). This is a large enough salary that it is published in the local newspapers and is considered to be an 'upper income'. Translating at official exchange rates (say one Canadian dollar is equal to US$ 0.65), this salary is equivalent, in US dollars, to roughly, $73 125. But, according to a recent issue of *The San Francisco Chronicle*, the salary of a newly minted fresh PhD in economics with strong recommendations from a top US graduate school could reach $70 000 annually, which is only slightly less than the University of Ottawa's ceiling salary.

## FURTHER DISCUSSION OF THE 'FIX' REGIME

Perhaps the prototype of a fixed rate regime is the old gold standard of the nineteenth and early twentieth centuries, where each country (or trading area) defined its monetary unit in terms of a gold content. Thus both the US and the Canadian dollars were defined as 23.22 grains of fine gold, which works out to US/Canadian $20.67 per ounce, as an ounce contains 480 grains. Every other country (at least those in the system) would have a similar definition of their monetary system, and so gold parity rates among currencies could easily be established. (Example: the British pound sterling was defined as 113.002 grains of fine gold, which gives a gold parity exchange rate of one pound sterling as the equivalent of US/Canadian $4.867.) Moreover, market exchange rates could not deviate far from the gold parity values, or else it would pay some economic agent to take gold in the undervalued currency area and ship it to where the currency was overvalued. This was the case because free convertibility and international movements of gold were part of the rules of the 'gold standard game'. In principle, it was a marvellous system; there was no need for government intervention to keep the system running, as Hume's price-specie-flow mechanism supposedly would keep the accounts balanced in the long term and in any case gold flows were assumed to have their principal effects on the level of prices, and not on the amount of aggregate economic activity. It had the great virtue that all money was effectively international money (after brokerage fees, of course).

In practice, the system did not function nearly as smoothly as the theory predicted. Already, in 1924 Jacob Viner noticed that the balance of payments moved into equilibrium much more rapidly than the classical price-specie-flow mechanism would have predicted. Of course, in the Great Depression of the 1930s, it became abundantly clear that employment effects were pronounced if not predominant. Gold-losing countries might well correct their balance of payments problems, but only at the cost of a major recession or depression. As Joan Robinson once commented, 'The invisible hand will always work, but it may work by strangulation'. The gold standard was doomed when it was observed that countries recovered from the Great Depression more or less in proportion to the date at which they left this system. Even in prosperous times, however, it seemed to some inappropriate to leave the total supply of the world's money to the vagaries of gold discoveries, such as those in Alaska in the 1890s.

After the Second World War, another system of fixed rates was established, and this system lasted until 1971 or 1973. This was the Bretton Woods system, where the major trading currencies were effectively fixed to the US dollar (it was nominally a gold exchange system among central banks, but the US dollar was the major international currency). It is to be recalled that this system could also be described as an 'adjustable peg'; devaluation (or, much more rarely, a currency appreciation) was permitted to remove 'fundamental disequilibrium'. As time passed, many thought that the system had a number of defects: it was a speculators' heaven (often at the expense of the public purse), it threw the burden of adjustment almost entirely on the deficit countries, and some (the

French in particular) thought that it gave too much advantage to the USA as the world's banker. Still, in retrospect, as Davidson (1997) and others have pointed out, the system was not so bad; the world economy in general was much more prosperous in the quarter-century between the end of the Second World War and the break-down of the Bretton Woods system than it has been since.

We are not through discussing fixed rates; a country can simply decide unilaterally that it will fix the rate of exchange to that of another country, usually its major trading partner. Then, provided the monetary authority has the international reserves to enforce its decision, such a regime can become viable. Thus, after a period of relatively free floating, Canada fixed the value of its dollar to that of the United States, at a rate of US$ 0.925 per Canadian dollar, during the period 1962–70. Two other examples are those of the Dutch guilder and of the Austrian schilling, both of which were fixed to the deutsche mark for most of the period between the break-down of Bretton Woods and the advent of the euro. In turn, this made perfect sense to the monetary authorities in these two countries, as Germany (the Federal Republic) was the major trading partner of both of these smaller economies, and the German mark was a relatively stable (low-inflation) currency.

Another possibility for a fixed rate is that of a currency board, which system requires a country to 'back' its currency with reserves of the currency of the country to which the domestic currency is fixed. Thus we have the example of Argentina, which has defined since 1991 the international exchange value of its peso as one US dollar. The system did stop endemic inflation dead in its tracks, and growth in Argentina between 1991 and 1998 was impressive. However, the system appears to have stagnated since then, and unemployment rates have been quite high (between 15 and 18 per cent of the labour force), with little prospect for an immediate turn-around. On the financial side, the charges for converting dollars to pesos or vice versa are impressively low – when I travelled to Argentina in 1998, a local bank charged me 0.23 per cent (roughly a quarter of one per cent) to convert my reimbursement in pesos to US dollars. (Compare that to spreads of 1 to 2 per cent that I routinely pay at the bank to convert to US dollars or back again to Canadian funds; as an economic agent, I *hate* floating rates.) On the other hand, in Argentina today, there is a huge spread (between 400 and 1200 basis points) between long-term interest rates for loans denominated in pesos and those denominated in dollars, which shows that many portfolio managers and other economic agents doubt the long-term sustainability of this system.

This last point suggests that fixed rate exchange rate systems may often be subject to financial instability, a point to be developed below.

## THE STRATEGY OF 'JOIN' AS AN EXCHANGE RATE REGIME

Of course one can avoid the problems of having an independent currency, Monaco has for years used the French franc, San Marino has adopted the Italian lira, and Panama has used the US dollar. It may even be noted that the Bélanger–Campeau Commission of 1991 proposed that an independent Quebec continue to use the Canadian dollar (see Bernard Fortin, 1991). All of these cases concern unilateral 'dollarization,' where the currency of the larger trading partner is adopted without compensation or special consideration from this major partner.

Another possibility involves sharing monetary sovereignty rather than surrendering it, as is presumably the case with the new European currency, the euro. Herb Grubel (1999) has recently proposed that Canada, the USA and Mexico enter into a monetary termed union, with the new currency to be termed the 'amero'. (Surprise: one amero would initially equal one US dollar.) In this way, Canadians and Mexicans could share some (small) portion of the seigniorage associated with the issue of new money and should not have to invest heavily in paper assets, i.e. US dollars. In turn, this reminds me of another story. Young Willy had been courting young Susie for a number of months and had never given any sign physically that he was interested in a romantic relationship. One day, excited as he ever got, he seized Susie's hand and enthused, 'Susie, let's get married!'. Susie looked at her usually phlegmatic beau, sighed, and said, 'Fine, Willie, but who will have us?' In particular, would the Americans have Canada in a monetary union? Robert Barro assures us that they would, but the price for their banking services may be more than Mexicans and Canadians would be willing to pay.

In any case, many have been tempted by the ideal of having a world currency and (nearly) full employment simultaneously, in other words, the advantages of the gold standard without the pains. Keynes wanted to make the IMF a real central bank and proposed the name of 'bancor' as the international monetary unit that would serve as the reserve currency in his schema. More than half a century later, Paul Davidson (1997) has proposed reviving Keynes's scheme for a world currency; he terms the international reserves (which would only circulate among central banks) IMCUs (for 'international monetary clearing units'). Incidentally, Davidson appears to be proposing that countries maintain fixed *real* exchange rates; to do this he is quite willing to limit capital mobility. Indeed, the title of his article, 'Are grains of sand in the wheels of international finance sufficient to do the job when boulders are often required?', suggests his critique of the Tobin Tax as an instrument insufficient for the purpose of ending destabilizing speculation in foreign exchange markets. Finally, mention may be made of the many writings of Ronald I. McKinnon (see McKinnon, 1993) on the subject. McKinnon appears to be arguing that, if the USA, Japan and Europe can agree on a rate of inflation, then it should be relatively easy to stabilize the exchange rates among these currency blocs. Many writers (not just Davidson) would consider this highly optimistic.

One cannot leave this section without a mention of the political considerations in deciding to merge one's currency with that of the major trading partner; these political considerations can be enormous. Indeed, some pan-Europeanists are hoping that the euro will be the first step towards a political union, a United States of Europe. (Indeed, some of its opponents oppose it for just the same reason.)

I might close this section by relating an encounter that I had when I first came to Canada in 1965 with the late John Deutsch, then the first Chairman of the Economic Council of Canada and later Principal of Queen's University. Deutsch had been a member of the Canadian delegation to Bretton Woods and had observed Keynes and Harry Dexter White, the chief American negotiator, in action. Keynes and White, the chief architects of what was to become the Bretton Woods system, had quite different ideas on how that system should be shaped, with Keynes wanting a much more international system, with a real world bank. According to Deutsch, Keynes was a brilliant man but White had the political power and was of course savvy enough to know it. 'Now tell me, Ron,' he quizzed this young political neophyte, 'In a conflict like that, who will win?'. After a moment's reflection, I replied, 'The man with the power, provided that he doesn't get flustered and allow himself to be talked out of his position.' 'Right, right,' Dr. Deutsch replied excitedly, 'And Harry Dexter White was one cool customer. Time after time, he would shoot down an idea of Keynes saying, "That's a brilliant idea, Lord Keynes, but I could never get it through my congress!"' In other words, politics often trumps mere economic arguments.

## ADVANTAGES AND DISADVANTAGES OF A FLOATING RATE REGIME

Let us begin this discussion by observing that David Laidler, of the University of Western Ontario, is an ardent defender of the current floating rate regime (Laidler, 1999). Laidler argues that the floating rate regime is the only one which is consistent with inflation targeting, which is the present monetary policy framework of the Bank of Canada. I think that this point is essentially correct and in fact goes back to Tinbergen and his analysis of instruments and targets. If we consider that monetary policy is essentially only one instrument (short-term interest rates), then one must choose only one objective to target. In particular, if one fixes a range for the rate of inflation (currently, an interval between 1 and 3 per cent annually), then one simply cannot fix the rate of foreign exchange as well. Of course, this assumes that inflation targeting is the best that one can do with monetary policy, which is surely a controversial proposition.

The second great advantage of the current regime is its presumed contribution to macroeconomic stability. There are many studies from the Bank of Canada (e.g. Daw et al. (2000) and Murray et al. (2000)) which purport to show that the structure of the Canadian economy is quite different from that of the United States, and so a common monetary policy for the two countries would be sub-optimal. This seems particularly relevant when one considers that free mobility of labour across the Canadian-US border does not exist; suboptimal monetary policy (from the Canadian viewpoint) could imply very high rates of unemploy-ment for the Canadian economy, perhaps even as high as are found in the Maritime provinces today.

We should probably also list two other advantages of a floating rate regime. First, the retention of one's own currency is a source of pride to many Canadians, but it is hard to put a dollar figure on what this may be worth. Second, the pres-ence of one's own currency to finance transactions is a source of social capital and as such generates seigniorage to the public authorities. If Canada has roughly $40 billions in high-powered money and if the social rate of return on capital is 10 per cent, then the estimated seigniorage would be roughly $4 bil-lions annually.

Now for the disadvantages of a floating dollar, which could also be consider-able. Immediately, there are the microeconomic costs of transactions; every international transaction involves someone in changing currencies, and this in-volves real resource costs. Of course, most of the fees paid to convert Canadian to US dollars and vice versa are economic rents to the moneychangers, but there are real resource costs entailed in these transactions. A few years ago I estimated such resource costs as roughly ¾ to 1 per cent of GDP, which today would entail transaction costs (in terms of foregone output and not just transfers to brokers) equal to $7–9 billions (Canadian) annually. Of course, when spreads on the buying and selling rates on the US dollar at Canadian banks are as large as 4 per cent, many will have no trouble believing that the real costs are so high. In any case, as both the Toronto–Dominion Bank study and the Governor of the Bank of Canada admitted recently, such costs are growing over time.

Perhaps the major cost of such a regime is one pointed up by Thomas J. Courchene (1998, 2001). It is possible that Canada's floating dollar with its long-run tendency to decline in terms of real purchasing power has served as a shield from competitive pressures. Thus, in the short run, the low dollar has served as a stimulus to exports, but it may have removed competitive pressures from Canadian businesses, thus allowing them to innovate less rapidly than American competitors. In turn, this could well explain lower productivity growth in Canada for some time (at least for the past decade), which in turn implies lower living standards for Canadians. In this regard, a diagram that Courchene

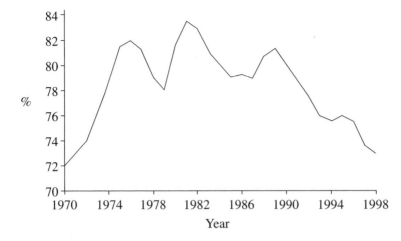

*Source*: Fortin, 1999 as reproduced by Courchene, 2001

*Figure 7.2*   *Purchasing power of total real national income per adult, Canada as a percentage of the USA (1970–88)*

(2001, p. 209) reproduces from Fortin (1999), and which in turn is reproduced here, is instructive. Note that real income per adult in Canada as a percentage of the equivalent measure in the United States has certainly been falling since the late 1980s and probably since the early 1980s. Could the floating exchange regime be partly to blame? Courchene and others certainly think so, and I find it difficult to reject their argument out of hand, given the money illusion in the system which affects most of us.

## ADVANTAGES AND DISADVANTAGES OF A FIXED RATE REGIME

In a sense, the advantages and disadvantages of a fixed rate regime are the mirror image of the floating rate regime, which have just been discussed. Of course, pride in one's own currency and gains from seigniorage still remain; the first disappears only with monetary union, which (if negotiated) may still permit some or all of the gains of seigniorage.

In principle, the big gains from a fixed rate come from reduced transactions costs, as an enormous source of short-run uncertainty is removed, and also from faster productivity growth, if Courchene (and others) are correct. (This could occur if many Canadian entrepreneurs are satisficers and will only innovate when forced to by competitive pressures, such as those that occur when there is no longer protection from foreign competition because of an undervalued exchange rate.) The much larger brokerage charges on foreign exchange in a system of floating rates (already alluded to above) are surely indicative of greater resource costs in converting currencies in such a regime, even if some of these additional costs to the clients are simply monopoly rents to the dealers.

The disadvantages of a system of fixed exchange rates (already mentioned above) are so well known that there is little point in discussing them in detail. Finding and maintaining an equilibrium exchange rate, especially one consistent with reasonably full employment and a tolerable absence of inflationary pressures, is an enormous headache for stabilization policy. In particular, on the Tinbergen criterion it cannot be done, as explained above. Now fiscal policy may add another instrument, but if we consider that both employment and price levels are targets, we are back to our position of being under-endowed in instruments. In particular, it often appears to be the case that the only way to defend a given fixed rate is to bleed the economy with excessive unemployment.

And this in turn suggests another great weakness of fixed exchange rates – their vulnerability to speculative attacks, so that when disruption finally comes, it is quite pronounced. The second half of the decade of the 1990s is replete with foreign exchange crises across the world that greatly harmed the international economy. In addition, successful speculative attacks entail huge profits for the speculators, at the expense of the public treasury. In consequence, many feel that fixed rates subject to periodic review (such as the Bretton Woods system or a 'crawling peg', which is allowed to vary within bands) are an unstable system that cannot be maintained indefinitely. As Stanley Fischer (2001) expressed the matter, floating rates can be sustained and hard pegs (such as currency boards or dollarization) can be sustained, but he is very suspicious of unanchored soft pegs. So perhaps it is not worth considering this option any further. Certainly, Canada's experience with the 'Diefenbuck' (the Canadian dollar pegged at US$ 0.925 over the period 1962–70) would not encourage one to adopt this system; speculative pressures (toward an appreciation) forced an abandonment of the system in mid-1970. (It is just as bad to accumulate barren foreign exchange reserves indefinitely as it is to run out of them!)

But if the Bretton Woods system was so bad, why was world economic performance from 1946 through 1971 or 1973 so much better than, in general, it has been since, as Davidson (1997) and others have pointed out? There are two answers to this question. First, it appears that a world of fixed exchange rates (even just fixed in the short run) can function only with much less international capital mobility than exists (and than powerful actors want to exist) today. The exploitation of growth opportunities immediately after the Second World War may not have required much international capital movement and, in any case, limited capital mobility may have permitted the maintenance of a much higher level of aggregate demand, on average. Second, the history of the Bretton Woods period is a history of periodic exchange rate crises, with some currency almost always targeted for change (usually, for a depreciation, because zero net reserves appears to possess such finality). My conclusion is that unless one is willing to discuss Professor Davidson's 'boulders' (Davidson, 1997), there is a limited future for this sort of foreign exchange rate regime.

## THE ADVANTAGES AND DISADVANTAGES OF THE 'JOIN' OPTION

Transnational currency unions as a solution to foreign exchange problems and shortcomings have existed for some time, but the method has recently become quite fashionable, perhaps as a result of the establishment of the European currency union and a common currency, the euro. The intellectual influence of Robert A. Mundell and the notion of 'optimal currency areas' should also not be discounted. As noted above, the 'join' option can include either straight 'dollarization' (unilateral adoption of another's currency) or a negotiated monetary union (in general, preferable if one has the political clout to negotiate such an arrangement).

What are the advantages and disadvantages of such a drastic change in institutional arrangements? In a sense, these are the opposite side of the coin of the advantages and disadvantages of competing foreign exchange regimes that we have already discussed, so that we may go over these briefly. First, the real resource costs of foreign exchange transactions to Canadian agents have been estimated at $7–9 billions (Canadian) annually, and all these would be saved by a common North American dollar. Even more importantly, if Canadian businesses started behaving more like American ones (achieving American productivity growth rates), then the relative slide in the Canadian standard of living would be arrested.

A story may illustrate this point. Back in 1988, when the Canadian–US free-trade agreement was being considered, Alain Parguez came to me and said, 'Ron, I hear that if free trade between Canada and the United States goes ahead, the Niagara wine industry will be completely ruined. [Pregnant pause for effect followed.] I can't think of a stronger argument for the proposed free trade agreement!'. However, an interesting development occurred. Far from being driven to the wall by its inferior product, the wine-growers of the Niagara peninsula improved their product, both by using better grapes and better technology, so that their product became competitive internationally. Moreover, they innovated and developed new products like ice-wines.

Two final advantages for Canada of a currency union with the United States should be mentioned. First, as Professor Barro has argued (Barro, 2001), currency unions tend to expand trade, and expanded trade fosters specialization, the division of labour and increased productivity. (This may be simply another aspect of the above argument.) A final advantage of the 'join' option is that, unlike a soft peg (like the Diefenbuck), one need never fear speculation against a separate, fixed Canadian dollar. After all, with a monetary union, the Canadian dollar would become indistinguishable from the New England dollar, the California dollar, the Michigan dollar, and so on.

What about the disadvantages? First, there would be transition costs; converting account books, price lists and labels, and organized securities exchanges to (effectively) US dollars would be a substantial exercise, just as the conversion of Canadian weights and measures to metric in the 1970s was. A second major cost would be the loss of an independent monetary policy; as noted above, the Bank of Canada has argued that such a loss would have very serious consequences for the Canadian economy, given the quite different structures of the US and Canadian economies. (Presumably these costs could be reduced by also negotiating free or nearly free labour mobility across the Canadian–US border, although such an agreement would move the two countries closer to political union.)

Two other disadvantages of a monetary union might be mentioned. First, if there is no negotiated agreement on a currency union with the United States, Canada would have to obtain its US dollars just as it obtains every other foreign investment, namely through purchase on the open market. This of course entails the outlays of real resources for what is currently obtained 'for free'. In particular, there would be a loss of seigniorage on high-powered money currently enjoyed by the Bank of Canada (and thus, from the transfer of its profits to general government revenues, by all Canadians). As indicated above, the loss of this seigniorage might be as high as $4 billions (Canadian) annually, although some of it could probably be recaptured as a result of a negotiated currency union. Professor Barro assures us (Barro, 2001) that the Americans would be willing to negotiate on this point; however, they will wish to be paid something for their brokerage services, so that it is unlikely that Canadians will be able to recapture all of this seigniorage. And one final disadvantage of a currency union, negotiated or not, may loom huge. If Canadians are emotionally attached to their multi-coloured money with its national symbols, the loss of one's own currency may be very difficult to compensate. Some Canadians may no doubt feel that, like the patriarch Issac's son Esau, they have sold their birth-right for a mess of potage. Others may fear that this will be the first step toward political union. One may recall Alain Parguez's advice never to join a monetary union unless a political union is in the offing.

We may close this section by observing that it may take many years to make a monetary union a success or even functional. Hugh Rockoff's fascinating account (2000) of the American monetary union suggests that it took a long time (perhaps a century and a half) for the United States to become a 'real world' approximation to the theoretical concept of an optimal currency area. In turn, this suggests that the gains from joining a currency union with the United States would be far from instantaneous and would emerge only gradually over time.

## CONCLUSIONS

The present system of foreign exchange rate regimes is not probably ideal. Indeed, Rudi Dornbusch (2000) presented a paper at a New Orleans meeting of the American Economic Association entitled, 'Fewer monies, better monies.' It should be possible to do better. But how?

Should we go for a cleaned-up Bretton Woods system, currency blocs, or dollarization (either formal or informal)? In considering major changes in the policy regime in Canada, I should remind you of what I like to call Bodkin's Rule of Economic Policy in Canada, to wit: it is almost impossible to better US macroeconomic performance, but it is very easy to do worse (perhaps a lot worse). This should give one pause when considering major changes.

Three other points remain to be stated. First, the issue of money, Professor Barro (2001) notwithstanding, is a major emotional issue. Even if the benefit–cost calculations to the surrender of currency sovereignty were all positive and of a large magnitude, this could not demonstrate conclusively that this step should be taken. In a sense, economic considerations have to bow to political factors in this context. An appropriate analogy may be that of a young person considering leaving home and setting up his/her own residence. There is little doubt that economic factors favour continuing to live with the birth family, but other considerations (maturation, independence, and so on) would surely favour setting up one's own household.

Next, it may be remarked that the choice of a foreign exchange rate regime entails considerable conflicts within a society.[1] I have the feeling that I should be better off (as a soon-to-be-retired university professor and incipient capitalist) with a common North American dollar, but my guess is that the majority of my fellow citizens are better off with the present regime. Of course, the owners of Canada's NHL hockey teams may well feel strongly on my side of the argument!

Finally, different exchange rate regimes are certainly warranted for different countries. The Swiss, for example, have no intention of joining the euro, for a variety of reasons. And who is to say that they're wrong? They (unlike the Canadians) have certainly made a success of a floating exchange rate!

## NOTE

1.  This point is dramatically illustrated by Beine and Coulombe (2003), who show that monetary union with the USA will presumably have, following the optimal currency area (OCA) theory, benefits for Ontario and Quebec (and possibly British Columbia), while the current regime has net benefits for the rest of Canada. A clearer conflict of interest would be difficult to find.

## REFERENCES

Barro, R. (2001), 'Currency Unions,' address given at Kalamazoo College, Michigan, USA, 11 May.

Beine, M. and S. Coulombe (2003), 'Regional perspectives on dollarization in Canada', *Journal of Regional Science*, **43** (3), 541–69.

Courchene, T. (1998), 'Towards a North American common currency: an optimal currency area analysis,' paper presented at a conference at Queen's University, Canada, November.

Courchene, T. (2001), *A State of Minds: Toward a Human Capital Future for Canadians*, Montreal: Institute for Research on Public Policy.

Davidson, P. (1997), 'Are grains of sand in the wheels of international finance sufficient to do the job when boulders are often required?' *Economic Journal*, **107** (442) (May), 671–86.

Daw, J., J. Murray, P. St-Amant and L. Schembri (2000), 'Revisiting the case for flexible exchange rates in North America,' mimeographed paper, Bank of Canada, February.

Dornbusch, R. (2000), 'Fewer monies, better monies,' mimeographed paper presented at the January 2001 meeting of the American Economic Association, December.

Fischer, S. (2001), 'Exchange Rate Regimes: Is the Bipolar View Correct?' Distinguished Lecture on Economics in Government, *Journal of Economic Perspectives*, **15** (2) (Spring), 3–24.

Fortin, B. (1991), 'Les Options monétaires d'un Québec souverain,' [The monetary options of an independent Quebec], text submitted to the Bélanger–Campeau Commission.

Fortin, P. (1999), *The Canadian Standard of Living: Is There a Way Up?*, C.D. Howe Benefactors' Lecture, Toronto: Howe Institute.

Grubel, H. (1999), *The Case for the Amero: Economics and Politics of a North American Monetary Union*, Vancouver and Toronto: Fraser Institute.

Laidler, D. (1999), 'What Economists Know about Canada's Regime,' mimeographed, Political Economy Workshop, Western Ontario (London, Ontario), September.

McKinnon, R. (1993), 'The Rules of the Game: International Money, in Historical Perspective,' *Journal of Economic Literature*, **31** (1) (March), 1–44.

Murray, J., M. Zelmer and Z. Antia (2000), 'International financial crises and flexible exchange rates: some policy lessons from Canada,' Bank of Canada Technical Report no. 88, April.

Rockoff, H. (2000), 'How long did it take the United States to become an Optimal Currency Area?' Historical Paper 124, NBER Working Paper Series on Historical Factors in Long Run Growth, National Bureau of Economic Research, Cambridge, MA.

Viner, J. (1924), *Canada's Balance of International Indebtedness: 1900–1913: An Inductive Study in the Theory of International Trade*, Cambridge, MA: Harvard University Press.

PART 3


Emerging markets and the financial architecture

# 8.    Can emerging markets float? Should they target inflation?

**Barry Eichengreen**[1]

## INTRODUCTION

The hot debate over the best monetary-cum-exchange-rate regime for developing countries shows no signs of cooling down. The Asian crisis and its fallout in Latin America and Eastern Europe convinced many observers that soft currency pegs are crisis prone and that emerging markets should embrace greater exchange rate flexibility. The Turkish crisis reinforced that view. But worries that greater flexibility will impede market access, hinder financial development, and undermine rather than underpin financial stability have led others to advocate moving in the opposite direction – that is, hardening the peg by installing a currency board or dollarizing.[2] While there are prominent examples of countries that have moved both ways – Ecuador and El Salvador have dollarized while Brazil has embraced greater flexibility – many developing countries continue to occupy the middle ground in the sense of making extensive use of their reserves so as to limit the variability of their exchange rates.[3]

The one thing all these regimes have in common is that none is an entirely comfortable solution to the monetary dilemma. Flexible rates tend to fluctuate erratically, especially if abandonment of a peg leaves a country without a nominal anchor, a clear and coherent monetary policy operating strategy or credibility in the eyes of the markets. Unilateral dollarization limits policy flexibility, gives the country resorting to it no voice in the monetary policy it runs and sacrifices seigniorage revenues. And ad-hoc intervention to limit the variability of the exchange rate in the absence of a credible commitment to a transparent, coherent and defensible monetary strategy is unlikely to inspire confidence; attempting to prevent the exchange rate from moving beyond set limits under these circumstances can render the central bank and its reserves sitting ducks for speculators. That none of these options is particularly appetizing is, if course, the dilemma of a world in which markets are international but governments are national. It is why some authors (such as Mundell, 1997, Cooper, 1999) see a global currency and a global central bank as logical consequences of the globalization of markets.

Notwithstanding this vision for the future, countries opening their economies to international capital flows will be forced for the present to choose from this limited menu of hard pegs (currency boards, dollarization), implicit target zones (de jure floating but de facto intervention to limit the variability of the exchange rate), and greater flexibility.[4] Other authors have made the case for the first two options, what can be called hard and soft or loud and quiet pegs.[5] In this chapter I consider the viability of the third.

Calling for emerging markets to abandon the exchange rate as an anchor for policy compels those issuing the call to offer an alternative.[6] The leading candidate is inflation targeting.[7] The task I take on in this chapter is to assess whether inflation targeting offers a viable, and even attractive, alternative to an exchange-rate based monetary policy regime.

There has been some analysis of inflation targeting in emerging markets, most of it recent (the pioneering work is Masson et al. 1997; see also Eichengreen et al. 1999; Christoffersen and Wescott 1999; Mishkin, 2000; Mishkin and Savastano, 2000; Bogdanski et al. 2000; Devereux and Lane, 2000; Jonas, 2000; Morande, 2000; and Schaechter et al. 2000). But none of these studies has considered the entire range of issues. And most have failed to distinguish between open-economy and developing-country aspects of inflation targeting.

I organize my discussion as follows. Section 2 defines inflation targeting and reviews some conceptual issues relating to its implementation. (Readers familiar with the literature on inflation targeting may want to skip or skim this material.) Section 3 then asks what is distinctive about inflation targeting in open economies. Issues that arise under this heading include susceptibility to external shocks and the sensitivity of output and inflation to the exchange rate. Section 4 then asks what is distinctive about inflation targeting in emerging markets. Topics under this heading include passthrough, the difficulty of forecasting inflation, liability dollarization and credibility issues.

The conclusion then returns to the question of whether inflation targeting is a viable option for emerging markets.

## GENERAL CONSIDERATIONS[8]

I define inflation targeting as a monetary policy operating strategy with four elements: an institutionalized commitment to price stability as the primary goal of monetary policy; mechanisms rendering the central bank accountable for attaining its monetary policy goals; the public announcement of targets for inflation; and a policy of communicating to the public and the markets the rationale for the decisions taken by the central bank.[9] Institutionalizing the commitment to price stability lends credibility to the pursuit of that objective and gives the central bank the independence needed to attain it. Mechanisms for accountability make this pursuit politically acceptable and impose costs on central banks that are incompetent or behave opportunistically. Announcing a target for inflation and articulating the basis for the central bank's decisions allow these mechanisms to operate.

The multi-dimensional nature of this definition explains why there is no consensus about which emerging markets are inflation targeters. Brazil, Chile, the Czech Republic, Israel, South Africa, Poland, Colombia, Thailand, Mexico, the Philippines and South Korea are all cited in this connection.[10] But while all of these countries have announced numerical targets for inflation, not all of them have put in place the other elements of inflation targeting as defined above. At the time of writing, most observers would probably draw the line between the first and last six countries, classifying only the former as full-fledged inflation targeters.

One can further distinguish strict inflation targeting from flexible inflation targeting. Strict inflation targeting is when only inflation enters the central bank's objective function, flexible inflation targeting when there is also a positive weight on other variables, output for example (Svensson, 1999). (Even with strict inflation targeting there is still a positive weight on output in the monetary policy reaction function insofar as the information content of the output gap is useful for forecasting inflation.[11]) Since few central banks and polities are prepared to disregard all other variables under all circumstances, flexible inflation targeting is the policy-relevant case.[12]

This has a number of implications. Most obviously, whereas a central bank that targets inflation strictly will attempt to hit that target as quickly as possible under all circumstances (where the feasible speed depends on the control lag from its policy instruments to inflation), a central bank that pursues flexible inflation targeting will more gradually push inflation toward its target. It will balance the benefits of minimizing the variability of inflation against the costs of creating additional variability in the other variables that enter its objective function.

So defined, inflation targeting is a target rule, where policy is formulated to hit an appropriately weighted set of ex ante specified policy objectives. The question is how to move from a target rule to an instrument rule – that is, settings for the policy instrument or instruments as a function of the information currently available to policy makers.[13] This is not straightforward in a complex economy.[14] Three imperfect solutions are to fly by the seat of the central bank's pants, inflation-forecast targeting, and the Taylor rule. I consider these alternatives in turn.

Seat-of-the-pants inflation targeting (using everything from in-house econometric models to central bankers' intuition to guide the setting of policy instruments) is what many central banks do – some, it would appear, with considerable success. But it is unlikely to be efficient insofar as it is not systematized.

And to the extent that the rationale for the central bank's decision cannot be fully articulated and defended, it will lack credibility.[15]

Targeting the central bank's inflation forecast (conditional on the information available at the time of the forecast) is an example of an intermediate targeting rule that specifies a vector of intermediate targets that are correlated with the ultimate policy goal but easier to control and observe than the ultimate goal (Svensson 1999). Inflation forecast targeting should be more efficient than formulating policy on the basis of an ad-hoc reaction function insofar as the policy instruments respond to all the information that is relevant to the forecast. It will have more credibility than the alternatives if the central bank has a track record of accurate forecasting.[16]

That seat-of-the-pants inflation targeting is arbitrary and that inflation-forecast targeting is no more reliable than the forecast have motivated a search for simple rules. The Taylor rule is the leading example. Taylor (1993) specifies a reaction function for a closed economy with positive weights on deviations from target inflation and from the natural rate of unemployment that closely tracks the actual policies followed by many central banks pursuing policies of low inflation. Contributors to the closed-economy literature have shown how a Taylor rule can be derived as the optimal reaction function for a strictly inflation-targeting central bank in a simple model.[17] Let the economy be represented as:

$$\pi_{\tau+1} = \pi_\tau + \alpha(y_t - y^*) + \varepsilon_{t+1} \tag{8.1}$$

$$y_{t+1} - y^* = \lambda(y_t - y^*) - \beta(r_t - r^*) + n_{t+1}. \tag{8.2}$$

Equation (8.1) is an accelerationist Phillips Curve, where the change in inflation ($\pi$) between this period and next is a function of this period's gap between actual output ($y$) and its natural level ($y^*$) and of a disturbance (denoted $\varepsilon_{t+1}$). Equation (8.2) is aggregate demand, where next period's output gap is a function of this period's output gap, of the deviation of the interest rate ($r$) from normal ($r^*$), and of a disturbance ($n_{t+1}$). The key assumption is that the control lag until inflation responds to the central bank's instrument ($r$) is longer than the control lag for aggregate demand.

Under strict inflation targeting, the optimal policy is to target inflation two periods ahead, setting $\pi_{t+2} = \pi^*$, where $\pi^*$ denotes target inflation. (Inflation one period ahead is given by output in the current period, which is predetermined; hence inflation one period ahead cannot be controlled.) To solve for the optimal reaction function, shift equation (8.1) forward, substitute in equation (8.2), and set $\pi_{t+2}$ (the two-year inflation forecast) equal to $\pi^*$ (thus adopting a version of inflation-forecast targeting). This yields:

$$r_t = r^* + \phi(\pi_t - \pi^*) + \chi(y_t - y^*). \tag{8.3}$$

This is a Taylor rule with positive weights on deviations of inflation from target and of output from its natural rate, where the weights $\phi$ and $\chi$ depend on the parameters $\alpha$, $\lambda$ and $\beta$. We see the point mentioned above, that even under strict inflation targeting there is still a positive weight on output in the reaction function because of its information content for future inflation.

However, equation (8.3) is a peculiar Taylor rule. Strict inflation targeting implies sharp changes in the interest rate in response to deviations of inflation from target and output from its natural level, since $\phi = 1/(\alpha\beta)$ and $\chi = (1 + \lambda)/\beta$.[18] For example, if $\lambda = 0.8$, $\alpha = 0.4$, and $\beta = 0.6$, values that most observers would agree approximate realistic conditions, then we would observe changes in the interest rate in response deviations to both variables of several times the magnitude suggested by Taylor as matching the actual behavior of central banks.[19] This in turn implies very considerable output fluctuations. This is a further indication, if one was needed, that central banks are not strict inflation targeters; they care also about the behavior of other variables such as output.

If it cares about the deviations of output from the natural rate as well as deviations of inflation from target, then an optimizing central bank, instead of adjusting two-year-ahead expected inflation all the way to the inflation target, will adjust it part way:

$$E(\pi_{\tau+2}) = \kappa\pi^* + (1 - \kappa)E(\pi_{\tau+1}), \tag{8.4}$$

where $\kappa$ is a constant between zero and one, and E denotes an expectation. Svensson (1996) derives this relationship in the present model and shows that $\kappa$ will be a decreasing function of the weight on output stabilization in the central bank's objective function.[20]

Life will be more complicated if the structure of the economy is more complex – for example, if the economy is open. It is to the complications that arise in the case of open-economy inflation targeting that I now turn.

## WHAT'S DIFFERENT ABOUT OPEN ECONOMIES?

The openness of emerging markets raises obvious questions about the relevance to them of the simple closed-economy inflation targeting framework. Openness exposes the economy to external shocks: there will be foreign shocks to both commodity and financial markets.[21] In addition, openness implies additional channels for policy. For example, the central bank's policy instrument ($r$) will now affect output not just directly, as in equation (8.2), but also indirectly through its impact on the exchange rate. While the direct interest-rate channel will dampen investment, as in a closed economy, the indirect channel will reduce net export demand by appreciating the exchange rate. This is easiest to see by starting from the interest parity condition that will hold in a financially open economy:

$$e_t - \mathrm{E}(e_{t+1}) = r_t - r' + v_t, \tag{8.5}$$

where the exchange rate $e$ is defined as the foreign price of domestic currency (an increase is an appreciation), $r'$ is the foreign interest rate, and $v$ is a financial market (or pure portfolio) disturbance.[22] Ball (1999) and Mishkin and Savastano (2000) consider a simplified version of this relationship where the expected future exchange rate is constant (so that $e_t = r_t - r' + v_t$).[23] For convenience, I adopt this simplification in what follows. The additional impact of the interest rate on output, operating through the exchange rate, then implies nothing more than a larger coefficient on the domestic interest rate in equation (8.2). Since it is assumed (for the time being) that the exchange rate and the interest rate affect the change in output with the same lag, (8.2) can be written as:

$$y_{t+1} - y^* = \lambda(y_t - y^*) - \beta(r_t - r^*) - \delta e_t + n_{t+1}. \tag{8.6}$$

Note that $\beta(r_t - r^*) + \delta e_t = (\beta + \delta)r_t - \beta r^*$. In open economies where the output response is larger, adjustments in the policy instruments will be smaller. But the reaction function is otherwise unchanged.

The implications are more complex if exchange rate movements also affect inflation directly with the same one-period lag as it is affected by the output gap.[24] In other words, we rewrite equation (8.1) as:

$$\pi_{\tau+1} = \pi_\tau + \alpha(y_t - y^*) - \gamma(e_t - e_{t-1}) + \varepsilon_t. \tag{8.1'}$$

Strict inflation targeting is the simple case (as always). Now a central bank that wishes to hit its inflation target in $t + 1$ and not just $t + 2$ can do so. It does this by using its instrument (the interest rate) to alter the exchange rate and hence import prices. But output is more variable than before, since the interest rate is no longer adjusted to push output back toward its natural level (that having been the only channel, in the closed economy, through which policy could affect inflation in the event of an aggregate demand shock). Thus, strict inflation targeting that puts a high weight on inflation stability will result in more output instability in an open economy.[25]

Intuition suggests that when the central bank values the stability of both inflation and output, the ratio of the two reaction function coefficients (the response to inflation deviations relative to the response to output deviations, that is, the ratio $\phi$ to $\chi$ in equation (8.3) above) will be smaller in more open economies.[26] In terms of equation (8.4), the central bank will move more slowly to restore inflation to its target level ($\kappa$ will be smaller). Because the policy instrument, operating through the exchange rate, has a more powerful first-period effect on inflation, tending not only to stabilize inflation but also to destabilize output, policy is used more moderately in response to a given ratio of deviations of inflation to deviations in output.

An open economy is susceptible to shocks emanating from international commodity and financial markets. Although both types of shocks will affect the exchange rate, the appropriate policy response by an inflation-targeting central bank will depend on the source. Consider first a shock emanating from financial markets – a change in the direction or availability of capital flows due to, say, a rise in foreign interest rates (or a deterioration in foreign investor sentiment toward the country). I refer to this in what follows as a *Calvo shock*, Guillermo Calvo having emphasized the impact of capital-flow-related shocks to emerging markets. This can be modeled as an increase in $r'$ (or as a low realization of v). A higher foreign interest rate implies less capital inflow for a given domestic interest rate and therefore a weaker currency, ceteris paribus. As the exchange rate weakens, higher import prices are passed through into inflation.[27] The optimal response is then to raise interest rates.

Note that this encourages *fear-of-floating* type behavior by an inflation targeting central bank, although the exchange rate may still be considerably more flexible than if it is pegged. If a Calvo shock displaces the exchange rate, then the interest rate adjustments that offset the inflationary consequences have the effect of moderating the change in the value of the currency (that is, of bringing the exchange rate back toward its previous level). If the currency weakens, the central bank raises interest rates, which strengthens it, ceteris paribus. If it strengthens, the central bank reduces rates, which weakens it, other things equal. This is not because the central bank cares about the exchange rate in and of itself but because it cares about inflation.

The intuition that central banks concerned about future inflation should adjust the interest rate to counter fluctuations in the exchange rate has been formalized as the idea of a monetary conditions index. The MCI, which indicates the overall stance of policy, is a weighted average of the interest rate and the exchange rate (since these two variables are linked by equation 8.5) where the former is adjusted to offset finance-induced fluctuations in the latter.[28] Using a simulation model of the New Zealand economy, Hunt (1999) shows that when the main source of shocks is from international financial markets to the exchange rate, it will be desirable to target an MCI which includes both the interest rate and the exchange rate (raising interest rates when the exchange rate weakens, other things equal).

What if the shock is temporary? A transitory shock to v that depreciates the exchange rate will still dictate a limited rise in interest rates to damp down future demand-induced inflation.[29] But because the direct impact on inflation through higher import prices is transitory, responding to it with sharply higher interest rates will only amplify the volatility of output and inflation, since v, and with it underlying inflationary pressures, will have returned to normal in the next period. Interest rates should be hiked to damp down only the domestic component of inflation (which derives from the persistent increase in aggregate demand), but not also imported inflation (which is temporary). Responding this period to a problem that will have disappeared by next period, using an instrument that takes one period to work, will only produce cycles of output and inflation.

In Ball's (1999) model, the implication is that the monetary conditions indicator (the weighted average of the interest rate and the exchange rate) should be adjusted not to movements in $\pi_t$ but to movements in $\pi_t + \gamma(e_t - e_{t-1})$, where $\gamma$ is the response of inflation to a change in the exchange rate. In other words, the authorities should target domestic and not CPI inflation. Bharucha and Kent (1998) use a simulation model of Australia to show that responding only to the domestic component of inflation (and not also to imported inflation) delivers better results when shocks to the exchange rate are temporary.[30] Since the interest rate response to movements in the exchange rate will be less, fear-of-floating type behavior will be less when capital market shocks are temporary.[31]

All this rests on the assumption that the source of disturbances is international financial markets. Assume instead that the disturbance is to the foreign component of aggregate demand (to the terms of trade or to export demand). I refer to this as a Prebisch shock. The exchange rate will again weaken, since export revenues will have declined while nothing else affecting the foreign exchange market will have changed in the first instance. In addition, aggregate demand will weaken, since foreigners are demanding fewer of the country's exports.[32] Now there are two offsetting effects on inflation: while higher import prices will be passed through into inflation, weaker aggregate demand will be deflationary.

Imagine that the second effect dominates. Then inflation will decline with the growth in the gap between potential and current output. The appropriate response for an inflation-targeting central bank is to cut interest rates, regardless of the weight it attaches to output variability. Now central bank behavior will not resemble fear of floating. To the contrary, the cut in interest rates will accentuate the change in the value of the currency. Because the decline in foreign demand requires a weaker exchange rate in order to stabilize output (and because the cut in demand also subdues inflation), the central bank does nothing to limit the adjustment of the exchange rate; to the contrary, it encourages it to adjust.

What if the Prebisch shock, by depreciating the exchange rate, is inflationary on balance? If the central bank attaches a high weight to output variability, it still may want to cut interest rates, knowing that inflation will decline subsequently due to the weakness of output. If on the other hand it attaches a high weight to deviations of inflation from target, it may instead raise interest rates to limit currency depreciation in the short run, while still allowing the exchange rate to adjust eventually to its new long-run equilibrium level. It will engage in exchange rate smoothing rather than succumb to fear of floating.

Note that the monetary conditions indicator now sends the wrong signal in response to this shock. Mishkin (2000) cites cases (such as New Zealand in 1997 and Chile in 1998) where the central bank either utilized a monetary conditions indicator or attempted to limit the variability of the exchange rate as part of its inflation targeting regime, inducing precisely the wrong response to a shock to external demand (tightening when the economy was weakening).[33]

To summarize, inflation targeting is more complicated in open economies, reflecting the additional shocks to which such economies are exposed and the additional channels linking policy instruments and outcomes. Insofar as policy has more powerful effects when it operates through the exchange rate as well as the interest rate, this implies, other things equal, that policy instruments should be adjusted less in response to the same shocks. Insofar as the additional exchange rate channel linking interest rates to inflation changes the structure of policy lags, openness also requires rethinking the relative weights on inflation and output in the reaction function. In general, the central bank of an open economy will respond less to inflation deviations relative to output deviations, since monetary policy, which also operates through the exchange rate, now has a more powerful, immediate effect on inflation.

Will open-economy inflation targeters exhibit fear of floating? The answer depends on the source of shocks. In response to export-demand (Prebisch) shocks, an inflation targeting central bank will let the exchange rate adjust. But it will want to lean against the exchange rate change in response to portfolio (Calvo) shocks. In this case, if the exchange rate depreciates, it will raise the interest rate. That higher interest rate will lead to a step appreciation of the exchange rate, offsetting a part of the initial depreciation. Behavior that resembles fear of floating will thus be observed in response to some shocks but not others.

## WHAT'S DIFFERENT ABOUT EMERGING MARKETS?

What is different about emerging markets is the speed of passthrough, the difficulty of forecasting inflation, liability dollarization, and credibility issues.

### A. Higher Passthrough

Calvo and Reinhart (2000) provide evidence that changes in import prices due to movements in the exchange rate are passed through into domestic prices faster in emerging markets than industrial countries. A history of inflation may have raised agents' awareness of and sensitivity to imported inflation or led to formal indexation. The commitment to price stability may lack credibility; hence, it may be feared that transitory shocks leading to depreciation of the exchange rate will be validated by policy and hence become permanent.[34]

Faster passthrough can be formalized as a larger $\gamma$ in equation (8.1'). A larger $\gamma$ was shown in the previous section to lead the central bank to raise the coefficient on output deviations relative to the coefficient on inflation deviations in its reaction function, since inflation has now become more sensitive to the policy instrument. But the preceding paragraph makes clear that passthrough is not an exogenous parameter that can be regarded as independent of the monetary regime. If an institutionalized commitment to price stability, central bank independence and accountability, and policies of communicating the rationale for monetary-policy decisions enhance the credibility of the commitment to low inflation, then agents will revise downward the likelihood they attach to the prospect that transitory shocks will be validated by policy and hence become permanent, and therefore how quickly they adjust prices in response to a weaker exchange rate.[35]

Under full (instantaneous, 100 per cent) indexation, monetary policy has no capacity to stabilize – or, for that matter, destabilize – output.[36] It can simply be used to target inflation. With full indexation, that target can be hit immediately.[37] Full indexation thus simplifies the inflation targeting problem since it reduces the central bank's objective function to the one variable that it can now influence and since it allows the authorities to hit that target immediately.

What this implies for exchange rate management depends on the source of shocks. If domestic monetary policy is the source of the instability, then stabilizing the exchange rate will force the central bank to undo such shocks immediately. If shocks are external, then the exchange rate should adjusted to offset them. Foreign deflation will induce an inflation-targeting central bank to expand the money supply and allow the currency to depreciate, while an inflationary shock will induce the opposite reaction. We are in what Calvo (2000b) refers to as the world of the traditional model.

## B.   Difficulty in Forecasting Inflation

Disturbances make it difficult for observers to evaluate the central bank's commitment to inflation targeting, since it is often hard to determine the extent to which divergences between actual inflation and the target are due to the monetary policy implemented several quarters ago as opposed to shocks occurring during the control lag. This uncertainty may reduce credibility – it will not be clear whether the central bank is in fact following the announced policy.[38] This is where the conditional inflation forecast comes in.[39] The central bank announces a point or range forecast for inflation and explains how its instrument settings are consistent with its forecast. If it misses the target, it must be able to point to unanticipated disturbances occurring during the control lag that can account for the discrepancy or risk losing credibility.

If reliable forecasting is not possible, then the markets may be unable to determine the intent of the authorities. A brutally honest central bank might surround its point forecast with a wide confidence interval. But a wide range of outcomes may be consistent with a wide range of policies, complicating efforts to determine the authorities' intent.

Forecasts based on historical relationships can be invalidated when there is a change in the policy process – that is to say, a change in the monetary regime. And what is the adoption of formal inflation targeting but a change in regime? Thus, the problem of forecasting inflation in the early phases of the new regime is general, not specific to emerging markets.

But there are reasons to worry that it is especially difficult in such markets. Emerging markets attracted to inflation targeting will typically be bringing inflation down from high levels. Thus, the change in regime is likely to be particularly sharp and inflation volatility particularly pronounced during the transition. Passthrough may change. De-indexation will be proceeding, with uncertain consequences. The shift from an alternative monetary policy operating strategy to inflation targeting will be part of a package of stabilization measures, typically including structural reforms of the public and private sectors that transform the inflation process in unpredictable ways. If the country is emerging from a period of strict central planning, price controls may be in the process of elimination, and there may be the prospect of sharp changes in excise taxes to augment public sector revenues and enhance the efficiency of tax collection.

While these are reasons why inflation forecasting may be especially difficult during the transition, they do not obviously challenge its feasibility once the aforementioned structural and policy reforms have been put in place. Revealingly, those emerging markets that have adopted full-fledged inflation targeting have not generally started from a position of high inflation; rather, they have first brought inflation down to moderate levels and pursued other reforms before installing the new regime.[40]

But are there also structural features of emerging markets that complicate the forecasting exercise even once these structural and policy reforms are complete? Emerging economies are more commodity-price sensitive than their advanced-industrial counterparts, and commodity price fluctuations can wreak havoc with the forecastability of consumer price inflation. There is the fact that foodstuffs, whose prices are affected by weather conditions, have a heavy weight in the CPI in low-income countries. The obvious solution to both problems is to target core (or underlying) inflation net of commodity prices, as is the practice of some industrial countries.[41]

Then there is such countries' disproportionate dependence on capital flows. Sensitivity of domestic financial conditions to international capital flows is, in a sense, the defining feature of an emerging market. The literature on asymmetric information suggests that unpredictable volatility is especially pronounced in the financial sphere, and nowhere more than in international financial markets. Because information is costly to acquire and process, investors tend to be imperfectly informed. They therefore herd in and out of markets in response to the movements of other investors, amplifying volatility. Because asymmetric information reduces the liquidity of financial assets in periods of stress (reflecting fears that assets liquidated in fire sales are damaged goods), illiquidity and balance sheet problems may transmit financial distress across borders, with destabilizing repercussions for innocent bystanders. (The now extensive literature on contagion is concerned with this point.) These problems will be most severe in international markets, where information must travel geographical and cultural distance, and in emerging markets, where the information environment is least developed.

The forecastability of inflation, ultimately, is an empirical issue. Hoffmaister (1999) has analysed it in South Korea, finding that inflation is roughly as forecastable there as in Sweden. Univariate models of inflation perform similarly in Korea and in high-income inflation targeters in the period immediately preceding their adoption of the strategy, although there is some evidence of positive kurtosis, as if inflation is subject more frequently to larger shocks than would be expected given its standard deviation. Christoffersen and Wescott (1999) and Rivas (2001) similarly find evidence of kurtosis and skewness for Poland in the period 1992–8 and Nicaragua in 1988–98, respectively. But upon eliminating some of the largest and smallest price changes each month among the 33 main categories in Poland's CPI to derive a measure of core inflation, Christoffersen and Wescott find that a limited set of economic variables forecasts one-period-ahead core inflation reasonably well by international standards.[42] Rivas similarly has considerable success in forecasting core inflation in Nicaragua so long as he focuses on the period of moderate inflation starting around 1993.

Thus, the difficulty of forecasting inflation may be an obstacle to effective inflation targeting in an economy in economic and financial disequilibrium. It is not realistic to hope to forecast inflation with the requisite reliability if the country is still bringing inflation down from high levels, comprehensively re-forming the tax and public spending systems, and radically restructuring the private sector. But where such reforms have been underway for some time and are proceeding at a measured pace – as in Poland, South Korea and Brazil – fore-casting difficulties would not appear to be an insurmountable obstacle to inflation targeting.

## C. Liability Dollarization

In many emerging markets, the obligations of banks, corporations and governments – their foreign obligations in particular – are denominated in foreign currency, while their revenues are domestic-currency denominated to a considerable extent. Insofar as banks and other intermediaries close their open foreign currency positions by issuing dollar-denominated loans, the liability dollarization of their customers will be greater still. When the exchange rate depreciates, their balance sheets will still suffer, and this financial accelerator will significantly depress output and employment.

The simplest way of thinking about liability dollarization is as reducing $\delta$, the positive response of output to currency depreciation in equation (8.2). While depreciation renders domestic goods more competitive, as before, it now also weakens the balance sheets of banks, firms, households and governments, depressing consumption and investment. The second effect partially offsets the first.[43]

Consider the response to a Calvo shock, compared to the benchmark case analysed in Section 2. Weaker consumption and investment due to adverse balance sheet effects now imply less inflation in the intermediate run compared to before. An inflation-targeting central bank will therefore feel *less* compelled to raise interest rates in order to push up the exchange rate and damp down the increase in import prices.[44] If the shock to the exchange rate instead emanates from commodity markets (a negative Prebisch shock), higher import prices will still be passed through into inflation, but now aggregate demand will be even weaker than before because of adverse balance sheet effects. Since output is lower and inflation is no higher than in the absence of liability dollarization, again there will be *less* pressure to hike interest rates in order to stabilize the currency and damp down inflation, and more incentive to cut interest rates to stimulate production (compared to the situation where balance-sheet effects are absent). This suggests that, regardless of the source of shocks, fear of floating will be *less* in the presence of liability dollarization.

While this may seem counterintuitive, it is simply an illustration of the general point that when the central bank worries more about variables other than inflation, either because of a heavier weight on those variables in its objective function, or because the parameters of the model cause those other variables to be displaced further from their equilibrium levels (where the latter is the case presently under discussion), it will move more gradually to eliminate discrepancies between actual and target inflation. Because the exchange rate must move more to increase output and employment, and because measures which would limit its fluctuation and thereby reduce imported inflation tend to destabilize the real economy, the now weaker tendency for depreciation to stimulate activity means that the central bank will do even less to limit depreciation.

The same is true when the problem in the financial system is maturity mismatches rather than currency mismatches. (This can be modeled as an increase in the coefficient β in the aggregate demand equation.) Again, the more the central bank fears that an interest rate hike designed to damp down inflation will cause financial distress (because the maturity of banks' liabilities is shorter than their assets, or because higher interest rates will increase default rates among bank borrowers), the less sharply it will raise interest rates in the intermediate run to strengthen the exchange rate and limit inflation.

Clearly, those who argue that liability dollarization creates fear of floating have something else in mind, presumably that the balance sheet effects of currency depreciation are so strong that they turn δ negative. Let $-δ > β$, so that a cut in the interest rate which weakens the exchange rate depresses output on balance. This constellation of parameter values is extreme (and it has some peculiar implications), but it would appear to be what the Cassandras of liability dollarization have in mind.

As before, a negative Calvo shock fuels inflation through higher import prices, encouraging the authorities to raise rates. It also now lowers output through the adverse balance sheet effect. The appropriate response, which damps down inflation *and* stabilizes output by limiting balance-sheet damage, is to raise interest rates and push the exchange rate back up to its pre-shock level.[45] Fear-of-floating type behavior results. If the disturbance is instead a Prebisch shock, the weaker exchange rate again means more imported inflation and lower levels of output. (The decline in output is even larger than before because the direct effect of the decline in foreign demand is reinforced by the indirect effect of exchange rate depreciation via its adverse impact on balance sheets.) Again, interest rate hikes are a desirable response to both problems, since a higher interest rate which strengthens the exchange rate not only damps down inflation but also strengthens balance sheets. Again, the central bank will not hesitate to raise interest rates. Again, its response will resemble fear of floating.

This formulation has some peculiar implications, as already noted. For one, a negative Prebisch shock that reduces export demand and depresses output must be offset in the new long-run equilibrium by an appreciated exchange rate, not a depreciated one. This is a world where overvaluation is good for output because its favorable financial effects dominate its adverse competitiveness effects. It may be objected that this is unrealistic – that it is implausible to assume that $-δ > β$. But relaxing this assumption means we are back in a world not just where the authorities allow the exchange rate to adjust to a new lower level following an adverse Prebisch shock but also where they do not jack up interest rates to significantly slow its movement. In other words, they display fear of fixing rather than fear of floating.

A possible reconciliation is that when the exchange rate depreciates by a large amount, the adverse balance sheet effects dominate, but when it depreciates by

a small amount, the favorable competitiveness effects dominate. Large depreciations are known to cause severe financial distress because they confront banks
and firms with asset prices for which they are unprepared, while doing little to
enhance competitiveness because of the speed with which they are passed
through into inflation. For small depreciations, the balance of effects is the opposite; small depreciations are more likely therefore to satisfy the conditions
for an expansionary devaluation. There is a range of exchange rates for which
$-\delta > \beta$, in other words, and another range closer to prior levels where $-\delta < \beta$.[46]
This nonlinearity in the effect of the exchange rate on output might seem arbi-
trary. But in fact it is precisely the way authors like Aghion et al. (1999) and
Krugman (2001) model the interplay of competitiveness and balance sheet effects: the latter dominates for small depreciations but the former dominate for
large ones, producing a nonlinear aggregate equation of precisely the sort being
assumed here.

If the exchange rate falls sufficiently to enter the first range, then an inflation-
targeting central bank will raise interest rates sharply and push the currency up
quickly in order to minimize financial damage to banks, firms and households.
But if the depreciation is modest, so too will be the rise in interest rates; the
central bank will allow the currency to fall to a new lower level so long as the
competitiveness effects continue to dominate the balance-sheet effects. In fact,
heavy intervention when the exchange rate drops precipitously but light intervention when it fluctuates around normal levels is not unlike the observed
behavior of central banks.

It is important to emphasize that liability dollarization, as analysed here, in
no sense precludes inflation targeting. The preceding propositions for how the
central bank should respond flow directly from the standard inflation-targeting
framework. But in the extreme case of liability dollarization where interest rate
cuts depress output as well as aggravating inflation $(-\delta > \beta)$, that response will
be such as to limit exchange rate variability. If the perceived advantage of inflation targeting is that it permits a greater exchange rate flexibility (compared to
the alternative of a hard peg), then the advantages of inflation targeting are in
practice correspondingly less in highly dollarized economies.

This discussion assumes that the output effects of liability dollarization are
independent of the policy regime. This assumption may be no more appropriate
here than it is for passthrough and indexation. The greater exchange rate variability that the shift from pegging to inflation targeting implies, even if it is
slight, will encourage hedging by banks and corporates. Whereas a policy of
pegging the currency is tantamount to providing implicit insurance against
currency risk, which discourages private purchases of currency hedges (why
hedge when doing so is costly and the government avers its commitment to
limiting currency fluctuations), the knowledge that the exchange rate is allowed
to move on a daily basis should strengthen the hand of a chief financial officer

trying to convince his CEO of the importance of purchasing a hedge. Precisely those banks and corporates most vulnerable to severe distress because the liability side of their balance sheets is dollarized will have the greatest incentive to hedge. Hence, even if banks and firms are unable to borrow abroad in their own currency in the aggregate, they will have an incentive to redistribute that foreign exposure in ways that limit the adverse output effects of depreciation. Thus, the adverse balance sheet effects that occur in a country that has traditionally oriented its monetary policy strategy around the level of the exchange rate may not be a good guide to the magnitude of these effects when the central bank shifts to an inflation targeting regime that implies even a modest increase in exchange rate flexibility. And even a modest increase in exchange rate flexibility that leads to a modest increase in hedging will make it optimal for an inflation-targeting central bank to allow a bit more exchange rate flexibility, which may encourage a bit more hedging, and so on. If the demand for unhedged dollar liabilities is endogenous, then behavior under the new regime – by the central bank as well as the private sector – may be quite different from behavior under the old one.

What if this response is not forthcoming, perhaps because the relevant hedging instruments are not available? If the authorities are concerned that inflation targeting still looks too much like a de facto soft peg, rendering the country vulnerable to a build-up of speculative pressure, then it may be possible to fulfill the desire for greater flexibility only through the imposition of regulatory limits on gross and net foreign currency exposures. The regulatory authorities will have to limit the gross foreign currency exposures of the banking system (and strengthen corporate governance and prudential practices in the financial sector so as to encourage banks to better manage and limit those exposures on their own). The central government will have to limit its foreign currency borrowing to the extent that its domestic-currency-denominated revenues are imperfectly indexed to the exchange rate, and it should similarly takes steps to discourage excessive foreign currency borrowing by states and municipalities.

Such measures are in fact integral to the agenda pushed by G7 governments and the multilaterals under the heading *new international financial architecture*. Greater exchange rate flexibility has also been an element of this agenda (in either a rare instance of internal consistency or a fortuitous coincidence). But if this ability to regulate markets (and for markets to regulate themselves) is beyond the capacity of an emerging economy, then evasion and regulatory laxity will result in destabilizing balance sheet effects, undermining the viability of an inflation targeting regime that aspires to permit increased exchange rate flexibility. It is revealing that those emerging markets which have moved to inflation targeting and have succeeded in achieving greater de facto exchange rate flexibility have generally had relatively well-developed financial systems and regulatory capacities.

One can question whether the solution is worth the price. If the exchange rate movements implied by inflation targeting are compatible with financial instability only when foreign borrowing is curtailed, then the cost may be slow growth and underdevelopment. The severity of this risk depends on one's evaluation of the importance of foreign capital for domestic development and of the extent to which gross (as opposed to net) exposures must be curtailed to reconcile exchange rate flexibility with financial stability. Those fearful that curtailing capital flows will hinder growth logically prefer full dollarization.

## D.   Credibility Problems

We have already seen how the difficulty of forecasting inflation can lessen the credibility of inflation targeting in emerging markets (although I have argued that the point should not be pushed too far). In addition, a history of arbitrary enforcement that lessens respect for constitutional and statutory law may limit the effective independence of the central bank, whose insulation from pressure to pump up activity before an election or to help meet the government's financial needs is a prerequisite for effective inflation targeting. Central bankers threatened with dismissal, notwithstanding laws ostensibly guaranteeing them long terms in office, will be more inclined to bow to pressure to purchase government securities on the primary market. And chronic budget deficits can convince even an independent central bank that it has no choice but to meet the government's fiscal needs if it wishes to preserve financial stability, sowing the seeds of time inconsistency.[47]

Historically, lack of effective central bank independence has been a major impediment to the pursuit of independent monetary policies in developing countries. At the same time, emerging markets have come a long way in recent years in creating a political consensus in favor of low inflation and buttressing the independence of their central banks.[48] Although budget deficits have been chronic problems, there has also been considerable progress in strengthening fiscal institutions and bringing down budget deficits.[49] The dozen or so transition economies seeking membership in the EU and its monetary union, for example, have made very considerable progress in bringing their deficits and debts to within the Maastricht Treaty's 3 and 60 per cent ceilings.

To the extent that inflation targeting is less credible in emerging markets, its benefits will be less. Absent confidence that the central bank is committed to low inflation, interest rates will not fall to the levels of other low-inflation countries. Shocks will raise questions about whether the authorities are prepared to stay the course. Sharp changes in interest rates, exchange rates and international capital flows may feed upon themselves: financial variables will be volatile, with negative implications for the economy. If policy is not credible, then firms will not reduce price increases to meet the inflation target. Hitting it will require an increase in interest rates sufficient to deliver a substantial reduction in import prices (through a sharp appreciation of the exchange rate), with destabilizing output effects.[50]

What are the implications for emerging markets contemplating inflation targeting? A wide variety of models of monetary policy point to the fact that there is a tradeoff between flexibility and credibility. Central banks most lacking in credibility will have an incentive to move along the frontier of feasible credibility-flexibility combinations in order to obtain it.

In particular, imperfect credibility may require the central bank to target inflation rigidly. Absent credibility problems, a central bank faced with inflation in excess of its target may want to raise interest rates and damp down inflation only gradually in order to avoid causing or compounding a recession. Faced with a weak banking system ill-prepared to absorb interest rate increases, which raise the cost of servicing its short-term liabilities and increase default rates by borrowers, it may want to limit interest-rate volatility and administer its anti-inflationary medicine in small doses. But if the monetary authorities fail to respond quickly when inflation heats up, observers may begin to wonder whether they are optimally trading off objectives or they are in fact not really committed to price stability. Asset prices and the variables they affect will not respond as hoped. Similarly, if the central bank targets core rather than headline inflation, observers may wonder whether this is because monetary policy should not attempt to offset temporary commodity price fluctuations, or whether the authorities are really just seeking an excuse to disregard inflationary pressures.[51] Monetary policy will thus have to respond more sharply to exchange rate and commodity price fluctuations than would be the case if it was being implemented by a highly credible central bank. The monetary authorities may not be able to afford even modest deviations from strict inflation targeting for fear of sending the wrong signal.

In addition, central banks in emerging markets will have an incentive to use transparency to further enhance their credibility. This means that they will have an incentive to adopt a fully articulated inflation-targeting framework rather than the seat-of-the-pants approach preferred by, inter alia, the Federal Reserve. Its hard-won credibility allows the Fed to hint at its inflation forecast rather than announcing it. It allows the Fed to sketch the model used to link its policy instruments to that forecast rather than describing it in any great detail. Most emerging markets do not enjoy this luxury.[52] To convince investors that they mean what they say, their central banks will have to publish the forecast and the model. Chile, for one, has moved in this direction, while Mexico has taken the first step of publishing a regular *Inflation Report.*

Another implication is that effective inflation targeting will require steps to eliminate fiscal dominance as a way of building credibility. In particular, inflation targeting must be supported by the reform and reinforcement of fiscal institutions as a way of delivering better fiscal outcomes. Fiscal policy making processes and procedures should be centralized to reduce free riding. Vertical fiscal imbalances should be reduced. The budget constraints facing subcentral governments should be hardened.[53] An example of progress in this direction is Brazil's Fiscal Responsibility Law, which bans the federal government from bailing out debt-ridden states and municipalities and has already produced visible improvements in state and municipal fiscal performance. The federal fiscal authorities, for their part, can invest in the new monetary regime so as to intentionally incur costs if it fails, further limiting problems of time inconsistency. Thus, inflation targets in a number of emerging markets are announced not by the central bank but by the government (Chile, Poland) or by the central bank and government jointly (Brazil, Israel), precisely as a way for the government to commit to the fiscal discipline needed to achieve the target.

These implications are evident in the behavior of those emerging markets that have embraced inflation targeting. Such countries have generally moved toward the adoption of a formal framework. Their central banks have been reluctant to miss the inflation target even temporarily, or to slow the pace at which deviations between target inflation and actual inflation are eliminated, for fear of undermining their anti-inflationary credibility.[54] The credibility problem has tended to dictate that the change in the CPI must be the operational measure of inflation, because it is widely understood and therefore more credible, even when core inflation purged of import-price fluctuations would be more appropriate in principle.[55]

Credibility problems make inflation targeting less attractive. They imply more volatility and less flexible policy implementation. The question is then how quickly credibility can be gained, and whether or not inflation targeting can be part of that process.

## CONCLUSION

Inflation targeting is the increasingly fashionable alternative for countries unable or unwilling to abolish the national currency.[56] It is seen as providing a coherent alternative to exchange-rate-based monetary policy strategies that are overly restrictive and crisis prone. But is it feasible for emerging markets?

In a nutshell, inflation targeting is difficult in emerging markets for three reasons: they are open, their liabilities are dollarized, and their policy makers lack credibility. Openness exposes their economies to external disturbances.[57] It opens additional exchange-rate related channels linking the central bank's instruments and targets that operate with very different control lags. Because an inflation-targeting central bank will want to respond differently to exchange rate changes depending on their source and persistence, these problems cannot be solved simply by adding the exchange rate to the standard reaction function. None of this is to suggest that inflation targeting is infeasible in an open economy, only that its implementation is more complex.

Liability dollarization introduces more fundamental complications. Financial institutions and their clients in the typical emerging market will be saddled with currency mismatches, given the difficulty these countries have in borrowing abroad in their own currencies. Under these circumstances, an inflation-targeting central bank will be reluctant to let the exchange rate move; it will be unable to partake of the greater flexibility ostensibly promised by the regime.

In practice, whether countries with partially dollarized economies reap any advantages from inflation targeting – whether the framework will provide even limited scope for policy autonomy, and in particular whether it will enable them to allow the exchange rate to fluctuate more freely – depends on the exact nature, extent and effects of their liability dollarization. If even a small depreciation of the exchange rate threatens to destabilize balance sheets and output (in other words, if the country immediately enters the zone where depreciation and lower interest rates are recessionary), then the central bank will be unwilling to let the exchange rate to move. Inflation targeting and a hard peg are then basically indistinguishable. If the perceived advantage of inflation targeting is that it permits greater flexibility than a hard peg, then the advantages of inflation targeting are correspondingly less in highly dollarized economies. Inflation targeting has no obvious advantages under these circumstances, while a hard peg has the advantages of simplicity, transparency and credibility.

For countries where the adverse balance sheet effects dominate only when exchange rate movements reach a certain point, conventional inflation targeting will be viable so long as shocks and corresponding exchange rate movements are small, while the desire to intervene and stabilize the exchange rate will dominate when they grow large. The greater exchange rate flexibility promised by inflation targeting will be possible, although the central bank's appetite for indulging in it will have limits.

Such countries will wish to implement inflation targeting in a flexible way, by adjusting monetary policy in response to large exchange rate movements, for example, while treating small movements with benign neglect. Unfortunately, flexibility can be destabilizing when credibility is lacking. A central bank that temporarily disregards a surge in inflation in order to, say, stabilize the financial system may find its commitment to price stability questioned. Credibility problems will force precisely those emerging markets where a flexible approach to inflation targeting is most valuable to adopt a relatively rigid version.[58]

These observations suggest what countries should find inflation targeting attractive. Inflation targeting will be less attractive the more open the economy, for the reasons detailed several paragraphs back. Note the consonance of this argument with a key implication of theory of optimum currency areas. Inflation targeting will be less attractive the dimmer the prospects of the central bank acquiring policy credibility. Note this time the consonance of this argument with the idea that countries in crisis whose credibility has been shredded should rebuild their reputations by dollarizing. Finally, inflation targeting will be more attractive where liability dollarization is limited and banks and corporations have markets on which to hedge their exposures, so that limited exchange rate fluctuations will not irreparably damage their balance sheets. Note here the consonance of this observation with popular explanations for the success of inflation targeting in Brazil.

On the other hand, emerging markets that are less open, that have well regulated financial institutions and markets on which foreign exposures can be hedged, and whose central banks possess a reasonable degree of policy credibility may prefer inflation targeting. The question is how many emerging markets may soon fall under this heading.

## NOTES

1.  An earlier version of this paper was presented at the Bank of England. For helpful comments I thank Lawrence Ball, Paul Masson, Rick Mishkin, Peter Sinclair, Lars Svensson, Ted Truman and John Williamson.
2.  I use the term dollarization generically to denote the adoption of a major (international) currency, be it the dollar, the euro or another unit.
3.  Calvo and Reinhart (2000) are leading exponents of the view that many emerging markets exhibit *fear of floating* – that, despite being reclassified by the IMF as embracing a greater degree of exchange rate flexibility, they continue to intervene heavily to limit the actual variability of the currency.
4.  A further option, the adjustable peg, may be viable for countries with capital controls, as the experiences of China and Malaysia have shown. I disregard this option here on the grounds that trends in technology and policy (domestic financial liberalization, in particular) will lead additional countries to liberalize their international financial transactions, limiting those to which this option is relevant.
5.  On dollarization, see Hausmann (1999) and Calvo (2000a). On bands and pegs for emerging markets, see Williamson (2000). In order to reduce effective options to three, I lump together under the heading of *intermediate regimes* pegs, bands and crawls à la Williamson with implicit strategies to limit exchange rate flexibility as described by Calvo and Reinhart (2000), since both are monetary policy strategies framed in terms of the level of the exchange rate, while neither hardens the peg to the extent of a currency board. This follows the policy literature on target zones, which encompasses both hard and soft zones (that is, with and without buffers and escape clauses) and loud and quiet zones (those that are announced and unannounced).
6.  Not all of the advocates of greater flexibility take this additional step. Calvo (2000b) criticizes contributions to this literature, with no little justification, for failing to specify the alternative to an exchange-rate based policy regime.
7.  Brazil, Chile, Colombia, Israel, the Czech Republic and Poland all adopted inflation targeting in conjunction with recognition of the need to widen or abandon an exchange rate band. South Africa, in contrast, had been targeting M3. Clearly, inflation targeting and flexible exchange rates are not synonymous, although, as Calvo (2000b, p. 28) writes, there is a tendency to erroneously identify inflation targeting with flexible rates. Flexible rates can be backed by no coherent monetary policy operating strategy of any kind or by a number of alternatives to in-

flation targeting. The other options for policy are monetary targeting, which is impractical in emerging markets (and most other places) because of the instability of the relationship between monetary aggregates and policy targets, and nominal income targeting, which has formidable data requirements and has never been tried. Another option is the so-called Taylor rule for monetary policy, whose connection to inflation targeting I elaborate below.

8.  There are many more complete and authoritative surveys of the literature on inflation targeting than I am able to provide here, for example, Bernanke et al. (1999).

9.  Others would add following an information-inclusive strategy where the variables to which the central bank responds are not limited to, say, current inflation and the output gap, and/or using an inflation forecast as the intermediate guide for monetary policy. I defer consideration of these aspects until later.

10. Since such lists are constantly changing, this one is almost certain to be outdated by the time this chapter sees the light of day.

11. I show this below using a simple model. De Brouwer and O'Regan (1997) also show using a simulation model that inflation targeting which ignores the information context of output deviations results in not just more variable output but more variable inflation as well.

12. Calvo (2000b, p. 28) asserts that 'Inflation targeting is equivalent to pegging the currency to a basket of goods.' This is true only of strict inflation targeting, not of its flexible counterpart.

13. The language here is from Svensson (1999). Other authors refer to this as the distinction between policy objectives and policy rules.

14. And where outcomes are uncertain. There is a growing literature on inflation targeting under uncertainty (for example, Levin et al. 1999, Kumhof 2000), which I leave aside in this chapter.

15. Something that is likely to be particularly problematic in emerging markets, as I analyse below.

16. This is another big if. It is likely to be especially problematic in emerging markets, as I discuss below. In addition, simply targeting the inflation forecast does not solve the problem that additional information about the structure of the economy and its reaction to policy is needed to inform the central bank's decision of how quickly to eliminate any discrepancy between the inflation forecast and the inflation target.

17. It is important to emphasize the *simple model* qualification. In general, the instrument rule will be an implicit function of all the relevant information. The reaction function will not, in general, be a Taylor-style reaction function except in the special case when current inflation and output are sufficient statistics for the state of the economy.

18. In the general case where the central bank cares not just about inflation but also about other variables like output, the reaction coefficients will also depend on the parameters of its objective function (see below). But that is not the case here.

19. Taylor identifies $\phi = 1.5$ and $\chi = 0.5$ as replicating the actual behavior of inflation-targeting central banks. Here we get $\phi = 4$ and $\chi = 3$.

20. Similarly, the higher the central bank's discount rate (the more it cares about the present relative to the future) and the less responsive is inflation to output fluctuations (the smaller $\alpha$), the less will be the weight on target inflation. If inflation two periods ahead is of less concern (because the discount rate is higher), then the central bank will be prepared to incur less output variability in order to stabilize it. And if output has to be pushed around a lot in order to hit the inflation target, then the weight on that target in the reaction function will be less. These relationships are easy to show for shocks to $\varepsilon_t$ when the control lag from the policy instrument to inflation is only one period – if we rewrite equation (8.2) as $y_t - y^* = -\beta(r_t - r^*) + n_t)$ for example, so that the interest rate affects output immediately but inflation only with a one period lag – but harder to show in the model in the text (again, however, see Svensson 1996). In contrast to the response to shocks to $\varepsilon$, in the variant in this footnote, the interest rate is adjusted immediately in response to shocks to aggregate demand (to $n_t$), so as to return both inflation to target and output instantaneously to the natural rate; equation (8.4) in the text is irrelevant.

21. I analyse these below.

22. This is a 'pure portfolio disturbance' in the sense that it appears only in this condition for fi-

nancial market equilibrium, not also in the aggregate demand equation. Later in the chapter I introduce an international commodity market (or 'export market') disturbance that affects financial and commodity markets simultaneously. The implications for policy turn out to be rather different.

23. One can attempt to justify this by arguing that since the expected values of the disturbances to equations (8.1) and (8.2) are zero, the exchange rate is expected to return to its (constant) level in the long run. But this of course ignores the distinction between temporary and permanent disturbances and between the long-run equilibrium level and the level one period out.

24. In the model of the previous section, the policy instrument could affect inflation only after two periods, since there was a one-period lag from policy to the output gap and a further one-period lag from the output gap to inflation. Ted Truman has raised the question (in private correspondence) of whether there is strong empirical support for this assumption that the impact of monetary policy on inflation is felt faster in open economies.

25. Note that it is current account openness as well as financial openness that matters for this conclusion.

26. While a closed-form solution demonstrating this result is not available, Ball (1999, pp. 132–3) obtains it in a simulation of the present model. Gomez (2000) conducts analogous exercises using the more elaborate model in Svensson (2000). For flexible CPI inflation targeting (the case relevant to the present discussion), he obtains this result over most of the relevant range: as the share of imported goods in the CPI rises from, say, 10 to 50 per cent, the reaction to innovations in domestic inflation declines relative to the reaction to output innovations. However, as openness begins to rise from very low levels, the reaction to inflation innovations falls relative to the reaction to output innovations. Since an increase in the share of imported goods affects several parameters of Svensson's model (notably the effects of both the exchange rate and the output gap on inflation and effect of the exchange rate in the Phillips Curve) in interdependent nonlinear ways, it is not surprising that the change in the ratio of the two reaction function coefficients is not the same over the entire range of possible values for openness.

27. The weaker exchange rate also implies future inflation insofar as it boosts export demand, but this is a secondary effect. That a decline in capital inflows would raise aggregate demand seems peculiar; it is a figment of the present thought experiment because the domestic interest rate (the other main determinant of aggregate demand) is held constant. The paradox is dissolved by the next sentence in the text.

28. Freedman (1994) has suggested that the weights in the composite indicator made up of the interest rate and the exchange rate (the 'monetary conditions indicator') should be proportional to the coefficients on $e$ and $r$ in the Phillips Curve (equation 8.2). That is, they should be proportional to the parameters $\beta$ and $\delta$. For representative parameter values, this means that when the exchange rate depreciates by 1 per cent, holding everything else constant, the interest rate has to be raised by some 30 basis points to damp down growth and the domestic inflation that it provokes. (In constructing this example I assume that it is the log exchange rate but the level of the interest rate that enter equation 8.2.) In reality, the optimal response depends on more than simply these two parameters, as should now be clear, but Ball (1999) shows that Freedman's intuition is basically correct: that the weights are likely to be fairly close to the ratio of coefficients on the exchange rate and the interest rate in the Phillips curve.

29. Under the assumption that even temporary shocks to the foreign exchange market have persistent output effects, as will be the case given the structure of equation 8.2.

30. Ryan and Thompson (2000) suggest that it may not be necessary to explicitly target the domestic price index if the CPI target is defined as an interval rather than a point. Australia's monetary policy framework, they show, deals adequately with this problem by permitting relatively small divergences from the 2–3 per cent target band over the cycle 'provided inflation is forecast to be back within 2–3 per cent in the medium term. The forward-looking nature of policy should also be sufficient to prevent the RBA from responding to exchange rate shocks which are only expected to have a temporary effect on inflation' (p. 2).

31. It may seem peculiar that the central bank will intervene less to neutralize transitory shocks to the foreign exchange market (which standard efficiency arguments suggest it might want to obviate) than in response to long-lived shocks. The result reflects the existence of control

lags between monetary policy on the one hand and inflation and output on the other; in this setup, responding as vigorously to a purely temporary shock as to a permanent shock just destabilizes the target variables.

32. We can model this by adding the commodity market disturbance $\mu$ to the exchange-rate and aggregate–demand relationships (8.5) and (8.2). The former becomes:

$$e_t - E(e_{t+1}) = r_t - r = + v_t + \mu_t, \tag{8.5'}$$

while the latter becomes:

$$y_{t+1} - y^* = \lambda(y_t - y^*) - \beta(r_t - r^*) - \delta e_t + \xi\mu_t + n_{t+1}, \tag{8.2'}$$

where $\xi$ is a parameter linking the terms-of-trade shock to aggregate demand. (The export-demand shock is assumed to affect output with the same lag as movements in the exchange rate emanating from other sources.)

33. Ball (2000) similarly analyses how the monetary conditions indicator may be an inferior indicator of the stance of policy in response to certain shocks.

34. The sources and further implications of limited credibility are left to Subsection D below.

35. There is some anecdotal evidence of this for Brazil and Mexico (Mishkin and Savastano 2000) and for Israel (Leiderman and Bufman 2001).

36. See Sachs (1980).

37. This is note to say that central bankers in fully indexed economies have necessarily had particular success in hitting that target, especially in those countries where fiscal deficits are chronic and central bank independence is limited.

38. See below.

39. As noted above, this can be interpreted as minimizing the loss function using all the relevant information. This should be the central bank's internal forecast and not a market forecast to avoid problems of multiple equilibria.

40. The point applies to Brazil, for example, which had considerable success in moderating inflation between 1994 and 1998.

41. There are likely to be credibility issues here as well. Again I defer these to a subsequent subsection.

42. Since their measure of core inflation is constructed transparently, this should be something that private agents are able to replicate.

43. As it turns out, this is not precisely what those concerned with the perverse effect of exchange rate changes in the presence of liability dollarization have in mind, as I explain momentarily.

44. We can also see this from Freedman's formulation of the monetary conditions indicator and from Ball's model, where the weight on the exchange rate in the MEI declines with $\delta$.

45. Here it is important to interpret $e$ as the *real* exchange rate and $r$ as the *real* interest rate, since even temporary depreciation will lead to inflation and a higher price level, whose implications for the real exchange rate are otherwise suppressed in this simple model by omitting that price level from the aggregate demand equation.

46. If, for example, default rates are not just proportional to the rate of currency depreciation but increase at an accelerating pace, this could plausibly be the case.

47. It is revealing that emerging markets have generally introduced full-fledged inflation targeting only after first attaining strong fiscal positions. See Schechter et al. (2000). Then there is the argument of whether inflation targeting is part of the solution to the problem of 'fiscal dominance', as the time inconsistency problem created by chronic deficits is known. This is, of course, the same argument made by some advocates of hard pegs and is open to the same objections. I return to this point below.

48. A comprehensive compendium of the relevant evidence is Mahadeva and Sterne (2000).

49. I say more on the reform of fiscal institutions below.

50. The same negative implications also follow, of course, for any other monetary regime if the financial system is fragile, the commitment to fiscal discipline is questionable, the monetary

authorities lack autonomy and independence, and the economy is subject to foreign disturbances. I return to this point in the conclusion.

51. In countries where the authorities have manipulated price indices in the past, they may question whether an index specially constructed for use in inflation targeting can be taken at face
value.

52. As Jonas (2000, p. 3) writes of the Czech case, 'The "just-do-it" approach to monetary policy
probably would not be very effective in bringing inflation expectations and actual inflation
down. Public announcements by the CNB about its expectations of future inflation would also
probably not suffice to anchor inflation expectations and persuade economic agents that
monetary policy would be actually conducted with the aim to achieve the announced
inflation.'

53. There is evidence that more centralized and hierarchical fiscal policy-making processes lead
to better fiscal outcomes and that large vertical imbalances heighten bailout and inflation risk
(von Hagen and Eichengreen 1996).

54. While the Czech Republic and South Africa have escape clauses spelling out in advance the
circumstances over which targets may be missed and requiring the central bank to indicate
the time frame in which it will attempt to return to the target inflation path, in practice neither
country has been willing to utilize the provision.

55. Chile is thus said to have chosen 'a clear and widely understood index like the headline
CPI....[precisely in order] to enhance the communicational effectiveness of inflation targeting.'
Morande (2000), p. 161. From this point of view it is no coincidence that emerging market
inflation targeters typically target the CPI, while industrial-country inflation targeters generally
target core inflation (Schechter et al. 2000).

56. Or, in the European case, by joining a monetary union in partnership with the issuers of a
recognized international currency.

57. In this respect, it obviously complicates the execution and effects of *any* monetary policy operating strategy, and not just inflation targeting. I return to this momentarily.

58. Even if they do, questions about the central bank's intentions and independence mean that financial variables and the nonfinancial magnitudes they affect will be more volatile than in a
country whose inflation-targeting central bank enjoys greater credibility. Under such circumstances, it is unrealistic to promise that volatility will fall to the levels enjoyed by
advanced-industrial economies that target inflation. The same is true, of course, of any other
monetary regime so long as the financial system is fragile, the commitment to fiscal discipline
is questionable, and the economy is subject to foreign disturbances. A dollarized emerging
market subject to these conditions will similarly be more volatile than the typical advanced-
industrial country. Some may argue that the very act of dollarizing can solve all problems of
financial fragility. Others will suggest that explicit inflation targeting can solve problems of
fiscal indiscipline. If either argument is correct, then it creates a strong presumption in favor
of one or the other of these regimes. But most readers presumably believe that financial
problems have deeper roots than simply the monetary regime, and that fiscal problems are a
function of more than just the availability of seignorage revenues. This is just another way of
saying that a mere change in monetary regime is unlikely to solve all problems of economic
development, miraculously transforming developing countries into G7 nations.

# REFERENCES

Aghion, Philippe, Philippe Bachetta and Abijit Banerjee (1999), *Capital Markets and Instability in Open Economies*, unpublished manuscript, Study Center Gerzensee.

Ball, Lawrence (1999), 'Policy rules for open economies,' in John Taylor (ed.), *Monetary Policy Rules*, Chicago: University of Chicago Press, pp. 127–56.

Ball, Lawrence (2000), *Policy Rules and External Shocks*, NBER Working Paper no. 7910 (September).

Bernanke, Ben, Thomas Lubach, Frederic Mishkin and Adam Posen (1999), *Inflation Targeting: Lessons from the International Experience*, Princeton, NJ: Princeton University Press.

Bharucha, Nargis and Christopher Kent (1998), *Inflation Targeting in a Small Open Economy*, Discussion Paper no. 98-07, Reserve Bank of Australia (July).

Bogdanski, Joel, Alexandre Tombini and Sergio Werlang (2000), *Implementing Inflation Targeting in Brazil*, Working Paper no. 1, Central Bank of Brazil (July).

Calvo, Guillermo (2000a), *The Case for Hard Pegs*, unpublished manuscript, University of Maryland at College Park.

Calvo, Guillermo (2000b), *Capital Markets and the Exchange Rate, with Special Reference to the Dollarization Debate in Latin America*, unpublished manuscript, University of Maryland at College Park.

Calvo, Guillermo and Carmen Reinhart (2000), *Fear of Floating*, NBER Working Paper no. 7993 (November).

Christoffersen, Peter and Robert Wescott (1999), *Is Poland Ready for Inflation Targeting?* IMF Working Paper no. 99/41 (March).

Cooper, Richard (1999), 'Exchange rate choices,' in Jane Sneddon Little and Giovanni Olivei (eds), *Rethinking the International Monetary System*, Boston: Federal Reserve Bank of Boston, pp. 99–123.

De Brouwer, G. and J. O'Regan (1997), 'Evaluating Simple Monetary-Policy Rules for Australia,' in Philip Lowe (ed.), *Monetary Policy and Inflation Targeting*, Sydney: Reserve Bank of Australia, pp. 244–76.

Devereux, Michael and Philip Lane (2000), *Exchange Rates and Monetary Policy in Emerging Market Economies*, unpublished manuscript, University of British Columbia and Hong Kong Monetary Authority.

Eichengreen, Barry, Paul Masson, Miguel Savastano and Sunil Sharma (1999), *Transition Strategies and Nominal Anchors on the Road to Greater Exchange Rate Flexibility*, *Essays in International Finance*, no.213, International Finance Section, Department of Economics, Princeton University (April).

Freedman, Charles (1994), *The Use of Indicators and of the Monetary Conditions Index in Canada*, in Tomas J.T. Balino and Carlo Cottarelli (eds), *Frameworks for Monetary Stability*, Washington, DC: International Monetary Fund, pp. 458–77.

Gomez, Javier (2000), *Inflation Targeting and Openness*, unpublished manuscript, Central Bank of Colombia.

Hausmann, Ricardo (1999), *Should There Be 5 Currencies or 105? Foreign Policy*, **122**, 44–53.

Hoffmaister, Alexander (1999), *Inflation Targeting in Korea: An Empirical Exploration*, IMF Working Paper no. WP/99/7, Washington, DC: IMF (January).

Hunt, Ben (1999), *Inter-Forecast Monetary Policy Implementation: Fixed-Instrument versus MCI-Based Strategies*, discussion paper no. G99/1, Reserve Bank of New Zealand (March).

Jonas, Jiri (2000), 'Inflation targeting in transition economies: some issues and experience,' in Warren Coats (ed.), *Inflation Targeting in Transition Economies: The Case of the Czech Republic.*

Krugman, Paul (2001), *Crises: The Next Generation*, unpublished manuscript, Princeton University.

Kumhof, Michael (2000), *Inflation Targeting Under Imperfect Credibility*, unpublished manuscript, Department of Economics, Stanford University.

Leiderman, Leo and Gil Bufman (2001), *Surprises on Israel's Road to Exchange Rate Flexibility*, *Emerging Markets Research*, Deutsche Bank, 23 March.

Levin, Andrew, Volker Wieland and John C. Williams (1999), 'Robustness of simple monetary policy rules under model uncertainty,' in John Taylor (ed.), *Monetary Policy Rules*, Chicago: University of Chicago Press, pp. 263–99.

Mahadeva, Lavan and Gabriel Sterne (eds) (2000), *Monetary Policy Frameworks in a Global Context*, London: Routledge.

Masson, Paul, Miguel Savastano and Sunil Sharma (1997), *The Scope for Inflation Targeting in Developing Countries*, IMF Working Paper no. 130 (October).

Mishkin, Frederic (2000), 'Inflation targeting for emerging-market economies,' *American Economic Review Papers and Proceedings*, **90**, pp. 105–9.

Mishkin, Frederic and Miguel Savastano (2000), *Monetary Policy Strategies for Latin America*, NBER Working Paper no. 7617 (March).

Morande, Felipe G. (2000), 'A decade of inflation targeting in Chile: main developments and lessons', in Charles Joseph and Anton Gunawan (eds), *Monetary Policy and Inflation Targeting in Emerging Economies,* Jakarta: Bank Indonesia, pp. 149–79.

Mundell, Robert (1997), *The International Monetary System in the 21st Century*, Latrobe, Penn.: St. Vincent's College.

Rivas, Luis A. (2001), *Underlying Inflation Measures as Short-Run Inflation Targets in Developing Economies: The Case of Nicaragua*, unpublished manuscript, Central Bank of Nicaragua.

Ryan, Chris and Christopher Thompson (2000), *Inflation Targeting and Exchange Rate Fluctuations in Australia*, Research Discussion Paper 2000-06, Reserve Bank of Australia (September).

Sachs, Jeffrey A. (1980), 'Wages, flexible exchange rates, and macroeconomic policy,' *Quarterly Journal of Economics*, **94**, pp. 737–47.

Schaechter, Andrea, Mark R. Stone and Mark Zelmer (2000), 'Adopting inflation targeting: practical issues for emerging market countries,' Occasional Paper no. 202, Washington, DC: IMF.

Svensson, Lars (1996), 'Commentary,' in Federal Reserve Bank of Kansas City, *Achieving Price Stability*, Kansas City: Federal Reserve Bank of Kansas City, pp. 209–28.

Svensson, Lars (1999), 'Inflation targeting as a monetary policy rule,' *Journal of Monetary Economics*, **43**, pp. 607–54.

Svensson, Lars (2000), 'Open-economy inflation targeting,' *Journal of International Economics*, **50**, pp. 155–83.

Taylor, John B. (1993), 'Discretion Versus Policy Rules in Practice,' *Carnegie Rochester Conference Series on Public Policy*, **39**, pp. 195–214.

Von Hagen, Juergen and Barry Eichengreen (1996), 'Fiscal restraints, federalism and European Monetary Union: is the excessive deficit procedure counterproductive?' *American Economic Review Papers and Proceedings*, **86**, 134–8.

Williamson, John (2000), 'Exchange rate regimes for emerging markets: reviving the intermediate option,' Policy Analyses in International Economics, **60**, Washington, DC: Institute for International Economics.

# 9. Integrating uneven partners: the destabilizing effects of financial liberalization and internationalization of Latin American economics

**Rogério Studart**

## INTRODUCTION

In the second half of 1980s and throughout the first half of the 1990s, there was a spectacular growth of financial markets in the developed economies. This growth was soon followed by a significant surge of capital flows from mature economies to developing countries. In particular, in Latin America the opening of capital account (in the context of liberalizing policies of the end of 1980s and beginning of the 1990s) led to a very significant surge of voluntary foreign capital inflows. These flows had strong destabilizing effects on key economic variables, such as exchange rates, domestic supply of credit and domestic asset prices – soon followed by significant macro and financial imbalance. This chapter claims that to some this instability was originated by the abrupt and careless integration of two financial markets of quite distinct structure, size, depth and pace of growth. Even though the international financial environment and the policy regimes did have an important role in creating the macro and financial imbalances of the 1990s in Latin America, here we want to focus on the 'domestic financial channels' – that is, the links between surges of financial capital in the context of a bank-based financial system with shallow credit and securities markets and of highly unstable growth performance.

The paper is structured in four parts in addition to this introduction. Section 2 contrasts the distinct structural features and pace of development of financial systems of developed and Latin American economies in the 1980s. Section 3 presents a theoretical account of the transmission channels of surges of capital inflows into a bank-based developing economy, focusing on the domestic financial channels – on which we want to focus our analysis here. Section 4 discusses, in the light of the analysis in the three previous sections, the impacts of the above-mentioned surges on macroeconomic performance and financial stability in the region. Section 5 summarises our findings and presents our conclusions.

## UNEVEN PARTNERS

Financial systems in a number of key mature economies (especially the US economy) changed dramatically in the 1980s and 1990s, as a consequence of domestic deregulation and external financial liberalization.[1] At least four strong trends are observed.

First, a well-known process of desintermediation occurred: the traditional banking institutions were transformed into new financial services firms – including those of institutional securities firms, insurance companies, and asset managers. In addition financial institutions other than banks – such as mutual funds, investment banks, pension funds and insurance companies – began actively competing with banks both on the asset and liability sides of banks' balance sheets. Second, the deregulation and growth of institutional investors – especially pension funds and insurance companies – have made their role in the provision of loanable funds more prominent. Finally external liberalization and significant improvements in information technology have increased across-the-border dealings of securities, and internationalization of the financial business.

The mere fact that new financially 'heavy-weight' agents (investment banks, mutual funds and institutional investors) were allowed to expand their securities trading led to a rapid growth of prices in the secondary markets. This created a virtuous circle of expansion of asset prices and markets: as financial wealth increased, investors' expectations were fulfilled, leading to further rounds of financial investment. Not surprisingly, the total financial assets in the hands of institutional investors almost tripled from 1987 to 1990, and again almost doubled from 1990 to 1996 (Table 9.1).

In addition, evidenced by Fornari and Levy (1999) the gross financial assets of the G6 doubled as a proportion of GDP between 1980 and 1994, whereas the liquidity of these assets increased substantially.[2] Just to give a measure of this trend, from 1989 to 1993, the outstanding amounts of debt securities issued in OECD economies increased over US\$ 6 trillion, and more than doubled from 1989 to 2000 (Table 9.2).

The surge of capital flows to developing economies in the 1990s is directly associated with the process described above. First of all, the rapid growth of financial wealth in the hands of private financial investors increased the demand for 'risk diversification'. This explains to a great extent the expansion of a variety of specialized securities markets in mature economies – especially in the USA – from investment asset-based securities (for instance, mortgage-based

Table 9.1 Financial assets in the hands of institutional investors in selected OECD economies

| | Investment companies | | | | Insurance companies | | | |
|---|---|---|---|---|---|---|---|---|
| | 1987 | 1990 | 1993 | 1996 | 1987 | 1990 | 1993 | 1996 |
| USA | 770 | 1069 | 2075 | 3539 | 1095 | 1900 | 2422 | 3052 |
| Japan | 305 | 336 | 455 | 420 | 271 | 1067 | 1620 | 1956 |
| Germany | 42 | 72 | 79 | 124 | 155 | 401 | 452 | 692 |
| France | 204 | 379 | 484 | 529 | 74 | 239 | 363 | 582 |
| United Kingdom | 68 | 89 | 131 | 188 | 190 | 454 | 667 | 792 |
| Other OECD | 161 | 184 | 517 | 533 | 180 | 565 | 645 | 908 |
| Subtotal | 1550 | 2129 | 3741 | 5333 | 1965 | 4626 | 6169 | 7982 |

| | Pension Funds | | | | Total | | | |
|---|---|---|---|---|---|---|---|---|
| | 1987 | 1990 | 1993 | 1996 | 1987 | 1990 | 1993 | 1996 |
| USA | 1606 | 2492 | 3449 | 4752 | 3471 | 5461 | 7946 | 11343 |
| Japan | 0 | 0 | 0 | 0 | 576 | 1403 | 2075 | 2376 |
| Germany | 22 | 52 | 47 | 65 | 219 | 525 | 578 | 881 |
| France | 0 | 0 | 0 | 0 | 278 | 618 | 847 | 1111 |
| United Kingdom | 224 | 537 | 682 | 897 | 482 | 1080 | 1480 | 1877 |
| Other OECD | 287 | 612 | 668 | 886 | 628 | 1361 | 1830 | 2327 |
| Subtotal / TOTAL | 2139 | 3693 | 4846 | 6600 | **5654** | **10448** | **14756** | **19915** |

*Source:* BIS (1998: 76–97). Data consolidated by the author.

Table 9.2  Outstanding amounts of debt securities issued in domestic markets (US$ billions and %)

| | 1989 | 1993 | 1997 | 2000 | 1989 | 1993 | 1997 | 2000 |
|---|---|---|---|---|---|---|---|---|
| | US$ billions | | | | % of total | | | |
| All issuers | 14042.4 | 20564.7 | 25464 | 29732.9 | 100.0 | 100.0 | 100.0 | 100.0 |
| *OECD* | *13558.7* | *19966.7* | *24452.4* | *28579.9* | *96.6* | *97.1* | *96.0* | *96.1* |
| United States | 6682.8 | 9226.7 | 12059 | 14545.9 | 47.6 | 44.9 | 47.4 | 48.9 |
| Japan | 2626.7 | 4010.1 | 4399.3 | 6072.3 | 18.7 | 19.5 | 17.3 | 20.4 |
| France | 557.6 | 995.7 | 1102.5 | 1068.1 | 4.0 | 4.8 | 4.3 | 3.6 |
| Germany | 668.4 | 1458.4 | 1732.1 | 1711.6 | 4.8 | 7.1 | 6.8 | 5.8 |
| UK | 332.9 | 446.1 | 777.7 | 895.9 | 2.4 | 2.2 | 3.1 | 3.0 |
| *Latin America* | *172.1* | *296.7* | *490.6* | *482.8* | *1.2* | *1.4* | *1.9* | *1.6* |
| Argentina | 113.5 | 39 | 70.1 | 85.2 | 0.8 | 0.2 | 0.3 | 0.3 |
| Brazil | – | 189.9 | 344.5 | 292.5 | – | 0.9 | 1.4 | 1.0 |
| Chile | 7.5 | 19.2 | 36.5 | 34.2 | 0.1 | 0.1 | 0.1 | 0.1 |
| Mexico | 51.1 | 47.9 | 37.6 | 67.3 | 0.4 | 0.2 | 0.1 | 0.2 |
| Peru | – | 0.7 | 1.9 | 3.6 | – | 0.0 | 0.0 | 0.0 |

*Source:*  BIS database; consolidated and elaborated by the author.

179

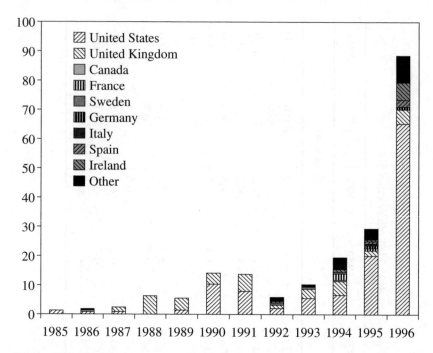

*Source*: BIS (1998: 43).

*Figure 9.1* *Announced asset-backed bonds in the international markets
(US$ billions)*

securities) to 'junk bonds'. This search for risk diversification also explains a
great deal of the expansion of across-the-border securities dealings, and the
development of foreign-asset based securities (such as ADRs and GDRs) in the
'international' markets – as for instance happened with the asset-based securities
issued in securities markets (Figure 9.1).

As in developed economies, but on a much smaller scale, Latin American financial markets increased substantially in the 1990s – as evidenced by Table
9.2 above.

However, in contrast to what happened in developed economies, and as in
most developing economies (Beck et al., 2000), Latin American financial systems
in the early 1990s continued to suffer from similar structural problems to those
described by Raymond Goldsmith (1969) in the 1960s:[3] (1) the banking sector
remained relatively small (Figure 9.1),[4] lending relatively little and concentrating
its operations on short-term activities, including the refinancing of government
debt, and was highly vulnerable to external shocks; (2) the supply of loanable
funds to specific sectors continued to be highly rationed.[5] This implies that credit

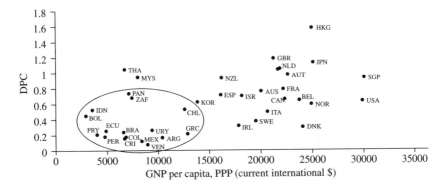

*Note*:   DPC = Private Credit by Deposit Money Banks to GDP.

*Source*:   World Bank (2001). Elaborated by the author.

*Figure 9.2*    *Private credit from deposit money banks to GDP – selected developed and developing economies (1997)*

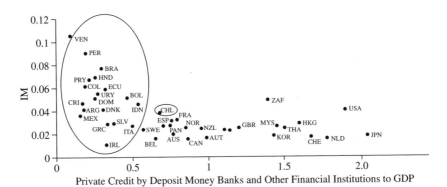

*Note*:   IM = Net interest margin (%).

*Source*:   World Bank (2001). Elaborated by the author.

*Figure 9.3*    *Interest rates margins in selected developed and developing economies (1997)*

market is *supply-constrained* in many sectors, and these expenditures tended to be highly sensitive to changes in the supply of loanable funds; (3) net interest margins in the banking sector were still much higher than those found in developed economies (Figure 9.2), an indication of very high *spreads*, leading to non-competitive financial costs to the domestic corporate sectors and high levels

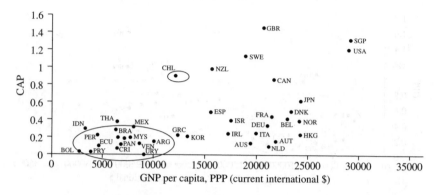

*Note*:    CAP = Stock market capitalization to GDP.

*Source*:    World Bank (2001). Elaborated by the author.

*Figure 9.4    Some indicators of the size of securities in selected developed
and developing economies (1997)*

of self-finance (which is a deterrent to economic expansion);[6] (4) securities
markets remained small (Figure 9.3), and the *primary markets* actually shrunk
in the 1990s, rather than expanded (cf. Dowers et al, 2000).[7]

In the late 1980s Latin American economies opened up their capital accounts
and their domestic financial markets to foreign investors. Given the characteristics of Latin American financial systems (vis-à-vis those of the US economies),
the microeconomic incentives for portfolio investors in investing in some Latin
American financial markets and domestic financial institutions and large corporations issuing became quite significant – as we will see below. This
microeconomically rational behavior was, to a great extent, the main source of
the process of increasing macro-financial vulnerability and instability in the
region in the 1990s.

In order to understand why this integration was destabilizing, we must depict
how this surge of capital flows affected key macro and financial variables in
Latin American economies. This is our next topic.

## A)    A Stylized Transmission Mechanism

All developing economies are soft-currency economies,[8] so that it is fair to assume that surges of financial flows affect their performance depending on:

- the international financial environment – the volume of these flows in relation to the size of the economy and their volatility;

- policy regimes – the exchange rate, trade, monetary and fiscal policy regimes 'chosen' by the specific economy;
- domestic financial channels:
  - structure of domestic financial markets – the size, development and
    depth of domestic financial institutions and markets;
  - growth dynamics – the domestic dynamics of investment, consump-
    tion and government expenditure in the economy.

The diagram below presents a visual guidance to our discussion.

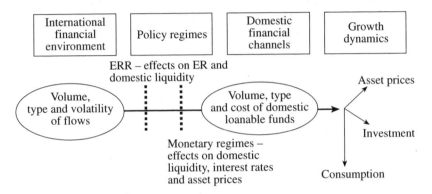

*Source*:  Elaborated by the author.

*Figure 9.5   Transmission channels of surges of foreign capital inflows*

## B)   International Financial Environment and Policy Regime

The international financial environment (IFE hereafter) determines the freedom
of capital flows between developed and developing economies. In contrast to
what was observed in the post-war period until the 1970s, financial development
and internationalization was significant in the 1980s and 1990s. The deregulation of capital accounts in both developed and developing economies allowed
for a significant increase of the volume, a diversification of flows (especially in
the direction of more portfolio flows) and more mobility (and volatility of these
flows) (see for example, Ocampo 1999). Given the *pull factors* (that is, risk-di-
versification by investors in mature economies), this opening allowed for a rapid
expansion of financial integration.

Given this IFE, the relative size of capital flows, *vis-à-vis* the size of the
economy matters in fundamental ways. Excessive capital flows (in relation to
the need to finance current account deficits) lead to excess supply of foreign
reserves in the economy, which creates pressure either to revaluation of the do-

mestic currency. This excess supply can be measured by the accumulation of reserves during a period of surge of capital inflows. This excess supply has consequences on the real (trade and output) as well as on the financial side (capital account and to the domestic financial markets) of developing economies, contingent on the policy regimes in place in the recipient economies.

The size of such flows vis-à-vis the size of host economies and of their domestic financial system determines the capacity of economies to absorb such flows productively. How such 'excessive flows' were to affect the domestic economies was very much a result of the policy regimes adopted.

Policy regimes can be seen as the 'filters' in the transmission mechanisms of surges of capital inflows. First, the capital account regime can *partly* restrict the volume and the type of flows allowed into the country. Second, exchange rate regimes determine how excessive flows of foreign capital are internalised: in a purely floating ERR, the impact of surges would fall only on the exchange rate, that is, the excess would be translated into exchange rate revaluation; whereas in fixed ERR, the surges will result in expansion of domestic liquidity, even if monetary authorities attempt to sterilize it (more on this below). Third, the trade regime will determine how the changes of exchange rate will affect the trade balance. Finally, monetary policy regimes determine whether domestic monetary authorities will be prepared to sterilize or not the additional liquidity created by a surge of capital flows. If the monetary authorities decide (or are able)[9] to sterilize, open market operations can maintain interest rates high. It is important to notice though that in such a case this will create further incentives for continued capital inflows, as well as put pressure on fiscal balance (more on this below).

There are obviously many combinations of the items above (IFE and policy regimes), so that for the sake of simplicity our theoretical discussion will be based on the characteristic policy and structural environments surrounding Latin American economies in the 1980s and 1990s (when the most recent surge of capital inflows started).

For a significant number of the economies in the region, the policy regime adopted in the early 1990s was a mixture of highly liberal capital account and trade policies – with an important exception, that is Chile where some policies towards selective entry of capital were implemented. Exchange rate policies were used as anchors for price stabilization policies, whereas the monetary policy maintained the differentials between domestic and international interest rates high enough to continue attracting capital flows (especially portfolio flows). Given the characteristics of the IFE, the policy regimes and the structure of domestic financial systems in Latin American economies, we can go on to analyse the domestic financial channels of surges of capital flows into the region – as we mentioned, the focus of our analysis in this chapter.

## C)   Domestic Financial Channels

The shallowness of secondary asset markets in developing economies makes domestic asset markets very sensitive to abrupt changes in liquidity. Unlike what happened in the US economy (as described above), the links between secondary and primary securities markets is weak, so that rapid expansion of the former does not lead necessarily to the expansion of the issues of securities. To the contrary, a rapid growth of the liquidity of these markets tend to become mainly speculative bubbles, which creates disincentives for both issuers and long-term investors to remain in the market.

Further, in the context of rapid financial integration and exchange rate stability, the larger size and greater depth of securities markets in mature economies makes them more attractive to large corporations (exactly those that issue securities in developing economies) to issue abroad. Paradoxically, thus, surges of capital flows in the context of the 'integration of uneven partners' tends to exacerbate the speculative nature of securities markets, and to create barriers for the long term development of these markets in developing economies.

A different logic applies to foreign direct investment in the 1990s: most FDI to developing economies has been associated with acquisitions of companies in the context of privatisation of public companies and banks. Of course these flows *per se* are only direct changes of the ownership of capital, and do not lead to expansion of aggregate demand. But they do tend to create rapid increases in share prices.

Even though securities markets are small, and their impact can be reduced in affecting expenditure decisions, the bursting of speculative bubbles can affect both key domestic financial players and expectations in the economy. In both cases, this can affect macroeconomic performance.

Now, let us consider flows generated by the domestic banks borrowing in the international market. Due to their balance-sheet structure, banks are usually suppliers of short-term credit. The shallowness of markets in long-term securities and the poor development of interbank deposits markets reduce their capacity to manage their liabilities in order to compensate for changes in their reserves. In these circumstances, banks tend to be very conservative: they tend to undertake short, restricted lending to privileged agents (large corporations and governments) and maintain high spreads. The access to international markets provides banks with expanded sources of funding at low interest rates (vis-à-vis domestic markets) and longer maturities. As long as the exchange rate is perceived as stable (as was the case in most economies in the region in the early 1990s), it is microeconomically rational to borrow long abroad to lend short domestically. Such an increase of external funding increases the domestic competition for expansion of bank loans.

How these surges will affect the macroeconomic performance of the domestic economy will, finally, depend on the inherited growth dynamics and the inherited vulnerability of domestic financial systems. These are our next topics.

## D)  Inherited Growth Dynamics

The supply and maturities of loanable funds represent a constraint on the expenditure decisions of different agents in the economy, being a more determined factor for some (for instance, consumers) than for others (such as firms and governments). Surges of financial flows tend to reduce these constraints, as the additional domestic liquidity, created by the domestic intermediation, pushes domestic intermediaries to expand their assets. But final distribution of these loanable funds depends on the dynamics of growth.

In some East Asian economies, for instance, the surge of capital inflows was associated with expansion of investment (see Park, 1998). This is not at all surprising given that one of the characteristics of the region in the recent past was sustained growth led by domestic investment and exports, and government deficits and debts were relatively small in the early 1990s.

In Latin America, by contrast, investment was depressed during the 1980s, whereas fiscal disequilibria were significant (more on this below). Given the macroeconomic uncertainties and the extent of competitive pressure put on investors, long-term expectations, and thus investment, tended to be highly depressed in the 1990s. As mentioned above, consumer credit in the region, due to the characteristics of the domestic financial structure mentioned below, is highly rationed. In contrast with investment, thus consumption responds rapidly to changes in the supply of credit. Thus in Latin America most of these surges are associated with 'over-consumption', rather than 'over-investment'.

In addition, given the same uncertainties and other characteristics of the financial sector, and as mentioned above, the intermediation *spreads* of even short-term credit tend to be very high, whereas the private supply of long-term loanable funds is simply irrelevant. All these supply and demand factors in the credit market in Latin America tend to create a significant causal relation between surges of financial flows, credit expansion and domestic consumption booms. These, in turn, affect financial stability, according to the inherited stage of financial fragility – as we will discuss below.

## E)  Inherited Financial Fragility

First, some words on financial fragility in the context of specific financial structures.

A market economy is characterized by the fact that some expenditures (for instance, the acquisition of durable goods) and long-term uncertain undertakings (fixed capital for instance) need to be financed via the issuance of short-term assets (such as bank deposits) or liquid marketable assets. This combination of uncertainty and maturity mismatching makes our economies inherently a financially fragile economy.

Keynes (1936) rightly noticed that in an economy with developed financial asset markets changes in the expectation of players in financial markets, which can be significant in periods of uncertainty, could lead to significant changes in the demand for money and interest rates. This in Keynes's view could not only create undesirable changes in relative prices of all other assets and goods, but also reduce productive entrepreneurs' capacity to repay their debts. Other authors, *inter alia* Minsky (e.g. 1982), based on Fisher's (1933) early description of debt-deflation processes, showed that if monetary authorities did not intervene in this case, this process would lead to decline in output, employment and bankruptcies.[10]

Both Keynes and Minsky based their views on a historically specific, anglosaxon capital market-based financial system. The same rationale can be applied to bank-based systems, of the type observed in Latin American economies, with some caveats. First of all, it is bankers' expectations (much more than expectations of traders in securities markets), which are obvious at the centre of changes of supply of liquidity in bank-based systems. This is not the appropriate place to discuss a Keynesian approach to the banking firm,[11] but it can be said that, given these expectations, banks will expand credit according to the supply of reserves available to them.

According to the approach above, surges of capital flows will affect the financial fragility of a given economy according to the way liquidity is expanded in the process and how this expanded liquidity affects domestic financial flows – and this has a lot to do with the domestic financial structure. In general, though, periods of surges of capital flows are associated with improved expectations, both of international investors and domestic players, on the future macroeconomic performance of the economy.

It is seemingly rational to assume that bankers' expectations also tend to improve in such periods. So, not surprisingly, surges of foreign capital flows to Latin America are often associated with the expansion of domestic credit, higher leverage of domestic banks and higher levels of indebtedness by private and public agents. That is, such flows tend to increase domestic financial fragility – as defined above. Fragility does not mean instability: it takes abrupt changes of certain key variables – for instance, an economic downturn, an abrupt change in interest rates and/or in the exchange rates (if a significant part of domestic liabilities are denominated in foreign currencies) – to turn financial fragility into financial instability.

Given the characteristics of developing markets described above, the policy regimes adopted in Latin America in the 1980s, and the analysis made in the previous paragraph, how did large surges of financial flows affect domestic macroeconomic performance and financial stability? This is the theme of our last topic before the conclusion.

## SURGES OF FOREIGN CAPITAL INFLOWS, MACROECONOMIC PERFORMANCE AND FINANCIAL STABILITY

### A) Types of Flows

As mentioned above, in the first half of the 1990s, there was a spectacular growth of financial markets in the developed economies. This growth was soon followed by a significant surge of capital flows to developing countries – which more than tripled from 1991 to 1995. As indicated by Table 9.3, these flows have only been a fraction of those between mature economies, but by all measures are signification vis-à-vis the size of developing economies and their domestic financial markets.[12]

The policy regimes in many Latin American economies had some distinctive features, but were also in a certain way influenced by the opportunity offered by such excessive flows. After one decade of balance-of-payments constraints (and net negative resource transfers) leading to very poor macroeconomic performance and high inflation in Latin America, the surge of capital inflows-*cum*-trade liberalization eased the external constraint on the expansion of domestic demand associated with expanding imports[13] (Table 9.4). In addition, given these exceptional external conditions, many economies in the region used some type of exchange-based price stabilisation programs, based on pegged exchange rate regimes and commercial liberalization, which were effective in reducing inflation.[14]

### B) Macroeconomic Performance

Using excessive capital inflows to stabilize prices and to grow had important costs in Latin America in the 1990s. First, in most of the growth dynamics was highly associated with consumption expansion (Chile being one of the very few exceptions).[15] In contrast, (1) domestic investment remained depressed; (2) domestic output grew at a lower pace than aggregate demand; (3) despite the growth of exports, the current account situation continued to deteriorate, owing both to the pace of growth of imports and to the increasing external debt. In sum, whereas in the short-medium run external imbalances, and thus external financial dependency, continued to grow, potential output was growing at a pace that was lower than needed to solve the macroeconomic imbalances created in the process.

Table 9.3 Developing-country shares (percentages except where stated otherwise)

| | 1991 | 1992 | 1993 | 1994 | 1995 | 1996 | 1997 | 1998 | 1999 | 2000 |
|---|---|---|---|---|---|---|---|---|---|---|
| In global total private capital flows | 11.8 | 12.4 | 12.6 | 12.8 | 12.4 | 13.2 | 14.4 | 9.9 | 7.6 | 7.6 |
| In global capital market flows | 9.7 | 9.4 | 9.4 | 9 | 9 | 9.8 | 10.8 | 6.2 | 4.7 | 5.5 |
| In global FDI flows | 22.3 | 27.4 | 29.5 | 35.2 | 32.3 | 34.9 | 36.5 | 25.9 | 18.9 | 15.9 |
| In global output | 19.8 | 19.2 | 19.7 | 20 | 20.7 | 22.1 | 23.2 | 21.6 | 21.7 | 22.5 |
| In global trade | 26.5 | 28.3 | 28.3 | 28.4 | 29.5 | 31.3 | 32.4 | 30.7 | 30.7 | 33.4 |
| In global population | 84.1 | 94.3 | 84.4 | 84.5 | 84.6 | 84.7 | 84.9 | 85 | 85.1 | 85.2 |
| | | | | | | | | | | |
| Memo items (billions of dollars) | | | | | | | | | | |
| Global capital market flows | 794 | 850 | 1226 | 1501 | 1928 | 2403 | 2929 | 3033 | 3910 | 4324 |
| Global FDI | 160 | 172 | 226 | 256 | 331 | 377 | 473 | 683 | 982 | 1118 |

Source: World Bank (2001).

189

Table 9.4  *Latin America: some key macroeconomic indicators*

| | 1991 | 1992 | 1993 | 1994 | 1995 | 1996 | 1997 | 1998 | 1999 |
|---|---|---|---|---|---|---|---|---|---|
| | | | | | % changes | | | | |
| GDP | 3.8 | 3.3 | 3.9 | 5.3 | 1.1 | 3.6 | 5.4 | 2.1 | 0.4 |
| Per capita GDP | 2.0 | 1.4 | 2.1 | 3.5 | −0.6 | 1.9 | 3.7 | 0.5 | −1.2 |
| CPI[a] | 199 | 414 | 877 | 333 | 25.8 | 18.2 | 10.4 | 10.3 | 9.6 |
| Terms of trade | 0.8 | −0.6 | −0.4 | 4.9 | 1.2 | 1.4 | 2.0 | −5.8 | 0.4 |
| Urban unemployment rate % | … | 6.5 | 6.5 | 6.6 | 7.5 | 7.9 | 7.5 | 8.1 | 8.7 |
| | | | | | % of GDP[b] | | | | |
| Balance of payments | | | | | | | | | |
| Trade account | 0.4 | −1.2 | −1.5 | −1.7 | −0.7 | −0.5 | −1.5 | −2.7 | −1.1 |
| Current account | −1.5 | −2.7 | −3.3 | −3.3 | −2.2 | −2.1 | −3.3 | −4.5 | −3.1 |
| Capital and financial Account a | 1.9 | 3.9 | 4.4 | 2.7 | 1.8 | 3.7 | 4.3 | 3.5 | 2.8 |
| BOP | 0.5 | 1.2 | 1.2 | −0.6 | −0.4 | 1.6 | 1.1 | −0.9 | −0.3 |
| Total disimbursed external debt | 39.4 | 37.7 | 38.1 | 35.8 | 37.2 | 35.5 | 33.7 | 37.9 | 43.4 |

*Notes:*  [a]Dec–Dec. [b]Estimated using current price dollars.

*Source:*  UN-ECLAC based on official figures.

As external dependency grew, so did the constraints on domestic policy. First, in order to maintain the attractiveness for international investors and domestic borrowers, monetary policies started targeting the maintenance of high interest differentials in many economies, whereas fiscal discipline was used as a tool for adding credibility to the stability of exchange rate regimes.[16] Thus, attracting capital flows became a crusade that often included policy package (beyond the exchange rate regime).

Second, the combination of high levels of interest rates made the process of fiscal adjustment difficult and led to the loss of international competitiveness of domestic corporations, low levels of economic activity and rising unemployment. Third, domestic financial markets became increasingly integrated with the international ones and dollar-denominated liabilities and assets became more widespread: in a significant number of the countries, the process of *policy-induced dollarization* was a fact,[17] – and this has profound effects on financial stability as we will discuss next.

## C)   Financial Fragility

On several occasions in the past (but more obviously in the 1990s), surges of capital flows in Latin America were also associated with domestic financial crises (mainly of the banking sector). These crises in turn prompted policies not only to avoid systemic effects, but also to restructure the domestic banking sector and improve prudential regulation and supervision.[18]

The reasons for these crises have varied, but certainly there are some important explanatory factors relating to four items.

First, there was a rise of intermediation risks associated with exchange rate mismatching. Rapid financial integration led to an *overborrowing syndrome*, to a rapid process of assets and liabilities dollarization and to volatility in the prices of domestic securities and other real assets. The overborrowing syndrome[19] leads to the increasing vulnerability of domestic borrowers to changes in international interest rates and exchange rates – a vulnerability that is related to the increasing mismatching of exchange rates.

In the region, this process took different forms and went to different levels, according to the characteristics of the policy package adopted – but it did happen in a significant number of economies. In Argentina, for instance, there was a rapid increase of dollar-denominated contracts (especially of financial contracts such as consumer and corporate loans) (Studart and Hermann, 2000). In contrast in Brazil, where the law forbids contracts denominated in foreign exchange, asset dollarization took mainly the form of dollar-indexed government bonds.[20]

Second, the domestic maturity mismatching increased, owing to the way financial flows are internalized into the economies of the region. A significant part of these took the form of portfolio investment, foreign direct investment, issues of corporate and government bonds. But another significant part was intermediated by domestic banks to domestic consumers, which was due to two facts. First, as mentioned earlier, banks in the region tend to be very *short-termist*. Second, the expansion of the supply of loanable funds reached the region in a period of high macroeconomic uncertainty and low investment.

Third, the volatility of prices of domestic assets rose, whereas domestic primary markets shrank. In the region, securities markets, when they exist at all, are quite small and affect only marginally the macroeconomic performance (through the formation of expectations for instance).[21] However, one important result of the financial integration of the 1990s was the shrinkage of primary markets, associated both with the delisting of large companies and their option to issue securities abroad (Dowers et al., 2000). This is likely to create further problems of investment finance, and thus growth in the long run.

Fourth, exchange rate crises have become more frequent, often associated with rapid devaluation and/or interest rate hike. In the context of high maturity and exchange rate mismatching and/or increased supply of credit, raising the domestic interest rates or devaluing exchange rates is a recipe for financial instability. And indeed there were many occasions when both had to be done in view of abrupt reversals of foreign capital flows. Indeed, in many economies of the region, banking crises were often associated with such reversals.

### D)   Recent Developments and a Inheritance of the Integration Among Uneven Partners

In the first half of the 1990s the combination of stable (and sometimes overvalued) exchange rates, commercial opening and financial opening, and fiscal discipline led to a virtuous circle in which a rapid achievement of price stability and exchange rate overvaluation further attracted foreign capital inflows.

The virtuosity of this circle proved however to be a double-edged sword in the second half of the 1990s, a feature that was already signalled by the 1994 Mexican crisis and the *Tequila* contagion effect. From that experience, it was already clear that the economies in the region were too dependent on foreign financial inflows and thus on the *moods* of international financial investors. However, the prompt recovery of the flows to Latin American economies reduced the overall concerns, and very few voices were heard against the continuing process of external fragilization that was in course in the region.

From the eruption of the East Asian crisis in 1998, a deterioration of the confidence of foreign investors was reflected in increasing country risk implicit in the need to maintain even higher levels of interest rates. This in turn led to the widening financial disequilibria in domestic public and private sectors, while the disequilibria of the trade and services accounts of the balance of payments persisted.

Ultimately the growing emerging-market crisis hit the LAC region, beginning with the contagion of the East Asian financial crisis and culminated with the 1999 speculative attack on Brazil – an attack that led (initially) to a chaotic process of devaluation of the Brazilian *Real*. The pressures on Brazil ceded and the price and output effects were far less drastic than expected (by the most optimistic analysts). Nevertheless the devaluation of the *Real* brought a severe misalignment of exchange rates in some important partners of Brazil in the region, especially those in the Mercosul bloc. As occurred in East Asia, the pressures for competitive exchange devaluation became significant and further increased the policy constraints and challenges faced by the region today.

A process of competitive devaluation *per se* can have drastic effects on domestic prices and output – as the experiences in Europe in the 1970s–1980s and, more recently, in East Asia indicate. In economies with low levels of domestic asset and liability dollarization, these effects tend to diminish with time, as real exchange levels are established around their equilibrium levels. However, owing to the degree of *dollarization* of domestic assets and liabilities in countries such as Argentina, Paraguay and Uruguay – just to mention a few – devaluation tends to have further consequences affecting their domestic financial systems. And financial instability, as is well documented, tends to have long-term negative effects on macroeconomic performance.

## CONCLUDING REMARKS

The nature and the transmission of surges of foreign financial flows seem to have become quite different since the 1980s. Financial globalization does not only mean an increase of financial flows between developed and developing economies, but also deeper financial linkages between the economic agents of these economies.

If our reasoning is correct, this integration is inherently destabilizing because of the wide (and widening) differences between financial markets in mature and developing economies. Domestic policies in developing countries can mitigate, but not avoid, these destabilizing effects. At least four complementary strategies need to be implemented in order to avoid surges of financial flows (and abrupt reversals of these flows) affecting the macroeconomic performance and financial stability in the region.

First, a better International Financial Architecture (IFA) is badly needed. Most proposals in this area focus on the need for improved transparency and information, better domestic and international regulation, increased provision of official liquidity in times of crises and more private sector involvement in preventing and resolving crises. Most of these proposals lead, at the end of the day, to a reduction in incentives for abrupt shifts of capital flows and the mitigation of their effects on developing economies, and to more incentives towards increased flows of productive capital into the latter.[22]

Second, until such a more stabilizing IFA is not built, Latin American economies should be able to 'shelter' their economies from the destabilizing effects of short-term volatile capital inflows. The major problem about imposing capital controls is that if this is a long-term policy it tends to affect flows of productive capital (FDI) (on this see Ocampo, 1999). In this sense, this policy cannot be but a medium-term one, in order to buy time for the development of mechanisms which make such short-term capital less harmful and even less necessary (on the need of capital controls, see *inter alia,* Ffrench-Davis, 1999 and Griffith-Jones and Kimmis, 1998).

Third, even if the conditions above are met, given the size and volatility of international financial flows, the maintenance of an autonomous monetary policy can be more of an asset than a liability. And in this case, a more flexible ERR is preferred to a less flexible one. *Choosing an ERR that permits active use of stabilizing monetary policy.* If our analysis is correct, a stabilizing monetary policy is required in order to avoid financial instability and to provide lender-of-last resort-facilities for the domestic banking system. In addition, as shown above, an active monetary policy is required if the rate of growth of developing economies is to be greater that that of developed economies – a requirement that few economists would doubt. Choosing an ERR that inhibits and surrenders policy autonomy in this case may be both counterproductive in terms of avoiding financial stability and in terms of making growth potential effective.

Finally, developing countries should make efforts in the long run to develop financial mechanisms to internally finance and fund production, consumption and investment. The question of financial development cannot be treated in this chapter, much less opened in a conclusion. We would refer the reader to some recent literature on this issue, including the *World Economic and Social Survey* (United Nations, 1999), which in addition to an updated bibliography on the theme has important policy conclusions. Studart (1999) analyses the growth of institutional investors within developing economies.

## NOTES

1.  For more detailed description of the changes in the financial systems of mature economies, see inter alia BIS (1986), Franklin (1993), Feeney (1994), Helleiner (1994), Bloomenstein (1995) and Group of Ten (2001).
2.  This process would probably end up in a tradition Mynskian asset crisis (Minsky, 1982; Taylor and O'Connell, 1985), were it not for the characteristics of the financial markets in some mature economies – especially the US financial markets. This characteristic has to do with the significant side and depth of securities markets and the strong link between secondary and primary markets. The result of this link was that the growth of capital markets provided new

sources of finance to the corporate sector (for instance, the IT sector, 'dot.com' companies and so on), a trend that has been highly leveraged by the use of financial derivatives to unbundle risks and securitize. This provided the financing required for the technological revolution and productivity expansion which in turn permitted the astonishing growth of the US 'new economy' in the 1990s.

3. As a matter of fact they continue to suffer from these problems to this date.

4. In the graphs below (Figures 9.2 to 9.4) the circles comprise most Latin American economies of our sample, as an indication of the comparative stage of development of financial systems in the region viz-a-viz mature economies and even some developing economies.

5. Especially to popular house financing, SME and poor consumers and long-term productive investments.

6. Even though it is possible to reduce such *spreads* through specific policies, as the recent Brazilian experience shows (BCB, 2000), these spreads seem to be highly related to the shallowness of credit markets in developing economies as indicated by Figure 9.3 below.

7. In Latin America, the external financial opening and domestic financial deregulation did change some microeconomic structural problems. But the structural problems described above remained (Beck et al. 2000). This is not surprising: as discussed in Studart (2000), overcoming these structural problems requires long-term financial and institution-building policies.

8. The fact that some developing economies adopt hard currencies as their means of payments (such as in the recent processes of dollarization) does not make them 'hard currency economies', due to the fact that their monetary authorities cannot issue the hard currency adopted. On this see Studart (2001).

9. In the extreme case of a fixed ERR, such as the Argentinean currency board, the option to sterilize is limited. In that case, constraining the expansion of liquidity will have to be placed on the domestic banks' capacity to expand credit, for instance through higher reserve requirements. Indeed this was the option taken in the early stages of the Brazilian stabilization plan in 1994.

10. If such a process of debt deflation becomes a self-filling prophecy, it will not be easily reversed by spontaneous means (Taylor and O'Connell, 1985). And it can create a path-dependent process: bankruptcies are irreversible changes, and if their number is significant, potential output is reduced and growth perspectives are lower. Rational long-term investors would have less confidence in such an economy, leading to lower investment and growth. The expectations that led to the debt-deflation process can become a long, persistent process of stagnation.

11. On this see Keynes himself (1930, vol. I).

12. Even though country-specific features did affect the *distribution* of such flows between developing economies, the *push factors*, related to the changes in financial markets in developed economies, seem to be the most important factor in explaining such growth. This can be seen by the growth of flows to both Latin America and the Caribbean (LAC hereafter) in the 1980s and 1990s, two regions known to have significant macroeconomic performances and that nonetheless had similar trends of capital flows in the 1990s.

13. The surge of capital flows significantly surpassed the needs to finance both the current and the capital account, generating systematic accumulation of reserves in the region.

14. This is not to deny that other measures were necessary to achieve rapid stabilization. In Argentina, for instance, the Plan de Convertibilidad, which led to the creation of a *currency board* system, was effective in breaking down the inflation dynamics mainly by dollarizing a significant part of spot transactions and forward contracts. In Brazil, with a long history of indexation, breaking up with the inflation dynamics also required monetary reform (implemented in 1994), which had the role of dismantling the main mechanisms of indexation of the economy.

15. Given the macroeconomic uncertainties and the extent of competitive pressure put on investors, long-term expectations, and thus investment, tended to be highly depressed in the 1990s. As mentioned above, consumer credit in the region, owing to the characteristics of the domestic financial structure mentioned below, is highly rationed. In contrast with investment, consumption responds rapidly to changes in the supply of credit. Thus in Latin America most of these surges are associated with 'over-consumption', rather than 'over-investment'.

16. Of course, fiscal discipline was also required for assuring sustainable growth of aggregate demand and supply in a context of low inflation.
17. There are four ways dollarization could be achieved. For a classification of types of dollarization see Studart (2001).
18. This is an important topic for several reasons: first, such processes were often with fiscal costs that made the maintenance of fiscal discipline even tougher; second, because the restructuring of the banking system was normally associated with opening up the domestic financial sector to foreign investors; third, because these regulatory and supervisory changes are affecting the way banks and other financial institutions intermediate loanable funds in the economy – a factor that is important for the long-term growth perspectives of some of the economies. These topics go far beyond the scope of these chapters, but see, for instance, Stallings and Studart (2001) for a discussion of this theme.
19. That is, the expansion of external debt in excess of the needs to finance current account deficits leading to accumulation of reserves in periods of surges of financial flows to the region.
20. For an analysis of the process of liability dollarization in the Mercosul region, see Studart and Hermann (2001).
21. An important exception is the Brazilian case, as is evidenced by Studart (2000).
22. Detailed analysis and proposals concerning this new international financial architecture can be found *inter alia* in Ocampo (1999), United Nations Task Force (1999), Fischer (1999) and Griffith-Jones et al. (1999).

# REFERENCES

Beck, T, A. Demirgüç-Kunt, R. Levine and V. Maksimovic (2000), 'Financial structure and economic development: firm, industry and country evidence', mimeo, available at www.worldbank.org, August.

BCB – Banco Central do Brasil (2000), 'Juros e Spreads: avaliação de um ano do programa', available at www.bcb.org.br.

BIS – Bank for International Settlements (1986), 'Recent innovations in international banking', mimeo, April.

BIS – Bank for International Settlements (1998), 68th Annual Report, Basle, June.

Blommestein, H.J. (1995), 'Structural changes in financial markets: overview of trends and prospects', in OECD (1995), pp. 9–47.

Dowers, K., F. Gomez-Acebo and P. Masci (2000), 'Making capital markets viable in Latin America', *Infrastructure and Financial Markets Review*, 6 (3), Washington: IMF, December.

Feeney, P.W. (1994), *Securitization: Redefining the Bank*, the Money and Banking series, General Editor John R. Presley), New York: St. Martin's Press.

Ffrench-Davis, R. (1999), *Reforming the Reforms in Latin America: Macroeconomics, Trade, Finance*, London, Macmillan.

Fischer, S. (1999), 'On the need for an international lender of last resort', *Journal of Economic Perspectives*, September, 85–104.

Fisher, I. (1933), 'The debt-deflation theory of great depression', *Econometrica*, **1**, 337–57.

Fornari, F. and A. Levy (1999), 'Global liquidity in the 1990s: geographical and long run determinants', BIS Conference Papers No. 8, available at www.bis.org/publ/confer08.htm.

Franklin, R. E. (1993), 'Financial markets in transition – or the decline of commercial banking', In Federal Reserve Bank of Kansas: *Changing Capital Markets: Implica-*

tions for Monetary Policy, Conference Proceedings, Jackson Hole, Wyoming, 19–21 August.

Goldsmith, R. (1969). *Financial Structure and Development*, New Haven: Yale University Press.

Griffith-Jones, S. and J. Kimmis. (1998), 'Capital flows: how to curb their volatility,' *Human Development Report* (1999), background paper.

Griffith-Jones, Stephany, José Antônio Ocampo and Jacques Cailloux (1999). 'The poorest countries and the emerging international financial architecture', mimeo.

Group of Ten (2001), 'Report on consolidation in the financial sector', Basel: Group of Ten, available at www.bis.org.

Helleiner, E. (1994), *States and the Re-emergence of Global Finance: From Bretton Woods to the 1990s*, Ithaca and London: Cornell University Press.

Keynes, J.M. (1930), *A Treatise on Money*, vol. I. London: Macmillan.

Keynes, J.M. (1936), *The General Theory of Employment, Interest and Money*, London: Macmillan, 1947.

Minsky, H.P. (1982), 'The financial-instability hypothesis: capitalist processes and the behaviour of the economy', in C.P. Kindleberger and J.P. Laffargue (eds), *Financial Crises*, Cambridge: Cambridge University Press.

Ocampo, José Antônio. (1999), 'Reforming the international financial architecture: consensus and divergence', *Série Temas de Coyuntura*, no. 1, Santiago, Economic Commission for Latin America and the Caribbean (ECLAC), April.

Park, Y.C. (1998). 'The financial crisis in Korea and its lessons for Reform of the international financial system', in J.J. Teunissen (ed.), *Regulatory and Supervisory Challenges in a New Era of Global Finance*, The Hague: FONDAD.

Stallings, B. and R. Studart (2001), 'Financial regulation and supervision in emerging markets:the experience of Latin America since the Tequila Crisis', ECLAC, Economic Development Division, mimeo.

Studart, R. (1999). 'Pension funds and the financing of productive investment: an analysis based on Brazil's recent experience', *Série Financiamiento del Desarollo*, 102, LC/L.1409-P.

Studart, R. (2001), 'Dollarization: an intellectual fad or a deep insight'? *Journal of Post Keynesian Economics*, Summer, **23** (4): 639–62.

Studart, R. and J. Hermann (2001). 'Sistemas financeiros no Mercosul: desenvolvimento recente e perspectivas de integração', in R. Baummann (ed.), *Avanços e Desafios da Integração*, Brasília: IPEA.

Taylor, Lance and Stephen A. O'Connell (1985), 'A Minsky Crisis', *Quarterly Journal of Economics*, **100** (Supp), 871–86.

United Nations Task Force (1999), 'Towards a new international financial architecture', report of the Task Force of the Executive Committee on Economic and Social Affairs (LC/G.2054), Santiago, Chile, Economic Commission for Latin America and the Caribbean (ECLAC), March.

United Nations (1999), *World Economic and Social Survey*, New York: United Nations.

World Bank (2001), 'Global Development Finance', Washington, DC: World Bank.

# 10. Exchange rate regimes and the need for elements for a new international financial architecture

## Stephany Griffith-Jones

### INTRODUCTION

The recent wave of currency and banking crises that began in East Asia, then spread to many other emerging markets (as described in depth in previous chapters), and even threatened briefly to spill over to the USA in the wake of Russia and Long-term Capital Management (LTCM) – generated a broad consensus that fundamental reforms were required in the international financial system. More recent crises, as in Brazil, as well as critical situations in Turkey and Argentina, reiterate the need for additional changes in the eyes of many observers. Existing institutions and arrangements were widely seen as inadequate for dealing with very large and extremely volatile capital flows, in which an important part of the volatility was caused by large imperfections in the financial markets themselves.

The seriousness of the situation is underlined by the fact that in the 1990s, during 40 out of 120 months, (that is 33 per cent of the time) there were important crises. This is particularly problematic for two reasons. Firstly, currency and banking crises – which have recently occurred mainly in emerging markets – have extremely high development and social costs. Indeed, deep and frequent crises in developing countries could undermine achievement of the UN target to halve world poverty by 2015. Secondly, there is always the very small – but totally unacceptable – risk that contagion and spillovers in an increasingly interdependent international financial system could lead to global problems. Both these problems implied that urgent action was required to overcome the risk that the important benefits that globalisation offers in other fields could be seriously undermined by international financial developments.

In the context of this volume, it is crucial to stress that, while large private capital flows remain so volatile, no exchange rate regime can provide by itself an adequate response, even though some exchange rate regimes may be 'less bad' than others. This is illustrated by events in the summer of 2001. Argentina is under serious pressure from the markets, and requires increasing support from the international financial community; clearly its exchange rate regime has become a major source of vulnerability, as has the great cost and difficulty of changing the exchange-rate regime. However, countries situated in the 'other corner' – floaters, like Brazil and Chile – are also affected by the turmoil in financial markets arising mainly from the situation in Argentina; indeed though committed very strongly to floating, they are being increasing forced to intervene.

There is therefore no 'silver bullet', or no panacea to be found just in an exchange rate system (see Studart, Chapter 9). To make any exchange rate regime function properly in emerging markets, in ways that help sustain growth, it is therefore essential that an international financial system exists in which capital flows are less prone to large surges and reversals.

Some progress has been made on reforming the international financial system, but it is clearly insufficient. Important changes have been implemented. For example, IMF lending facilities for both crisis prevention and management have been quite usefully expanded and adapted and the Fund's total resources increased.

Important institutional innovations have been introduced, such as the creation of the Financial Stability Forum (FSF), to identify vulnerabilities and sources of systemic risk, to fill gaps in regulations and to develop consistent financial regulations across all types of financial institutions. As capital and credit markets become increasingly integrated both amongst each other and between countries, it is essential that the domain of the regulator is the same as the domain of the market that is regulated in order for regulation to be efficient. Given that regulation is still national and sectoral, an institution like the FSF is valuable to help coordinate regulation globally and across sectors. The creation of the G20, a body to discuss international financial reform, that includes both developed and developing countries, is also a positive development.

Developing countries have been asked to take a number of important measures to make their countries less vulnerable to crises; these include the introduction of a large number of codes and standards. Though introducing standards is very positive, there are however concerns in developing countries that the number of standards (more than 60) is too large; developing countries also are worried that standards are too uniform, in the assumption that 'one size fits all'. At a major conference organised with the IMF and the World Bank, held at the Commonwealth Secretariat in June 2000, senior policymakers from developing countries called for greater selectivity and flexibility in the standards they are asked to implement (see Griffith-Jones and Bhattacharya, 2001). A more inclusive process is also necessary, whereby developing countries could participate in the development of these standards and codes, which at present they are asked to implement without having been involved in their design.

Even though there has been quite significant progress on reform of the financial architecture, it has suffered from two serious problems. First, it has been insufficient, given the magnitude of the changes required to create a financial system that supports – and does not undermine – growth and development in the dramatically changed context of the twenty-first century, which is characterized by very large, but extremely volatile and highly concentrated private capital flows. It is essential to develop a clear vision of an appropriate financial architecture in the new circumstances; drawing parallels from the institutional mechanisms developed nationally as domestic credit and capital markets have grown, a new international architecture requires: (1) appropriate transparency and regulation of international financial loans and capital markets, (2) provision of sufficient international official liquidity in distress conditions; and (3) standstill and orderly debt workout procedures at an international level. The mechanisms that exist and the adaptations made so far, do not fully meet the new requirements.

Second, the progress made has been asymmetrical in three key aspects, in which a more balanced approach is urgently needed.

A first asymmetry in the reform process is that far more progress has been made on important measures taken by developing countries, which are being asked to introduce a very large number of codes and standards, so as to make them less vulnerable to crises. However, far less progress is being made on equally important and complementary international measures. As much of the literature has argued, crises, such as in Asia, were not just caused by national problems but also by imperfections in international capital markets, that lead to rapid surges and reversals of massive private flows. To deal with the problems in the international financial markets, it is thus essential that international measures both for crisis prevention and management are also taken.

As the G24 (2000) group of developing countries has pointed out, standards in the area of transparency are being pressed upon developing countries to improve information for markets without equal corresponding obligations for disclosure by financial institutions, including highly leveraged ones, such as hedge funds, who have no reporting obligation. Better information on financial markets would be of great value to policymakers, especially in developing countries. Transparency should not be a one-way street. Furthermore, while valuable progress is being made on attempting to improve regulation of domestic financial systems in developing countries, there is painfully slow progress in filling important gaps in international regulation, of institutions such as mutual funds or hedge funds, or of modifying regulations, as of banks, where current regulations may have contributed to, rather than prevented, greater short-termism of flows (as discussed in more detail later). In the field of international regulation, valuable studies have been carried out particularly by the Financial Stability Forum Working Parties, but recommendations made are implemented very slowly.

Passing from crisis prevention to crisis management, it seems important that the IMF's own resources are large enough to meet the financing needs of a systemic crisis involving several economies simultaneously, while also retaining sufficient liquidity to meet normal demands on the Fund's resources. Michel Camdessus (2000) and others, including the influential US Council of Foreign Affairs (1999), have suggested that this expansion of official emergency financing could be funded in part by temporary and self-liquidating issues of SDRs. Such a mechanism would not add to total world liquidity, except in a temporary manner during a crisis situation – when it would be compensating for reductions or the reversal of private flows. This proposal deserves serious analysis and consideration and there seems to be considerable merit in the G24's call for a study of this matter and discussion at the autumn 2001 meeting of the IMFC. More speedy progress on orderly debt workouts is also urgent.

A second source of asymmetry in the reform process that needs to be urgently overcome is the insufficient participation of developing countries in the key fora and institutions. As regards the international financial institutions, more representative governance needs to be discussed in parallel with a redefinition of their functions. It is particularly urgent that developing countries (which are now only represented in a very limited way in the FSF Working parties) are fully represented in the Financial Stability Forum itself, as the issues discussed there have very profound effects on their economies and as their insights can make an important contribution to the Forum's valuable work. It is important to note that after their 2000 annual meeting Commonwealth Finance Meetings called for such developing country participation in the Forum. The inclusion of major developing countries in the G20 is clearly a welcome step, but it might be of value to include also some smaller developing nations, to reflect their specific concerns. Above all, it would also be helpful if the agenda of the G20 could be broadened, to include more explicitly the key issues of international financial reform. (For a more detailed discussion of the issue, see Griffith-Jones and Kimmis, 2001, on the participation of developing countries in global financial governance).

A third asymmetry that has emerged in recent discussions on reform of the system is that we have all placed excessive focus on crisis prevention and management, mainly for middle-income countries. Important as this is, it may have led us to neglect the equally (if not more) important issues of appropriate liquidity and development finance for low-income countries. As regards liquidity, it is important that existing IMF facilities for low-income countries – such as the Compensatory Financing Facility and the Poverty Reduction and Growth Facility – should be made more flexible, in case terms of trade shocks affect such countries. More generally, the role of the IMF in providing liquidity to low-income countries is crucial. As regards development finance, low-income countries need sufficient multilateral lending and official flows, as well as speedy debt relief. It is a source of concern that multilateral lending to low-income countries, especially via IDA, has recently fallen sharply. Furthermore, in a world of rapidly increasing private flows, it is important that low-income countries, donors and international organisations collaborate to help attract more significant private flows to them. Mobilizing sufficient and stable development finance, both private and official to low-income countries is an essential precondition to help ensure growth and poverty reduction in the poorest countries.

It is important that significant further progress on reforming the international financial system is done quickly, as the risks and potential costs of not doing so are unacceptably large, especially for poor people in developing countries.

Given the focus of this volume on exchange rate regimes, the policy discussion that follows in this chapter focuses on two aspects: (1) on better international information on markets and financial regulation; these are international measures for crises prevention where there has been very little action, or even analysis and (2) provision of sufficient international liquidity to developing countries in distress situations and of sufficient development finance to help support their growth and poverty reduction. We will not discuss here very important issues, probably the main being private sector involvement and burden sharing on which there is already a large literature (for a seminal contribution, see Eichengreen and Portes, 1995) even though again relatively little action. Furthermore, the type of preventive measures – à la regulation – suggested here seem to us somewhat more appropriate than burden sharing measures to be taken mainly ex-post, as the former seem more market friendly, and therefore less likely to discourage excessively private flows to developing countries, or increase their cost too much.

A final point is important about the discussion of international financial architecture. This discussion arose mainly out of the Asian crises, and concerns about excessive volatility and reversibility of private capital flows, especially but not only short-term bank lending. Many of the proposals have been dominated by those concerns. However, in the last three years, the nature of flows to emerging countries has changed in two fundamental ways. Firstly, their level has fallen significantly, with net bank and bond lending – as well as net portfolio equity flows – becoming negative. Secondly, their structure has changed dramatically, with foreign direct investment becoming not only the dominant flow, but also the only positive one. Whilst the increased importance of FDI is on balance very positive, the sharp reduction of overall flows and the negative net flows for most categories is very problematic.

Should these new tendencies in capital flows continue, the discussion of international financial architecture must shift to include not just measures to prevent and manage excessive surges of capital flows to developing countries, but also measures to encourage sufficient private flows to take place. In this context, care should be taken in designing measures for orderly debt workout to avoid them further discouraging private flows. Furthermore, as we discuss below, in designing measures such as the new Basle Capital Accord, care must be taken not to design systems that could excessively discourage private bank lending to most developing countries.

## BETTER INTERNATIONAL INFORMATION AND FINANCIAL REGULATION

### 1. Additional Information on Markets to Developing Countries

As pointed out above, better information to markets on developing countries has to be complemented by better information on international financial markets available to policymakers, especially but not only in developing countries. Particularly during the crisis that started in Asia, emerging country policy-makers have found important limitations in the essential information available on the functioning of international capital and banking markets. The type of information required is particularly on almost day-to-day changes in the functioning of markets – and their key actors – globally and regionally.

The IMF has led the way in improving information, and its dissemination, on emerging market economies, which is of particular use to markets. A parallel symmetric effort needs to be done to gather and provide timely information on market evolution to emerging markets' policy makers. This task should perhaps be led by the BIS, and co-ordinated by the newly created Financial Stability Forum (FSF). Inputs would be very valuable from the IMF and the private sector (for example, the Institute of International Finance, IIF). The growth of financial innovations, such as over-the-counter derivatives, while designed to facilitate the transfer of market risk and therefore enhance financial stability, have also made financial markets more complex and opaque. This has created difficulties in monitoring patterns of activity in these markets and the distribution of risks in the global financial system for market participants, regulators, central banks and other authorities, including particularly those in developing countries. It would seem appropriate for major central banks and the BIS to attempt to improve registration of derivatives and institutions like hedge funds, by making it obligatory. Unfortunately, such initiatives to make reporting obligatory have until now been blocked, especially in the US Congress.

Given the speed with which markets move, it seems particularly important that the frequency with which relevant data is produced is very high (and possibly higher in times of market turbulence, when it becomes particularly crucial), and that dissemination to all countries' central banks is instant. Indeed, a special additional service could be provided by the BIS in which it would play the role of clearing house of information. For this purpose, it could draw not just on information it can gather directly from markets, but by collecting and centralizing information that individual central banks have on their markets, and where the aggregate picture is not easily available to any individual central bank. This could possibly include both quantitative and qualitative information. Via the internet, the BIS could standardize the information requirements, collect the information, aggregate it and disseminate it rapidly to all central banks, as well as to other relevant institutions. Such a service would be of the greatest usefulness to developing country policy-makers, especially immediately before and during crises; however, it would naturally also be very valuable to developed country policy-makers and international institutions (including the BIS itself) in handling crisis prevention and management.

## 2.   Improved International Financial Regulation

### The case for regulation
A strong case can be made that international financial regulation is welfare increasing. At the domestic level, it is broadly accepted that financial markets, due to problems such as asymmetries of information, behave erratically at times, and that the first best response to these problems is regulation and supervision (Greenwald et al., 1984; Wyplosz, 2001). Major efforts are now being made to develop and improve financial regulation in developing countries. But as financial markets have become globalized, similarly, it is increasingly accepted that financial regulation has also to be globalized. The welfare-increasing effects of global financial regulation will be larger if – as we discuss below – such regulation has explicit counter-cyclical elements, to compensate for inherent pro-cyclical behaviour by financial actors that can also partly characterize traditional financial regulation.

Indeed, there is growing support for a view that the process of international financial intermediation has a second-best element, in which welfare for both source and recipient countries can be increased by regulatory changes (through measures in source and/or recipient countries), which would reduce excessive lending or investing. It is noteworthy that Chairman Alan Greenspan proposed – for the case of interbank lending – that it might be appropriate for either borrowing countries or lending ones to impose reserve requirements to 'deter aberrant borrowing: sovereigns could charge an explicit premium, or could impose reserve requirements, earning low or even zero interest rates, on interbank liabilities. Increasing the capital charge on lending banks, instead of on borrowing banks, might also be effective' (Greenspan, 1998).[1]

There is growing recognition that it may often be desirable to regulate excessive surges of potentially reversible capital flows in recipient countries. Indeed, an important part of the responsibility with discouraging excessive reversible inflows – as well as managing them – lies with the recipient countries. However, the experience of the 1990s, with very large scale of international funds – compared to the small size of developing country markets – leads to the question whether measures to discourage excessive short-term flows by recipient countries are sufficient to deal with capital surges and the risk of their reversal.

Aizenman and Turnovsky (1999) have formalized such analysis, by developing a rigorous model that analyses the impact via externalities of reserve requirements on international loans (both in lending and recipient countries) on the welfare of both categories of countries. They thus evaluate the macroeconomic impact of reserve requirements in a second-best world, where there is moral hazard owing to likely bail-outs on the lender's side and sovereign risk on the borrower's side; both generate large negative externalities on welfare.

The broad theoretical rationale for such measures is that, unlike in the case of trade in goods and services where most mainstream economists agree that free trade is beneficial, there is no such consensus as regards capital flows. Indeed, many mainstream economists have identified circumstances in which unlimited capital mobility may be sub-optimal; such views have become more widespread as currency crises became more frequent. This does not imply advocating closed capital accounts, as many flows are beneficial. However, it does lead to the conclusion that – globally as well as nationally – the optimum result may be appropriate regulation.

The general conclusion of the Aisenman and Turnovsky model is that the introduction of a reserve requirement in either country reduces the risk of default and raises the welfare in both the source and the emerging market borrowing country. More specifically, they show that:

1.  the introduction of a reserve requirement by the lending country will raise welfare in both economies; this is particularly true when there is no reserve requirement in the borrowing nation;
2.  starting from a situation where there are no reserve requirements, the introduction of a reserve requirement by the borrowing country will raise welfare in both economies;
3.  more generous bail-outs, that encourage borrowing and increase default risk, effectively raise the level of the lender's optimal reserve requirement. If such higher reserve requirements are applied, world welfare is unchanged by higher bail-outs;
4.  on the other hand, more generous bail-outs in the absence of reserve requirements, or if they are optimally set only by the borrowing nation, will reduce welfare due to the increase of default risk;
5.  given that it is unlikely that a 'non bail-out policy' can be totally credible, reserve requirements – particularly in source countries – are clearly welfare-enhancing;

6. comprehensive reserve requirements – independently of their size – will most probably improve information about countries' exposure; this may improve the supply of credit to them, and especially its stability.

The aim of such regulatory changes is to help smooth capital flows to emerging markets, without discouraging them excessively. This is in contrast with views based on a belief that crises in emerging markets are due only to moral hazard, and that the appropriate way to combat such moral hazard is by scaling down the role of the IMF in providing financial packages before and during crises. The latter view has acquired some prominence in developed countries, particularly but not only in the USA; in particular, the majority Meltzer Report, (2000) took such views to the extreme. However, such reduction of the role of the IMF could either make crises even more costly and/or lead to a sharp reduction in private flows to developing countries. These are both highly undesirable effects which could significantly diminish welfare, particularly but not only in the developing economies, as well as undermine support for open economies and market-based economic policies in developing economies. Therefore, an approach based on better regulation is clearly better and more welfare-enhancing than one which cuts back the IMF.

**Filling gaps**
The broad welfare case for applying reserve requirements in both source and recipient countries can also be applied to institutional investors and in particular to mutual funds, which became increasingly important in relation to banks in the 1990s. This growing importance occurred both within the developed countries, and particularly within the USA – where mutual funds receive more than 50 per cent of total deposits in the financial system – and in capital flows from developed to developing countries (see D'Arista and Griffith-Jones, 2000). The narrowing of differences between banks and institutional investors like mutual funds, and the fact that securities markets and thus mutual funds also have access to the lender of last resort – nationally in the USA but more importantly in our context also internationally, owing to the frequent rescue packages put together by the IMF in recent serious currency crises – suggests the importance of improving prudential standards for institutional investors such as mutual funds.

It is also important to stress that the risks being borne by institutional investors, such as mutual funds, are increasingly similar to those facing banks, including both liquidity management problems and a higher exposure to macroeconomic problems and to macroeconomic effects. As regards the latter macroeconomic effects, institutional investors seem up to now insufficiently aware of the risks that macroeconomic problems and developments can have on their investments, which would seem to justify regulatory actions such as those suggested below to help take account of macroeconomic risks when investment decisions are made.

Another source of concern is liquidity management by international institutional investors; such liquidity management in the face of heavy redemptions – for example as a currency crisis threatens or explodes – may become an issue not just for the mutual funds concerned but for the countries in which they are invested. As institutional investors attempt to meet redemptions – or even accumulate cash for possible large redemptions – this will encourage them to liquidate their investments very quickly, sometimes even quicker than their liquidity needs warrant. This will contribute to short-term excessive and rapid outflows from developing countries' securities markets. Better arrangements for managing mutual funds' liquidity – such as the cash requirements suggested below – would, by lowering the need for mutual funds to liquidate their cash holdings, dampen the reversibility of investment flows out of developing markets. Equally important, such cash requirements would also boost investors' confidence in the financial strength of such funds, lowering the trend towards large redemptions in unfavourable circumstances.

Both aspects promote more gradual changes in investment holdings and thus smooth international capital flows overall.

As regards portfolio flows to emerging markets, there is an important regulatory gap, as at present there is no regulatory framework internationally, for taking account of market or credit risks on flows originating in institutional investors, such as mutual funds (and more broadly for flows originating in non-bank institutions). This important regulatory gap needs to be filled, both to protect retail investors in developed countries and protect developing countries from the negative effects of excessively large and potentially reversible portfolio flows.

The East Asian crisis (and even more the 1999 Brazilian crisis) confirms what was particularly clearly visible in the Mexican peso crisis (Griffith-Jones, 1998). Institutional investors, like mutual funds, given the very liquid nature of their investments, can play an important role in contributing to developing country currency crises. (For recent evidence, see Kaminsky et al., 1999). It seems important, therefore, to introduce some regulation to discourage excessive surges of portfolio flows; this should not affect normal portfolio flows to emerging markets, which play an important role such as helping to develop domestic financial markets. This could perhaps best be achieved by a variable risk-weighted cash requirement for institutional investors, such as mutual funds. These cash requirements would be placed as interest-bearing deposits in commercial banks. Introducing a dynamic risk-weighted cash requirement for mutual funds (and perhaps, other institutional investors) is in the mainstream of current regulatory thinking and would require that standards be provided by relevant regulatory authorities or agreed internationally. The guidelines for macroeconomic risk, which would determine the cash requirement, would take into account such vulnerability variables as the ratio of a country's current account deficit (or surplus) to GDP, the level of its short-term external liabilities to foreign exchange reserves, and the fragility of the banking system, as well as other relevant national risk factors. It is important that quite sophisticated analysis is used, to avoid simplistic criteria stigmatizing countries unnecessarily; this could be based on the large literature on vulnerability indicators. The views of the national central bank and the Treasury in the source countries and of the IMF and the BIS should be helpful in this respect. The securities regulators in source countries would be the most appropriate institutions to implement such regulations, which could be coordinated internationally by the International Organization for Securities Commissions (IOSCO), probably best in the context of the Forum for Financial Stability.

The fact that the level of required cash reserves would vary with the level of countries' perceived 'macroeconomic risk' would make it relatively more profitable to invest in countries with good fundamentals and relatively less profitable to invest in countries with more problematic macro or financial sector fundamentals. If these fundamentals in a country deteriorated, investment would decline gradually, which should force an early correction of policy, and a resumption of flows. Though the requirement for cash reserves on mutual funds' assets invested in emerging markets could increase somewhat the cost of raising foreign capital for them, this would be compensated by the benefit of a more stable supply of funds, at a more stable cost. Furthermore, this counter-cyclical smoothing of flows would hopefully discourage the massive and sudden reversal of flows that sparked off both the Mexican and the Asian crises, making such developmentally costly crises less likely.

Given the dominant role and rapid growth of institutional investors in countries such as the USA, the UK and France, this proposal – for a risk-weighted cash requirement on mutual funds – could possibly be adopted first in those countries, without creating significant competitive disadvantages, soon after international harmonization was introduced. However, an alternative route would be for such measures to be studied and implemented internationally being discussed initially within IOSCO, and/or in the broader context of the Forum for Financial Stability. International coordination of such a measure would prevent investments by mutual funds being channelled through different countries, and especially off-shore centres that did not impose these cash requirements (the latter point draws on communication with the Federal Reserve Board).

Such IOSCO international guidelines would be formulated through international consultants similar to those employed by the Basle Committee in developing the 'Core Principles for Effective Banking Supervision'. The guidelines could be developed by a working group consisting of representatives of the national securities' regulatory authorities in source countries together with some representation from developing countries, in the context of IOSCO. Due account should be taken of relevant existing regulations, such as the European Commission's Capital Adequacy Directive.

Finally, it is important to stress that additional regulation of mutual funds should be consistent with regulation of other institutions (e.g. banks) and other potentially volatile flows.

It is encouraging that the September 1998 IOSCO Emerging Markets Report, *Causes, Effects and Regulatory Implications of Financial and Economic Turbulence in Emerging Markets*, has in fact described in some detail and evaluated rather positively the above proposal. This report emphasised that 'there appears to be scope – and an urgent need for further work. This is very likely to require a multilateral effort – i.e. by regulators from both source and recipient countries in collaboration with the industry'. It is therefore to be hoped that this type of proposal will be analysed in further detail, with a view towards possible implementation, either within IOSCO and/or within the Financial Stability Forum.

### Removing regulatory distortions and dampening exuberance of bank lending

As regards bank lending, there has firstly been concern that the 1988 Basle capital accord contributed to the build up of short-term bank lending and its reversal in East Asia and elsewhere, owing to significantly lower capital adequacy requirements for short-term lending than for long-term lending. The new proposal published in January 2001 attempts to address this distortion by reducing somewhat (though perhaps not sufficiently) the differential between capital adequacy for short-term and other lending. However, the new proposed Basle Capital Accord, though including many positive elements also have suggestions that are widely seen as problematic, particularly for developing countries (see Griffith-Jones and Spratt 2001, and Reisen 2001).

In recent years criticisms from many quarters have been levelled at the functioning of the 1988 Accord, with critics arguing that the regulatory requirements do not correspond to actual levels of risk. The consequences of this have been distortions and biases in the practices of the banking industry. Consequently, the proposals aim to increase the risk-sensitivity of capital requirements and thereby more closely align these requirements with actual risks. To this end, a major proposal is to move towards ever-greater use of banks' own internal risk management systems. However, although the focus of the proposals is aimed towards the needs of major banks from the G10, it is likely that the new Accord, when implemented, will have significant, and broadly negative, repercussions for the developing world.

Developing sovereigns, corporations and banks wishing to borrow in international markets will find the lending environment greatly worsened, as the major banks' lending patterns are significantly changed by the adoption of internal ratings based (IRB) approaches. The outcome of these changes is likely to be a significant reduction of bank lending to the developing world, and/or a sharp increase in the cost of international borrowing for many developing countries. Drawing on calculations by Reisen (2001), based on estimates by Deutsche Bank, we can see in Table 10.1 that the adoption of the IRB approach as currently proposed could result in speculative grade borrowers (BBB– or lower) being effectively excluded from international bank lending – the median sovereign rating for non-OECD countries in 2001 was BB, with 31 of the 53 rated non-OECD countries being rated below BBB–. We believe that the proposed changes will be neutral or broadly positive for sovereigns rated triple-B or higher. However, for sovereigns rated below that, the situation is very problematic. For example, for sovereigns such as Brazil and India, rated double-B under the current Accord, each $100 lent requires an $8 capital requirement. Under the new standardized approach this would be unchanged, however, under the IRB approach and (based on the assumptions reflected in Table 10.1) it can be seen that the capital required for the same $100 could rise to $30.3 and spreads could increase by 1115 bp (11 per cent). Even more dramatically, for countries such as Argentina and Pakistan, rated at single-B, spreads could increase by 3709 bp (that is 37 per cent) under the IRB approach to produce an equivalent level of risk adjusted return as under the existing Accord.[2] The implications of this are clear: large parts of the developing world would no longer be able to access international bank lending on terms likely to be acceptable. The impact of this is likely to be felt even more severely in the lowest rated countries – such as those in Sub-Saharan Africa, the very countries in most need of such access.

The effect is extreme because the Basle Committee proposes a strongly exponential, rather than a linear, rise of risk weightings along the spectrum of probability of default. Thus, once ratings fall below BBB the capital requirements increase sharply, implying that for the lowest-rated borrowers the cost of loans from banks operating an IRB approach is likely to be prohibitively high. Therefore, it is not the principle that increased riskiness should be reflected in higher-risk weightings that is being challenged, but a concern that the IRB approach increases the weights far more rapidly than is objectively justified as one moves to lower creditworthiness ratings.

A second highly problematic likely effect of the new Basle Capital Accord if the January 2001 proposals were implemented, would be sharply increased pro-cyclicality. This would imply that both for developed and developing countries in periods of slow-down or recession, the perceived riskiness of loans would increase, which would imply far higher capital requirements, which would lead to sharp reductions in bank lending that would in fact deepen any slow-down or recession.

*Table 10.1*   *Sovereign borrowers*

|  | Risk weight | Capital required per $100 | Breakeven spread change bp.* | Examples of countries in category |
|---|---|---|---|---|
| *Double-A (OECD)* | | | | |
| Current | 0 | 0 | – | Belgium |
| Standardized | 0 | 0 | – | Bermuda |
| IRB approach | 7 | 0.6 | +3 | Canada |
| | | | | Italy |
| | | | | Italy |
| | | | | Portugal |
| *Triple-B (non-OECD)* | | | | |
| Current | 100 | 8.0 | – | China |
| Standardized | 50 | 4.0 | –50 | Malaysia |
| IRB approach | 40 | 3.2 | –60 | Korea |
| | | | | Tunisia |
| | | | | Egypt |
| | | | | Latvia |
| *Double-B (non-OECD)* | | | | |
| Current | 100 | 8.0 | – | Brazil |
| Standardized | 100 | 8.0 | – | Costa Rica |
| IRB approach | 379 | 30.3 | +1115 | Colombia |
| | | | | Morocco |
| | | | | India |
| | | | | Kazakhstan |
| *Single-B (non-OECD)* | | | | |
| Current | 100 | 8.0 | – | Argentina |
| Standardized | 100 | 8.0 | – | Mongolia |
| IRB approach | 630 | 50.4 | +3709 | Jamaica |
| | | | | Paraguay |
| | | | | Pakistan |
| | | | | Venezuela |

*Note*:   * Estimated.

*Sources*: Reisen (2001) and Standard and Poor's Sovereign ratings, 6 June 2001, www.standardandpoors.com.

It is ironic and particularly problematic that these proposals (which would imply less and more costly lending to developing countries, as well as more pro-cyclical lending which is particularly damaging for developing countries), have emerged at the same time as developing countries are being urged to make greater use of private capital flows, and as these flows – especially bank lending – are not only slowing down, but are negative in net terms.

### Counter-cyclical elements in regulation

The answer thus may lie in the implementation of an explicit counter-cyclical mechanism which would, in boom periods, and in contrast to ratings, dampen excess bank lending. Counter-cyclical elements can also be introduced in regulating other actors (see above, for mutual funds). On the contrary, in periods of slowdown and of scarcity of finance the new mechanism should not further accentuate the decline in lending as exemplified by the 1997–8 Asian crisis, and to a lesser extent the 1999–2001 period, but rather encourage such lending. (For an excellent discussion of counter-cyclical issues in regulation, see the 2001 Bank for International Settlements (BIS) Annual Report.)

There would be two linked objectives for introducing elements of counter-cyclical regulation. One would be to help smooth capital flows and the other would be to smooth the domestic impact of volatile capital flows on the domestic financial system and therefore on the real economy. Introducing counter-cyclical elements into regulation would help build a link between the more microeconomic risks on which regulators have tended to focus till recently and the macroeconomic risks which are becoming increasingly important, both nationally and internationally.[3] Counter-cyclical elements in regulation related to bank lending could be applied, either internationally, nationally or at both levels.

Several mechanisms could be used to introduce a counter-cyclical element into regulation of bank lending. One mechanism would be to get the required capital ratio higher in times of boom, and to allow banks to use the additional cushion provided by the higher capital ratio, so they could sustain lending in times of recession at a lower capital asset ratio (when increased bad loans are likely to be reducing their capital). Some practical difficulties may arise in implementing such a mechanism, of which the most serious one may be getting international agreement on a general formula for cyclically-adjusted capital asset ratios.

A second mechanism for introducing counter-cyclical elements in bank lending regulation is for regulators to encourage higher general provisions to be made for possible loan losses (i.e. subtracted from equity capital in the books of the bank) to cover normal cyclical risks (Turner, 2000). This would allow for provisions built up in good times to be used in bad times, without affecting reported capital. The way to ensure this would be to maintain higher general provisioning that applies to all loans. The main problem for this mechanism, according to Turner, may be that tax laws often limit the tax deductibility of precautionary provisioning; however, it is possible to change such tax laws, as indeed was done in the late 1980s in the UK. It is encouraging that the Spanish central bank has already introduced such a 'forward-looking' provision, and that other central banks and regulators are beginning to evaluate provisioning, that would attempt 'to see though the cycle'.

A third mechanism, relevant particularly for domestic bank lending, is for regulators to place caps on the value of assets (such as real estate stocks, or shares) to be acceptable as collateral, when the value of such assets has risen sharply in a boom and is at risk of declining sharply in a recession. Rules could be used such as averaging values for the last five years, or accepting only 50 per cent of current prices in the peak period of a boom. The latter mechanism seems to have the least problems of implementation (indeed, reportedly it is already applied in some jurisdictions, such as Hong Kong).

A fourth possible counter-cyclical mechanism is that, as suggested by McKinnon and Pill (1999), monetary authorities could monitor and try to limit or discourage lending for property, construction and personal consumption, as those items tend to increase substantially – and often even be a major factor – in booms. A possible implementation problem would be that it may be difficult to verify final use of credit, and such measures could be partially evaded.

Furthermore, regulators should be flexible in the downturn, particularly to allow banks to easily use cushions (for example of capital or of provisioning) in times of recession; it may even be advisable, if a recession is very serious, to allow ratios to fall below normally required levels (to help sustain lending) in the understanding that they will be rebuilt as soon as the economy starts recovering. A tension may arise here between the regulatory concerns about individual bank liquidity and solvency and the macroeconomic externalities of their actions, particularly in recessions.

Specific issues seem to require further study. How best can the distinction between a temporary boom and a permanent increase in growth be made? After what period of 'boom' should regulatory changes be introduced? How large should such changes be? What are the best mechanisms through which counter-cyclical measures should be introduced (flexible capital adequacy ratios, higher provisioning against losses more 'realistic' pricing of collateral)? Should such measures be introduced for both international and domestic lending, or preferably for either one of them? This chapter provides only initial thoughts on these important issues. We suggest that further research in this area is important, and we are initiating some work ourselves, at the time of writing.

## EMERGENCY AND COUNTERCYCLICAL FINANCING

The enhanced provision of emergency financing during financial crises is another pillar of the system to prevent them and or manage their effects. Indeed, although the direct focus of emergency financing is crisis management, it also has crisis prevention effects, as it plays an essential role in avoiding the destabilizing expectations that are responsible for deepening and spreading of crises (contagion) and, ultimately, for systemic failures. This has been, in fact, the essential defence for the role that central banks play at the national levels as lender of last resort. Current international arrangements are weaker in this regard. Indeed, the IMF provides 'emergency financing' but certainly not liquidity, a fact that is reflected in the lack of automaticity in the availability of financing during crises. Although the Fund has the capacity to create fiat money, through the issue of special drawing rights (SDRs), it was used only in the past and in a very limited way.

It is important to emphasize that, in this regard, emergency financing is not a substitute but a complement to strong regulation and debt workout procedures. Regulatory changes help smooth capital flows to emerging markets. Together with private sector involvement in crisis resolution, through adequate debt workouts, they are essential to avoid moral hazard. However, the view that the appropriate way to combat such moral hazard is by scaling down the role of the IMF in providing financial packages during crises would make them even more costly and/or lead to a sharp reduction in private flows to developing countries. Indeed, as discussed, there may be a case in the current context of large and volatile private flows even for significantly larger emergency official emergency financing than currently exists. The great majority of recent reports support this view (Williamson, 2001), with the major exception of the majority Meltzer Report (although the minority view in Meltzer also strongly values the broad role of the IMF).

The main lessons from recent crises are, indeed, that: (1) as a preventive measure, wider use should be made both of private and official contingency credit lines that are agreed during periods of adequate access to capital market, following the (partly successful) pioneering experiences of some 'emerging' economies; (2) large-scale funding may be required, though not all of it (and maybe even none of it) needs to be disbursed if support programmes rapidly restore market confidence; (3) funds should be made available before – rather than after – international reserves reach critically low levels; and (4) owing to strong contagion effects, contingency financing may be required even by countries that do not exhibit fundamental disequilibria. Positive measures have been adopted in this area, including a significant expansion of IMF resources through a quota increase and the New Arrangements to Borrow, which finally entered into effect in late 1998; the launching of a new window in December 1997 to finance exceptional borrowing requirements during crises; and the creation of the Contingency Credit Line in April 1999 to provide financing to countries facing contagion and its redesign in September 2000.

The major controversies relate to inadequate funding and the design of some specific credit lines and the broadening scope of conditionality. With respect to the first issue, bilateral financing and contributions to the IMF will continue to be scarce during crises. This might reduce the stabilizing effects of rescue packages, if the market deems that the intervening authorities (the IMF plus additional bilateral support) are unable or unwilling to supply funds in the quantities required. As bilateral financing and contributions to the IMF will continue to be scarce and unreliable in crises, the best solution may be to allow additional issues of special drawing rights (SDRs) during episodes of world financial stress; these funds could be destroyed once financial conditions normalize. This procedure would create an anti-cyclical element in world liquidity management and would give SDRs an enhanced role in world finance, a principle that developing countries have advocated in the past and should continue to endorse in the future.

A key role in crisis prevention could be played by the Contingency Credit Line (CCL). The CCL was created as 'a precautionary line of defence readily available against future balance of payments problems that might arise from international financial contagion' (IMF, 1999). The philosophy of the IMF moving more strongly into precautionary lending that would reduce the chances of countries being caught by contagion, and give leverage to the IMF to encourage countries to pursue policies that would make crises less likely, is clearly the right one. However, the fact that the CCL had not been used at the time of writing since its creation in April 1999 reflects design problems that were only partly corrected in the 2000 redesign of this facility. These include: (1) the limited scale of the facility; (2) the lack of automatic triggering in the original design, which was partially corrected by making 'activation' a fairly automatic process, though still requiring a 'post-activation' review that would result in a conditional adjustment programme; (3) the 'two-phase' or 'double conditionality' that characterizes such design; and (4) the fear of countries that private lenders and investors might see the use of the CCL as 'the ambulance outside the door', which could contribute to rather than deter a speculative attack or withdrawal of flows.

To overcome problems of the CCL and the reluctance of countries to use the CCL, in spite of its modification, a further change could make it more effective. This would imply that any country that had been very successfully evaluated during its Article IV consultation and that continued to perform well during the next three months, could automatically get a CCL. Should a crisis linked to contagion hit such a country, the CCL could be disbursed automatically for a relatively short period. As pointed out above, if the CCL is to be made more effective, and easier to disburse, it must be accompanied by better regulation, to avoid problems of excessive moral hazard. Debt standstills and orderly debt workouts would also help reduce the excessive cost borne by debtor countries in crises under present arrangements (for detailed discussions, see UNCTAD, 1998, and United Nations Task Force, 1999). However, as mentioned above, care must be taken in designing such measures so they do not excessively discourage private flows to developing countries nor significantly increase their cost (Soros, 2000).

## NOTES

1. Remarks made by Alan Greenspan before the 34th Annual Conference of the Federal Reserve Bank of Chicago, 7 May 1998.
2. Other estimates were somewhat lower, but still showed major increases in spreads for borrowers below investment grade.
3. I thank Andrew Crockett for his suggestive remarks on this point.

## REFERENCES

Aizenman, Joshue and Stephen J. Turnovsky (1999) 'Reserve requirements on sovereign debt in the presence of moral hazards – on debtors or creditors?' NBER working paper no. 7004.

Bank of International Settlements (BIS) (2001), *Annual Report 2001*, Basle, Switzerland.

Camdessus, Michel (2000), 'An agenda for the IMF at the start of the 21st century', Remarks at the Council on Foreign Relations, New York, February.

Council on Foreign Relations, Task Force Report (1999), *Safeguarding Prosperity in a Global Financial System: The Future International Financial Architecture*, Carla A. Hills and Peter G. Peterson (chairs), Morris Goldstein (Project Director), Washington, DC, Institute for International Economics.

D'Arista, Jane and Stephany Griffith-Jones (2000), 'The Boom of Portfolio Flows to Emerging Markets and its Regulatory Implications', M. Montes (ed.), *Short-Term Capital Movements and Balance of Payments Crises*, Helsinki: World Institute for Development Economics Research.

Eichengreen, Barry and Richard Portes (1995), 'Crisis? What Crisis? Orderly Workouts for Sovereign Debtors', London: Centre for Economic Policy Research.

FSF (2000a), Working Group Report on Highly Leveraged Institutions.

FSF (2000b), Working Group Report on Offshore Centers.

Greenspan, Alan (1998), Remarks before the 34th Annual Conference of the Federal Reserve Bank of Chicago, 7 May.

Greenwald, B., J. Stiglitz and A. Weiss (1984) 'Informational Imperfections in the Capital Market and Macroeconomic Fluctuations', *American Economic Review*, **74** (2), 194–9.

Griffith-Jones, S. (1998), 'Global capital flows, should they be regulated?', London: Macmillan.

Griffith-Jones, Stephany and Armar Bhattacharya (2001), *Developing Countries and the Global Financial System*, London: Commonwealth Secretariat.

Griffith-Jones, S. and J. Kimmis (2001) 'The reform of global financial governance arrangements', report prepared for the Commonwealth Secretariat, London.

Griffith-Jones, S. and S. Spratt (2001), 'Will the proposed new Basel Capital Accord have a negative effect on developing countries?', mimeo, Institute of Development Studies.

Group of 24 (2000), Communiqué, 23 September.

IMF (1999), 'Report of the Acting Managing Director to the Interim Committee on progress in strengthening the architecture of the international financial system', Washington, DC, September.

IOSCO (1998), *Causes, Effects and Regulatory Implications of Financial and Economic Turbulence in Emerging Markets*, September.

Kaminsky, G. Schmukler, and R. Lyon (1999), 'Managers, investors and crises: mutual fund strategies in emerging markets', mimeo, Washington, DC: World Bank.

McKinnon, R. and H. Pill (1999), 'Exchange-rate regimes for emerging markets: moral hazard and international overborrowing', *Oxford Review of Economic Policy*, Autumn, **15** (3).

Meltzer, Allan H. (chair) (2000), Report to the US Congress of the International Financial Advisory Commission, March.

Reisen, H. (2001), 'Will Basel II contribute to convergence in international capital flows?', mimeo, OECD Development Centre, OECD, Paris.

Soros, George (2000), *Open Society: Reforming Global Capitalism*, New York: Public Affairs, First Edition.

The Eminent Non-G7 Report (2001), 'Financial Instability in the Third World'.

Turner, Philip (2000), 'Procyclicality of regulatory ratios?', in John Eatwell and Lance Taylor (eds), *International Capital. Markets Systems in Transition*, New York: Oxford University Press.

UNCTAD (1998), *Trade and Development Report, 1998* (UNCTAD/TDR/1998), Geneva. United Nations publication, sales no. E.98.II.D.6.

UNCTAD (United Nations Conference on Trade and Development) (1999), *Trade and Development Report, 1999* (UNCTAD/TDR/1999), Geneva.

United Nations Task Force of the Executive Committee of Economic and Social Affairs (1999), 'Towards a new international financial architecture', report of the Task Force of the United Nations Executive Committee of Economic and Social Affairs (LC/G.2054), Santiago, Chile, Economic Commission for Latin America and the Caribbean (ECLAC), March.

Williamson, John (2001), 'The role of the IMF: a guide to the reports', in S. Griffith-Jones and A. Bhattacharya (eds), *Developing Countries and the Global Financial System*, Commonwealth Secreatriat, London.

Wyplosz, C. (2001), 'How risky is financial liberalization in the developing countries?', paper presented at the 7th Dubrovnik Conference on Current Issues in Emerging Market Economies, June 28–9.

Zedillo, E. et al. (2001), 'Technical report of the high-level panel on financing for development', report commissioned by the Secretary-General of the United Nations, June.

# 11. Capital flows to emerging markets under the flexible dollar standard: a critical view based on the Brazilian experience

## Carlos Medeiros and Franklin Serrano[1]*

## INTRODUCTION

The purpose of this chapter is to contribute to the discussion of a number of issues concerning macroeconomic policies that should be appropriate for
developing countries. We shall take into account the broader political picture of
changes in the international economy, reflected objectively in terms of the nature
of the balance of payments constraints facing the 'emerging markets' and specially the Latin American economies since the early 1990s. It is within this wider
context that we present our account of the particular case of Brazil.

The Brazilian experience has some peculiarities that make it an interesting
testing ground for the presumed benefits of the process of financial globalization
and the policies of trade and financial opening.

Many will agree that the slow growth and extremely high inflation experienced in Brazil in the 1980s had much to do with debt crisis and the subsequent
interruption of capital flows towards Latin America. Indeed, in what became
known as the 'lost decade' Brazil experienced a severe balance of payments
constraint that slowed growth and triggered the acceleration of inflation. Since
the early 1990s, foreign capital started again flowing towards Brazil in large
quantities, first mainly as portfolio capital but towards the end of the decade
more and more as foreign direct investment. One could well have expected that
this large amount of foreign capital would improve 'quality' (presumably increasingly 'cold' rather than 'hot' money), by alleviating the balance of
payments constraint, and would have had a big effect on both inflation stabilization and in the resumption of fast economic growth.

However, what the actual record shows is that the impact on inflation stabilization, although starting a bit late, only by mid-1994, was in fact more drastic
than anybody could have reasonably expected. Inflation fell spectacularly and

has remained extremely low ever since. On the other hand, the growth performance was, to say the very least, extremely disappointing. This chapter will try to make sense of this experience using a combination of some features of the international situation and of particular policies followed by the Brazilian state.

Most Latin American economies followed more or less the same broad pattern of fast disinflation and slow growth with the notable exception of Chile and partial exception of Argentina. Therefore the Brazilian story, in spite of its peculiarities, may arguably be seen to reflect a more general pattern.

We shall begin our discussion in the following section with a brief account of the operation of the current international monetary system, a system that we call the 'floating dollar standard', and of other salient features of the international trade and financial environment faced by the 'emerging' developing economies since the early 1990s. The third section shows how this new international environment affects and changes the nature of the balance of payments constraint facing the developing countries. The fourth section discusses the Brazilian experience within the context of the resumption of large capital flows towards Latin America since the early 1990s. The last section contains a few concluding remarks.

## THE FLOATING DOLLAR STANDARD, FINANCIAL GLOBALISATION AND THE EMERGING MARKETS

### The Floating Dollar Standard

At the end of 1979 there was a major change in American monetary policy, with the Volcker interest rate shock. The dollar interest rate in both nominal and real terms reached unprecedented levels and this was followed by a wave of financial innovations and policies of financial deregulation, which has ever since been spreading a combination of large and increasingly unregulated short-term capital flows and volatile exchange rates all over the world.

This policy change quickly brought down international commodity prices and slowed down international inflation. The USA has since then regained complete control over the international monetary and financial system. The other developed countries, finally convinced of the futility of trying to question the centrality of the dollar (as they had been doing in the 1970), increasingly accept the reality of the new system: the floating dollar standard.

In this system, the dollar is still the key international currency. The difference now is that the USA is free from the two limitations that the previous gold–dollar standard imposed on its policies, namely, the need to keep a fixed nominal exchange rate (to prevent a run towards gold) and the need to avoid running current account deficits (in order to prevent a decrease in the US gold reserves) (Serrano, 1999; Medeiros and Serrano, 1999).

In the current floating dollar standard, the USA can incur overall balance of payments deficits and finance them by giving assets denominated in its own currency as in the gold–dollar standard that ended in 1971. However, the lack of convertibility in gold allows the USA to change by its own initiative the exchange parity against other currencies, mainly through changes in dollar interest rates. This occurred when it engineered trends both of dollar appreciation (as in 1980–5 and 1995–2001) and of depreciation (in 1986–94). In the latter case there is no big direct inflationary effect since international commodity and oil prices are set in dollars and there is also no reason to fear a gold run anymore because the current standard is the dollar itself. The dollar is the international means of payment and the main standard in contracts and price quotes in the international markets (as it happens, for instance, even in Asian trade which is mainly invoiced in US dollars), properties that make it an important store of value (because of its superior liquidity).

The main advantage of the current floating dollar standard for the USA is therefore the complete elimination of its external or balance of payments constraint. Now the USA can and does run current account deficits without worrying much about the increase in its net external liabilities because these 'external' liabilities are mainly denominated in dollars anyway (without gold convertibility the problem of losing gold reserves when a current account deficit happens has simply been eliminated, see Serrano, 1999).

This floating dollar standard, which Nixon and Kissinger tried to impose in the turbulent 1970 and which became a fact in the 1980s , allows the USA to run permanent current account deficits, as has been happening almost every single year since 1971 (except in 1973–6 and 1980–81). In the current system, the total value of American deficits in the balance of payments as a whole is automatically financed by an identical capital inflow corresponding to the increase of other countries' reserves. These countries, if they want to participate in the international economy, simply must agree to accumulate dollar assets (often in the for of US public debt). In fact, the dollar is the reserve asset of the whole international financial system, as it is clear both from the central role of American interest rates and from the 'flight to quality' movements in times of turbulence, where 'quality' always means US government bonds.[1]

It is very important to stress these characteristics of the current international monetary and financial system and the extreme extent to which they benefit US interests. That may perhaps temper a bit the well-meant calls for major changes in the 'international financial architecture', which often do not specify how or why the USA will accept those changes, a small detail that makes such proposals sound rather utopian.

## Financial Globalization and Emerging Markets

Curiously enough, in spite of the absence of overall balance of payments problems, American trade policy during the 1990s turned progressively tougher, both directly and indirectly, through its overwhelming influence in international organizations such as the WTO, the World Bank and the IMF. US trade policy has systematically attempted to reduce bilateral trade deficits with most countries and to protect its 'old' industries (such as, steel, orange juice, and so on) and at the same time to open foreign markets in sectors (such as services) where the US has a clear competitive edge (software, entertainment services, and so on).

The 1990s was characterized by relatively low growth of the world economy as whole, unfavourable terms of trade for the developing countries and the hardening of the trade policies of the USA, Euroland and of the international organizations. World trade still grew by more than world GDP but the export markets for developing countries grew relatively slowly and under an increasingly fierce competition. This competition has been aggravated by the repeated competitive exchange rate devaluations of a number of developing countries relative to the dollar, which creates problems for developing countries that adopt fixed exchange rate regimes.

Foreign direct investment since the 1980 has grown at very high rates, predominantly between industrial countries (for example, Japanese and European investment in the USA, investment between European Union countries) and also in a number of developing countries in Asia and increasing in China. In Latin America, Mexico (because of NAFTA) and more recently Brazil have received large flows of FDI.

As far as developing countries are concerned, these flows have been substantial only for a selected group of them. Furthermore, as a rule these flows towards developing countries have not always been geared towards import substituting or export sectors, since many emerging countries are attracting FDI through privatization of non-tradable utilities and services and/or by making local firms a cheap buy due to the arbitrage gain allowed by keeping large interest rate differentials (far above expected exchange rate devaluation). Only under very few specific circumstances such as in the East Asian economies in the 1980s, were FDI flows strongly connected with an acceleration of exports and a structural improvement in the balance of payments position.[2] Moreover, these flows, partially because of these attraction policies and in part because of the very once-and-for-all nature of a lot of FDI flows, have not been very stable or regular over time.

Over this period, increasing financial deregulation made it deceptively easy for most developing countries, even many of those who had been cut off from the circuit of international finance since the debt crisis in the early 1980s, to finance current account deficits through private international capital markets (mainly through short-term portfolio investments but also through bank loans). In the 1990s there was a marked expansion of these gross capital flows towards the developing countries, flows which in spite of numerous crises have continued, albeit with large fluctuations, ever since.

In the last five years, the global trend of capital flows towards developing countries has shifted again towards a faster growth of FDI relative to debt or portfolio flows. This has led in many places to a renewed optimism about 'globalization' and development since the 'quality' of the flows seems to be improving, but this optimism, at least in what regards growth performance, appears as we shall presently see to be rather exaggerated.

## LARGE CAPITAL FLOWS AND THE EXTERNAL CONSTRAINT FOR THE DEVELOPING COUNTRIES

### Capital Flows to 'Emerging Markets'

The balance of payments situation in the 'emerging' developing countries with the current floating dollar standard seems quite peculiar. For on the one hand, in terms of the balance of trade and growth of exports, the trends in general are quite unfavourable (in comparison with the 1970 for instance) since now the growth of export volumes are lower, the terms of trade worse and the pressure from the rich countries on those countries to increase imports is rather strong.[3] On the other hand, it has become even easier than it was in the 1970 for developing countries to attract large flows of foreign capital.

This contradiction is aggravated by the fact that, in general, it becomes easier to attract larger capital inflows the more an 'emerging' economy follows policies of financial deregulation and opening its markets: policies that invariably lead to exchange rate appreciation and loss of competitiveness. This increases the gap between the large accumulation of foreign liabilities and the real possibility of servicing these liabilities that requires a rapid increase in export earnings.

It is important to note that this problem cannot be solved by changing the form of the capital inflows. It is true that the more a financially open economy attracts and relies on short-term speculative capital the more it will be prone to foreign-exchange and liquidity crises.[4] However, even when capital inflows consist mainly of FDI the longer-term structural external fragility is not reduced. As it has been pointed out by Prebisch (1950), Kalecki ([1972] 1982) and more recently by Kregel (1996) among others, unless FDI is continuously and steadily expanding and is directly connected to the expansion of export capacity (or import substitution), it does not generate long-run positive effects on the balance of payments position of recipient countries (see below).

In this very unstable international environment, we observe that the best performance in terms of economic growth has occurred in the developing countries that have managed (in many countries for as long as they have managed) to resist the temptation of (and the pressures for) uncontrolled financial opening deregulation, and have kept some sort of control especially over the capital inflows; this has kept exchange rate and industrial policies geared towards export promotion. In other words, the growth performance has been much better in countries in which financial globalization did not lead (or for as long as it did not lead) to the abandonment of state-led development strategies (such as Chile from the 1980s, and China, India and Asian countries until the late 1980s).

## Long-term Sustainability and Growth

When discussing capital flows and the balance of payments situation we must be clear about what are the limits on the possibility of economies growing while incurring current account deficits.

In the first place it is important to look at the question of the sustainability (or solvency) of this type of growth trajectory. We must examine under what conditions the growth of net foreign liabilities in the economy will remain under control and not follow an explosive path. This can initially be thought of independently of the specific manner in which the current account is financed, whether it is in terms of external debt or foreign direct investment.

The central element, as far as the sustainability of a strategy of growing with current account deficits is concerned, is given by the relative evolution of the net external liabilities and exports, since the latter are necessarily the ultimate source of the cash flow in foreign exchange that allows the servicing of these liabilities.

The net external liabilities, like any debt that is rolled over, grow at a rate equal to the effective interest rate paid on these liabilities. The crucial relationship regarding the sustainability of this growth with debt is thus given by the difference between the rate of growth of the value of exports and that of the effective interest rate.

As demonstrated originally by Domar (1950), if the rate of growth of exports is systematically below that interest rate, even a small trade deficit will make the ratio between net external liabilities and exports grow without limit and at some point it will be inevitable that the economy will have to generate a trade surplus in order to stabilize the growth of its external liabilities. It is therefore extremely important, for countries that are growing and experience current account deficits, that the rate of growth of their exports should be sufficiently high to satisfy the Domar stability condition.

Considering this discussion of the sustainability of external liability, the only relevant difference between foreign direct investment and external debt, whether the latter is short-term or long-term, is their relative costs in terms of payments of foreign exchange.

Although foreign direct investment is considered the cheapest form of external finance because some of their profits are reinvested, some authors such as Kregel (1996) claim that the cost of this alternative may in fact well be higher than long-term external debt. Kregel claims that this is because the rate of profit tends to be higher than the rate of interest. In that case the 'reinvestment' of profits should be seen as a new gross foreign direct investment flow (implying new rights to future repatriation of profits) and should this not be deducted from the cost of previous flows.

Another problem is that the cost of attracting capital through a large difference between domestic and foreign interest rates is very probably much closer to the current dollar value of the domestic rate of interest rather than the rate at which the country gets credit in the international market. This happens because these capital flows are normally invested in funds that are, in one way or another, linked to the internal debt of the country (see Serrano, 1998).

Given these possibilities and the notorious practical difficulty of measuring accurately and separately the rates of return of all types of foreign liabilities – including the payments for royalties, licenses, patents and so on – a good empirical indicator that can be considered a reasonable measure of the sustainability of the country's external position is the ratio between its current account deficit and its exports.

This simple indicator has the further advantage of reflecting well the impact of the increases in the import coefficients and the volume of imports that has been such a marked feature of the experiences of trade and financial opening of the so-called 'emerging markets' in the 1990s.

## Short Term Liquidity and Crises

Note that while an unsustainable trajectory of net foreign liabilities will sooner or later lead to some slowdown in growth, it will not necessarily lead to a financial or foreign exchange crisis. An external liquidity crisis generally only happens when the creditors suddenly refuse to roll over debts that are due in a particular period. This, even in a situation where the current account deficit (the net inflow of capital over a given period) is not very big, may make the total stock of non-renewed credit lines appear as a rather large gross outflow of capital which can quickly deplete the country's foreign exchange reserves and trigger a serious crisis.

The conditions that will trigger an external liquidity or foreign exchange crisis depend on the magnitude of the foreign liabilities that are maturing in relation to the country's reserves of foreign exchange. It is in regard to the latter relationship that the distinction between short-term debt, long-term debt and foreign direct investment acquires great importance. It is clear that the greater the maturity of external debt and the more the current account deficit has been financed with foreign direct investment, the smaller will be the value of foreign liabilities that are due in a particular period. On the other hand, the more urgent the servicing of short-term external debt the greater will be the country's external 'financial fragility' and the risk of a liquidity crisis.

We can say then that a good indicator of the external financial fragility of a country and even of the probability of a foreign exchange crisis is given by the ratio between the country's short-term external liabilities and its foreign exchange reserves.

When this ratio becomes very high, any interruption of capital flows caused by a decision not to renew the credit lines that are due can trigger, and often does trigger, a speculative process. This process is magnified by the expectations of default or of exchange rate devaluations as the magnitude of the gross capital outflows involved are such that they can quickly wipe out the country's foreign exchange reserves.

Indeed, if we examine the circumstances of the foreign exchange and liquidity crises that have happened in various 'emerging' economies in Latin America, East Asia and Eastern Europe we can distinguish clearly between the problems of foreign debt sustainability and that of external liquidity with the help of the two indicators discussed above.

Some basic common features of all of these experiences can easily be enumerated. First of all, factors exogenous to the developing countries, such as financial innovations and deregulation, together with a reduction in US interest rates in the early 1990s, played a central role in originating capital flows towards these economies.[5]

A second feature is that crises, (i.e. sudden reversals of capital flows together with a collapse of asset prices and of the exchange rate) have always been preceded by a significant increase in the ratio between short-term external liabilities and foreign exchange reserves and also by an appreciation of the exchange rate.[6]

A third salient feature is that the imposition of controls on short-term capital flows, whether of the inflows as in Chile in the first half of the 1990s or even of outflows as in Malaysia after 1997, have worked well in terms of reducing the volume and increasing the maturity of the external liabilities of these countries.[7]

Based on the liquidity indicator discussed above, Table 11.1 below ranks a few 'emerging market' countries in terms of their short-term external financial fragility.

These facts and figures indicate that amidst the abundance of foreign short-term capital flows, the accumulation of short-term liabilities relative to available reserves (as happened in Mexico in 1994, Thailand, Malaysia, Indonesia and Korea in 1997, Russia in 1998, Brazil in 1999 and Argentina in 2000), has al-

*Table 11.1    External short-term bank liabilities relative to official forex in selected countries (stocks in December 1998)*

| Country | Short term debt/reserves |
|---------|--------------------------|
| Taiwan | 0.18 |
| China | 0.21 |
| India | 0.28 |
| Malaysia | 0.36 |
| South Korea | 0.57 |
| Chile | 0.57 |
| Thailand | 0.83 |
| Mexico | 0.92 |
| Brazil | 0.93 |
| Indonesia | 1.04 |
| Argentina | 1.37 |
| Russia | 2.26 |

*Source*:    (downloaded from www.oecd.org/dac/debt), OECD data from the World Bank, IMF and BIS. Calculated by the BIS.

ways led to a situation of worsening financial fragility and, with different national variations, to a foreign exchange crisis.

The international evidence shows also that speculative bets against countries in which the ratio between short-term foreign liabilities and reserves is small simply do not work (see the case of Hong Kong in 1997). This does not seem to depend very much on the type of exchange rate regime or the 'credibility' of the finance ministers of these economies, nor on any generic fiscal fundamentals favoured by the orthodox view.

Although the instability of financial markets and uncertainty about short-term movements of asset prices seem to have increased in the 1990s, the financial crisis that happened in these countries was based on an objective condition: the accumulation of short-term foreign liabilities relative to foreign exchange reserves.

This accumulation of short-term debt was not inevitable and it shows that the behaviour of central banks and finance ministries of the emerging markets and their attitudes in terms of controlling the process of financial liberalization and the conduct of monetary and exchange rate policy in general is a key determinant of the possibility of crisis.

We observe from these experiences that there is no strong correlation between the expansion of foreign trade and the increase in short-term capital flows. Both the very dynamic, export-led East Asian economies and the slower-growing and less open Latin American economies have been hurt by liquidity crises. Thus it seems that it is not necessarily the size of the current account deficit per se that explains the liquidity crisis.

**Exports, the Current Account and Growth**

Turning now to the question of the long term sustainability of the foreign liabilities/export relationship, we may note that, except under extreme circumstances, as this ratio gradually deteriorates, it can be and often is improved by devaluation and/or by slowing the growth of aggregate demand and the economy, and thus the containing the growth of imports. Thus an economy which has sustainability problems with its external debtor position tends to be slowed down. From this slowdown a foreign exchange crisis may or may not 'emerge' depending on the maturity structure of the country's foreign liabilities and the size of its central bank foreign exchange reserves.

For instance, over the first half of the 1990 the slowdown of the growth rate of Korean exports and the increase in its import coefficients clearly signalled that growth could not continue at the very fast rates of the 1980s. That, however, was not the reason for the collapse of the won in 1997, which was due to excessive short-term borrowing following the financial opening of the economy (Chang and Yoo, 1999; Medeiros, 1998).

There is significant autonomy between the problems of longer-term sustainability and that of short-term liquidity although one can and does affect the other. The main connections between then are transmitted through the rate of interest and the exchange rate. Short-term capital inflows increase when the difference between domestic and international interest rates is big enough to compensate for the expected devaluation of the currency and the country's sovereign risk premium. Capital flows tend to hurt the competitiveness of exports and cheapen imports to the extent that when large, they tend to lead to exchange rate appreciation. This ends up affecting negatively the current account to exports ratio. This, by its turn, may well lead to deflationary demand policies that further increase the domestic interest rate and attract even more short-term capital inflows, increasing the external financial liabilities. The result may be a crisis, or else a 'stop-and-go' pattern of growth with a tendency towards overvaluation.

While the view that sustaining growing current account deficits (even in relation to exports) is possible as long as they are financed by 'cold' rather than 'hot' money is still the dominant one, we observe no empirical evidence in the current conditions of the international economy that previous gross flows of foreign direct investment will signal the future persistence of those flows, as we pointed out above. That result puts in question the idea that foreign direct investment is inherently stable (Claessens et al., 1995, Kregel, 1996).

The historical record and the problems mentioned above show that large in-flows of foreign direct investment do not seem to constitute a stable solution for the sustainability problem, unless it generates in the host economy a sufficient acceleration of exports that can finance the expansion of imports and other out-flows of dividends, royalties and so on which are traditionally associated with this type of investment.

## CAPITAL FLOWS TO LATIN AMERICA AND THE CASE OF BRAZIL

### Latin America: from the Export Drive to the Import Boom

After the 1982 Mexican default, most of Latin America found itself without fresh external sources of finance in a period when the terms of trade had wors-ened; the demand for its exports had fallen with the recent world recession and international interest rates were at record levels. This combination of events imposed a severe and prolonged balance of payments crisis on the region.

This crisis resulted in an interruption to the State-led industrial development strategy in countries such as Brazil and Mexico.

In general the regional reaction to the crisis was based on the control of im-ports both through policy-induced recessions and administrative controls and by the promotion of net exports through exchange rate devaluations. These policies led to an increase in exports and at the same time to economic stagna-tion and an explosive acceleration of inflation. As the European economy was in recession in the early 1980, the counterpart of increased factor service pay-ments and capital outflows of the region was an increase of Latin American trade surplus with the USA. However, since its main purpose was to service the debt rather than increasing the capacity to import (that had been constrained throughout the decade in the region) the Latin American export drive in general came together with slow growth and high inflation.

With the abundance of international liquidity and after the 'securitization' of the external debt in the early 1990s, the external financing conditions of Latin America changed drastically. From a strategy of promoting exports, exchange rate devaluation and rigid control of imports (responsible for the stagnation and high inflation) the Latin American economies in general turned to a strategy geared towards attracting growing external capital inflows in order to remove the external constraint and resume some growth, controlling inflation through control of nominal exchange rate and integrating domestic financial markets with the international financial circuit.

With the exception of Chile (which did not allow excessive real exchange rate revaluation or impose capital controls on the inflows) and of Colombia, the biggest economies in the region followed the 'southern cone' strategy that had been tried and had failed in the late 1970s in Argentina and Chile.[8] Following trade and financial liberalization, countries like Argentina, Mexico and Brazil started to receive large inflows of international speculative capital. Many of them seized this opportunity and applied inflation stabilization plans based on the relative stabilization of nominal exchange rates (this time accompanied with measures to drastically reduce or eliminate inflation indexing of contracts).

This was on the whole quite successful in bringing inflation down. The combination of large capital inflows in a context of economic recovery, dismantling of import controls and overvalued real exchange rates (due to the stabilization plans) led to a large increase in imports across the whole region, particularly from the USA (Medeiros, 1997, Medeiros and Serrano, 1999).

The case of Mexico, one of the very few countries of the region that, because of NAFTA, actually saw a high rate of growth of exports, is a very good example of how the deterioration of the current account deficit to exports ratio, due to the import boom, leads to a situation of constrained growth even when the inflow of FDI is quite large. In fact, in 1990, Mexican exports reached US$ 40.7 billion, which was about 28 per cent of all Latin American exports. In 1998 Mexico exported US$ 117.5 billion dollars increasing its share of Latin American exports to 46 per cent.

However, rather than bringing fast growth, the Mexican exports came together with an even more spectacular expansion of imports. Since the 1994 crisis that led to a 6 per cent fall in GDP in 1995, the trade balance shifted back into surplus. On average, the Mexican economy grew modestly in the 1990s, in spite of having had an above-average performance compared with the rest of Latin America. What happened in Mexico was a very fast increase in the import coefficient and of the remittances associated with the foreign direct investments that elevated the ratio of current account deficit to exports from 15.3 per cent in 1990 to 41.7 per cent in 1994. With an increasing share of Mexican exports being concentrated in the maquiladoras where the creation of domestic value added is very low and with the non-tradable sector constrained by a relatively by a relatively restrictive macroeconomic policy, the Mexican economy did not manage to transform its export growth into an engine for overall economic growth. When, after 1994 the real exchange rate was devalued and kept low, and particularly in the last few years when oil prices increased sharply, the current account was stabilized and the expansion of exports did come together with a higher rate of economic growth. These years of faster expansion however merely compensated for the big 1995 recession and in the end in both halves of the 1990s Mexico (after growing on average only 1.9 per cent in the 1980s) kept the disappointing average rate of growth, for a country with so much catching up to do, of around 3.5 per cent as can be seen in Table 11.2 below.

*Table 11.2    Growth and the current account/export ratio in Mexico*

| | GDP growth rate (percentage) | Current account deficit/exports |
|---|---|---|
| 1990 | – | 15.3 |
| 1991 | 4.2 | – |
| 1992 | 3.6 | – |
| 1993 | 2.0 | – |
| 1994 | 4.4 | 41.7 |
| 1995 | –6.2 | 1.8 |
| 1996 | 5.2 | 2.2 |
| 1997 | 6.8 | 6.1 |
| 1998 | 4.9 | 12.2 |
| 1999 | 3.7 | 9.4 |
| 2000 | 7.0a | – |

*Note*:   a = preliminary estimate.

*Source*:   ECLAC statistical yearbook 2000 (ECLAC, 2001).

### The Debt Crisis, Stagnation and the Acceleration of Inflation in Brazil

Just like the other Latin American countries, the Brazilian economy was very much affected by the interruption of capital flows in the 1980s and their resumption in the 1990s.

This relatively sudden resumption of capital flows was decisive for economic recovery in the early 1990s and the dramatic reduction and successful stabilization of the rate of inflation was obtained in mid-1994 with the Real Plan, which was based on the comprehensive elimination of the indexation of the economy and (more crucially ) on strict control of the nominal exchange rate.

The external debt crisis and interruption of capital flows in the 1980s although as in other Latin American countries they had different effects on the Brazilian economy because of some distinctive features of this economy and its economic development strategy (see Serrano, 1998).

One of these peculiarly Brazilian features was the very high degree of domestic price indexation of the economy. In fact, widespread indexation in Brazil can be traced back to the mid-1960s. The military government of the time decided to follow a development strategy in which the local currency should not be allowed to become persistently overvalued relative to the US dollar. This led to a crawling peg adjustable exchange rate regime with quite frequent minidevaluations. This continuous nominal devaluation of the currency by its turn led to the need to formally index interest rates on government bonds (the so called 'monetary correction' mechanism) in order to prevent capital flight. Indexation then spread to all financial contracts and also to taxes and tariffs on public utilities and introduced an element of inertia in inflation which at the same time made necessary or perhaps inevitable (even in a politically repressive regime) a partial but later increasing indexation of nominal wages. The latter by its turn reinforced the inflationary inertia in inflation rates giving further stimulus to widespread indexation of all contracts.

Therefore, when the external shocks of the early 1980s and the debt crisis hit Brazil, the economy already had a very high degree of indexation and a relatively high persistent rate of inflation. This explains why inflation accelerated so much and reached such high and persistent levels in Brazil during the 1980s. The debt crisis led to the so called 'maxi-devaluations' over and above the crawling peg as an attempt to alter the real exchange rate, to promote exports and cut imports in order to obtain a trade surplus large enough to service the debt and make up for capital flight (the latter being a less serious problem in Brazil because of capital controls and the indexed, and on the average quite positive in real terms, interest rate). Those maxi-devaluations led to an acceleration of inflation and led to further increases in interest rates and then wages. On the other hand, the system of generalized indexed contracts allowed the economy to operate normally in spite of record high rates of inflation. Thus, indexation at the same time made inflation rates much higher and more persistent than in other countries of the region but at the same time prevented the disorganization of the economy that happens under open uncontrolled hyperinflation.

In the period between 1982 and 1994 many different types of inflation stabilization plans were attempted. But, regardless of such efforts, until the Real Plan the Brazilian economy lived under permanent inflationary conditions with strong trends towards hyperinflation, briefly contained by increasingly ineffective stabilization attempts. By the end of the decade annual inflation rates reached four digits.

Another feature of Brazilian development strategy that was crucial in explaining the peculiar performance of the economy in the 1980s was that, in marked contrast with many other Latin American countries (where the external debt financed capital flight) from the mid-1970s a good part of the Brazilian external debt was used to finance the Second National Development Plan which invested heavily in the capital goods sector and infrastructure. Those investments were instrumental in reducing the dependency of the economy on some imports (such as oil, for instance) and more importantly, served to complete the local industrial base (including some indigenous technological capacity) and provided the cost externalities (in transportation, energy and basic inputs) that allowed the country to become a major exporter of industrial commodities within a short space of time. This successful export performance coupled with the policy-induced stagnation of the economy and other measures to ration imports, allowed the country to produce large trade surpluses after 1983 for ten years. Brazilian exports increased from US$ 15 billion in 1979 to around US$ 34 billion in 1989.

Although relatively successful in servicing the debt and preventing economic collapse this export performance appears differently when compared with other developing countries outside Latin America. Indeed, the average rate of growth of exports in the 1980s, of about 4.5 per cent a year was below the growth of world trade and around only one-third that of countries such as China or Korea over the same period.

Under these circumstances the control of imports was made inevitable and even then foreign exchange reserves were not stabilized. By 1990 Brazilian imports in current dollars were still below the 1980 levels (see Table 11.4 below). The whole export expansion was absorbed by the debt service and did not improve the capacity to import. When the Brazilian economy returned to the international financial circuit in the early 1990s, its industry and its overall international competitiveness were significantly inferior, relative to the rest of the world than at the beginning of the 1980s.

This whole process made Brazil achieve an average GDP growth rate of only 1.6 per cent in the 1980s. This was a little worse than Mexico, substantially lower than Chile (3 per cent) and Colombia (3 per cent), countries where the capital flows where not cut off so drastically and were resumed earlier, but still much better than Argentina (–0.7 per cent) and many of the other smaller countries in the region.[9]

**The Resumption of Capital Flows, the New Exchange Rate Policy and the End of Inflation**

Import liberalization started in Brazil in 1990 when, following very closely World Bank advice, Brazil dismantled a number of non-price import restrictions and started reducing tariffs. However, since the economy was in recession at the beginning of the decade the value of imports only started growing more substantially after 1993 when a more sustained economic recovery began.

In May 1991, an important regulatory change in Brazil (the so called 'Annex IV'), which allowed foreign ownership of domestic portfolio investments marked the beginning of a large inflow of capital, after almost ten years of very small flows.[10] In that same year the central bank started the policy of creating an interest rate differential between internal and external rates way beyond any possible expectation of devaluation of the exchange rate (which was still indexed to inflation to avoid overvaluation). This policy started attracting large capital inflows. Given that the value of exports was growing at a relatively high rate in the period 1992–4, that imports had not yet started growing and that there had been cuts in the international interest rate that eased the servicing of the 'old' external debt, the result of these initial surges of capital inflows was a fast accumulation of reserves, which more than doubled between 1991 and 1992.

These events show clearly the exogenous character of these inflows. When they began to mount, the economy was stagnated, inflation was more than 400 per cent a year, and the so-called fundamentals were far from right. Indeed, capital inflows picked up so much momentum that in spite of the subsequent import boom and slowdown of exports and more generally of the increase in the current account deficit, the growth of foreign exchange reserves between 1991 and 1996 was of 539 per cent.

For a number of reasons, mostly related to the domestic political situation and the election calendar, it was only in 1994 that the government took full advantage of this new external situation to launch a new (and this successful) radical stabilization plan, the Real Plan.

This plan, like the failed 1986 Cruzado Plan, was based on stabilizing the nominal exchange rate and eliminating indexation of wages, prices and financial contracts.

The main differences were a certain lack of preoccupation with possible real wage losses, a long preparatory phase to synchronize relative prices and other contracts[11] and the maintenance of record high interest rates in order to ensure a continuation of the inflow of foreign capital.

Interest rates were set so high when the monetary reform began that they quickly led to a nominal appreciation of the new currency, which was supposed to be pegged on a one-to-one basis to the US dollar but eventually went as high as 85 cents of Real to the Dollar for a short while. The Brazilian central bank then followed a policy of frequently and gradually making small devaluations. This policy was run until early 1999 but, as subsequent events have shown, was not enough to correct the chronic overvaluation. The plan was extremely successful in bringing inflation down and keeping it low. Inflation rates of 43.1 per cent a month in the first half of 1994, fell to 3.1 per cent in the second half of that year and to 1.7 per cent in the first half of 1995 (Calcagno and Sainz, 1999, p. 13). Annual inflation was brought down to less than 5 per cent in 1998 and 1999, in spite of the large devaluation in the latter year, showing that the government did really succeed in eliminating indexation and 'real wage resistance.'[12] The behaviour of the rate of inflation and the nominal exchange rate can be gauged from Table 11.3 below.

The Real Plan represents a complete break with the macroeconomic policy of relative real exchange rate stability which had been maintained more or less consistently (in spite of everything) since the 1960s in order to avoid compromising the export performance of the economy.

*Table 11.3 Yearly rates of inflation and nominal exchange rate devaluation*

|  | Implicit<br>GDP deflator | Real/US$<br>average exchange rate |
|---|---|---|
| 1991 | 416.7 | 497.9 |
| 1992 | 969.0 | 1011.4 |
| 1993 | 1996.1 | 1853.9 |
| 1994 | 2240.2 | 1888.9 |
| 1995 | 77.5 | 43.6 |
| 1996 | 17.4 | 9.6 |
| 1997 | 8.2 | 7.3 |
| 1998 | 4.7 | 7.7 |
| 1999 | 4.3 | 56.4 |
| 2000 | 8.6 | – |

*Source*: IPEADATA database (www.ipeadata.gov.br).

The government shifted to a policy of trying to achieve the maximum possible stability of the nominal exchange rate in order to control inflation and prevent the return of indexation. This policy seemed also to be strictly necessary for the strategy of financing growing trade and current account deficits.

## The Unsustainable Current Account and Slow Growth

The combination of an appreciated currency in a new environment of liberalized imports (which were further liberalized in the first months after monetary reform) with a credit boom that followed the stabilization naturally led to an explosion of imports.

Very quickly, monthly figures for the growth of imports more than doubled. As exports could not and did not follow suit, Brazil ran a trade deficit in 1995, after more than a decade of surpluses. The fear of a Mexican-style balance of payment crisis quickly made the authorities put brakes in the economy mainly through monetary policy (credit controls and stratospheric interest rates), but also by attempts at controlling the growth of public expenditure and tax increases.

Indeed, in spite growing interest payments (reaching 7.5 per cent of GDP in 1998) that seem to have had little if any effect on aggregate demand, the highest primary deficit in the period was around one per cent of GDP in 1996 and 1997.

These policies of containing the trend growth of aggregate demand have been followed more or less consistently from 1995 to the beginning of 1999, avowedly to control demand inflation but in fact dictated mainly by the surprising and unexpected ever-worsening current account figures, and doubts about their ability to finance it adequately.

During this period GDP growth was brought down from 5.8 per cent in 1994 to a meagre 0.2 per cent in 1998. Even then the current account deficit as a proportion of the GDP measured in current dollars swung from practically zero in 1994 to 4.3 per cent in 1998.

Remittances for payments of profits and interests grew from 23 per cent of exports in 1994 to 39.9 per cent in 1998, reflecting the high dollar interest rates paid to foreign investors in Brazilian assets and also increasing payments of royalties, patents and licenses, as Brazil progressively abandoned its policy of creating local technology and the shift in its diplomatic position in terms of payments for 'intellectual property rights'.

If we look at our favourite measure of the sustainability of the current account, which is a change in the ratio of the current account deficit to exports, we see that in the period 1994–8 this indicator shifted from 3.9 to 65.8, a deterioration of approximately 1580 per cent. This had the inevitable consequence of increasing the growth of Brazil's net external liability position, i.e. the sum of foreign debt plus accumulated FDI. This position, according to some estimates increased from approximately US$ 165 billion in 1994 to around US$ 303 billion in 1998. The country's net external position, calculated as a ratio to exports, shifted from 3.8 to 5.9 over that same period.

Table 11.4 below contains data for the many of the indicators discussed above for Brazil in the 1990s.

Given the overvaluation and the misguided industrial policy strategy, the current account was clearly on an unsustainable path, even with ever-slowing growth. To make matters worse, the increase in reserves and large and growing current account deficits were originally financed through the accumulation of a high level of short-term debt and portfolio investments.

After the Russian crisis of mid-1998 that led to a fall in international commodity prices of many Brazilian exports and to the downgrading of Brazil by the credit rating agencies, the situation became critical. A 'preventive' IMF agreement was made and it was meant to avoid a major devaluation. In the months that followed, short-term capital quickly flowed out of Brazil, and the country lost a large amount of foreign exchange reserves in a few months. A major devaluation became increasingly expected by the market in spite of repeated denials by both government and IMF officials.

Banks started reducing their exposure to Brazil. According to Baig and Goldfajn's (2000) estimates, international banks reduced their overall exposure to Brazil from US$ 84.6 to 62.3 billion during 1998. The net outflow of short-term capital which started in 1997 was of more than US$ 30 billion during 1998 (see Table 11.4).

Table 11.4  *Macroeconomic indicators for Brazil*

| | Exports | Imports | GDP (growth) | Ratio of net factor payments abroad to exports | Ratio of current account deficit to exports | Ratio of current account deficit to GDP* | Ratio of net foreign liabilities to exports | Foreign direct investment | International Reserves (million US$) | Short-term capital flows |
|---|---|---|---|---|---|---|---|---|---|---|
| 1991 | 0.6 | 1.8 | 1.0 | – | –4.4 | 0.0 | 4.73 | – | 9406.4 | –7406 |
| 1992 | 13.2 | –2.3 | –0.5 | – | 17.2 | 1.5 | 4.15 | 1 924 | 23 754.3 | –2844 |
| 1993 | 7.7 | 22.9 | 4.9 | – | –1.5 | 0.0 | 4.09 | 801 | 32 211.2 | –4432 |
| 1994 | 12.9 | 31.0 | 5.8 | 23.0 | –3.9 | 0.0 | 3.81 | 2 035 | 38 806.2 | –3824 |
| 1995 | 6.8 | 50.7 | 4.2 | 27.7 | –38.6 | 2.5 | 3.64 | 3 475 | 51 840.3 | 15523 |
| 1996 | 2.6 | 7.0 | 2.7 | 33.4 | –484 | –3.0 | 4.15 | 11 666 | 60 110.1 | 4857 |
| 1997 | 11.0 | 12.0 | 3.3 | 36.6 | –58.1 | –3.8 | 4.70 | 18 608 | 52 172.7 | –15517 |
| 1998 | –3.5 | –3.3 | 0.2 | 39.9 | –65.7 | –4.3 | 5.93 | 28 541 | 44 556.4 | –30032 |
| 1999 | –6.1 | –14.7 | 0.8 | 41.2 | –52.2 | –4.5 | 7.02 | 30 254 | 36 342.3 | –1943** |
| 2000 | 14.0 | 13.2 | 4.5 | – | –44.7 | –4.2 | 6.68 | | – | – |

*Notes:*    * GDP in US$; ** Up until November 1999.

*Sources:*    IPEADATA (www.ipeadata.gov.br/), ECLAC (2001), Miguel and Cunha (2001; Baig and Goldfajn (2000).

The debt rollover rate for short-term loans fell to 0.62 between 1 October and 31 December 1998. In January 1999 a new director was appointed to the Brazilian central bank who tried to accelerate the devaluations gradually according to a new formula. The decision seems to have taken the IMF by surprise. It led to a lot of confusion and apparently the Brazilian central bank was not allowed to intervene to support the new regime using funds which were de facto under IMF control. That, amidst intense speculation, led to the quick collapse of the new scheme. The currency was allowed to float, and the new central banker was duly removed and replaced. The exchange rate suffered wild gyrations for some time, and only when yet another central banker with tacit IMF permission to intervene was appointed did the market calm down.

After that Brazil officially adhered to a 'free' floating exchange rate regime and to a monetary policy of 'inflation targeting' mainly through nominal interest rate changes. The floating however was far from 'clean' and interest rate management was not independent of balance of payments considerations. Interventions were frequent and some of the interest rate changes were clearly made with the exchange rate in mind. In any case, the fact that formal indexation of interest rates, exchange rates and wages were eliminated prevented the exchange rate supply shock turning into an accelerating inflation spiral. The crisis, and a very tight fiscal policy aimed at stabilizing the internal debt-to-GDP ratio in a situation of very high real interest rates, brought the economy to a standstill.

However, from the second semester of 1999 a recovery began and the economy actually grew 0.7 per cent in that year. After the situation was normalized, capital flows were resumed. Banks reopened credit lines although now with a permanently reduced exposure to Brazil.[13] This turned out not be a pressing problem since by then foreign direct investment, which was already following a very fast rising trend since 1994, increased even further to record levels for a few years. FDI flows increased from little more than US$2 billion in 1994 to more than US$ 30 billion in 1999. After peaking in 2000, the FDI flow started decreasing again in 2001 raising new fears about the external financing of the country.

The main feature of this FDI boom is the predominance of acquisitions of existing local firms, whether already in the private sector or through privatization, instead of the installation and expansion of the operations of foreign firms in the country as in the 1970s. Also these capital flows, contrary to naive official expectations, have not had a major positive impact on export performance, nor are the investments geared to import substitution. On the contrary, given the concentration of these flows on largely non-tradable sectors (especially services such as telecommunications) and the natural tendency of multinationals (when allowed by policy) to import a large fraction of their inputs and components the FDI has helped to increase the import coefficients of a number of sectors of the Brazilian economy that have very high income elasticity.

Before looking at the data one would have expected that after the 'preventive' IMF agreement in 1998 and the devaluation and crisis in early 1999, things would have changed and the Brazilian economy and in particular its current account would by now be on a sustainable growth path. That unfortunately does not seem to have been the case. In spite of the very slow growth in 1999 and the large real devaluation, the current account deficit fell by about US$ 8.5 billion, a little more than the fall in imports. Exports actually fell in 1999 because of the fall in international commodity prices and had not recovered their current dollar value of 1998 by the end of 2000.

The change in the exchange rate regime led to a substantial reduction in interest rates and easing of credit, which together with some spontaneous import substitution induced by the devaluation made the economy grow 4.4 per cent in the year 2000 in spite of the tight fiscal policy. However, the current account deficit seems to be stuck at around 4 per cent of GDP. Recent studies show that such deficits would require very high average rates of export growth, in excess of 10 per cent a year, almost twice the historical average, in order to be sustainable (Miguel and Cunha, 2001).

On the other hand, as economic growth recovers imports are beginning to grow fast again. Moreover the recent (2001) fall in flows of FDI, precisely as the global markets are getting turbulent over the troubles of Argentina, has made the Brazilian central bank abandon its forecast of 4.5 per cent growth in 2001 and emit some signs, by raising interest rates, that it might be getting ready to slow the economy down reverting to its moderately more expansionist policy stance adopted after the dust of the big devaluation settled.

In the end, what Brazil has to show for this immense accumulation of foreign liabilities is an average growth rate of GDP in the 1990s of merely 2.6 per cent, a single percentage point more than in the so-called 'lost decade' of the 1980s and almost a whole point less than the 3.3 per cent average growth rate for Latin America from 1991 to 2000 (ECLAC, 2001).[14]

The structural reasons behind this continuing external fragility are related to a number of factors. First, to the size of the already accumulated net foreign liability position and the associated remittances of factor services' income. Another problem is the very high income elasticity of industrial imports and the rather low income elasticity of exports that is being observed even after the big devaluation. These very unfavourable elasticities are mainly the result of the re-specialization of the Brazilian industry and in particular of the capital goods and intermediate goods and components sectors. This re-specialization of Brazilian industry was induced by policies and disincentives that were explicitly meant as an abandonment of the state-led development strategy, a strategy that made Brazil one of the fastest growing economies in the world until the early 1980s but that was seen by the Collor (1990) and later the Cardoso administrations (1995–2002) as having produced an inefficient and outdated manufacturing sector that would be modernized without the need of traditional industrial policy merely by exposing the system to strong foreign competition.

The current difficulties that Brazil faces are the direct result of these policies. Facing the loss of subsidies and incentives, the dismantling of a large part of the incipient technological efforts of national research institutes, state-owned enterprises and universities, the disorganization of a messily privatized infra-structure,[15] an unfavourable exchange rate, a much higher cost of capital and a slow-growing domestic market (that did not help in terms of economies of scale), it is not very surprising to find that since the early 1990 the structure of Brazilian industrial exports has changed back a bit towards more natural re-source-based goods and standardized industrial commodities.[16]

On the other hand, many of the same factors, and the opening of the economy to foreign competition, have given a strong impetus to the growing use of im-ported capital goods components and inputs (Brazil is now a net importer of raw cotton and there is not a single microchip factory in the country) even of the products that are still being produced in the country. The 'competitive' re-specialization of the Brazilian economy has resulted in a reduction of its industrial diversification, in exports more concentrated in sectors with lower technological content and lower international demand growth rates.[17] At the same time this re-specialization brought with a large increase in import coeffi-cients,[18] creating an inherent tendency towards growing deficits. It seems that the reversal of this situation will take much more than a sensible exchange rate policy (although that does really help) and would require restarting the state-led development strategy which would entail rebuilding the state's regulatory and incentives framework and a major new industrial policy effort. That is as difficult to do as it sounds even if there is the political will (since it has been done in the past) but it is extremely unlikely to happen in the near future.

## CONCLUDING REMARKS

In this chapter we have argued that in the current floating dollar standard the balance of payments situation facing the emerging markets is characterized by a basic contradiction. On one hand, it is extremely easy to attract large amounts of foreign capital. On the other hand, it becomes more and more difficult to de-liver the fast growth of exports that is a necessary condition for the financial servicing of these inflows.

This basic contradiction is greatly strengthened in countries that have fol-lowed more closely the 'Washington-consensus' fashionable package of trade and financial liberalization together with the control of nominal exchange rates. In these cases, the amounts of capital attracted are even bigger but at the same time the tendency towards overvaluation, deindustrialization and dismal export performance are much stronger. Moreover, the relative lack of control of short-term capital movements does add to the unsustainable trend of that current account a large probability of an exchange rate collapse and an external financial crisis. In our view the case of Brazil in the 1990 illustrates very well these dangers.

## NOTES

\*     Associate professors at the Instituto de Economia, Universidade Federal do Rio de Janeiro (UFRJ), Brazil. E-mail addresses: ca29@centroin.com.br and franklin.s@openlink.com.br.
1.   In what was to be his last book Hicks (1989) noticed that from the beginning of the 1980s, the USA had taken for itself the responsibility of making the US dollar the international currency and thus correctly adopted a 'passive' attitude towards its balance of payments results. However, Hicks asked himself if this role could be performed by a 'weak' currency like the dollar. By 'weak' Hicks means the currency of a country that tends to run current account deficits. More than ten years later, the answer seems to be yes, it can and it does.
2.   Medeiros (1997) showed how the FDI export connection found in Asia in the 1980s was a product of particular circumstances involving US trade policies, the Japanese reaction to yen revaluation and local state development policies and could not be generalized to Latin America. More recently Agosin and Mayer (2000) have confirmed econometrically that FDI did seem to 'crowd in' investment in Asia while it seems to 'crowd out' investment in Latin America.
3.   Indeed, for most developing countries the same rates of growth are associated with much bigger trade deficits than in the past.
4.   As shown by Kregel (1996), if the capital account is really open, even the capital that came in as FDI may quickly and easily transform itself in to speculative capital, something that weakens somewhat the idea that external financing via FDI would expose the economy less to exchange rate speculation and external liquidity crises.
5.   See among others Calvo et al. (1993). The capital flows toward Latin America in the early 1990s depended heavily on the lowering of interest rates and regulatory changes in the USA: 'the most salient changes were the approval of Regulation S. and Rule 144a which reduced transaction and liquidity costs faced by developing countries in approaching capital markets there' p. 128.
6.   See Rodrik and Velasco (1999) and Kaminski et al. (1998).
7.   See Ffrench-Davis and Reisen (1997).
8.   Initially Chile and Argentina followed a policy of pegging the nominal exchange rate between 1978 and 1982 (without eliminating domestic indexing clauses in wages and contracts), preceded by wide-ranging trade and financial liberalization. Capital flight plus the fast growth of external liabilities, at a moment when international interest rates where at record high levels, led to a serious crisis and the insolvency of the domestic financial system. In both countries this led the State to take over the private sector external debt, to nationalise many banks and control imports again.
9.   Data from ECLAC (2001).
10.   See Carneiro (1997).
11.   Synchronization was achieved through a special transitory unit of account, the URV (Unit of Real Value) by which wages were compulsorily converted at their average level over a period, while other prices were freely and voluntarily converted at any desired rate.
12.   In this the government was helped not only by weakened unions and high unemployment but also by the favourable trend of relative prices of foodstuffs, which have been following a longer-run downward trend due to the modernization of large-scale Brazilian agriculture since the 1980s and by the resumption of easy (but not cheap) consumer credit, which gave to a large number of poorer Brazilians the opportunity to buy consumer durables.
13.   Note that in the case of Brazil, the devaluation did not cause banking crises. Domestic banks

were not much in debt in foreign currency and had been 'strengthened' by a major central bank programme, Proer, just after the 1994 stabilisation. See Calcagno and Sainz (1999).

14. Brazil which grew around 7 per cent a year from 1945 until the late 1970s became a low-growth country. In the 1990s it grew less than Argentina, Bolivia, Chile, Costa Rica, El Salvador, Guatemala, Honduras, Mexico, Nicaragua, Panama, Peru and the Dominican Republic (ECLAC, 2001).

15. The most glaring case is that of electricity. The partial privatization lack of an adequate regulatory framework, together with the government not allowing the still state-owned power generators to invest have made investment in that sector fall from around US$ 8 billion a year in the 1980s to around US$ 3 billion in the 1990s. Not surprisingly energy rationing schemes are probably going to be introduced in the next few months.

16. As a result of this anti-export policy bias in 1998 the Brazilian share of world exports in 1998 was lower than 1980 while over the same period Korea's share doubled and China's trebled.

17. According to a recent study, the Brazil's share in export markets classified as 'very dynamic' fell from 20 per cent to 13 per cent during the two halves of the 1990s. These changes happened in the composition of exports not of imports that remain concentrated in the 'very dynamic' sectors. See IEDI (2000).

18. According to Mesquita (2000) the share of imports on the value of gross output in Brazilian manufacturing industry increased from 5.7 in 1990 to 20.3 in 1998. Over the same period the ratio of exports to gross output increased from 9.4 per cent to 14.8 per cent.

# REFERENCES

Agosin, R and R. Mayer (2000), 'FDI in developing countries: does it crowd in domestic investment', UNCTAD Discussion Paper no. 196, February.

Baig, T. and I. Goldfajn (2000), 'The Russian default and the contagion to Brazil', Texto para Discussão No 420, Departamento de Economia, PUC-Rio, May.

Calcagno A. and P. Sainz (1999), 'La Economia Brasilena ante el Plan Real e su crisis', Temas de Coyuntura no. 4, CEPAL, Santiago, July.

Calvo, G., L. Leiderman and C. Reinhart (1993) 'Capital Inflows and Real Exchange Rate Appreciation in Latin America', IMF, staff papers, **40** (1).

Carneiro, D. (1997), 'Flujos de Capital y Desempeño Económico en Brasil', in R. Ffrench-Davis and H. Reisen (eds), *Flujos de Capital e Inversion Productiva*, Santiago: CEPAL, McGraw Hill.

Chang, H.-J. and C.-G. Yoo (1999), 'The triumph of the rentiers? The 1997 Korean crisis in a historical perspective', Center for Economic Policy Analysis, New School, New York.

Claessens, S.; M. Dooley and A. Warnes (1995), 'Portfolio capital flows: hot or cold?', *World Bank Economic Review*, **9** (1), January.

Domar, E. (1950), 'The effect of foreign investment on the balance of payments', *American Economic Review*.

ECLAC (2001), *Statistical Yearbook 2000*, Santiago.

Ffrench-Davis, R. and H. Reisen (1997), *Flujos de Capital e Inversion Productiva*, Santiago: CEPAL, McGraw Hill.

Hicks, J. (1989), *A Market Theory of Money*, Oxford: Clarendon.

IEDI, (2000), 'Abertura, Política Cambial e Comércio Exterior Brasileiro – Lições dos Anos 90 e Pontos de Uma Agenda para a Próxima Década', at http://www.iedi.org.br/.

Kaminsky, G., S. Lizondo and C. Reinhart (1998), 'Leading indicators of currency crises,' IMF, staff papers, **45** (1), March.

Kalecki, M. ([1972] 1982), 'Formas de Ajuda Externa: Uma Análise Econômica', in J. Miglioli (ed.), *Kalecki*, São Paulo: Ática.

Kregel, J. (1996), 'Riscos e Implicações da Globalização Financeira para a Autonomia das Políticas Nacionais', *Economia e Sociedade*, 7, December.

Medeiros, C. (1997), 'Globalização e Inserção Internacional Diferenciada da Ásia e da America Latina', in M. Tavares and J. Fiori (eds), *Poder e Dinheiro*, Rio de Janeiro: Vozes.

Medeiros, C.A. (1998), 'Raizes Estruturais da Crise Financeira Asiática e o Enquadramento da Coréia', Economia e Sociedade, 11, Campinas.

Medeiros, C.A. and F. Serrano (1999), 'Padrões Monetários Internacionais e Crescimento', in J. Luís Fiori (ed.) Estados e Moedas no Desenvolvimento das Nações, Vozes. Rio de Janeiro.

Mesquita, M. (2000), 'A Indústria Brasileira nos Anos 90. O que já se pode Dizer?', USP, IPE, texto para Discussão.

Miguel P. and J. Cunha (2001), 'A Vulnerabilidade Externa do Brasil', *República* , April.

Prebisch, R. (1950), 'Estudo Econômico da América Latina', in R. Bielschowsky (ed.) (2000), *Cincuenta Anos de Pensamento na CEPAL*: Rio de Janeiro, Record.

Rodrik, D. and A. Velasco (1999), 'Short-term capital flows', World Bank, processed.

Serrano, F. (1998) 'Tequila ou Tortilla: Notas sobre a economia brasileira nos noventa', *Archetypon*, 6, (18) September–December.

Serrano, F. (1999), 'Do Ouro Imóvel ao Dólar Flexível', IE-UFRJ, processed.

# PART 4

# Final reflections

# 12. From capital controls to dollarization: American hegemony and the US dollar

## Matías Vernengo

### INTRODUCTION

The recent turmoil in the world's financial markets has prompted cries for innovative ways of dealing with uncertainty and volatile capital flows. The wave of financial crises from the Mexican Tequila to the more recent Argentinean one have only revived a long-standing debate on the merits of flexible versus fixed exchange rate regimes. The consensus for a while was that only corner solutions were efficient ways of dealing with capital flows (Fischer, 2001).[1] In other words, countries should adopt either a rigid peg or a flexible exchange rate regime.

In this view, dollarization is only an extreme form of a fixed peg, and as such is one possible alternative for emerging markets. In fact, some countries in Latin America have moved in that direction recently, most notably Ecuador and El Salvador. Further, several countries in the region maintained relatively fixed pegs with respect to the dollar for a good part of the 1990s, such as the Argentinean Currency Board. According to this definition of dollarization the decision to dollarize is based on the notion that the gains in economic efficiency arising from the elimination of transaction costs, and the reduction of risk arising from uncertain movements in exchange rates, outweigh the costs of dollarization. Those costs are associated with the loss of national sovereignty in conducting monetary policy. Interestingly enough the discussion of the effects of dollarization on the balance of payments adjustment have been neglected. An overview of the literature suggests that the conventional wisdom assumes that balance of payments adjustment would be relatively smooth.

Furthermore, the debate on dollarization should not be circumscribed to the question of adoption (or not) of the dollar by developing countries. The term dollarization may also refer to the extension of the international role of the dollar as both reserve currency and vehicle currency, which represents the cornerstone of the US political and economic hegemonic position. Dollarization in this sense is more widespread in Latin America than in any other world region. In most Latin American countries the use of the dollar is not restricted to international transactions. In some Latin America countries banks take deposits in dollars. Also, in most countries in the region either the public sector or the private sector or both have sizable debts in dollars. Currency substitution is an important challenge to domestic monetary sovereignty.

The key role of the dollar in the international markets has provided extensive advantages to the USA, as indicated by the persistence of a trade deficit for more than 20 years. In fact, the USA has actively encouraged the dominant role of the dollar by pressing for a more open international financial order. Cohen (2004) argues that the US policy with respect to dollarization should be described as benign neglect. Cohen is only correct when dollarization is interpreted in the narrow sense as the decision to adopt the dollar or tie the domestic currency to the dollar. The opposite is true when dollarization is interpreted in a broader sense.

In this chapter two points are explored. First, it is argued that dollarization does not imply an automatic adjustment of the balance of payments in the periphery. Instability may very well increase, with dire consequences for employment and growth. Second, it is suggested that the collapse of Bretton Woods implied that dollarization is more rather than less widespread. In other words, US hegemony has increased in the post-Bretton Woods dollar system *vis-a-vis* the gold–dollar system of Bretton Woods, and that this has been actively pursued by the USA. This is not to say that the current position of the dollar is invulnerable. The limits to the system are also taken into account.

## BALANCE OF PAYMENTS ADJUSTMENT

Mundell's discussion of an optimum currency area is still the main reference in the literature on the adoption of a common currency and, as an extension, on dollarization. According to the theory a monetary union is optimal if the economies are subjected to similar shocks, so that the depreciation or appreciation of the common currency solves the problems of all the countries. If shocks have asymmetric effects on the economies, an optimal currency area implies that there is either sufficient wage flexibility or there is sufficient labor mobility, so that countries can adjust without resorting to variations of the exchange rate.[2]

It is assumed that the costs of monetary union in an optimal currency area will be very small. On the other hand, the gains in economic efficiency arising from elimination of transaction costs, and the reduction of risk coming from uncertain movements of exchange rates are seen to be considerably high. Also, an additional advantage for the USA in the case of dollarization is the increase in revenues from seignorage.

The first question posed by the optimal currency literature is whether countries, in the case at hand dollarizing countries and the USA, are subjected to symmetric shocks. That is, if the economic cycles converged in all participant economies, than the lack of independent monetary policy is of secondary importance. Yet it is important to consider that it is quite possible that a correlated cycle might not be sufficient to guarantee that the absence of independent monetary policies will have no effects.

In particular, countries that are at different stages in the process of development might need different monetary policies, irrespective of their position in the cycle. Several authors have suggested that some degree of financial repression is necessary for underdeveloped countries. That is, in developing countries the use of interest rate limits, subsidized credit, and discretionary allocation of credit are all-important parts of the system.[3]

However, in order to decide whether to dollarize or not one has to weigh the costs and benefits associated with dollarization. On the benefit side, it is generally assumed that dollarization reduces transaction costs, and also eliminates foreign exchange risk. As a result of these two advantages, trade flows between the countries involved increase dramatically. The idea is that countries that share a common currency engage in substantially higher levels of international trade.[4]

The most important gains from higher trade, in turn, are the higher rates of growth. This has been a dominant theme in the literature on development, in the last 25 years. The contrasting experiences of the relatively closed Latin American economies and the relatively open East Asian countries led many authors (e.g. Dollar, 1992; World Bank, 1993) to argue that outward oriented development strategies are more conducive to growth.

However, the literature on the advantages of economic openness is far from being consensual. Measures of openness do not seem to be consistent across studies (Pritchett, 1996). Taylor (1991, p. 100) argues that 'structuralists models of both commodity and capital flows suggest that openness or a hands-off policy in either market will not necessarily lead to faster growth or less costly adjustment to external shocks'. Further, Rodriguez and Rodrik (1999) find little evidence that open trade policies are significantly associated with higher growth. In their recent study on the effects of the structural adjustment reforms in Latin America, Stallings and Peres (2000), find that capital and current account liberalization had a significant but small effect on growth.

The weakness of the link between trade and growth suggests that any decision to dollarize based on the effects of the reduction of transaction costs on trade, and hence on growth, should not be over-emphasized. If this is the main reason for dollarization by developing countries, the rewards seem hardly enticing. From an American perspective, on the other hand, the main advantage for dollarization, according to the standard arguments, would be the increase in seignorage revenues.

The standard arguments surrounding seignoriage can be divided neatly into two secondary propositions. First, there is a discussion of how to measure the precise value of revenues accruing to a government out of seignoriage. Second, the debate then concerns itself on how much the United States should repatriate to any given country that chooses to dollarize: that is, the precise nature of the sharing rule.

Seigniorage arises because currencies are worth more than their printing costs. Printing money, therefore, generates revenues, since it allows the government to finance real purchases. The more a country prints money, the more revenue it accrues up to a certain point. In general the literature assumes that a seignorage Laffer curve (or inflation–tax Laffer curve) exists. The existence of this curve is justified as follows. The quantity of real spending financed through money creation is equal to the nominal increase of the money stock over the price level (seignorage). It is easily shown that in steady state, when the real stock of money is constant, seignorage will equal the tax rate (rate of depreciation of the real value of money) times the amount being taxed, that is, the real money balances (Agénor and Montiel, 1996).

As a result, the government can increase its revenues by printing money and generating inflation, since a higher rate of inflation represents a higher tax on money holders. However, beyond a certain inflation level, agents will substitute money for interest-bearing assets, so a rise in the tax rate (inflation) is accompanied by a decrease of the tax base (real money balances).[5]

Estimates on the actual size of seigniorage revenues vary from 0.5 to more than 4 per cent of GDP depending on the country and the author making the calculations. Despite these considerable divergences on the actual size of seignorage revenues, there is no doubt that dollarization represents a windfall gain for the United States. This brings us to the second issue, namely the nature of the sharing rule. Several economists in this field believe the United States should, on an annual basis, compensate dollarized countries for the loss of seignorage revenues.

However, many authors argue that losing seigniorage revenues is good for countries that have a history of hyperinflation, since it forces fiscal discipline upon populist governments. Dollarized countries then would enjoy price stability compatible with US standards. Two sets of problems are posed by the view that dollarization leads to lower inflation rates. On the one hand, it is quite possible to have inflationary processes even if governments do not have any seigniorage revenues. Supply shocks, increased labour bargaining power with pressures for higher wages, indexation rules and other mechanisms could lead to higher inflation, and more likely causes of inflation in the developing world (Taylor, 2004).

Furthermore, the argument of seignorage brings into question the finance of public spending. Under a dollarized economy, domestic governments would have to issue bonds in dollars. Given the incapacity to print dollars, one would expect that these bonds would pay a premium over American bonds. Moreover, even if foreign exchange risk is eliminated by dollarization, country risk will still exist leading to a spread over US treasury bonds. The higher interest rates in the dollarized countries would in turn make government spending more costly, creating a permanent contractionary fiscal stance.[6] This would lead to reduction in social spending or to the impossibility of increasing spending in social programs when needed. This is probably the most important cost of any dollarization attempt.

Finally, the literature on dollarization in the narrow sense neglects the effects of dollarization on the balance of payments adjustment. One gets the sense that most studies assume that when a country dollarizes, it ceases completely to have balance of payment problems. In other words, the dollarized country does not have a balance of payments constraint. Fiscal discipline and price flexibility would ensure that dollar flows are in the right direction, and that the balance of payments adjusts automatically, as in Hume's specie flow mechanism or the Gold Standard system.

However, De Cecco (1984) has forcefully argued that the automatic stability of the Gold Standard system is a myth. Arthur Bloomfield (1963, p. 2) argued emphatically against the nostalgic references to the 'good old days of the international gold standard ... [since] disequilibrating movements of short term capital, destabilizing exchange speculation, capital flight, threats to the continued maintenance of convertibility, concern as to the adequacy of international reserves and the volume of floating international indebtedness – all these at times were in evidence in the pre-1914 system and in some cases necessitated measures going well beyond routine application of discount-rate policy'.

An alternative view to the one based on Hume can be derived from Kindleberger (1973), based on the theory of hegemonic stability.[7] In this view, the stability of the Gold Standard system resulted from the effective management by the leading hegemonic member, i.e. the UK. According to Kindleberger (pp. 289–90) the Bank of England stabilized the system by acting as the lender of last resort, ensuring the coordination of macroeconomic policies, and providing counter-cyclical long term lending.

This suggests that it was the relevance of the UK's position in world trade and finance that allowed for the stability of the system. De Cecco (1984, p. 20) argues that 'the system was really based on sterling rather than gold'. In this view, neither credibility nor cooperation was at the centre of the working of the international Gold Standard. Hegemonic power was instead.[8]

The role of the City of London as the financial centre of the world allowed the Bank of England to manage the international monetary system. The City of London could lend long and borrow short, functioning as the banker of the world (Stallings, 1987). Whenever the exchange rate fell to the gold export point, an increase in the Bank rate would avoid the outflow of gold. The command over gold flows was asymmetric, since changes in the interest rates of other countries had less effect than the Bank of England's discount rate.

Furthermore, in the case of peripheral countries, adjustment tended to be in the quantities rather than in prices. Hence, outflows of capital caused by a crisis in the centre led to a severe contraction of the domestic economy. Stagnation was the only instrument to avoid deficits in the current account of the balance of payments. Also, most countries in the periphery of the system were regularly forced to suspend payments in gold. As Ford (1962, p. 189) notes, 'automatic income adjustment forces ... provided the main adjustment mechanism, whilst the gold standard "medicine" of higher interest rates in the face of gold losses played a subsidiary role in promoting long term adjustment'.

During the Bretton Woods system peripheral economies were able to increase the insulation from international financial markets. Balance of payments adjustments still depended on a painful combination of contractionary depreciation, and contractionary macroeconomic policies. However, foreign exchange controls reduced the risks of runs on the domestic currency, and allowed governments to set the interest rate for domestic purposes as Keynes had suggested during the negotiations of Bretton Woods (Vernengo and Rochon, 2000).

The most important consequence of low rates of interest was that they allowed financing public spending at low costs. In other words, capital controls enabled not just the use of monetary policy to achieve full employment, but also the expansion of the role of the state. Monetary sovereignty is not just about monetary policy, but fundamentally about the ability of the state to promote social policies in a sustainable way.

The demise of Bretton Woods and the increasing challenges to national monetary sovereignty that followed, leading eventually to dollarization in some cases, is in many ways a return to the pre-Bretton Woods era. Capital mobility is reinstated, and the US dollar takes the place of gold. Nostalgia about gold may lead some peripheral countries to dollarize. However, the lesson for dollarizing countries today is that balance of payments problems will not disappear with dollarization. Understanding that the costs of balance of payments adjustments were quite high in the pre-Bretton Woods era should be a stern warning.

Current account deficits, in the absence of the devaluation alternative, are corrected by contraction of domestic demand. Historically, monetary arrangements that reduced national sovereignty constrained both monetary and fiscal policy, leading to pro-cyclical macroeconomic policies. Hence, the main risk of dollarization is not associated with reduced seignorage revenues, but the imposition of a quasi-permanent contractionary stance on fiscal policy.

## THE POST-BRETTON WOODS SYSTEM

The period of prosperity that followed the end of the Second World War and that lasted until the end of the Bretton Woods arrangement has become known as the golden age of capitalism. The golden age can be characterized as a 'period of rapid and sustained ... advance in economic performance' (Glyn et al., 1990, p. 40). Moreover, 'the length, steadiness, speed, and spread of the post-war boom are revealed to be so exceptional in the history of capitalism as to suggest that an explanation for its occurrence must be found in a unique economic regime rather than in a chance set of particularly favorable economic circumstances' (ibid.).[9] The Bretton Woods regime was exceptional in at least two important respects. First, the existence of a set of rules that included fixed exchange rates, capital controls and domestic macroeconomic policy autonomy was in place. Second, the USA became the hegemonic power, in a bipolar world.

The Bretton Woods system represented 'the first successful systematic attempt to produce a legal and institutional framework for the world economic system' (James, 1996, p. 27). The need for this legal framework was unanimously accepted as a way of avoiding the negative consequences of the inter-war period.

Ragnar Nurkse (1944) forcefully presented the consensus view. According to Nurkse (1944, p. 16), 'the flow of short term funds, especially in the thirties, often became disequilibrating instead of equilibrating, or instead of simply coming to a stop'. This was partially true of the pre-1914 system as Bloomfield showed, but the main difference was the absence of a hegemonic power capable of controlling capital flows through the variation of the interest rate (Kindleberger, 1973). Further, according to Nurkse (1944, p. 22),

> in the thirties, there was a gradual but persistent change in economic opinion. The price-level came to be regarded more and more as a secondary criterion of economic stability. The state of employment and national income tended to become the primary criterion.

This change was to a great extent part of the effects of the Keynesian revolution.

The approach followed by Nurkse is congenial with Keynes's own views at that time. During the 1920s and early 1930s, Keynes argued against the return to gold, since he believed that the effects of devaluation would be less pronounced than the effects of deflation. One might conclude from Keynes's attack on the return to gold that he was committed to flexible exchange rate policies. However, it would be more correct to argue that Keynes's objective was always the management of the exchanges to achieve domestic policy goals (Vernengo and Rochon, 2000).

Hence, the change in Keynes's view is not related to the fixed/flexible exchange rate dichotomy, but to the causes of unemployment, and the ways to avoid it. The development of the principle of effective demand led Keynes not only to support expansionary fiscal policies, but also low interest rate policies, whose ultimate impact would be to reduce the significance of the rentiers' income share, the so-called euthanasia of the rentier.

To guarantee the euthanasia of the rentier, Keynes pointed out that the central bank should be able to set the rate of interest independently from any international pressures. Keynes especially insisted upon the idea that movements of capital could not be left unrestricted, during the preparatory works and the negotiations for the Bretton Woods agreement. He argued that 'we cannot hope to control rates of interest at home if movements of capital moneys out of the country are unrestricted' (Keynes, 1980, p. 276).[10]

The control of capital flows means that the central bank does not need to use the bank discount rate to attract inflows of capital, or avoid capital flight. As a result the bank rate can be maintained as low as possible. A fall in the bank rate leads to a transfer from the finance or rentier sector to the industrial capitalist and working classes, leading to an increase in consumption and investment spending. Even more crucial is the fact that low rates of interest reduce the burden of debt servicing, so that active fiscal policies can be pursued by the state without leading to a explosive increase of the debt to GDP ratio.[11] Thus, the prosperity of the golden age period is associated to a great extent with the so-called euthanasia of the rentier.[12]

However, despite the intense preoccupation with capital controls, capital movements began to play an important role in the late 1960s. A pool of unregulated capital emerged as early as the late 1940s, when the Chinese communist government placed its dollar earnings with a Soviet bank in Paris. This was the origin of the Euromarket (James, 1996, p. 179). However, it was not until the late 1950s, with return of the convertibility of the European currencies, and the removal of the current account restrictions that the transition from a dollar shortage to a dollar surplus took place.

The growth of the Euromarket is also directly connected to the expansion of the US multinational firms, and the consequent expansion of US banking abroad. The collapse of Bretton Woods is related to increasing speculative capital flows. Helleiner (1994, p. 82) argues that the Euromarket was stimulated by the US and British governments, and 'by the mid-1960s, US officials were actively encouraging American banks and corporations to move their operations to the offshore London market'. The globalization of finance is, thus, less a feature of the markets and more a creature of the state.

The breakdown of the Bretton Woods system does not represent the demise of American hegemony. In fact, by closing the gold window the US eliminated the speculation against the gold–dollar parity, and the dominant position of the dollar in international trade and finance enhanced the ability of American officials to manage the international economy for domestic purposes. The material representation of this hegemonic power is the accumulation of trade deficits in the last twenty years. Pivetti (1992, p. 377) correctly pointed out that in the 1980s 'the role of the dollar in the international monetary system, which in practice eliminated any insolvency problems for the United States, was the factor which reconciled domestic growth with worsening of the balance of payments'. The USA can grow at higher rates without incurring in a balance of payments crisis, given the hegemonic role of the dollar.

The end of Bretton Woods allowed the USA to borrow in international markets directly in its own currency, without the fiction of gold. That is, before that the USA borrowed internationally, but other countries had a claim on gold in exchange for dollar-denominated assets. Hegemonic countries were always able to borrow in international markets, one should note. Yet the maintenance of fixed rates with gold limited the ability to borrow, since a risk of default was always present. In that sense, the USA is the first financial hegemon for which there is truly no distinction between foreign and domestic debt.[13]

This peculiar situation allowed the US to become the first financial hegemon – whose currency is the international reserve and vehicle currency – to be a debtor country rather than the creditor of the world. Note, however, that national governments are always debtors, not only as a result of government borrowing in domestic financial markets, but also as providers of the domestic currency. Domestic debt is usually deemed necessary to operate monetary policy through open market operations, and to provide a safe (low-risk) asset for financial markets. Hence, the USA is the first global financial hegemon that can operate macroeconomic policy on a global scale.

This should reduce the fears regarding a possible collapse of the dollar. The risk is not that the USA is an international debtor, a position that no other global financial hegemon had before. A proper hegemon must be a debtor. The question is whether, as with any other debtor, the accumulation of debt is sustainable. Despite the fear of its eminent collapse, the dollar is still the lingua franca, in Frankel's words (Frankel, 1995). As noted by Frankel, the volume of dollar reserves in foreign central banks has increased in the 1990s. Other measures of the hegemonic role of the dollar point in the same direction. According to Blinder (1996, p. 133) 48 per cent of world trade transactions in 1992 was in dollars, and 83 per cent foreign exchange transactions in financial markets involved the dollar on one side of the transaction. D'Arista (2004, p. 558) argues that in 2002, 46 per cent of all cross-border loans were denominated in dollars, and about the same proportion of outstanding international debt securities were in US dollars.

The special position of the dollar implies that the benchmark for the sustainability of the US trade deficit is substantially higher than most analysts are prepared to believe. There is considerable room for US foreign indebtedness to grow, since the ratio of US foreign liabilities to GDP stands at approximately 25 per cent, which is low by international standards (D'Arista, 2004).

This is not to say that the post-Bretton Woods dollar system does not have its own limitations.[14] The global market is supposed to constrain the capacity of national governments to pursue independent policies. For example, if a country decides to follow an expansionary policy, capital flight and depreciation will ensue, so that fiscal and monetary discipline are imposed. This has created a deflationary bias in the post-Bretton Woods system (Eatwell, 1996). The commitment to deflationary policies dates back to the appointment of Paul Volcker as the chairman of the US Federal Reserve Board in 1979 (Greider, 1987). Glyn et al. (1990, p. 72) argue that '1979 can be taken as symbolic of a much broader recognition that the post-war economic regime had ended'.

Bhaduri and Steindl (1985, pp. 60–2) argue that the rise in real interest rates in the post-Bretton Woods period reflects 'a shift of power from industry to the banks,' since 'a high interest rate policy is generally beneficial to banks under normal circumstances (i.e. as long as they do not become the victims of financial crisis)'. The shift in power reflects the revenge of the rentiers, to use the expression introduced by Pasinetti (1997).

Pasinetti (1997) concludes that the ultimate purpose behind the conservative prescriptions is to maintain and increase the real rate of return to financial capital. In this view, the main cause of the political shift in power in the late 1970s is associated with the fact that the social pact of the post-war system was broken when real rates of interest became negative in the mid-1970s. In that sense, the political shift to the right was also a change in the centre of gravity from industrial to financial sector.

According to Pasinetti (1997) the causes of the lower rates of growth in the post-Bretton Woods period can be directly related to the fall of investment that results from higher interest rates. Also a rise in the real rate of interest affects income distribution between wages and profits, leading to a change in favor of profits. If the propensity to spend out of profits is smaller than the propensity to spend out of wages, then there will be a fall in effective demand, and hence higher unemployment rates.

It must be noted that even if the higher rates of interest were introduced in the midst of a conservative revolution, it is also true that higher interest rates were introduced to deal with the new environment of liberalized and deregulated financial markets. That is, the demise of Bretton Woods – in particular of the system of capital controls – is as important as the new commitment against inflation that was expressed by several central banks by the late 1970s. The building of a more open international financial environment was evident when the USA announced in December 1974 that it would abolish its own capital controls. The main reason for this policy change was, according to Helleiner

(1994, p. 113), that 'the dollar's position as a world's currency ... would be preserved and reinforced in an open financial system because US financial markets and the Eurodollar market would still be the most attractive international markets for private and public investors'.

One of the main consequences of the breakdown of Bretton Woods has been the worldwide imposition of a deflationary fiscal stance. The increase in interest payments intensified the pressures for cutting expenses in social programmes, as much as the previous era of low interest costs stimulated social spending. To the extent that the rise of the dollar standard has led to lower levels of capital accumulation and on average higher rates of interest around the globe, consequently increasing the degree of indebtedness (private and public), it has increased the degree of financial fragility of the world economy.

## CONCLUDING REMARKS

Dollarization in the narrow sense does not imply an automatic adjustment of the balance of payments. Capital outflows in the face of a current account deficit are not impossible, and very likely if country risk is perceived to be high. In that case, output contraction would be the only instrument left to dollarized economies. The deflationary stance imposed on dollarizing countries is, however, only a recent variation of a longer story.

The collapse of Bretton Woods implies that dollarization is more rather than less widespread. In other words, US hegemony has increased in the post-Bretton Woods dollar system *vis-a-vis* the gold–dollar system of Bretton Woods, and this has been actively pursued by the USA. The move away from capital controls and in favour of a more open financial regime was seen by US officials as a way of extending the international role of the dollar. However, this dominance of the dollar has served financial interests and a conception of the economy that puts more emphasis on price stability than full employment. Hence, in the last 30 years the process of dollarization in the broad sense has also imposed a contractionary stance on macroeconomic policy.

## NOTES

1. This view has been considerably softened in recent years.
2. In the second case the theory implies that wage flexibility can automatically adjust the labor market. There is an extensive literature in the Keynesian tradition that shows that increased flexibility can in fact make matters worse.
3. The argument is not that credit markets are imperfect, since they are subject to asymmetric information or other imperfections, which may very well be true. The point is that imperfections had to be created in order to promote growth. In other words, the State took deliberate action in getting prices wrong. The argument follows Gerschenkron's notion of the advantages

of backwarderness. Gerschenkron (1962) emphasized the importance of banks for late industrializers.

4. However, given that by all reasonable estimates transactions costs involved in dealing with more than one currency are fairly small, one tends to believe that increasing trade is related to the trade liberalization, that is, the elimination of quotas and reduction of tariffs rather than the common currency.

5. This is in fact the conventional wisdom on hyperinflation. Alternative view would emphasize the role of the balance of payments constraint, and inertia rather than the fiscal requirements of the State. See Câmara Neto and Vernengo (2004–5).

6. Câmara Neto and Vernengo (2004–5) argue that the Washington Consensus did just that. In other words, by forcing countries to maintain credibility, a permanent contractionary fiscal stance resulted in the periphery.

7. The term hegemonic stability theory was coined by Keohane (1984), and is related to Gramsci's concept of hegemony (Gilpin, 1987, p. 73). De Cecco (1984) developed a similar position, even tough it is not generally classified as part of the hegemonic stability theory.

8. Power in world financial markets has usually been seen as State-centered by International Political Economy (IPE) scholars. Susan Strange (1976) emphasized that single national currencies always tended to dominate trade and credit creation on a global scale. For a modern Historical International Political Economy (HIPE) approach see Langley (2002).

9. The economic regime encompasses a macroeconomic structure that deals with the relations between wages, profits and productivity; a system of production dealing with the techniques of production and organization of work; and an international order that implies a certain configuration of trade and capital flows which reflect, in turn, a hierarchy of competitiveness (Glyn et al., 1990, pp. 40–41).

10. The fact that Keynes accepted, and even defended the final agreement at Bretton Woods, which diverged in several points from his Bancor proposal, can be attributed to the maintenance of capital controls in the final document. For a full discussion of the subject see Crotty (1983).

11. One can argue that whenever the rate of interest is below the rate of growth of the economy prosperity will follow, and vice versa in the case of a rate of interest above the rate of growth (Pasinetti, 1997). In that sense, the euthanasia of the rentier is the sine qua non of economic prosperity.

12. This is not to say that other factors were irrelevant, but that the crucial element is to be associated with the social pact that allowed maintaining cheap money policies.

13. Arrighi (1994) argues that there were four long financial cycles in the capitalist system, associated with four major financial hegemonic powers, namely: Genoa, Holland, Britain and the USA.

14. Arguably if foreigners decide to reduce their exposure to dollar-denominated assets, a run on the dollar could take place. It appears that most economists agree that the ratio of foreign debt-to-GDP must somehow be stabilized in the long run. There is however little agreement about the level at which to stabilize it. Some argue that there exists a ceiling beyond which it would be unwise to push the debt ratio for fear of jeopardizing the government's creditworthiness and risking the specter of bankruptcy. Once we note that the American foreign debt is equivalent to its domestic debt, though, a functional finance argument may be considered. Economists in the functional finance tradition argue that a high debt-to-GDP ratio, as long as the borrowing is done internally in the country's own currency, does not imply any appreciable risk for State bankruptcy. Further, wealth effects – through which public debt fuels private spending – tend to spontaneously establish a certain level to which the debt-to-GDP ratio converges in the long run. Therefore, the debt problem takes care of itself in the long run, and there is little cause for concern.

# REFERENCES

Agénor, P. and P. Montiel (1996), *Development Macroeconomics*, Princeton: Princeton University Press.

Arrighi, G. (1994), *The Long Twentieth Century*, London: Verso.

Bhaduri, A. and J. Steindl (1985), 'The rise of monetarism as a social doctrine,' P. Arestis and T. Skouras (eds), *Post Keynesian Economic Theory*, Armonk, NY: Sharpe.

Blinder, A. (1996), 'The role of the dollar as an international currency,' *Eastern Economic Journal*, **22** (2).

Bloomfield, A. (1963), 'Short-term capital movements under the pre-1914 Gold Standard,' *Princeton Studies in International Finance*, 11.

Câmara Neto, A. and M. Vernengo (2004), 'Allied, German and Latin theories of inflation,' in M. Forstater and R. Wray (eds), Contemporary Post Keynesian Analysis, Cheltenham, UK and Northampton, MA, USA: Edward Elgar.

Câmara Neto, A. and M. Vernengo (2004–5), 'Fiscal policy and the Washington Consensus', *Journal of Post Keynesian Economics*, **27** (2), Winter, 333–43.

Cohen, B. (2004), *The Future of Money*, Princeton: Princeton University Press.

Crotty, J. (1983), 'On Keynes and Capital Flight', *Journal of Economic Literature*, 21, March, 59–65.

D'Arista, J. (2004), 'Dollars, debt, and dependence: the case for international monetary reform,' *Journal of Post Keynesian Economics*, **26** (4), Summer, 557–72.

De Cecco, M. (1984), *The International Gold Standard: Money and Empire*, New York: St. Martin's Press.

Dollar, D. (1992), 'Outward-oriented developing economies really do grow more rapidly: evidence from 95 LDCs, 1976–1985', *Economic Development and Cultural Change*, **40** (3).

Eatwell, J. (1996), 'International capital liberalization: the record', CEPA, Working Paper Series I, No 1.

Fischer, S. (2001), 'Exchange rate regimes: is the bipolar view correct?', *Journal of Economic Perspectives*, **15** (2), Spring, 3–24.

Ford, A.G. (1962), *The Gold Standard, 1880–1914: Britain and Argentina*, Clarendon: Oxford University Press.

Frankel, J. (1995), 'Still Lingua Franca,' *Foreign Affairs*, **74** (4).

Gerschenkron, A. (1962), *Economic Backwarderness in Historical Perspective*, Cambridge, MA: Harvard University Press.

Gilpin, R. (1987), *The Political Economy of International Relations*, Princeton: Princeton University Press.

Glyn, A., A. Hughes, A. Lipietz and A. Singh (1990), 'The Rise and fall of the Golden Age', S. Marglin and J. Schor, (eds), *The Golden Age of Capitalism*, Oxford: Oxford University Press.

Greider, W. (1987), *Secrets of the Temple*, New York: Simon and Schuster.

James, H. (1996), *International Monetary Cooperation since Bretton Woods*, New York: Oxford University Press.

Helleiner, E. (1994), *States and the Reemergence of Global Finance: from Bretton Woods to the 1990s*, Ithaca, NY: Cornell University Press.

Keohane, R. (1984), *After Hegemony: Cooperation and Discord in the World Political Economy*, Princeton: Princeton University Press.

Keynes, J. M. (1980), *The Collected Writings of John Maynard Keynes, Vol. XXV: Activities 1940–1944, Shaping the Post-War World: The Clearing Union*. London: Macmillan.

Kindleberger, C. (1973), *The World in Depression*, Berkley: University of California Press.

Langley, P. (2002), *World Financial Orders: An Historical International Political Economy*, London: Routledge.

Nurkse, R. (1944), *International Currency Experience*, Geneva: League of Nations.

Pasinetti, Luigi (1997), 'The social burden of high interest rates,' in P. Arestis, G. Palma and M. Sawyer (eds), *Capital Controversy, Post-Keynesian Economics and the History of Economics: Essays in Honour of Geoff Harcourt*, Volume I, London: Routledge.

Pivetti, M. (1992), 'Military spending as a burden on growth: an "underconsumptionist" critique,' *Cambridge Journal of Economics*, **16**, pp. 375–84.

Pritchett, L. (1996), 'Measuring outward orientation in LDCs: can it be done?', *Journal of Development Economics*, **49** (2), 307–35.

Rodriguez, F. and D. Rodrik (1999), 'Trade policy and economic growth: a skeptic's guide to the cross-national evidence', NBER Discussion Paper, No 7081.

Stallings, B. (1987), *Banker to the Third World*, Berkeley: University of California Press.

Stallings, B. and W. Peres (2000), *Growth, Employment, and Equity: the Impacts of the Economic Reforms in Latin America and the Caribbean*, Washington, DC: Brookings.

Strange, S. (1976), *International Economic Relations of the Western World, 1959–1971*, Oxford: Oxford University Press.

Taylor, L. (1991), 'Economic openness: problems to the century's end', in T. Banuri, (ed.), *Economic Liberalization: No Panacea*, Oxford: Clarendon Press.

Taylor, L. (2004), *Reconstructing Macroeconomics*, Cambridge: Harvard University Press.

Vernengo, M. and L-P. Rochon (2000), 'Exchange rates and capital controls,' *Challenge*, **43** (6), November–December, 76–92.

World Bank (1993), *The East Asian Miracle: Economic Growth and Public Policy*, Washington, DC: Oxford University Press.

# 13. A framework for analysing dollarization

**Paul Davidson**

## INTRODUCTION

A precise taxonomy is necessary for any analytical discourse. Otherwise the discussion often collapses into semantic obfuscation. In order to understand the implications of a foreign nation adopting the dollar as its internal currency, it is necessary to make clear distinctions between open and closed economies and between unionized monetary systems (UMS) and non-unionized monetary systems (NUMS). Table 13.1 presents the four possible combinations of these features.

The closed economy in a UMS in this table is the equivalent of the traditional closed economy model which was utilized with great success by Keynes in *The General Theory* to demonstrate the possibility of underemployment equilibrium. If, in this rarefied simple case, it was possible to show why market-oriented,

*Table 13.1   A classification of economic systems by trading patterns and monetary systems*

|  | Closed economy $(f = 0)$ | Open economy $(f > 0)$ |
|---|---|---|
| Unionized monetary System [UMS] $(Q = 0)$ | (1) No external trading partners (2) Single money for contracts | (1) External trading partners (2) Single money for contracts |
| Non-unionized monetary system [NUMS] $(Q > 0)$ | (1) No external trading partners (2) Various monies for contracts, no fixed exchange rate | (1) External trading partners (2) Various monies for contracts, no fixed exchange rate |

entrepreneurial economies could yield undesirable levels of unemployment and price instability, then it was reasonable to believe that the more complicated open economies (in the second column of the table) were even less likely to achieve a socially desirable level of output, employment and price stability without some governmental and private institutional planning and control.

The open economy in a UMS can be associated with an analysis of a home (local) regional economy trading solely (or primarily?) with other regions (usually in the same nation) where the trading regions have a legal (or customary) currency union which, either by law or by practice, uses the same monetary unit to denominate all private contracts.

The closed economy in a NUMS would be applicable to a global analysis where the various trading partners use one monetary unit for denominating contracts between domestic residents and different monetary units for contracts between foreigners and domestic residents. The exchange rate is expected to vary over the life of a contract. Finally, an open economy in a NUMS is applicable to the analysis of an individual real world national economy which has foreign trading partners with different currencies and variable exchange rates.

Money is a human institution that is directly related to the civil law of contracts and the customs established in the economic system under investigation. Money is the thing that discharges legal contractual obligations. Money, however, need not be limited to legal tender. In modern societies money is anything the state or the central bank undertakes to accept in payments to itself or in exchange for compulsory legal-tender money. Thus when people speak of 'dollarization', they usually mean that the state has mandated that the US dollar is legal tender for all contracts between domestic residents. In practice, however, if things other than legal tender are customarily accepted in discharge of debts to the state or the central bank, they will be accepted to discharge all contractual obligations, and hence are money.

As we have already indicated, there are two basic types of monetary systems – a unionized monetary system (UMS) and a non-unionized monetary system (NUMS). If *all* spot and forward contracts between transactors (in either a closed or open economy) are denominated in the same nominal unit, such a contracting system is a pure UMS. The system is still essentially a UMS even if various nominal units are used in different contracts between different transactors, as long as the exchange rates among the various nominal units are (a) currently fixed (with negligible conversion costs) and (b) are expected to remain unchanged over the life of the contracts. Any system which permits different contracts denominated in various nominal units while maintaining a fixed exchange rate amongst these units can be considered a UMS where the various currencies are fully liquid assets.[1] Thus when Argentina adopted a currency board, which assured two-way convertibility at an unchanging exchange rate with the US dollar, Argentina effectively dollarized.

If there is more than one fully liquid asset, and if law or custom permits contractual settlement of any contract with any of the available fully liquid assets at the option of the payer, then the system can be considered a pure UMS. If, however, law or custom requires fully liquid assets to be actually converted into the money of contractual settlement at the option of the payee, then the system is one step removed from a pure UMS where the size of the step depends on the cost of conversion.

Where different contracts are denominated in different nominal units, expectations of fixed exchange rates are therefore a necessary requirement for any system to approach UMS status. Moreover, since forward contracts for production, hiring, investment and other economic activities do not have any uniform duration, and since an ongoing economy is always operating under a (contracted for) future!

For example, one can conceive of the State of Tennessee as an open economy ($f > 0$) dealing with the rest of the United States in a pure UMS since all contracts between Tennessee residents and trading partners throughout the USA are in dollar terms. It should be noted that each district US Federal Reserve Bank issues its own bank notes and that, until the mid-1970s, Federal Reserve notes found circulating in the USA outside the district of issue were sent back to the issuing Federal Reserve District Bank for redemption. Nevertheless, notes from any Federal Reserve District Bank are legal tender for paying any contractual obligations within the USA. Furthermore, the exchange rate between Boston Federal Reserve dollars and, say, San Francisco Federal Reserve dollars are fixed and unchanging no matter what the payment flow imbalance between these districts. Thus, the 12 Federal Reserve districts are part of one single UMS, even though each individual district can be considered an open economy trading with the other 11 districts in a UMS (and with the rest of the world in a NUMS).

Similarly, Scotland and England can be looked upon as open economies trading with each other (and others), even though the Scots use very different-looking bank notes compared to English currency. These two 'nations' are part of the UMS of Great Britain and even if devolution ultimately comes to Scotland and the political openness of the two nations increases, this should not per se affect the magnitude of $f$. The basic UMS of Great Britain is likely to remain.[2]

In a NUMS, regional or national contracts are denominated in local monetary units, while interregional or international contracts are denominated in various nominal units. The exchange rate between units is expected to exhibit significant variability over the contract period. In essence then, the UMS can be thought of as a limiting case, of a NUMS when any domestic currency can be used as the means of contractual settlement for the exchange rate are expected to remain absolutely unchanged during the period.

Since the degree of unionization of the monetary system depends on expectations about the fixity of future exchange rates, we cannot measure it directly. We could quantify the degree of 'non-unionization' of the monetary system ex post, by the variability of exchange rates between trading partners over past periods, but in an uncertain world the historical record (looking back) need not reflect what past populations expected the future to be (looking forward). Of course, if the historical record showed $Q = 0$ (for example for the exchange rate between the English and Scottish pounds), then it is probably true that past populations considered the two nations to be a UMS. If the historical record shows $Q > 0$, however, it is likely that in the past, citizens thought they operated in less than perfect UMS, but the degree of non-unionization is unknown except if we make the historic (and unlikely) assumption that the historical path accurately tracked people's expectations at the time.

In sum, our classification system has been devised in such a manner that it is theoretically possible to have variations in the degree of openness and degree of non-unionization. Thus an expanded Table 13.1 would have as many rows and columns as desired, with the upper left hand corner cell having the parameters $f = 0$; $Q = 0$, the magnitude of $f$ increasing towards unity as we go across columns and the magnitude of $Q$ increasing towards unity as we go down columns.

It should be possible to classify all real world nations for any period into one of the cells of Table 13.1. The closer to the upper left hand corner of the matrix, the more closed and more unionized will be the monetary system of the local economy vis-a-vis its trading partners; the closer to the lower right hand corner, the more open and the more non-unionized the monetary system of the local economy with its trading partners. In a non-unionized economy, there is always some uncertainty as to the domestic monetary value of a contract denominated in terms of a foreign currency.

If the forward exchange market reaches far enough into the future to cover the date of contractual settlement, then there is a market mechanism for shifting (but not eliminating) this additional uncertainty from entrepreneurs to speculators. This possible shifting of the cost of exchange uncertainty (a real cost which does not exist in a UMS) is similar to the possibility of shifting the real costs of future production and marketing uncertainties from producer-hedgers to speculators via futures markets in a closed UMS. But in either case the existence of forward contracting does not eliminate the real costs involved.

Thus the existence of a NUMS inflicts a real cost on the economic system which, ceteris paribus, would not exist otherwise. This real cost, which is due solely to the way economies organize the medium for discharging a contract in a NUMS, must be borne by someone. Moreover, since organized forward exchange markets are limited to short durations (e.g. 90 days), long-term exchange uncertainties associated with contracts that are of longer duration cannot be shifted but must be willingly borne by the original transactors if they are to consummate a 'deal'.

## CASH FLOWS AND BANK CLEARING

As a first approximation, assume that all contractual payments are processed through the banking system of a closed economy (rather than via hand-to-hand currency disbursements). Whenever the current level of production is one of stationary equilibrium, agents are, over the period, in a matching cash flow position. In other words, on average, each individual's cash outflows are matched by his cash inflows. Finance is a revolving fund flowing through the banking system. All banks will be, over the production period, in balance at the clearing house and the aggregate value of bank deposits held by the public are unchanged.

Any planned expansion is unlikely to be equally dispersed over all sectors and regions of the economy. Accordingly, any expansion of production will increase entrepreneurial spending and thereby force some banks into deficit at the clearing house as the additional productive inputs are paid for before the finished products are available for sale. If the Central Bank is sensitive to these expansionary financial problems amongst sectors and regions, then additional reserves can be provided to the deficit banks, permitting them time to tide entrepreneurs over the production period until purchases by other sectors (because of higher incomes) create a return cash flow through the clearing house.

There is a significant time lag between the date when expansion of bank reserves are necessary until a return cash flow for banks in the expanding sector is observed at the clearing house. This time lag is even more apparent when expansion of production involves interregional and international trade.

During times when there are no trade imbalances and trade flows are neither increasing or decreasing, contractual settlements occurring at the interregional (and international) clearing house are such that on average all regional and national banking systems are in balance.

If, however, one region steps up the production pace it is likely to begin to import more from its trading partners as soon as production expansion plans are activated. An immediate trade payments deficit will occur. This payments imbalance causes interregional (and international) bank clearing house problems which will be immediately resolved by any one of three processes (or some combination of all three). These processes are:

1. by the loss of previously stored reserves by the banks of the deficit region; or
2. by the creation of additional reserves for the deficit banks; or

3.   by the borrowing of reserves by deficit banks from surplus banks.

The ability of the combined interregional and international banking system to resolve these immediate clearing house payment difficulties will be a measure of the capacity of trading partners to overcome any obstacles to growth which, by the very nature of an entrepreneur economy, must begin with some changes in net cash flows among agents and their bankers.

## FOREIGN LENDING AND FINANCE

Whether an economy is open or closed, planned aggregate expansion of production processes to meet expected or actual forward orders of either domestic or foreign buyers will require the domestic money supply to increase in proportion to the increase in domestic factor input and material production costs. Of course, if some factor owners or raw material suppliers are foreigners, then foreign money supplies will have to increase *pari passu* with the increase payments for these foreign inputs into the expanding aggregate working capital.

Any planned increase in country A's expenditure flows on imports from country B, which is in addition to the existing total flow demand for goods produced in nation B, will require B's banks to increase the supply of B's money (real bills). This additional finance will be required by B's entrepreneurs to meet A's increased demands as they are manifested today in additional forward contractual orders. In other words, during the production period needed for B's entrepreneurs to increase export output, additional finance is needed in B to facilitate additional hiring in B's export industries. When, at the end of the production period, increased output flows from B's factories are available for export to A, then A's residents will require additional liquidity from holders of B's money in order to pay the hypothesized increased in A's trade deficit.

The foreign lending balance ($L$) is a variable which reflects the net differences in loan (and equity) transactions between residents in B and the rest of the world. In the absence of unilateral international transfers (or gold movements), an excess of the amount of B's money claims loaned to its trading partner A, over the amount of A's money claims lent to B's residents at the current exchange rate, i.e. a positive net foreign lending position by nation B, is a necessary ceteris paribus condition for B to finance an export surplus to A.

In the balance of payments accounting system foreign lending is always expressed as a net figure over the accounting period. Every agreement involving foreign loans ultimately places domestic money at the disposal of a foreigner in return for either title to foreigner's property or a foreigner's promise to pay.

When net foreign lending is zero, then there will be a balance in the goods and services trade account. Starting from this balanced position, any expansion of international trade will initially involve some positive increase in net foreign lending by those nations whose exports are expanding more rapidly as the world's aggregate liquidity is required to increase concomitantly.

## FINANCING TRADE DEFICITS VIA FOREIGN LENDING IN THE ABSENCE OF A CHANGE IN GLOBAL AGGREGATE DEMAND

Assume that A's demand for imports from B increase at the expense of A's home produced goods. This would increase A's demand for foreign currency as a running asset while lowering A's transaction demand for domestic money. Since the increased demand for imports is solely a substitute for domestic production, by hypothesis there is no change in A's total demand for money (domestic plus foreign).

In a closed UMS system, as region A merely substitutes imports from B for its own regional production there will be no change in the public's aggregate cash holdings throughout the UMS, only an initial redistribution of cash flows between regions A and B. To the extent that residents of A had idle balances (reserve money assets), they could draw these down to finance the ongoing interregional trade deficit. Over time, however, if this interregional trade deficit persists, then the interregional redistribution of domestic bank balances via a change in clearing house patterns would threaten some banks in A (and their customers) with a lack of liquidity. Assuming no policy actions by the central bank or the state to recycle funds from B to A, asset holders in the deficit A region (or their bankers) would have to sell either marketable fully liquid (or liquid) assets to the surplus region in order to reflux money to A's banks so that A's residents will be able to continue to purchase the products of B.

In a laissez-faire system, if the interregional trade deficit persists (B's net foreign lending remaining positive), then A will ultimately run out of marketable assets and/or acceptable promises it can pledge to gain replenishment of its money holdings for transaction purposes. Consequently, A will find that it is unable to continue financing its import deficit. A's real income will decline until either the trade deficit or A disappears.

Most orthodox economists argue that net interregional trade deficits and off setting net foreign (regional) lending on production and income accounts cannot go on indefinitely. In the long run, orthodox theorists claim a market adjustment process will bring to an end any persistent trade deficit. This 'long-run' view that trade deficits and net foreign lending (refluxing of funds) cannot endure assumes the absence of either (1) a government fiscal policy which deliberately recycles income and money balances from the surplus to the deficit region, (2) unilateral grants (private or governmental) as a reflux mechanism, or (3) the continuous creation of additional bank reserves for the deficit region's banks by the central bank.

In a completely laissez-faire system, factors (1), (2) and (3), by definition, will be absent and, in the long run, persistent deficits cannot endure. In the real world, however, these options for regional refluxing of cash flows do exist. If, however, the system does not exercise one or more of these refluxing policy options, then the deficit region's banks will find that they are having increasing difficulty in meeting clearing house obligations associated with the current rates of economic activity. Because of these liquidity problems, A's bankers will be forced to reduce the level of lending to customers. The resulting shortage of bank credit will make the A region a depressed economic area and a poor customer of industries located in A as well as in B. The shortage of liquidity forces agents in A to reduce all expenditures on goods and services increasing unemployment in both A and B. But, as long as regions A and B are in the same UMS, there will be no change in the exchange rate between the money used to denominate contracts in region A and the money used as the basis of contracts in B. Recession will permeate the UMS.

The willingness of a central bank either to directly and continuously 'make' a market in the local commercial paper and other debt instruments of deficit regions, or to act as lender of last resort for deficit regions can ease interregional payment pressures and avoid liquidity problems at the interregional clearing house. The need of the deficit region's bank to sell securities can be offset by the desire of the surplus region's, central banks, or public to buy liquid assets. Deficits due to regional imbalances in export–import flows can be, if the central bank is perceived to be willing to support local financial asset markets, readily offset by reverse deficits in net interregional lending. In the short run, a central bank's activity or support in spot markets for regional financial assets can prevent any interregional liquidity problems due to interregional balance of trade deficits from depressing aggregate economic activity.

Of course, if the central bank is not sufficiently active in supporting the market for local financial assets, then the market value of these assets will weaken as they are continually liquidated to finance the recurring deficit. The deficit region's banks perceive that their reserves at the central bank relative to their business activity are declining over time. This reduction in the value of reserves relative to initial turnover causes some banks in the deficit area (or their regulators) to worry that the banks' liquidity position is being impaired. Each deficit bank will be encouraged to restrict credit availability to its customers in order to regain liquidity. This in turn will reduce aggregate demand for goods and services which can weaken other banks and thereby encourage the remaining healthy banks and entrepreneurs to attempt to improve their liquidity position. If the money supply has any endogenous component, the result will be a decline in the liquidity available to all.

If the Central Bank is not sufficiently active in the regional asset markets to prevent an overall asset deflation, there will not be sufficient liquidity for the current level of interregional activity, and each bank in the deficit region will have to reduce its lending operations, forcing a decline in regional employment activity as well as a reduction in the region's imports. Continuing asset deflation, therefore, is a symptom that the economy is in a critical condition. In the absence of substantial rapid action by either the central bank or the government, the problem may be solved by recognizing that 'in the long run, we'll be dead'.

On the other hand, if the Central Bank supports (directly or indirectly) the market for these assets, asset deflation can be avoided. The resulting creation of liquidity will permit planned aggregate demand spending to be financed despite the persistent trade deficit. The result will be a higher total level of income and wealth of both trading partners (for otherwise idle resources are employed) vis-a-vis the situation where there is no financial intervention to support asset prices by the central bank. The development of national banking systems headed by *pro bono publico* central bankers has therefore often served to offset or at least limit the deflationary forces which interregional trade deficits can generate.

Orthodox theorists insist that there is no need for central bank or government intervention to enhance asset prices. It is claimed that the free market is efficient so that it will permit a trade deficit to be financed only as long as (1) the deficit region possesses sufficient saleable reserve assets to weather the expected period of the deficit or (2) the deficit region has sufficient expected future prospects to make the present value of any expected cash flow large enough to equal or exceed the current deficit. The surplus region, it is assumed, will be economically rational about its economic relations to the deficit region and, therefore, will not continuously allow A claims to current real goods indefinitely into the future for promises (to pay back real goods) that are never redeemable. In other words, there is a presumption that the deficit will not be financed indefinitely by unilateral transfer payments, gifts or promissory notes which are never called. But is it more sensible for surplus region B to stop net foreign lending if the end result will be to lower economic activity in B's economy?

If regions A and B are both encompassed within the same national boundaries, then the central government's taxation and spending policy can act as a transfer device and help finance at least some, if not all, of the deficit indefinitely. The magnitude of trade deficit finance government will provide depends on the tax burdens of each region vis-a-vis the central government's propensity to spend in the deficit region compared to the surplus region. If, for example, the deficit region is either undeveloped or an area of high unemployment, modern enlightened central government taxing and spending patterns are likely to permit the financing of deficits as long as these economic discrepancies between regions persist. The resulting income and money redistribution is likely to enhance the well being of all the nation's citizens!

In the absence of government fiscal policy or private unilateral transfers, the primary private sector mechanism for financing regional deficits involves the banks or the residents of the deficit region selling assets to the surplus region. This requires that the assets held by residents of the deficit region and/or their bankers are readily marketable in the surplus region. Consequently, any institution that makes regional assets more widely marketable will ease the difficulties in providing finance for interregional payments.

## FINANCING TRADE DEFICITS BETWEEN NATIONS IN A NON-UNIONIZED MONETARY SYSTEM

There are two important additional complications to financing trade deficits if regions A and B are in different nations using different monies and possessing independent banking systems in a NUMS. First, there is no overriding central government authority that can engage in taxing and spending policies to recycle liquidity at an international clearing house in order to offset the trade deficit-induced losses in liquidity. Second, in the absence of a prior agreement between the governments of the trading nations that each will be willing to purchase liquid assets from the other at a fixed price without limit (i.e. a UMS), persistent trade deficits can unleash speculative forces which can cause continuing devaluation in the exchange rate of the deficit nation. This devaluation threatens to reduce further the market value of the deficit region's remaining marketable assets. Foreigners will be loathe to further extend lending that might create a further reduction in liquidity (market value of assets relative to turnover) for those banks in the deficit region that finance trade between the nations in the NUMS. To avoid this potential liquidity crunch, the deficit region's banking system will have to hold a significant portion of its running and reserve assets in terms of foreign-denominated assets or fully liquid international assets such as gold.

Neither of these severe complications is inevitable! Grants and/or loans from the surplus nation's government can prevent a liquidity problem due to a trade deficit. For example, in the 1940s, the United States' Marshall Plan and the US Lend–Lease Agreement with England a decade earlier were planned programmes for the surplus government to recycle liquidity in order to finance the otherwise non-financeable (under the traditional rules of the game) huge trade deficits of England and Western Europe. This liquidity refluxing may have been found acceptable for political rather than economic reasons. Nevertheless it impressively demonstrated that there is no natural or national law which prevents authorities in trade surplus areas from redistributing (recycling) purchasing power and assets for as long a period as they wish – with obvious and widespread economic benefits to residents of both the surplus and the deficit region.

Even in the absence of intergovernmental unilateral transfer payments to ease the financing problem of interregional trade imbalances, as long as the banks of each region are members of banking systems cooperating in an international clearing house system which possesses certain powers to cure excessive reserve holdings, then the rules of the clearing house can be designed to permit creation of sufficient balance sheet reserves to promote expansionary conditions for international trade.

For much of the twentieth century, national central banks have not been willing to become members of a well-organized international clearing house system possessing *pro bono publico* powers to provide sufficient international liquidity to promote global full employment. Consequently, the ability of any national central bank to provide liquidity in the face of an external trade deficit is closely circumscribed by its gold and other foreign reserve assets holdings. Thus, the ability of each nation's central banker to accommodate its clients' international liquidity needs is often less than even that of regional bankers in a modern national banking system to meet clients' domestic liquidity demands. In the absence of an international institution able to 'make' a market in international liquidity, each national central bank has to hold overwhelmingly large international reserves in order to ensure it would be able to finance clearing house deficits due to interregional trade imbalances.

Furthermore, in a NUMS system, there is no fully liquid international reserve asset (other than to hold quantities of foreign currencies) to finance international transactions. This results in the uncertainty of exchange rate changes – an additional uncertainty that all entrepreneurs must face if they decide to engage in international transactions rather than domestic ones. Consequently, in an open NUMS economy, because of the multiplication of uncertainties about the value of running and reserve financial assets (which must be held to manage international cash flows as a result of spot and forward contractual obligations), each nation requires, ceteris paribus, a larger stock of reserve assets for any given volume of trading with external partners than a similar region operating within a UMS.

When the nations of the world operated under an automatic gold standard, the possession of gold was the primary running and reserve asset of international finance which could buy the time to make whatever economic adjustments were deemed necessary while sustaining a trade deficit. Except for minor fluctuations between the gold points, the exchange rates were fixed and therefore nations could operate as if they were in a UMS system with (near) fixed market values for gold and foreign exchange in terms of either local currency. Consequently, given the magnitude of trade flows, each nation's international running and reserve asset holdings could be lower than if the exchange rates were not fixed. Alternatively, larger trade flows could be financed given the global holdings of gold. The magnitude of gold holdings of reserve assets determined the length of calendar time in which adjustments and policy changes could be phased to minimize disrupting economic dislocations for any nation experiencing a persistent trade deficit. In a NUMS on the other hand, whenever any nation runs a trade deficit, uncertainty regarding the international value of its marketable assets are increased and therefore the time frame for phasing in orderly adjustments and avoiding wrenching changes is reduced. Thus, trade deficits (which are inevitable in a world of change) occurring in a NUMS tend to encourage hasty and potentially destructive financial reactions relative to the adjustments to similar circumstances occurring under a UMS.

## THE ASSET OF ULTIMATE REDEMPTION IN A UNIONIZED MONETARY SYSTEM

In the present state of the world, any attempt to form an international UMS (for at least some of the more developed nations) requires contractual agreement among the central banks of these nations. The central banks must agree on the 'rules of the game' which permit the fixing of exchange rates and they must accept or invent a common reserve asset, which each central bank agrees in advance to buy with domestic currency under pre-specified rules. This agreed obligation of the central banks ensures that if any national banking system gets into trouble at the international clearing house, the deficit banking system or its Central Bank can sell (at its own option) its 'reserve' assets to cure its clearing imbalance, while undertaking adjustments to phase out the trade deficit.

Any true reserve asset can ultimately be conceived in terms of an asset of ultimate redemption. The desirable and necessary characteristics of an asset of ultimate redemption are:

1.  it must be a fully liquid asset denominated in the same unit in which any future liabilities are expected to fall due;
2.  it is denominated in terms of a unit whose purchasing power in terms of future producible goods is expected to be relatively stable – and hence in units which make wages 'sticky'; and
3.  it must possess relatively very low carrying costs so that the cost of holding the asset of ultimate redemption does not, in itself, require the holders to give up significant claims of future real resources merely by carrying the inventory of this asset.

As long as international reserve assets are well distributed among the participants, the game of international trade can continue and flourish, with potential real gains to all who play.

But, as in the famous Parker Brothers board game that children play named 'Monopoly', if any participant runs out of the means of settlement when he lands on a square which requires a payment to another participant, then that player defaults and is forced out of the game. In the Monopoly board game, play can continue for long periods of time because there are pre-existing rules for replenishing liquid assets, such as 'When you pass "Go", collect $200'.

This rule expands aggregate liquidity as economic development in terms of building houses and hotels on properties is being undertaken. Such an inflexible rule of collecting a fixed $200 each time one passes 'Go' does not ensure that a player will never become insolvent and have to default; it merely ensures the possibility of $200 excess of cash outflows over revenue inflows for each trip around the board. This rule of the game ensures that the medium of contractual settlement in the hands of the public (players) can expand as players move more actively around the board. This, in turn, ensures that the game can go on longer than if the money supply were constrained to a zero, independent of the performance of the players.

This absolute rule for expanding the money supply as players pass 'Go' is not ideal in terms of providing for an elastic currency. The costs of landing on properties rises geometrically as economic development occurs, while the money supply increases arithmetically as players pass 'Go'. Ultimately the game of Monopoly ends as each player except one overextends his 'investments' and then experiences, by landing on someone else's property, an obligation which they are unable to finance by liquefying current asset holdings (i.e. when a liquidity shortage occurs).

In the real world game of 'Enterprise' in an entrepreneur economy, on the other hand, it is a socially desirable objective that every possible player be a winner and that economic development continue forever. We hope the game of Enterprise never ends! This goal of a perpetual game in which players' activity promotes increasing prosperity for all would require a more flexible rule for costlessly expanding liquidity than the one underlying the board game of Monopoly. Consequently, in the real world game of international enterprise, trade and finance, any agreement to form a UMS must have some rules for replenishing reserve assets holdings in general, and redistributing such assets from surplus to deficit banking systems whenever a liquidity shortage threatens. Replenishment is essential to growth, while relative redistribution is required whenever holdings become overly concentrated. Humans can surely devise financial rules and institutions which encourage such outcomes and thereby perpetuate the game of Enterprise and the resultant prosperity it provides.

To keep the game going and growing, an international UMS would require each central bank to relinquish some of its desire to engage in a completely independent domestic monetary and reserve holding policy. This perceived fear of loss of national autonomy consequent on joining a supranational banking and clearing system is largely a bogus anxiety. The loss of complete economic self-determination is the cost of any permanent trading relationship. Economic independence must always ultimately mean either complete economic isolation or complete dominance of others. Autarky and independence can only be purchased at some cost. Once a nation decides to join a community of nations for both political and economic reasons then interdependence and feedback effects among the trading partners are inevitable. The trick is to make these feedbacks provide for economic stimulus as much as possible before global full employment is achieved.

Trepidation over the loss of the current degree of national autonomy has been a fundamental factor preventing rational nations from organizing some international institution to coordinate more efficiently the liquidity-financing methods for generating additional income among trading partners. Nevertheless, it is obvious that a well designed organization, staffed by a management that comprehends the need for additional liquidity as a prerequisite for generating additional income for entrepreneur economies, could contribute significantly to the more rapid global growth of real income and employment. Until national governments recognize this elemental truth, private sector banking interests will, on their own, continue to develop makeshift institutions (such as eurocurrencies) which provide additional international liquidity for the expansion of world trade. Unfortunately, these private sector expedients often tend to fail at the least propitious time as they are unable to weather a liquidity crunch, especially when cash flow imbalances inevitably develop with expansion. Hence, in a crunch, central bankers will have to underwrite liabilities of these makeshift arrangements in order to avoid a global liquidity crisis.

# INTERNATIONAL LIQUIDITY AND RESERVE RECYCLING – NECESSARY

## Conditions for World Prosperity

A necessary, but not a sufficient condition, for a significant expansion of production to occur in any market-oriented, entrepreneur economy is a monetary payments system which endogenously expands to meet the needs of trade. Whenever entrepreneurs are unable to obtain sufficient additional financial commitments from bankers today to undertake expanded activities tomorrow (no matter how profitable these future production activities are expected to be in the more distant future when output is sold to the final buyer), firms will not hire additional resources and expand their working capital positions. This requirement of increasing liquidity provisions to entrepreneurs to permit expansion of productive activities has a long history in economics known as the real bills doctrine.

If, in addition to this endogenous monetary system, there is also provision for one or more institutions to act as a 'balancing wheel' either as spender or liquidity sponge as conditions require maintaining full employment effective demand, then the resulting economic system has built-in necessary and sufficient conditions for economic prosperity.

In capitalist economic systems in 'normal' times there is a tendency for a shortage of effective demand due to liquidity hoarding, and/or inadequate endogenous monetary responses to entrepreneurial financial needs and/or insufficient private 'animal spirits'. There are two general cases where monetary (liquidity) shortages, resulting from a payments system that does not adequately accommodate entrepreneurs' liquidity needs, can limit production flows before full employment:

1. The recessionary case occurs when income earners allocate current 'savings' into idle surplus liquid reserves and refuse either to spend these savings directly on the products of industry or to lend (or give) them to others who wish to spend on current output.
2. The inability to expand production case occurs when the payments system is unable, or unwilling, to expand financial reserves as rapidly as profit-seeking entrepreneurs desire to expand output. Without financial facilities to meet increased payrolls and raw material costs, entrepreneurs cannot undertake increased production activities, no matter how profitable they expect the sales from these expanded activities to be.

Accordingly, any well-designed international payments mechanism should provide for an accommodating (endogenous) system which not only supports, but encourages, spending to approach global full employment levels. This means that the system must provide entrepreneurs with financial facilities on favourable terms. The system must be able to create and maintain an adequate volume and distribution of an asset of ultimate reserve as quickly as entrepreneurs are capable of expanding production flows for global full employment and international trade.

Any international payments mechanism should contain a built-in bias of not only recycling idle reserves, preferably at little or no cost to the user, but also a bias towards increasing members' reserves as global productive capacity grows. As long as there is a shortage of global effective demand, the user of otherwise liquid idle reserves is providing a useful social function by employing these funds to hire otherwise involuntarily unemployed resources to produce goods. By definition, spending these liquid reserves on the products of industry provides additional utility to society in excess of the disutility involved in producing the additional goods without diminishing the world's liquid reserves one iota. From a global utilitarian standpoint, as long as there are people who prefer employment to leisure we should not permit those with surplus reserve assets either to hoard reserves or to drain them from the system thereby imposing leisure on workers willing to work for a living.

### Recycling Liquidity at Less Than Full Employment

Given some initial level of global effective demand, the development of any trade imbalances between regions – even those in a common market with a un-ionized monetary system [UMS] – can induce recessionary liquidity problems which ultimately reduce overall production and thereby lower the real income of inhabitants of both the trade deficit and trade surplus regions. Since the trade deficit region's spending (cash outflow) on production from the surplus region exceeds its earnings on sales (cash inflow) from those who have deposits in the surplus region's banks, it quickly runs out of export earnings to maintain its import purchases. In the absence of deliberate offsetting action by the monetary authority and/or the central government, these cash flow imbalances will creates a loss of reserves and hence liquidity from the deficit region's banks. Experience has shown that offsetting regional transfers can create economic benefits for both regions if used to promote economic expansion and hence real income for the deficit region and markets for the industries of the surplus region, e.g. the development of the TVA (Tennessee Valley Authority) during the Great Depression.

National monetary and fiscal policy administered by *pro bono publico* officials can help to offset the deflationary pressures which interregional trade deficits can generate. Unfortunately no global supranational *pro bono* monetary and/or fiscal authority is likely to be created in the foreseeable future, although the US Marshall Plan and US government military and economic aid programmes to LDCs have often played that fiscal role since the Second World War. In the days of 'Cold War' politics, superpowers provided unilateral transfers to LDC client states. As long as the Cold War did not escalate to actual hostilities, superpower politics played an important role in fostering economic growth in Europe and many LDCs. With the sudden end of the Cold War in 1989, the political need of the superpowers to provide economic aid to client states has diminished and, ceteris paribus, the gap between the rich and poor increased.

## RELEVANCE TO LATIN AMERICAN CRIES FOR DOLLARIZATION

Those in Latin America who advocate dollarization are trying to achieve a UMS with the USA which is typically a major (but not the only) trading partner with these Latin American countries. Will making the less developed nations of Latin America members of a UMS with the United States solve their trade, employment and price stability problems?

Dollarization merely makes the nation part of the UMS that is the USA. Obviously, it does not solve the problem for the dollarized nation, if that nation maintains a significant trading relationship with the Eurozone nations and/or with other countries whose currencies are not tied to the dollar, for then its exports and imports will be affected by changes in the exchange rate between dollars and other currencies. For example, although Argentina did not officially dollarize, its adoption of a currency board effectively made it part of a UMS with the USA. Argentina's economic problems were, for a few years, solved by the currency–board UMS solution. But when its large trading partner, Brazil, allowed its currency to depreciate relative to the dollar, Argentina entered a multi-year recession a liquidity problem in which it cannot service its debts. This threatens Argentina's ability to survive in the modern global economy. Obviously dollarization, or its currency board equivalent, did not solve the trade and ultimately the employment problem of this large open economy.

But even if a dollarized nation traded only with the USA, its balance of payments problem might still exist, just as the trade between federal reserve districts are not normally in balance-of-payments equilibrium. The difference is that if a large region of the USA developed a balance of payments deficit with other regions of the federal reserve, federal fiscal policy that spent significantly more in the deficit region could deliberately reflux the reserves within the federal reserve system and thereby alleviate the problem. No such fiscal option exists for the dollarized nation.

## NOTES

1. A fully liquid asset is any durable that is resalable in a spot market where the market maker guarantees an unchanged market price.
2. In effect Scotland has been, and is increasingly likely to be, 'poundized'.

# 14. Dollarization in Latin America: 2004 and beyond

**Kenneth P. Jameson**

## INTRODUCTION

At the time of the conference in May 2001, it seemed possible that the entire Western Hemisphere would soon move toward adopting the dollar as the uniform currency. Ex-President Menem of Argentina was positioning himself for another run with full dollarization one of his major proposals. Theoretical articles (Courchene and Harris, 2000) supporting Canadian monetary union with the USA and abandoning its own 'loony' had been joined by favourable statements from politicians and from important public intellectuals (Grubel, 1999). El Salvador had switched from a fixed exchange rate to a dollarization process, and Guatemala had begun to allow transactions in dollars and expected the dollar to displace the quetzal. Stanley Fischer (2001), from his powerful position as the First Deputy Managing Director of the IMF, espoused the 'bi-polar' view: countries should either float or adopt a hard peg such as dollarization. Many predicted that the entire western hemisphere would soon be dollarized (Schuldt, 2001; Trejos, 1999; Tuculet, 2001).

Now, several years into the millennium, a western hemisphere monetary union no longer seems likely; the dollarization momentum has diminished. After providing an update on the status of dollarization in 2004, this chapter examines the reasons for the reversal of dollarization's fortunes, with an eye to future exchange rate regime developments in Latin America. The conclusion is that official dollarization remains on the policy table, if for no other reason than continued unofficial dollarization. However, the prevalence of official dollarization will expand only if a number of the circumstances that gave dollarization its impetus at the century's turn become important once again.

## DOLLARIZATION IN LATIN AMERICA IN 2004

None of the western hemisphere dollarized countries has reversed course and set out to recreate a national currency.[1] This is not even an issue in Panama, the earliest dollarized country. However, opposition to dollarization in Ecuador remains (Acosta, 2002) and one influential group, the Foro Económico Alternativo, has proposed a process for moving away from dollarization. On the other hand, President Gutierrez has backed continued use of the dollar, despite the doubts he expressed as a candidate. In addition, the indigenous elements of his coalition that were most adamantly against dollarization have left the government. Ecuador's economy weakened in 2003; GDP actually declined in the first half of the year. However, there is relative stability in prices and employment, and exports actually increased during 2003. While Gutierrez's popularity has fallen, and his presidency faces some danger from allegations of drug money infiltration into his election campaign, there is little likelihood of any imminent reversal in dollarization under current economic and political conditions.

In El Salvador, the dollarization policy cornerstone was the government mandate that financial transactions be carried out in dollars. This advantaged the dollar and represented an attempt to create network externalities for the dollar. The requirement immediately meant that 90 per cent of economic transactions were dollarized. However, the pace of substitution in currency transactions was much slower, 46 per cent by the end of 2001 and 87 per cent by the end of 2002 (NotiCen 2002: 2). Emigrant remittances facilitated the growth of dollar transactions. In 2002, they reached $1.6 billion by October, three times the amount of currency in circulation and over 60 per cent of the total value of exports. By November, 2003, they achieved an additional $1.89 billion. As a result of a long period of citizen emigration to the United States, 'El Salvador' exists both in the original geographic area and as a sub-national reality within the United States (de la Campa, 1999). This suggests that what affects the reality of El Salvador as a 'split nation' may ultimately determine the course of dollarization. The ruling Arena party has raised fears of disruptions in this area if the FMLN wins the 2004 elections, a result that appears increasingly unlikely. However, the FMLN has claimed that there would be no policy reversals, only changes in emphasis and direction. Their political commission has specifically stated that there is no problem with the free circulation of the dollar (NotiCen 2003: 4). Therefore, dollarization in El Salvador appears robust and unlikely to reverse in the near future.

On the other hand and in contrast to this dollarization continuity, there have been two significant exchange rate regime changes elsewhere in Latin America. Argentina's 2002 rejection of convertibility, after a four-year recession and resultant political instability, immediately put the bi-polar view on ice. The floating peso crashed from 1 peso:1$ to 3.50 pesos:1$, before appreciating to 2.90 pesos:1$ by 2004. The 11 per cent GDP decline in 2002 reversed to a 7 per cent increase in 2003. The lesson was that a hard peg could result in fundamental disequilibrium, even though Argentina had implemented virtually every policy that should have ensured convertibility's success.[2] Making monetary policy dependent on foreign exchange backing had lowered inflation. Annual inflation was actually negative after 1999, thus aiding Argentina's international competitiveness. The financial system had been internationalized so that seven of the eight largest banks were foreign-owned, which should have committed their parents to act as lenders of last resort to ensure banking stability. Argentine financial regulation had become a model: 'Argentina has been at the fore in imposing high liquid reserve requirements on its banks ... and they have continued to provide insulation through the market turbulence of 1997–99' (Caprio and Honohan, 1999: 60–61). They added '... the Argentine experiment is being watched closely and may well become mainstream in time' (pp. 56–7). Capital was attracted to Argentina. For example, foreign direct investment reached $22 billion in 1999, as capital account inflows offset current account deficits. Finally, labour productivity increased 46 per cent between 1990 and 1996, further aiding Argentina's international competitiveness (Fanelli and Keifman, 2002). Nonetheless, Argentina's convertibility died in 2002.

This was virtually the only case where the studied neutrality of the USA on dollarization was publicly broken. Under-secretary of the Treasury John Taylor in his 2002 testimony on Argentina suggested that a bank deposit freeze might have been avoided if they had moved to a different exchange rate system: 'moving away from the peg toward solid dollarization or if you moved to a flexible ... I at that point in time thought that dollarization would have been good for Argentina' (Taylor, 2002: 21–2).

The other regime change came in 2003 when Venezuela moved to a fixed exchange rate with stringent capital controls. While this policy swims against today's strong liberalization current, and observers expect extensive evasion and inefficiency, much time will be required before any assessment of this policy can be undertaken.[3] Internal political strife and conscious economic disruption will also confound any conclusions about this effort to return to a Bretton Woods regime. Capital controls remain highly unpopular, despite their relative success in Malaysia during the Asian crisis. Nonetheless, Venezuela's experience will have implications for this approach to resolving countries' policy trilemma.

These changes took place at the same time that Latin American exchange rate regimes were undergoing a more gradual evolution. The first, noted in ECLAC (2004: 42) was an apparent movement toward flexible exchange rates. By ECLAC's categorization, the six countries with flexible rates in 1996 increased to 11 in 2003. Crawling peg or moving band countries decreased from ten to four over the same period. The reality is that these are 'dirty floats' in almost all cases, where the new element is the wider array of tools governments are using to influence the exchange rate. Inflation targeting, interest rate policy or even debt negotiations have all become mechanisms utilized primarily to reassure international markets. The goal is to avoid 'sudden stops' in capital flows

(Calvo et al., 2002), which is the currently favoured explanation for exchange rate crises.

The second evolutionary element is the continuation of unofficial dollarization in Latin America. The Bretton Woods system established after the Second World War encouraged 'national currencies', along with capital controls, to ensure national macroeconomic stability and independence. The most notable exponent of this policy was Robert Triffin, who was the chief of the Latin American section of the US Federal Reserve from 1943–6. As Helleiner noted (2003a, 411): '(These money doctors) encouraged Southern governments to eliminate the use of foreign currencies within their territory wherever that practice was widespread.' Economic instability in the 1970s reversed this policy and encouraged widespread currency substitution of dollars for national money. The dollar's role in the domestic monetary system has continued in subsequent decades, regardless of the stability or instability in national economies. The most important determinant of the degree of unofficial dollarization appears to be hysteresis or inertia (Lora, 2002). The degree of dollar substitution that occurred during the 1970s and 1980s is the best indicator of the current degree of unofficial dollarization. There are cases where currency substitution has clearly increased, for example, Guatemala, whose policy change was designed to encourage a form of dollarization. The same was true in Argentina at the end of convertibility, though the appreciation of the peso has apparently reversed the process to some degree. By mid-2001, 80 per cent of time deposits were in dollars as were 50 per cent of savings deposits (de la Torre et al., 2003, Figure 4). The effect of instability and exchange controls in Venezuela will bear watching. In any case, significant changes in unofficial dollarization would have important implications for the likelihood of official dollarization.

The conclusion at this point in time is that official dollarization has lost momentum in the last three years. The probability that the three dollarized countries will revert to a national currency under current international conditions appears low. Currently there is also little likelihood that other countries will follow their lead and adopt official dollarization.

This does not imply that dollarization is dead or completely off the policy table. However, conditions would have to change to give it new momentum. Understanding the changes since 2001 that slowed dollarization will allow us to understand the changes that could accelerate the process. What diminished the policy appeal of dollarization after 2001?

## WHY THE LOSS OF MOMENTUM?

Since 2001, there are four factors that account for the attenuation of dollarization's popularity: the exhaustion of efforts to win tangible US support for dollarization; increasing empirical evidence that dollarization's macroeconomic benefits were oversold; the growing interest in sub-regional currency arrangements; and the vertiginous growth of China's international importance combined with the depreciation of the dollar against the Euro and yen. Let us examine each in turn.

## Continued US Indifference

If the US government actively supported dollarization in the hemisphere, there would certainly be other countries that would take the step. This would require specific concessions by the USA: mechanisms to share seigniorage, shared influence over monetary policy, coordination of macroeconomic policy, and 'lender of last resort' support. Specific proposals along these lines had been broached at the end of the century. Senator Mack held hearings on dollarization, and proposals for sharing seigniorage had been discussed (United States Senate, 1999). Economists in Argentina's Treasury had proposed an agreement on dollarization and discussed it with US policymakers even before Carlos Menem's 1998 public embrace of dollarization. They proposed a mechanism for sharing seigniorage, based on interest that would have been earned on the reserves that would be converted into dollars. In addition, they proposed that financial instruments be developed to provide the resources for a lender of last resort, by allowing access to the resulting financial resources under extreme conditions (Guidotti and Powell, 2001). Discussions of the Argentine proposal in the US Treasury did not lead to clear rejection. There was widespread feeling in Latin America that the USA would welcome unilateral official dollarization, though the public US stance remained neutral (Summers, 1999). Finally, Courchene and Harris (2000) suggested that Canada – and Mexico – could dollarize and become new districts of the Federal Reserve System, thus gaining a role in setting US monetary policy.

By 2004, it has become clearer that there is very little chance of any such US concessions. Even in an administration with little consistent economic policy, there has been no overt and apparently no tacit encouragement of dollarization. All the proposals are off the table.[4] Cohen's (2002) analysis of the benefits and costs to the USA of dollarization persuasively argues that benign neglect is in the US interest. In addition, Helleiner (2003b) analysed the debate in Canada on monetary union with the USA. There are constituencies that favour adopting the US dollar, but only if Canada could have some influence on federal monetary policy. Helleiner's analysis of the institutional structure and actual functioning of the US Federal Reserve effectively discounted the viability of a Canadian role in a monetary union as the Thirteenth Federal Reserve District.

## Empirical Evidence

A 1999 Cato Institute study (Moreno-Villalaz, 1999) characterized Panama's macroeconomic performance as uniquely successful. Panama had exhibited 'high and relatively stable' economic growth, had 'low and stable' inflation, low interest rates, and ample capital flows. The conclusion was that dollarization could improve macroeconomic performance in Latin America. Closer examination showed that Panama's record was more mixed (Goldfajn and Olivares, 2001). Dollarization had not enforced fiscal discipline, reduced GDP growth instability or removed the volatility of interest rate spreads on sovereign debt. Much of Panama's success in lowering interest rates could be traced to the internationalization of its banking system rather than the absence of exchange rate risk. Finally, lower inflation and fixed exchange rates go hand-in-hand. Indeed, Edwards suggested that the major accomplishment of Panama's dollarization had been its ability to use the IMF as a 'lender of first resort' (Edwards, 1999).

Later empirical studies also reach less optimistic conclusions. Edwards and Magenzdo's (2003) study of 'strictly dollarized' countries found that they do have lower inflation. On the other hand, their economies are significantly more volatile and have lower GDP growth, though this last difference is not statistically significant. Karras (2002) used data from 1950–97 to assess the costs (loss of policy autonomy) and benefits (lower inflation) of dollarization to 19 Latin American countries. His most significant result was the high correlation of costs and benefits. In other words, the countries with high historic rates of inflation, which dollarization should reduce, are also the countries whose cyclical behaviour is very different from the USA's, and who therefore have the most need of policy independence. Finally, Duncan (2002) developed a dynamic equilibrium model that relied on Peruvian parameter estimates to simulate the effects of moving from partial to complete dollarization. Again, dollarization led to lower inflation and volatility of inflation. However, output and investment were more volatile, there was greater volatility in the fiscal deficit, and terms of trade changes had a larger effect on output. The sum of these results and their consistency raise questions about the economic value of dollarization.

As a final unkind cut, Williamson's (2003: 6) effort to address the shortcomings of the Washington Consensus rejected dollarization: '(e)xcept in countries that have close relations with the United States in terms of both trade and financial flows, where full dollarization makes sense, [countries should] aim to minimize use of the dollar both as an asset in terms of which residents hold savings and in terms of which loans are contracted'.

## Regional Currency Arrangements

There has been increased interest in creating regional currency blocs. This is partly the result of Europe's adoption of the euro and of its increased credibility since its introduction. The appreciation of the euro beginning in 2002 has added to its appeal. This is reflected in discussion of regional currency blocs for the Andean nations (Jaramillo, 2001) and for Mercosur (Kronberger, 2002; Arestis and de Paula, 2003). The articles in the Arestis and de Paula volume and in this volume specifically investigate the lessons the euro may have for Mercosur.

The Presidents of Brazil and Argentina have committed themselves to closer coordination in Mercosur, and this does not exclude moving toward a common currency. The benefit of some exchange rate agreement became clearer from the fundamental disruption of Mercosur occasioned by the unsynchronized collapses of the real and the peso after 1998.

The relative stability of the French franc bloc over a long period provides added support, though East Asia may be a more persuasive example. McKinnon (2000) suggests that a major contributor to their continuing success is an 'East Asian dollar standard'. Historically, the entire region retains a stable relation with the dollar. Even after the 1997–8 exchange rate crisis, where existing rates fixed to the dollar depreciated chaotically, the countries moved back to stability against the dollar. The new element in this later period is that the linchpin has become China, who has maintained a fixed rate with the dollar. This has allowed a rapid increase in intra-zone trade and a reorientation of the economies from producing finished products to producing components for finishing in China. As a result, dollarization is not the only change in exchange rate regime that could provide the basis for economic growth and stability. Regional currency arrangements might play this role, allowing regional coordination and modifying the loss of national sovereignty implied by dollarization.

## China and the Dollar

The driver of the world economy in recent years has been the extreme imbalance between trade/saving surplus countries and those in deficit.

> In the United States and Japan, the ratio of the current account balance to trade flows … have risen to levels almost never seen in industrial countries in the postwar period. As a result, Japan is exporting 1½ per cent of world saving and the United States is absorbing 6 per cent … One of the major concerns associated with the global imbalances is the possibility of an abrupt and disruptive adjustment of major exchange rates. (IMF, 2002: 66).

Since 2002, the dollar has depreciated by 40 per cent against the euro and by 25 per cent against the yen. This has been characterized as an 'orderly depreciation'; however, such a rapid decline in the value of the dollar and the continuing imbalances, now exacerbated by China's incredible manufacturing export growth, suggest that any exchange rate regime a country might adopt is likely to come under pressure. During the 1980s, it appeared that the world would move toward a system of three currency blocs, centered on the dollar, the Deutschmark, and the yen (Frankel and Wei, 1995). Stagnation in Japan and Germany's problems integrating the East while adopting the euro combined to make the dollar the 'great currency' of the decade (Mundell, 1998). Thus there was an incentive to hold dollars, for the dollar was literally better than gold. This provided an incentive to unofficial dollarization or currency substitution. The experience in the new millennium has been quite different. Gold prices rose from $280 per ounce in early 2002 to over $400 by 2004. As a result, anyone holding dollars, including citizens who use them as their primary currency, would have lost substantial international purchasing power. Belated recognition of the effects of this instability led the G7 finance ministers to adopt a coordinated verbal effort to slow the dollar depreciation on 7 February 2004. Whether this will lead to coordinated intervention, despite US resistance, remains to be seen. The future course of the dollar's value is hard to determine in early 2004. However, the continuing US trade deficit and questions about whether countries will continue to absorb the US financial assets required to finance the deficit suggest that dollar weakness will continue.[5] Nonetheless, the reversal of the dollar's fortune since 2002 should discourage any country from adopting the dollar. The expected return on dollar holdings will continue to under-perform compared with other returns until there is massive and coordinated intervention.

## WILL DOLLARIZATION RETURN TO THE TABLE?

In 2004, any voices favouring dollarization in other Latin American countries are faint at best. The move toward greater flexibility has been accompanied by relative stability, largely because capital flows to Latin America have resumed. President Lula of Brazil has calmed fears about Brazil and Argentina's growth has opened new possibilities while its debt default is worked out. The resurgence of the euro and yen has taken some of the gloss off the dollar as the world's great money. The dollar has certainly not been as good as gold since the new millennium. The US stance has not changed; trade liberalization is still the driving force for economic policy in the hemisphere. While US Treasury Secretaries talk of supporting the 'strong dollar', they have clearly acquiesced in the dollar's depreciation and making concessions to potential dollarizing countries is not on the radar screen.

On the other hand, these conditions support the maintenance of dollarization in the already dollarized countries. The depreciating dollar has helped their export competitiveness, especially with countries in Latin America and the rest of the world whose currencies have appreciated. Ecuador has been further aided by the high price of oil, which OPEC has allowed to increase in dollar terms to offset the dollar depreciation.

Nonetheless, experience since 1973 suggests that the sheer magnitude of international financial flows makes the stability of exchange rate regimes temporary at best. Changes in the four underlying factors noted above could easily result in renewed exchange rate crises in Latin America. The new year of 2004 has already provided one example. The Dominican Republic's political stalemate in early 2004 spilled over into a currency crash. The Dominican peso rate was 35 pesos per dollar on 22 January. By 2 February, it had fallen to 52 pesos per dollar, a 50 per cent decline in ten days. In mid-June of 2003 the exchange rate had been 17 pesos per dollar. It was in just such a crisis that Ecuador dollarized, and its success in stabilizing financial relations may appear attractive under certain political circumstances.

Another possible facilitating change would be an improvement in the relative performance of dollarized countries. The Asian dollar standard countries continue to outperform Latin America, partly because of their tight link to the dollar. In addition, the depreciating dollar may help the dollarized countries differentially.

Finally, it is possible that US economic policy could begin to give relations with Latin America a higher priority, as a counter to the growing economic importance of Europe and the Asian dollar standard countries. That could lead to greater willingness on the part of the US to offer support and even concessions for countries that would tie themselves more completely to US economic policy by dollarizing. While this last change is the least likely, especially in a second Bush administration, the others are entirely possible. If they were to occur, dollarization would suddenly be very much back on the policy table and the momentum that was lost in these last few years would suddenly return.

## NOTES

1. While Panama does have fractional coins termed balboas, their minor role does not qualify them as a national currency. The last effort to print paper balboas and reestablish a national currency by Arnulfo Arias after his election in 1940 was a complete failure.
2. One could argue that other mistakes caused convertibility's demise, e.g. the failure to deal with the fiscal deficit and the resultant need for debt financing. However, these elements became problematic mainly as a result of the extended recession that began in 1998, which had its roots in the policy constraints imposed by convertibility.
3. The opposition claims that the black market rate at the start of 2004 was almost double the official rate.
4. Kurt Schuler remains a voice favouring dollarization as a staff member of the Joint Economic Committee. He also maintains a web site http://www.dollarization.org/.
5. In November 2003, Japan held $525 billion in US securities, an increase from $501.9 billion

in October as Japan attempted to prevent yen appreciation. China held $143.9 billion and the United Kingdom $111.7 billion (Lagomarsina, 2004).

# REFERENCES

Acosta, Alberto. 2002. 'Si se puede salir de la dolarización!' Presentation, Quito, Ecuador (9 July).
Arestis, Philip and Luiz Fernando de Paula. 2003. 'Monetary union in South America: lessons from EMU'. Cheltenham, UK and Northampton, MA: Edward Elgar.
Calvo, Guillermo, Alejandro Izquierdo and Ernesto Talvi. 2002. 'Sudden stops, the real exchange rate and fiscal sustainability: Argentina's lessons.' IADB Working Paper no. 469.
Caprio, Gerard and Patrick Honohan. 1999. 'Restoring banking stability: beyond supervised capital requirements.' *Journal of Economic Perspectives*, **13** (4) (Fall): 43–64.
Cohen, Benjamin J. 2002. 'America's interest in dollarization.' Working Paper. Available at http://www.polisci.ucsb.edu/faculty/cohen/working/fordham.html (accessed 9 April).
Courchene, Thomas J. and Richard G. Harris. 2000. 'North American monetary union: analytical principles and operational guidelines.' *North American Journal of Economics and Finance*, **11**, 3–18.
De la Campa, Román. 1999. *Latin Americanism*. Minneapolis: University of Minnesota Press.
De la Torre, Augusto, Eduardo Levy Yeyati, and Sergio Schmukler. 2003. 'Living and dying with hard pegs: the rise and fall of Argentina's currency board.' Typescript: Washington, DC, World Bank.
Duncan, Roberto. 2002. 'Exploring the implications of official dollarization on macroeconomic volatility.' Typescript, Central Bank of Chile (October), 1–36.
ECLAC. (Economic Commission for Latin America and the Caribbean). 2004. 'Preliminary overview of the economies of Latin America and the Caribbean.' Santiago, Chile.
Edwards, Sebastian. 1999. 'The IMF is Panama's Lender of First Resort.' *Wall Street Journal* (24 September, A15).
Edwards, Sebastian and Igal Magendzo. 2003. 'Dollarization and economic performance: what do we really know?' *International Journal of Finance and Economics*, **8** (1) (October), 351–63.
Fanelli, José María and Saúl Keifman. 2002. 'Finance and changing trade patterns in developing countries: the Argentine case.' In Fanelli, José María and Rohinton Medhora (eds) *Finance and Competitiveness in Developing Countries*, London: Routledge, 20–44.
Fischer, Stanley. 2001. 'Distinguished Lecture on Economics in Government: Exchange rate regimes: is the bipolar view correct?' *Journal of Economic Perspectives*, **15** (2) (Spring), 3–24.
Frankel, Jeffrey A., and Shang-Jin Wei. 1995. 'Emerging currency blocks.' In Hans Genberg (ed.), *The International Monetary System*, New York: Springer Verlag.
Goldfajn, Ilan and Gino Olivares. 2001. 'Full dollarization: the case of Panama.' *Economía* **1** (2), 101–56.
Grubel, Herbert. 1999. *The Case for the Amero: The Economics and Politics of a North American Monetary Union*. Vancouver: Fraser Institute.

Guidotti, Pablo and Andrew Powell. 2001. 'The dollarization debate in Argentina and Latin America.' Typescript: Universidad Torcuato Di Tella.

Helleiner, Eric. 2003a. 'Dollarization diplomacy: US policy towards Latin America coming full circle?' *Review of International Political Economy*, **10** (3) (August), 406–29.

Helleiner, Eric. 2003b. 'What political architecture for North American monetary union? The Canadian debate.' Paper presented at the International Studies Association Meetings, Portland, Oregon (February), 1–22.

IMF. 2002. *World Economic Outlook*, Washington, DC: IMF.

Jaramillo, Fidel. 2001. Cinco, Una o Ninguna: Las Opciones Cambiarias para los Países Andinos. Bogota (typescript).

Karras, Georgios. 2002. 'Costs and benefits of dollarization: evidence from North, Central, and South America.' *Journal of Economic Integration*, **17** (3) (September): 502–16.

Kronberger, Ralf. 2002. 'A cost–benefit analysis of a monetary union for MERCOSUR with particular emphasis on the optimum currency area theory.' *Integration and Trade* (January–June), 29–93.

Lagomarsino, Deborah. 2004. 'Foreign inflows boosted US securities in November.' *Wall Street Journal* (19 January), A2.

Lora, Oscar. 2002. 'Sustitución de Activos en Bolivia: Evidencia Reciente.' *Revista de Análisis Económico*, **17** (2) (December), 31–47.

McKinnon, R. 2000. 'The East Asian Dollar standard, life after death?' *Economic Notes*, 29 (1), February, 31–82.

Moreno-Villalaz, Juan Luis. 1999. 'Lessons from the monetary experience of Panama: a dollar economy with financial integration.' *Cato Journal* (Winter): 421–39.

Mundell, Robert. 1998. 'What makes a great currency?' Processed presentation to Fourth Dubrovnick Conference on the Transition Economies: 23–26 June.

NotiCen. 2002. 'El Salvador deals with new rules for remittances.' (21 November), 1–3, available at http://ladb.unm.edu.noticen/.

NotiCen. 2003. 'El Salvador: US seen interfering in electoral process.' (12 June), 1–5, available at http://ladb.unm.edu-noticen/.

Schuldt, Jürgen. 2001. 'Latin American official dollarization: political economy aspects.' In James Dean, Steve Globerman and Tom Willet (eds), *Dollarization in the Americas?*, Boulder, Co: Westview Press.

Summers, Deputy Treasury Secretary Lawrence. 1999. 'Testimony.' Senate Banking Subcommittee, 22 April.

Taylor, John. 2002. 'Testimony.' Subcommittee on International Monetary Policy and Trade of the House Financial Services Committee (6 February).

Trejos, Alberto. 1999. 'Dolarización en América Latina. Es Deseable e Implementable? Es Inevitable?' San José, Costa Rica: Academia de Centroamérica.

Tuculet, Eduardo. 2001. 'La Dolarización Será Una Realidad en la Próxima Década.' *Tiempos del Mundo*, 19 July, B24–7.

United States Senate. 1999. 'Encouraging official dollarization in emerging markets.' Joint Economic Committee Staff Report. Washington, DC: (April).

Williamson, John. 2003. 'Washington Consensus and beyond.' Typescript. Washington, DC: Institute for International Economics.

# 15. Monetary integration and dollarization: what are the lessons?

## Alcino F. Câmara Neto and Matías Vernengo

### INTRODUCTION

Globalization, it is sometimes argued, diminishes the capacity for state intervention in the economy. Monetary integration and dollarization are ultimately strategies to cope with financial globalization. They are seen as a solution for high inflation countries that want to stabilize their economies and import credibility in doing so. Countries that successfully achieve macroeconomic stability are seen as trustworthy and should receive higher levels of foreign investment. Growth should naturally follow. The evidence in that respect is mixed at best.

It is clear that during the 1990s levels of inflation in the periphery fell to international levels. Exchange rate based stabilization programmes were part of the story, and in that respect it seems correct to argue that greater monetary integration and less autonomy in monetary policy went hand in hand with lower inflation. However, inflation fell all around the globe, and it is not absolutely clear that the reasons for that are associated with tighter macroeconomic policies resulting from a more integrated international financial system.[1]

Inflation is now virtually nonexistent in industrialized countries, and generally subdued in the developing world. The victory over inflation was however bought at a high cost in terms of sluggish growth, high unemployment and income inequality in many parts of the world, giving rise to a host of economic and social problems that take their toll. The question then is whether monetary integration and dollarization are not particularly important to reduce inflation – that is, can stabilization be achieved by other means – since they are so costly in terms of employment generation and growth.[2]

We believe that four fundamental lessons were highlighted by the participants of the conference, upon which this chapter is based.

1.  In the first place, the consensus at the conference was that monetary integration and dollarization are no panacea. They may solve some problems, but they imply significant costs.

2.  Monetary integration and dollarization affect the ability to conduct independent monetary policy, but also impose severe constraints on fiscal policy. Any successful integration strategy must provide for alternatives for fiscal policy.
3.  Balance of payments problems and increasing dependency from foreign capital flows may increase with monetary integration and dollarization. In that respect, financial fragility may actually increase.
4.  The three lessons above suggest that a great resistance to monetary integration and dollarization will maintain a relatively great diversity of national currencies.

In particular, it should be noted the relatively successful launch of the euro,[3] on the one hand, and the recurrent international financial crises in developing countries, on the other, serve as examples of the potential gains and risks from monetary integration and dollarization.

## MONETARY INTEGRATION AND FISCAL POLICY

The Bretton Woods period, broadly from 1944 to 1973, was characterized by fixed but adjustable exchange rates, widespread capital controls, which fostered high international transaction costs in foreign exchange markets. This framework was designed in order to promote national sovereignty, allowing the central banks to set interest rates for domestic purposes, with full employment as the main goal. More importantly, by allowing rates of interest to be on average at relatively low levels, the Bretton Woods arrangement favoured debtors in general, and states in particular.

Not surprisingly, the conventional view among academic economists after the Keynesian Revolution was that government debt is not a burden on future generations. Keynesians argued that government deficits, and the consequent accumulation of debt, should be instruments for the maintenance of full employment. This view became known as the functional finance approach to deficits and debt. Economists in the functional finance tradition argue that a high debt-to-GDP ratio, provided that the borrowing is done internally in the country's own currency, does not imply any appreciable risk for default. Nor does it limit the scope for active, counter-cyclical policy measures in any relevant sense.

Starting in the 1950s, the benign view of public debt gave gradually away to a more pessimistic position, partly as a result of the growth in non-war related debt. Also, the process of globalization – the liberalization of movements of goods, services and capital – since the end of Bretton Woods, led to the proliferation of tax heavens, and an increase in tax competition making public debt more costly to service. Finally, the stagflation of the 1970s, and the conservative revolution that followed fed a tax revolt that made increasing tax burdens to finance public debt unlikely. Measures to contain spending, and to reduce the burden of debt became more common. The most well-known policy measure to curb debt is undoubtedly the Maastricht limits on public debt to Gross Domestic Product (GDP) ratios imposed on the European countries.

In the last three decades the Keynesian belief in the positive effects of deficits – at least in the short run – has been turned upside down. Some authors argue that a fiscal contraction – reduction in government spending – could have an expansionary effect on the economy, provided that the cuts in government spending lead to a perception of permanently lower taxes. That is, if the government decides to spend less, then taxpayers would have to pay less in the future and would increase both consumption and investment. This increase in consumption and investment may outweigh the decrease in government consumption, leading then to a growing economy and higher levels of income.

All the research on the effects of fiscal consolidation is associated with the idea that a lower burden of debt would lead to higher growth. However, there is very little evidence that lower debt is associated with capital accumulation. In fact, the literature is inconclusive on the question of the optimal size of government debt. For that reason, some authors have argued that fiscal consolidation has gone too far. For example, Stiglitz (2003, p. 49) argues that the current mood with respect to fiscal policy around the world is related to the apparent success of Clinton's fiscal consolidation, even though Clinton 'pushed deficit reduction too far'.

It is not surprising that anti-Keynesian policies have had the upper hand in the post-Bretton Woods period, in which the relative isolation of domestic markets allowed monetary and fiscal policy to be fundamentally devoted to the maintenance of full employment at home. Greater integration with international financial markets implies that interest rates have to be used to attract capital flows and/or avoid capital flight. Also, higher interest rates increase the burden of debt servicing. In this view, the problem of debt accumulation results less from a Keynesian increase in social spending, but from the combination of high rates of interest and low rates of growth in the last 30 years.

Pasinetti (1997, p. 168) argues that the growth of debt is not caused by Keynesian profligacy, and that the vulnerability of fiscal accounts 'usually attributed to the high size reached by the debt … is in fact due to the high level reached by interest rates'. The causes of high interest rates and low rates of growth are highly complex and related to the demise of the accumulation regime that was in place during the so-called Golden Age of capitalism (Glyn et al., 1990). However, Pasinetti (1997) argues convincingly that a revenge of the rentier – the reverse of Keynes's euthanasia of the rentier – resulting from income distribution conflict is at the heart of the process.

*Table 15.1   Interest rate burden (% of GDP)*

|         | 1970 | 1980 | 1995 |
|---------|------|------|------|
| Canada  | 1.2  | 2.5  | 4.3  |
| France  | 0.5  | 1.5  | 3.2  |
| Germany | 0.4  | 1    | 2.5  |
| Italy   | 1.8  | 5.4  | 11.1 |
| Japan   | 0.4  | 2.4  | 3    |
| UK      | 2.7  | 4.7  | 3.7  |
| USA     | 1.3  | 2.3  | 3.2  |

*Source*:   Tanzi and Schuknecht, 2000.

Interest payments as a share of total GDP – which represent the burden of interest payments associated with government debt servicing – have increased, crowding out social spending (Table 15.1). The Bretton Woods period, in which capital controls were widespread, and interest rates were set with the view to generate full employment, allowed government social spending to increase without leading to explosive increase in government debt. That particular period vindicates the Keynesian benign view of deficits and debt.

In this view, then, the problem of a growing burden of debt should not be dealt by measures like the Maastricht limits imposed in Europe, or balanced budget amendments, as often suggested in the USA. These solutions tend to emphasize the need to curtail spending, which more often than not means social spending. A Keynesian perspective would emphasize the need for reintroducing the euthanasia of the rentier favoured by Keynes, and reduce the burden of interest payments.

Note that greater integration with international financial markets has affected all European countries, and, hence, has reduced as a whole the ability to pursue expansionary macroeconomic policies. The EMU, on the other hand, although it limits monetary sovereignty for all participants, it allows for significant fiscal transfers from the richer countries in the union to those in need. Hence, it does not worsen the situation of peripheral countries within Europe.

Hence, it seems that even with the EMU, less stringent limits on budget deficits and debt-to-GDP ratios, coupled with a European Central Bank (ECB) policy geared to both price stability and full employment maintenance – rather than strictly limited to inflation targeting – would allow for higher levels of employment in Europe. Monetary integration per se is not the problem.[4] The lesson for the Americas is that without the possibilities of fiscal transfers, as in the European case, the costs of monetary integration and dollarization may be too high.

The problem of monetary integration in the Americas is qualitatively different than in Europe. In the case of Latin America, as one participant commented, the problem is the other Monroe.[5] The Monroe Doctrine said that Latin America was an American area of influence. Monetary integration in the Americas means by definition dollarization, since there is no reasonable possibility that the USA would part with the dollar. The special relation of Latin America as part of the US periphery is central to any discussion about dollarization. No fiscal transfers should be expected, and, hence, the cost of monetary integration provides almost no rewards.

## DOLLARIZATION AND FINANCIAL FRAGILITY

Monetary integration and dollarization do not guarantee that countries would not have balance of payments crises. Conventional wisdom seems to suggest that fiscal discipline and price flexibility would ensure that the dollar flows in the right direction, and that the balance of payments adjusts automatically. On the contrary, by reducing the instruments available for balance of payments adjustment they may tend to make crises worse.

In the absence of the possibility of devaluation, current account deficits are corrected by contraction of domestic demand. Historically, monetary arrangements that reduced national sovereignty constrained both monetary and fiscal policy, leading to pro-cyclical macroeconomic policies.[6]

Greater integration with international financial markets and a reduced role for government regulations imply that on average interest rates tend to be higher. As we saw in the previous section, governments spend increasing shares on debt servicing as a result of this increase in interest rates in the late 1970s.[7] High interest rates and lower rates of growth had led to unsustainable debt dynamics. Table 15.2 shows the increase in the burden of debt in the same countries as Table 15.1. It is clear that the fiscal crisis of the state is related to the financial burden of a more globalized economic environment, than the excesses of the Welfare State.

Traditionally an increase in the public sector's debt burden results from periods of war. The increase in the debt burden in the last 30 years has taken place in a relatively peaceful period, and at a time when a backlash against the Welfare State and Keynesian policies has led to a halt in the increase of government social spending. As noted, the main cause behind the increased debt burden is higher financial costs that ultimately are connected with the more integrated international financial regime that emerged after Bretton Woods.

In the case of developing countries, not only there has been an accumulation of domestic denominated debt but, in line with the increasing integration of international financial markets, foreign debt has surged. This has led to an increase

*Table 15.2  Burden of debt (% of GDP)*

|         | 1970 | 1980 | 1990  | 1997  |
|---------|------|------|-------|-------|
| Canada  | 51.9 | 44   | 72.5  | 93.8  |
| France  | 53.1 | 30.9 | 40.2  | 64.6  |
| Germany | 18.4 | 31.1 | 45.5  | 65    |
| Italy   | 41.7 | 58.7 | 104.5 | 121.7 |
| Japan   | 12.1 | 51.2 | 65.1  | 87.1  |
| UK      | 81.8 | 54   | 39.3  | 60.3  |
| USA     | 45.4 | 37   | 55.5  | 61.5  |

*Source*:   Tanzi and Schuknecht, 2000.

in the number of debt crises in the developing world. The debt crisis of the 1980s, the Mexican Tequila of 1994, the Asian crisis of 1997, the Russian of 1998, the Brazilian of 1999, and the Argentinean of 2001 are the most prominent examples.

These crises can be seen as the unfolding of a story that began in August 1982 with the Mexican default. In that respect, then, the debt crisis of the 1980s was the first of a series, and was part of a long-standing pattern of cyclical lending flows to developing countries.[8] Table 15.3 shows the evolution of debt indicators for all developing countries during the last debt cycle. In 2000 the total debt of the developing world stood at around 2.5 trillion dollars.

Table 15.3 shows that the total debt to Gross National Product ratio increased from less than 10 per cent to almost 38 per cent. In terms of the amount of foreign resources that developing countries are able to rise through exports the burden of debt peaked in 1990s at 160 per cent, and in 2000 was around 114 per cent. Debt service consumed 17 per cent of exports in 2000, up from 12 per cent in 1980. The share of short-term debt was in 2000 close to 16 per cent of total debt.

*Table 15.3  External debt (US$ billion)*

|                 | 1970 | 1980  | 1990   | 2000   |
|-----------------|------|-------|--------|--------|
| Total debt (TD) | –    | 568.7 | 1459.9 | 2527.5 |
| TD/GNP          | 9.8  | 18.2  | 30.9   | 37.4   |
| TD/exports      | –    | 84.4  | 160.7  | 114.3  |
| Debt service/TD | –    | 12.8  | 18.1   | 17     |
| Short term/TD   | 12.9 | 23.7  | 16.8   | 15.9   |

*Source*:   World Bank, 2003.

Finally, the foreign-denominated debt of the developing world has increased, but also American foreign debt has expanded in the last two decades. According to D'Arista (2004) the ratio of US foreign liabilities to GDP stands at approximately 25 per cent.

Unsustainable debt is certainly one of the many reasons behind balance of payments crises. To the extent that the more financially integrated regime that emerged from Bretton Woods – based on deregulation of capital accounts of the balance of payments and of domestic banking sectors – led to higher rates of interest, and increasing domestic debt, on the one hand, and persistent balance of payments imbalances, and increasing foreign debt accumulation, on the other, the financial fragility of the international economy has also increased.

## CONTRACTION OR RESISTENCE?

The limitations of monetary integration and dollarization are then considerable from a domestic point of view. They involve not only loss of seigniorage, but more restrictive fiscal policies and greater chances of external crisis. The social costs of those crises are such that it is reasonable to expect social resistance to monetary integration and dollarization. For that reason the number of national currencies in circulation may very well expand, as governments defend their monies.

It is also important to notice that the costs of globalization are unevenly distributed in society, and this implies that in general an increased role for the state as a provider of a safety net is demanded. To the extent that monetary integration and dollarization reduce the ability of the state to actually expand social spending, they increase the social conflicts associated with globalization. Countries integrating into the world economy have an incentive to maintain monetary autonomy to ease the pains associated with the process of globalization.

## NOTES

1. The surge in worldwide inflation in the 1970s was related to a host of factors, including steadily rising taxes, an unanticipated slowdown of productivity, shock increases in commodity prices, and the depreciation of the dollar following the breakdown of the Bretton Woods system. Discontent and social tensions rose leading to conflicting income claims, and wage price spirals. In that respect, stabilization was the result of the reversal of several of the above-mentioned inflationary factors.
2. Edwards (2001) finds that dollarized countries have lower inflation, lower growth and higher output volatility than countries with a domestic currency. The conjecture is that lower rates of economic growth in dollarized countries are the result of difficulties in accommodating to external disturbances, such as major term of trade and capital flows shocks.
3. Almost all authors in the book agreed that the EMU has imposed severe macroeconomic restrictions on European economies. While that is true, it is clear that restrictive macroeconomic

policies in Europe precede the EMU, as much as the relatively high levels of unemployment. In that respect, a more accurate claim would be that the Euro did not solve European macroeconomic problems.

4. De Grauwe (2002) for example favours EMU, but believes that the Stability and Growth pact allows EU economies 'to be subjected to control by European institutions that even the International Monetary Fund does not impose on banana republics'.

5. Robert Barro gave the Monroe Lecture during the Conference. K.S. Jomo suggested sardonically that the theme of dollarization reminded him of the other Monroe, the doctrine, that is.

6. Krugman (2001) insightfully compared the Argentinean 'cross of dollars' with the American support for the Gold Standard in the late nineteen century and Bryan's 'cross of gold'.

7. Homer and Sylla (1996, pp. 366–435) provide a detailed description of the low interest rates of the Breton Woods period and their subsequent rise in the late 1970s in the USA.

8. Marichal (1989) argues that debt crises in peripheral countries are usually associated with financial cycles in central countries. Cycles of growth and expansion of international trade lead to surges in lending to developing countries, as the funds in central countries grow faster than their needs, leading to a frenzy of speculation. Ultimately investors became overextended and retrenchment occurs leading to a reversal of capital flows and eventually to default.

# REFERENCES

D'Arista, J. (2004), 'Dollars, debt, and dependence: the case for international monetary reform,' *Journal of Post Keynesian Economics*, **26** (4), Summer, pp. 557–72.

De Grauwe, P. (2002), 'Europe's instability pact,' *Financial Times*, 25 July, p. 11.

Edwards, S. (2001), 'Dollarization and economic performance: an empirical investigation,' NBER Working Paper, no. 8274, May.

Glyn, A., A. Hughes, A. Lipietz and A. Singh (1990), 'The rise and fall of the golden age,' in S. Marglin and J. Schor, (eds), *The Golden Age of Capitalism*, Oxford: Oxford University Press.

Homer, S. and R. Sylla (1996), *A History of Interest Rates*, New Brunswick: Rutgers University Press.

Krugman, P. (2001), 'A cross of dollars,' *The New York Times*, 7 November.

Marichal, C. (1989), *A Century of Debt Crises in Latin America: From Independence to the Great Depression, 1820–1930*, Princeton: Princeton University Press.

Pasinetti, Luigi (1997), 'The social burden of high interest rates,' in P. Arestis, G. Palma and M. Sawyer (eds), *Capital Controversy, Post-Keynesian Economics and the History of Economics: Essays in Honour of Geoff Harcourt*, Volume I, London: Routledge.

Stiglitz, Joseph E. (2003), *The Roaring Nineties: a New History of the World's Most Prosperous Decade*, New York: W.W. Norton.

Tanzi, V. and L. Schuknecht (2000), *Public Spending in the 20th Century*, Cambridge: Cambridge University Press.

World Bank, the (2003), *Global Development Finance*, Washington, DC.

# Index